Readings in
Estate Planning I

Huebner School Series

Gary K. Stone, Editor

Readings in Multiline Insurance Law and Operations

Charles E. Hughes (ed.)

Fundamentals of Financial Planning

Robert M. Crowe (ed.)

Readings in Income Taxation

James F. Ivers III (ed.)

Group Benefits: Basic Concepts and Alternatives

Burton T. Beam, Jr.

Retirement Planning for a Business and Business Owner

Kenn Beam Tacchino

Retirement Planning for Individuals

K. B. Tacchino, W. J. Ruckstuhl, E. E. Graves, and R. J. Doyle, Jr.

Readings in Wealth Accumulation Planning

Robert J. Doyle, Jr., and Eric T. Johnson (eds.)

Readings in Estate Planning I

Ted Kurlowicz (ed.)

Readings in Estate Planning II

Jeffrey B. Kelvin

Planning for Business Owners and Professionals

Ted Kurlowicz, James F. Ivers III, and John J. McFadden

Financial Planning Applications

James F. Ivers III and William J. Ruckstuhl

Retirement Planning Handbook

Robert J. Doyle, Jr., and Donald Wright (eds.)

Tax Planning for Business Operations

Eric T. Johnson

Computerizing a Financial Planning Practice

Edmund W. Fitzpatrick

The primary purpose of this series is to provide timely reading materials tailored to the educational needs of those professionals pursuing the Chartered Life Underwriter and Chartered Financial Consultant designation programs offered by the Solomon S. Huebner School of The American College. These publications should also be of interest to other persons seeking further knowledge in the broad area of financial services.

Huebner School Series

Readings in
Estate Planning I

Seventh Edition

Edited by Ted Kurlowicz

The American College/Bryn Mawr, Pennsylvania

This publication is designed to provide accurate and authoritative information about the subject covered. The American College is not engaged in rendering legal, accounting, or other professional service. If legal or other expert advice is required, the services of an appropriate professional should be sought. No patent liability is assumed with respect to the use of the information contained in the computer applications accompanying this course. While every precaution has been taken in the preparation of this material, the authors and The American College assume no responsibility for errors or omissions. Neither is any liability assumed for damages resulting from the use of the information contained in the computer applications.

Library of Congress catalog card number 90-82841
ISBN 0-943590-16-7

Printed in the United States of America

Contents

Acknowledgments

I would like to acknowledge Gary K. Stone, PhD, vice president of academics at The American College and editor of the Huebner School Series, for providing the support and encouragement necessary to keep this Series at the highest standards.

I would also like to thank the following individuals for their work in authoring and/or editing earlier editions of this book:

- Susan M. Harmon, JD, LLM, former faculty member of The American College, for her contributions to chapters 1, 2, 5, 6, 7, 9, 10, 13, 14, 16, 17, and 18
- Gwenda L. Cannon, JD, former faculty member of The American College, for her contributions to chapters 1, 2, 5, 6, 9, 10, 17, and 18
- Donald P. Vernon, JD, former faculty member of The American College, for his contributions to chapters 14, 17, and 18
- James E. Quigley, Jr., of the Delaware Trust Company for this contribution to chapter 18

The individuals above contributed significantly to the material contained in this text. The material has been since updated, and I retain full responsibility for any errors.

I would also like to express appreciation to Jill Schoeniger for editing the manuscript and Patricia Marruchella for production assistance.

Ted Kurlowicz

Readings in Estate Planning I

The estate planner must combine the talents of an artist with those of an artisan. In developing the necessary rapport with a client, the sometimes fragile threads woven into the tapestry of the client's life must be dealt with lightly but deftly. As an artisan, the estate planner must have a solid understanding of the tools of the field, including knowledge of property and tax laws as well as financial planning. The art lies in the ability to put clients in touch with their true feelings, dreams, and aspirations as well as to assist them in the crystallization of their estate plans. Estate planning is inherently complex because of the technicalities of the applicable law and the foresight required to develop a program that best suits the client's immediate as well as anticipated needs and desires.

PURPOSE

There is a common misconception that an estate is only the property that one leaves at death. In reality, it is much more than that. The term *estate planning* in its broadest sense encompasses the accumulation, conservation, and distribution of an estate. The overall purpose of the estate planning process is to develop a plan that will enhance and maintain the financial security of clients and their families. Estate planning has come to include lifetime financial planning that may lead to increases in a client's estate as well as the conservation of existing assets. Estate planning should provide financial security during retirement years and facilitate the intended and orderly disposition of property at death.

HISTORY

Before exploring the art of estate planning, it is important to understand the historical meaning of the term *estate* as well as its meaning today. Under old English common law (discussed in more detail below), an estate referred primarily to an interest in land and the buildings or other permanent improvements on the land. An estate described the proprietary rights of the estate owner projected over time. Different types of estate ownership were classified on the basis of (1) the rights an owner could exercise over the property and (2) the duration of the owner's interest. A life estate, for example, is a property interest for the life of the estate owner with certain limitations on the life tenant's use of the property. It is therefore a lesser interest than an estate in fee simple absolute, which is an interest that belongs absolutely to the estate owner, the heirs, and assigns forever without condition or limitation. Over the course of time, an estate has come to mean more than an interest in land. It encompasses all the property or property rights that a

1.1

person owns, even those from which a lifetime benefit will never be received, such as life insurance proceeds or survivor annuities. Modern estate planning focuses on all property-ownership rights (real, personal, tangible, and intangible), attempting to make appropriate arrangements for them during the estate owner's life and to provide for their orderly transfer at death.

The need for an orderly disposition of property at the death of the owner of that property has existed since humans began to accumulate and value possessions. Various cultures have resolved this need in different ways. In some cultures, all possessions belonged to families or tribes, so the death of an individual did not affect their ownership. Other cultures that did recognize individual property provided for a system of inheritance to persons related to the deceased through the mother, father, or both. It was a system not totally dissimilar to today's laws of intestate succession, which provide a rigid scheme for inheritance of a deceased person's property by the heirs, although the degree of relationship required to inherit as well as the method of tracing that relationship may have varied considerably from the criteria utilized for intestate succession today. Even in the early days of civilization, a rigid system of inheritance did not meet the needs of every family and it does not do so today. One child may have been favored by the estate owner over others or may have required special assistance because of physical or mental frailties or prowess. In short, no one knows as much about the interrelationships and needs of a family as the members of that family. Various cultures have recognized that fact for thousands of years by allowing adult family members to provide for postdeath property transfers designed to meet individual or family needs.

As early as the Fourth Egyptian Dynasty (2900–2750 B.C.), there appeared a testamentary disposition by an official to endow his tomb. In 2548 B.C. an instrument was written on papyrus and witnessed by two scribes in which an Egyptian provided for certain property to be settled on his wife and appointed a guardian for his minor children. The Code of Hammurabi (1750 B.C.) does not mention wills directly but suggests that the culture had a scheme of intestate succession that the individual could alter, if the individual so desired. The provision referred to is the right of an estate owner to favor the eldest son by *sealed deed*. If the sealed deed was executed, the eldest son would have had an absolute right to receive the property described within, sharing equally in the remaining property with his brothers. In the absence of a sealed deed, all male children presumably inherited equally. Total disinheritance of a son was allowed only by judicial proceeding during the lifetime of the father.

Both the Greek and Roman civilizations allowed a testamentary disposition of property pursuant to the wishes of the deceased party. In fact, prior to 40 B.C., Roman citizens could totally disinherit children or other relatives. Because part of the state's interest in the orderly disposition of property at death has always been the support of the deceased's dependents to prevent them from becoming burdens of the state, the Romans developed a system of forced heirship for a portion of the deceased's property. This system continues to this day in civil-law jurisdictions (those jurisdictions tracing their judicial system to the ancient Romans and the Napoleonic Code rather than to

English common law). Louisiana is the only true civil-law state in the United States and has a forced heirship provision that affects not only Louisiana residents but also Louisiana property owned by nonresidents. Other states, however, may also have some form of forced heirship provisions.

Although our modern statutes retain some traces of ancient Roman law, the most prevalent influence is the English common law that developed after the invasion of William the Conqueror in 1066 A.D. In that feudal society, the only property of consequence that a person could potentially pass at death was interest in land. All land in feudal England belonged ultimately to the king. Vast interests in land were granted by the king to the great nobles in return for various payments and services. The nobles, in turn, granted interests in smaller portions of land to lesser members of the nobility in exchange for services. It is readily apparent that an inherent conflict of interest existed between the tenant in possession of the land, the presumptive heirs, and the immediate overlord. In bargaining for the land grant, the tenant wished to give up as few payments or services as possible and the overlord wished to receive maximum benefits. The overlord wanted the land returned to him at the death of a tenant so that he could make a new and possibly more advantageous bargain with another tenant. On the other hand, the tenant in possession wished to be able to dispose of the land to his or her own heirs who, in turn, desired the certainty of knowing they would not be dispossessed. Conflicts were eventually resolved primarily in favor of the tenant in possession of the land by allowing the lifetime transfer by the tenant, thereby defeating both the claims of the presumptive heirs and the overlord (Statute of Quia Emptores, 1290 A.D.). A testamentary right of disposition over property, however, did not exist until the Statute of Wills in 1540 gave all those except married women, infants, idiots, and the insane the right to dispose of most of their property by written instrument.

The English common law (both the statutes and the case law that construed them) became the foundation for American law in most legal areas including the area of estates. Likewise the English *use* (by which legal title to property was conveyed to a person in whom the owner had confidence with the instruction that the property be used for the benefit of the original owner's family or other designated persons) became the basis for the modern law of trusts.

Two other historical occurrences are also important in estate planning. The first occurred in the late 19th century when various state legislatures in this country began to enact state inheritance tax laws based on the value of property distributed to a decedent's beneficiaries. The second occurrence was the federal government's taxation of gratuitous transfers of property (property passing at death [1915] and lifetime gifts [1932]).

As the legal complexities surrounding transfers of property at death became complicated further by federal and state estate, gift, or inheritance taxes, more people began to be concerned about protecting their property from erosion by taxes. Consequently, the process we refer to as estate planning evolved. In essence, estate planning today is the art of accumulating, conserving, and possibly transferring portions of one's property during lifetime and disposing of property at death in a manner that minimizes taxes, probate costs, and other related expenses but is consistent with one's lifetime goals.

IMPEDIMENTS TO A WELL-PLANNED ESTATE

Failure to Plan

Most people do not realize that even if they have not created an estate plan and executed the appropriate documents to implement their plans, a plan has been created and imposed on them by the state in which they reside. Everyone, no matter how poor, has an estate plan. Each state has drafted its own statutory scheme for the disposition of its citizens' property at death in the event that the resident dies either without a valid will or having made an incomplete disposition of property.

Each state legislature has drafted a statutory plan that clearly lays out the way in which the property one owns at death will be distributed if the decedent dies without a valid will. These statutes are called *intestate succession statutes*, or statutes of descent and distribution. In each of these statutes, the state has set out a standardized line of succession that controls who will succeed to ownership of the deceased person's property. These intestate succession statutes are based on spousal relationships and degrees of consanguinity (blood relationship) to the decedent rather than on the distribution of property according to the intentions and desires of the deceased individual. Without a will, one may not leave property to charity. Neither may a friend who is not related inherit any property from the deceased. If no relatives exist, the property will revert to the state. The property is said to have *escheated* to the state. It would appear that a decedent who died intestate (without a will) had little concern for property, family, friends, or any other potential beneficiary such as a charity.

The same limitations apply to today's statutes of intestate succession that applied to the intestate distribution vehicles of earlier cultures already noted. They are highly standardized and rigid. As a result, they take no account of any special circumstances within families or any special relationships with nonrelated parties. Furthermore, lack of planning can destroy family relationships unintentionally, thereby causing bitterness and hardship for innocent family members. Because of those facts, distribution by intestate succession is only used when decedents have failed to advise the state in a legally acceptable manner through a will or similar document what they intend to do with their accumulated property at death.

The most basic legal instrument of all estate plans is a will. A will is a legal instrument whereby a person makes disposition of his or her property to take effect after death. Once a valid will has been executed, the statutes of intestate succession are largely displaced by the provisions of the will. While the intestate succession statutes may be largely displaced by a will or other personal disposition by the decedent, they may not be totally displaced. Since the state is concerned with the support of a spouse and minor children so that these individuals will not become a financial burden to the state, most, if not all, states either have common-law rules or have enacted statutory provisions that protect a portion of the decedent's property for a surviving spouse under laws that are labeled variously as dower, curtesy, and homestead rights, or other statutory provisions, such as a spouse's right of election. These provisions may be operative only if the spouse and children have not been provided for by the will, or they may be absolute rights regardless of the will's provisions, such as forced heirship. The specific provisions of such laws vary from state to state, but they are a form of intestate succession. Individuals should understand what form these provisions take in their states and whether or not they can be displaced by the provisions in a will. The surviving spouse's rights can often be enforced only by an election to take against the provisions in a valid will.

The Outdated Plan

While a valid will is a good beginning point for an estate plan, the will must be reviewed periodically to assure that a property owner's most recent intentions are honored at death. Will provisions may be altered by an amendment (called a codicil) or completely rewritten by the property owner at any time. If family circumstances or laws have changed dramatically since the will was written, the will's provisions may be seriously out of touch with the property owner's current wishes, but the existing will is the one that will be followed until and unless it is replaced with a later valid will. This situation can produce some disturbing results. Perhaps that cousin who was a great friend 10 years ago and was a substantial beneficiary under the existing will has fallen into disfavor, and is now seldom spoken to and heartily disliked. Despite this change in attitude on the part of the property owner, the property set out in the existing will would still go to the cousin if the owner died, unless the will had been reviewed and revised to reflect the change in the relationship.

Improper Tax Planning

The potential estate and gift tax relief that changes in the federal estate and gift tax laws appear to have provided may make many more individuals think that they no longer have a need for a carefully planned estate. The truth is contradictory to this viewpoint—only by utilizing the new tax laws to maximum advantage through professional advice can property owners carry out their postdeath intentions and prevent the unnecessary erosion of their estates due to taxes. For example, the unlimited marital deduction that allows an individual to pass an entire estate free of federal gift and estate taxes to a spouse appears to offer relief from taxation. In reality, use of the unlimited marital deduction (covered in later readings) may be enormously expensive at the death of the second spouse, since property will pass unprotected by the marital deduction (assuming the surviving spouse does not remarry). Thus the combined taxes on two estates may be greater than if the unlimited marital deduction had not been used in the estate of the first spouse to die. In short, the need for estate planning has never and does not now depend solely on whether there is a federal estate tax payable in one particular estate.

While there are important tax planning options that can be utilized in estate planning, tax relief should not be the primary objective of estate planning. The best estate plan is one that accurately reflects the client's wishes, needs, and objectives in a manner that minimizes the potential tax liability to the lowest level consistent with the client's aims. This means that various tax options must be balanced against rigidity, loss of control over assets, tax liability, etc., and will have to be explained to clients in order to allow them to understand both the limitations and the benefits of these options, and to choose those that reflect their desires and intentions. An estate plan that reduces the estate tax liability to zero is a poor plan if the cost is the perversion of the client's wishes.

Improper Position or Ownership of Assets

Many times the estate tax liability and even the ultimate ownership of an asset is predetermined by the form of ownership in which it is held prior to the owner's death. An example of an asset that is frequently improperly owned or positioned is life insurance. If the insured retains any incident of ownership in life insurance, the proceeds are subject to estate taxation. This unnecessary estate tax drain can be eliminated and more net dollars can be made available to the estate or its beneficiaries by removing all incidents of ownership from the insured and giving them to a spouse or trust. However, the unlimited marital deduction may now make it more desirable for the decedent to retain ownership of life insurance. Proper ownership of assets, including life insurance, must be analyzed on a case-by-case basis.

Another form of property ownership that can be problematic in estate planning is joint ownership with right of survivorship. This includes ownership as joint tenants with right of survivorship (ownership by the deceased and any other person including the surviving spouse), or as tenants by the entireties (a form of joint ownership restricted to married couples). The postdeath succession of property that is owned in either of these forms is not controlled by the provisions in a valid will. Ownership is transferred automatically by operation of law to the surviving joint tenant or tenant by the entireties. If all or most property is owned in this form, this situation can be the cause of an improperly balanced estate in which the surviving spouse may inherit too much of the property relative to the children, possibly resulting in an excessive estate tax liability at the second death.

Failure to Plan for the Cost of a Protracted Period of Disability or Last Illness

The cost of a protracted period of disability or a prolonged last illness may so erode an otherwise adequate estate that the estate owner leaves nothing to the beneficiaries at death, except a crushing amount of debt. The ownership of adequate medical expense and disability income insurance protection is an important consideration in planning any estate. Disability protection, in particular, is often ignored or misunderstood by clients, despite the fact that statistically there is a greater likelihood of a significant period of disability before retirement age than there is of an early death.

Failure to Consider the Effects of Inflation on Estate Tax Liability and Estate Assets

Another impediment to effective estate planning that should not be underestimated is the rate of inflation experienced over the past few years. At the very least, continuing inflation necessitates periodic reviews of existing estate plans to keep abreast of projected estate tax liabilities, as these can be affected by inflation through *tax bracket creep*. It is also necessary to review asset valuations, projected income from assets held, and amounts of life insurance in terms of constant dollars to assure that the estate owner's family would continue to be adequately protected.

An inflated economic climate will have a direct impact on all estates as the value of the dollar is eroded. Failure to take inflation into consideration when projecting the adequacy of an estate 10, 20, or 30 years into the future will probably result in the impossibility of carrying out the estate owner's desires.

Lack of Liquidity

Lack of liquidity may be a major problem in an otherwise well-planned estate. Three factors are particularly important in assessing liquidity needs in estate planning: (1) the amount and terms of debt of the estate owner, (2) the projected estate tax liability, and (3) the type of assets that make up the estate.

At the time of an estate owner's death, the amount and terms of debt for which a decedent is personally responsible may dramatically reduce either the actual assets or the net income stream that would be available to the beneficiaries. The same is true of the estate tax liability.

The types of assets owned at the time of death will also affect the cash available to the beneficiaries for their income needs. For example, when a closely held business is the primary estate asset and has been the source of income to the decedent and family through the decedent's salary and bonuses, there is frequently a family cash shortage when salary and bonuses cease. This results in financial stress to a family that is trying to deal with the death of a family member. It is most important that the possibility of such a situation be considered prior to its occurrence, and that both the estate owner and the family make appropriate decisions to avoid these problems. If adequate planning has been done, salary continuation plans are a possible way to soften the financial shock of a breadwinner's death, and additional liquidity may also be available from retirement plans and life insurance proceeds.

If the business is to be sold, it is imperative that the arrangements for the sale be reduced during the lifetime of the shareholder to legally enforceable agreements that are equitable to all parties, including both the persons who will continue the business and the decedent-shareholder's family.

If no such advance planning is done, the estate may be forced to sell assets hurriedly to pay its bills or taxes, and assets may have to be sold under disadvantageous market conditions at greatly reduced prices.

Psychological Impediments

Dealing with One's Own Mortality

Many people avoid making an estate plan because it encompasses planning for the transfer of assets after their death. It is almost as if by failing to participate in estate planning these individuals will avoid confronting the fact that death will happen to them. They perpetuate their denial of death. Implementation of an estate plan includes provision for the disposition of assets after death and requires an individual to acknowledge the reality of his or her mortality. Very few people can deal comfortably with this. There are many sophisticated and successful professionals who are very comfortable in the highly pressured atmosphere of finance and international business, but who are so distressed when attempting to deal with the inevitability of death that they never implement a cohesive estate plan. In this case, it is the family of the estate owner who ultimately suffers when their standard of living is impaired at the decedent's death, or when they try to impose some semblance of order on an estate that is in disarray.

Estate planners must make every reasonable effort to work with clients who are avoiding a confrontation with the inevitability of death. They should avoid getting involved in an intense psychological encounter for which they are not trained; therefore they must be sensitive in handling the difficulties presented by clients in this situation. It may be possible to assist a client past this obstacle by suggesting that estate planning is purely precautionary, and prudence requires that one be prepared for any eventuality. It is also important to educate such a person to the consequences of failing to do estate planning, including the very real possibility that an unplanned estate may cause the dissolution of the achievements of a lifetime of effort devoted to accumulating and preserving wealth.

Procrastination

While procrastination may be another indication that clients are delaying a confrontation with their own mortality, a more common belief accounting for this delay is the feeling that planning for the distribution of an estate is so large that it is impossible to achieve. The client becomes overwhelmed by its enormity and simply does nothing. In this circumstance, it is often sufficient for the estate planner to accept a significant part of the responsibility for completing the estate plan and to divide that portion of the task that must be done by the client into manageable chores.

THE ESTATE PLANNING PROCESS

The estate planning process has a number of identifiable stages. First, data must be obtained. Then the existing estate plan must be evaluated for potential impairments. After that, a plan is designed that is approved by the client. After the client reviews the plan, it must be implemented. This stage includes the execution of any necessary legal documents and transfers for arrangements of property. Last, the client should be made aware that there should be a periodic review of the plan particularly at times of change in life or tax laws.

Fact Finding

The initial stage in creating an estate plan is to gather all relevant facts from the estate owner and to compile them in a systematic manner. These facts should include full disclosure regarding all property ownership (both assets and liabilities), including expected gifts or inheritances. Any known problems connected with particular property, such as the problems surrounding a closely held business interest, should be noted. Detailed information must also be obtained regarding the family structure, the names of all persons in the family who have some connection with the estate owner, and the relationships and attitudes of family members toward each other. For example, it is important to elicit the attitude of the estate owner toward a spouse and younger generations. Information must be obtained regarding philosophy about assets as well as feelings about work, money, risk, philanthropy, and financial security.

Some questions and areas of exploration that will help the estate planner discover the client's personal attitudes are the following: Does the estate owner have strong feelings about charitable giving or particular charitable organizations? Many individuals who have accumulated a substantial estate do have special feelings for some of the institutions that have aided them in achieving their goals and arriving at positions of financial, professional, or business success. What are the estate owner's obligations to a former spouse or to children of a first marriage? In estate planning today, one cannot ignore the subject of divorce. When an estate owner comes to see you with his or her spouse, it is possible that this may not be the first spouse. Also, there might be an elderly parent or a handicapped person in the family for whom the estate owner has some concern. Does the estate owner have a legal or moral obligation to support such a person? The estate owner should also be questioned regarding gifts that have been made during his or her lifetime as well as gifts that the estate owner anticipates making to various persons.

Review of Existing Plan

Information should be obtained regarding the provisions of the estate owner's current estate plan, if any. Does the client presently have a valid will? Has the client created trusts that may or may not serve his or her needs? These documents and other legal documents should be brought to the interview to assist the estate planner in evaluating the client's current plan and making recommendations for improvement.

Financial and Estate Planning Fact Finder

At the end of this reading, a sample copy of a Financial and Estate Planning Fact Finder that is designed to gather data systematically for financial and estate planning will be found. While a detailed discussion of the data-gathering process is beyond the scope of this reading, students desiring to improve their data-gathering skills are encouraged to peruse the fact finder closely and to review the reading on this subject in HS 320. If one is doing comprehensive financial planning, the fact finder should be used in its entirety. If only estate planning is being considered, relevant portions of the fact finder can be excerpted. The portions that are relevant in a particular case will depend on the facts and circumstances of the individual case, and estate planners must make decisions by exercising their professional judgment based on their relationships with clients and their assessment of the clients' problems.

It is crucial in gathering facts and information to obtain both objective and subjective information. No questionnaire or fact finder has any value if the personal objectives of the estate owner are not extracted during the interview. Estate planning involves property but more than that, it is planning for human beings. As such, it should be highly personalized. Good estate planners will make sure that they have elicited from clients all their goals and intentions regarding their property as well as their feelings about all family and nonfamily members whom they may want to protect or benefit in some way.

There are pros and cons regarding the submission of a fact finder to a client before an interview. While mailing the questionnaire in advance saves time during the initial interview, the amount of information requested may intimidate or overwhelm a client. In addition, there are many things the estate planner cannot determine from numbers and names on a piece of paper. It is only in a direct, personal interchange that a climate of trust can be established that will enable the estate owner to be comfortable in fully revealing personal information, beliefs, concerns, and attitudes to the estate planner. A good estate planning practitioner will usually be able to establish rapport with and gain the confidence of a client fairly quickly.

Client Interview

In eliciting or reviewing facts in the initial data-gathering interview, problems that would impede the estate plan should be noted, defined, and explored with the client. As part of the data-gathering process, the estate planner also has a duty to explain to the client various potential options that are available under the current law. The client's response to these various options will provide significant guidance to the estate planner in determining the type of plan that is most suitable for meeting the client's needs and objectives. This involves explaining the law to the client and making certain that it is understood. The plan is the client's plan as is the ultimate decision regarding the arrangement of assets and transfers to beneficiaries. Many clients are intimidated by the professional person, are unfamiliar with the professional's language or terminology, and do not quite know how to ask questions that would help them understand and feel comfortable with the estate plan. It is very important to make certain that clients know what they are doing and why. This can be accomplished by giving the client an analysis of problem areas the planner has identified as well as areas where there may be a choice among alternative solutions. The analysis will only be helpful to the client if it is explained in understandable terms.

The next stage is the actual development of an estate plan. This includes the preparation and presentation of the plan to the client for review and final approval.

The third stage is the implementation of that plan. This entails the execution of the necessary legal documents and making arrangements for any current transfer of ownership as well as provision for liquidity needs. In choosing between alternative planning options, the estate planner will utilize to the greatest extent possible those vehicles consistent with the client's wishes that will provide the most benefits in the areas of estate, gift, and income tax. Once the appropriate documents are reviewed and executed, the estate owner should be advised that a periodic review of them is essential as a final stage of estate planning to reflect, in the original estate plan, any changes in the tax laws that are occurring at an unprecedented rate as well as changes in financial and interpersonal situations.

Once an estate plan is fully implemented and a review procedure is adopted, estate owners should have the satisfaction of knowing that they have taken an active role in the direction of their lives' plans, and they should have greater peace of mind in the knowledge that they have provided for the financial security of themselves and their families.

The Estate Planning Team—Who the Estate Planners Are and How They Operate

Individuals from more than one professional discipline are qualified to assist clients in estate planning. The greatest benefit and the best results for a client can be obtained from an approach that enlists the assistance of a variety of advisers in total financial planning, including estate planning. If, however, the client is interested in either estate or death planning only, the estate planner should perform those tasks. It is hoped that the client can be interested in more complete planning through a successful relationship, but the estate planner should not insist that the client either plan comprehensively or not plan at all.

The estate planning team has traditionally consisted of an attorney, an insurance specialist, a bank trust officer, an accountant, and an investment counselor. A newer member of the team is the financial planner. It is frequently the financial planner or the insurance specialist who has made the first contact with the client, sensitized the client to the need for estate planning, and motivated the client to become involved in the process. This is because both the life underwriter and the financial planner can advertise their services and otherwise solicit business. Attorneys and accountants may engage in advertising only in a very limited and highly regulated manner; other solicitations of business are prohibited.

Financial planning is a new discipline that has emerged in the last few years. The financial planner has the education and background to do a comprehensive financial plan based upon much of the same data as that used by the estate planner. The financial planner may be an independent businessperson or may be affiliated with a large investment, insurance, accounting, or other institution. The financial planner may provide services solely for a fee, or, if permitted by state law, the fees for planning may be offset, in whole or part, by commissions on the sale of financial products. Financial planning has come to mean a process for arriving at comprehensive solutions to a client's personal, business, and financial problems and concerns. The term covers a wide range of financial services and products. The field of financial planning has grown substantially in the past 10 years and is growing still. It is the ability of financial planners to cooperate with other members of various disciplines to develop an overall plan for the client that is one of their most significant contributions to client service and to the estate planning team.

The next member of the estate planning team, the accountant, is the adviser most likely to have annual contact with the client through preparation of the client's tax returns. This gives the accountant the opportunity to be familiar with the size, amount, and nature of the client's estate. The accountant may be the person who can most easily provide a valuation for any asset in the estate where it is not easily ascertainable. Valuation might be particularly crucial if one recommendation in the estate plan is a buy-sell agreement to provide for a transfer of a business interest upon death or disability. The accountant may also be of help in preparing a final estate tax return.

The trust officer is the next member of the team. This may be the person to whom the client has initially turned for information and estate planning services if professional management is desired in the administration of an inter vivos or testamentary trust. A good trust officer will be familiar with the field of estate planning and the various estate planning tools that can be used. As executors or trustees, trust officers have primary responsibility for settling the estate, investing estate assets during the administration period, and making distribution—as necessary—to the estate or trust beneficiaries. The bank trust department may also be responsible for filing estate and fiduciary income tax returns.

The insurance specialist plays an important role on the estate planning team because he or she can provide products that will give the estate the necessary cash to pay the estate tax and other liabilities as well as to fund the income needs of the surviving family. Life insurance may be the primary asset of some estates and, consequently, the major source for family income after an estate owner dies. Life insurance agents who have become CLUs are knowledgeable in the fields of insurance as well as estate planning and taxation, and can provide an invaluable service as an informed member of the team.

The next member of the team is the attorney. The attorney is a crucial member because planning cannot be accomplished nor can a plan be executed without using an attorney's knowledge of the law. The attorney is the professional who must draft all the legal documents that are necessary to implement the plan. These documents will virtually always include wills, and may include trusts, buy-sell agreements, or other documents if a more sophisticated estate plan is elected. The attorney is responsible for assuring that the intentions of the client are expressed in legally enforceable documents that will serve as the basis for carrying out the client's postmortem plan.

The creation of a comprehensive and creative estate plan is a highly rewarding experience for the estate planning practitioner regardless of the discipline from which he or she emerges. Although there may be a different emphasis in various estate plans stemming from the knowledge and background of the practitioner, the primary objective of a good planner should be to effectuate and implement both the desires and objectives of the individual for whom the plan is created. The client is the director of the plan. The professionals are the producers. An estate plan reflects the personality of the client. It may evidence the client's cares and concerns for other human beings as well as for himself or herself. On the contrary, the plan may reflect or focus on the client's own self-interest, grievances, and grudges. Much will be revealed about the client's character, philosophy of life, and attitudes by the types of planning options he or she selects, and the reasons for which they are selected.

Estate planning has become vastly more complicated and challenging as a field of practice. In order to be an effective estate planner, one must be familiar with applicable local and federal law. One must also have a working knowledge of subject matter pertaining to property, probate, wills and trusts, federal and state taxation, corporations, partnerships, business, insurance, and divorce. An estate planner must be able to explain relevant portions of these subjects in plain language to a client. If the client is spoken down to or expected to deal with technical jargon, the client will not feel confident and may well abandon the project. A client has an absolute right to fully understand all the options and make his or her own decisions.

UNAUTHORIZED PRACTICE OF LAW

Because much of the knowledge necessary for estate planning deals with legal concepts, there is often concern over whether one is or is not practicing law without a license. Indeed, the line between unauthorized practice and other advice is sometimes a fine one.

What is the unauthorized practice of law? There is no definitive answer to that question. The American Bar Association's Model Rules of Professional Conduct takes the position that the definition of the practice of law is established by the law of the different jurisdictions. This seems to imply that what constitutes the unauthorized practice could vary from jurisdiction to jurisdiction. The Model Code's predecessor, the ABA's Code of Professional Responsibility, took the position that "[i]t is neither necessary nor desirable to attempt the formulation of a single, specific definition of what constitutes the practice of law. Functionally, the practice of law relates to the rendition of services for others that call for the professional judgment of a lawyer. The essence of the professional judgment of the lawyer is his educated ability to relate the general body and philosophy of law to a specific legal problem of a client. . . ."

Neither expertise in a particular subject matter area nor knowledgeability of the law is sufficient to allow anyone other than a lawyer to give legal advice. Giving such advice is clearly reserved to those who are licensed to practice law.

Even with the Bar Association's ambiguous definition of the unauthorized practice of law, there are activities that are universally recognized as the practice of law; therefore they are to be engaged in only by lawyers. The drafting of legal documents is one such activity.

The area of giving advice is much more problematic. For example, when does giving advice about the taxation of a particular trust arrangement that is properly within the province of the CPA or trust officer become *legal advice* and thereby solely within the province of the attorney? This is the crucial question in this difficult area. Some general guidelines are available, however, to assist the nonlawyer. If the advice is generally informational (that is, if the general principles of a proposal or technique are outlined for the client's information), there should not be a problem. Even if the advice is specifically related to the client's situation, there is no unauthorized practice violation if the advice is given on a settled area of law that is a matter of common knowledge in the estate planning field.

Since this problem is so difficult to resolve and potential penalties can be severe, the early and continuous involvement of an attorney in the estate planning process is perhaps the best way to deal with the unauthorized practice issue.

FINANCIAL AND ESTATE PLANNING FACT FINDER

The information collected and maintained in this document will be held in the utmost confidentiality. It will not be shared except as may be required by law, or as may be authorized in writing by the client.

(signed) _____

The American College

CONTENTS

PERSONAL DATA

Name (file no.)						
Spouse's name						
Legal home address						
Business address	*Client*					
	Spouse					
Phone	Home		Business:	*Client* *Spouse*		
Dates of counseling sessions	*Initial Interview*					
Dates Checklist for Financial Planning Review was sent						

Consultants for Financial and Business Planning*

		Name	Address	Phone
Attorney	personal			
	business			
Accountant	personal			
	business			
Trust officer				
Other bank officer				
Life insurance agent				
Property and liability insurance agent				
Securities broker				
Primary financial consultant				

*Indicate source of client with a check.

Notes

PERSONAL DATA (continued)

Client and Spouse

	Date of Birth	Social Security Number	Occupation	Amount of Support by Client/ Spouse	Health Problems/ Special Needs
*Client**					
*Spouse**					

*If not U.S. citizen, indicate nationality.

Children†/Grandchildren

†Indicate whether by prior marriage, adopted, or stepchild.

Client's Parents, Siblings‡

Spouse's Parents, Siblings‡

‡If possible, obtain addresses, phone numbers, and social security numbers of family members, especially those who are, or may become, beneficiaries, executors, guardians, etc.

Notes

Marital status	☐ Married ☐ divorced ☐ widowed (check appropriate status) date:
	Any former marriages? ☐ yes ☐ no If yes, to whom? client: spouse:
	Are you paying alimony? ☐ yes ☐ no If yes, amount: Are you paying child support? ☐ yes ☐ no If yes, amount:
	Are there prenuptial or postnuptial agreements? ☐ yes ☐ no
Estate plan	Do you have a basic estate plan? ☐ yes ☐ no If yes, describe briefly.
Wills	Do you have a will? ☐ yes ☐ no date of will:
	Does your spouse have a will? ☐ yes ☐ no date of will:
Executor nominations	Who has been named as executor in your will? in your spouse's will? Name: Name: Address: Address: Phone: Phone:
Guardian nominations	Have guardians been named for your children? ☐ yes ☐ no If yes, who? Name: Address: Phone:
Trust/trustee nominations	Have you created grantor, Clifford, insurance, or testamentary trusts? ☐ yes ☐ no If yes, who is the trustee?
	Who are the beneficiaries?
	Has your spouse created grantor, Clifford, insurance, or testamentary trusts? ☐ yes ☐ no If yes, who is the trustee?
	Who are the beneficiaries?
Custodianships	Have you or your spouse ever made a gift under the Uniform Gifts to Minors Act? ☐ yes ☐ no If yes, in which state?
	Who is the custodian?
	Who are the donees?
Trust beneficiary	Are you or any members of your immediate family beneficiaries of a trust? ☐ yes ☐ no If yes, who? Amount expected:
Gifts/inheritances	Do you, your spouse, or your children expect to receive gifts/inheritances? ☐ yes ☐ no If yes, who? How much? from whom? when?
Education	What is the level of your education?
	What is the level of your spouse's education?
Military service benefits	Are you or your spouse eligible for any benefits deriving from military service? ☐ yes ☐ no If yes, explain.

FINANCIAL OBJECTIVES

Rank from 1 to 8 the importance of having adequate funds in order to do the following:

_____ maintain/expand standard of living
_____ enjoy a comfortable retirement
_____ take care of self and family during a period of long-term disability
_____ invest and accumulate wealth
_____ reduce tax burden
_____ provide college education for children
_____ take care of family in the event of death
_____ develop an estate distribution plan
_____ any others important to you (specify)

Do you have a formal monthly budget?   ☐ yes   ☐ no   If yes, indicate amount:

How much do you save annually?   in what form?   why?

How much do you think you should be able to save annually?   for what purpose?

How much do you invest annually?   in what form?   why?

How much do you think you should be able to invest annually?   for what purpose?

FACTORS AFFECTING YOUR FINANCIAL PLAN

Have you or your spouse ever made substantial gifts to family members or to tax-exempt beneficiaries?   ☐ yes   ☐ no
If yes, give details.

What special bequests are intended, including charity?

Are you satisfied with your previous investment results?   ☐ yes   ☐ no
Explain.

Are there any investments you feel committed to (for past performance, family, or social reasons)?   ☐ yes   ☐ no
If yes, explain.

Is your spouse good at handling money?   ☐ yes   ☐ no

If you die, would your spouse be able to manage family finances?   ☐ yes   ☐ no

In the event of your death, what is your estimate of the emotional and economic maturity of your children?

In the event of your death or of divorce, what are your feelings about the possible remarriage of your spouse?

At what age would you like to retire?

Tax considerations aside, in what manner would you want your estate distributed?

What do you think financial planning should do for you?

OBJECTIVES REQUIRING ADDITIONAL INCOME/CAPITAL

Do your children attend public or private schools?	
If private, annual cost: (elementary)	(secondary)
Do you plan for your children to attend private schools later? ☐ yes ☐ no	
If yes, when?	

Education Fund

Name of Child	Age	No. Years until College	Estimated 4-Year Cost		Estimated Graduate School Costs	Capital Allocated	Monthly Income Allocated
			If Private	**If Public**			

Support for Family Member(s)

Name	Age	Relation	Estimated Cost	Estimated Period of Funding	Capital Allocated	Monthly Income Allocated

Other Objectives

Objective	Target Date	Estimated Cost	Estimated Period of Funding	Capital Allocated	Monthly Income Allocated

Notes

SOURCES OF INCOME

Annual Income

	Client	Spouse*	Dependent Children*
Salary, bonus, etc.			
Income as business owner (self-employment)			
Real estate rental			
Dividends			
Investments (public stock, mutual funds, etc.)			
Close corporation stock			
Interest			
Investments (bonds, money market funds, T-bills, etc.)			
Savings accounts, certificates of deposit			
Loans, notes			
Trust income			
Life insurance settlement options			
Child support/alimony			
Other sources (specify)			
Other sources			
Other sources			
Other sources			
Total annual income			

*If spouse or children are employed, give details here.

Income Tax Last Year

Federal			
State			
Local			
Total income tax paid last year			
Estimated quarterly tax this year			

Future Annual Income Estimate

Next year			
Three years			
Five years			
How often do you expect a salary increase or bonus?			
On the average, how much of a salary increase or bonus do you expect annually?			
Has your total annual income fluctuated significantly during the past three years?			

CASH-MANAGEMENT STATEMENT

Annual Income

	Current Yr.	Projections for Subsequent Years				
	19_____	Assumptions	19_____	19_____	19_____	19_____
Salary, bonus, etc.						
Income as business owner (self-employment)						
Real estate rental						
Dividends						
Investments						
Close corporation stock						
Interest income						
Investments						
Savings accts., CDs						
Loans, notes, etc.						
Trust income						
Life insurance settlement options						
Child support/alimony						
Other sources (specify)						
Total annual income						

Annual Expenditures: Fixed

Housing (mortgage/rent)						
Utilities and telephone						
Food						
Clothing and cleaning						
Income and social security taxes						
Property taxes						
Transportation (auto/commuting)						
Medical/dental/drugs/health insurance						
Debt repayment						
House upkeep/repairs/maintenance						
Life, property and liability insurance						
Child support/alimony						
Current education expenses						
Total fixed expenses						

Annual Expenditures: Discretionary

Recreation/entertainment/travel						
Contributions/gifts						
Household furnishings						
Education fund						
Savings						
Investments						
Other (specify)						
Total discretionary expenses						
Total annual expenditures						
Net income (total annual income minus total annual expenditures)						

INVENTORY OF ASSETS

Cash, Near-Cash Equivalents

Items	No. Units or Shares	Date Acquired	Amount, Cost, or Other Basis	Market Value and Titled Owners					
				Client	Spouse	Joint (survivor rights)	Joint (no survivor rights)	Community Property	Other*
Checking accounts/cash									
Savings accounts									
Money-market funds									
Treasury bills									
Commercial paper									
Short-term CDs									
Cash value, life insurance									
Accum. divs., life insurance									
Savings bonds									
Other (specify)									
Subtotal									

*Children, custodial accounts, trusts, etc.

U.S. Govt., Municipal, Corporate Bonds, and Bond Funds: Issuer, Maturity, Call Dates

Subtotal									

Preferred Stock: Issuer, Maturity, Call Dates

Subtotal									

Common Stock: Issuer, Listed (L), Unlisted (U), Nonmarketable (NM)

Subtotal									

Warrants and Options: Issuer, Expiration Date

Subtotal									

Mutual Funds and Type: Growth (G), Income (I), Balanced (B), Indexed (IX), Speculative (S)

Subtotal									

INVENTORY OF ASSETS

Cash, Near-Cash Equivalents

Annual Yield %	$	Amount Available for Liquidity	Amount of Indebtedness	Location, Description, Client's Reasons for Holding Asset, etc.	Items
					Checking accounts/cash
					Savings accounts
					Money-market funds
					Treasury bills
					Commercial paper
					Short-term CDs
					Cash value, life insurance
					Accum. divs., life insurance
					Savings bonds
					Other (specify)
					Subtotal

U.S. Govt., Municipal, Corporate Bonds, and Bond Funds: Issuer, Maturity, Call Dates

					Subtotal

Preferred Stock: Issuer, Maturity, Call Dates

					Subtotal

Common Stock: Issuer, Listed (L), Unlisted (U), Nonmarketable (NM)

					Subtotal

Warrants and Options: Issuer, Expiration Date

					Subtotal

Mutual Funds and Type: Growth (G), Income (I), Balanced (B), Indexed (IX), Speculative (S)

					Subtotal

INVENTORY OF ASSETS (continued)

Real Estate

Items	No. Units or Shares	Date Acquired	Amount, Cost or Other Basis	Market Value and Titled Owners					
				Client	Spouse	Joint (survivor rights)	Joint (no survivor rights)	Community Property	Other
Personal residence									
Seasonal residence									
Investment (residential)									
Investment (commercial)									
Land									
Other (specify)									
Subtotal									

Long-term, Nonmarketable Assets

Long-term CDs									
Vested retirement benefits									
Annuities									
HR-10 plan (Keogh)									
IRAs									
Mortgages owned									
Land contracts									
Limited partnership units									
Other (specify)									
Subtotal									

Personal Assets

Household furnishings									
Automobile(s)									
Recreational vehicles									
Boats									
Jewelry/furs									
Collections (art, coins, etc.)									
Hobby equipment									
Other (specify)									
Subtotal									

Miscellaneous Assets

Interest(s) in trust(s)									
Receivables									
Patents, copyrights, royalties									
Other (specify)									
Subtotal									
Totals of all columns									

INVENTORY OF ASSETS (continued)

Real Estate

Annual Yield		Amount Available for Liquidity	Amount of Indebtedness	Location, Description, Client's Reasons for Holding Asset, etc.	Items
%	$				
					Personal residence
					Seasonal residence
					Investment (residential)
					Investment (commercial)
					Land
					Other (specify)
					Subtotal

Long-term, Nonmarketable Assets

					Long-term CDs
					Vested retirement benefits
					Annuities
					HR-10 plan (Keogh)
					IRAs
					Mortgages owned
					Land contracts
					Limited partnership units
					Other (specify)
					Subtotal

Personal Assets

					Household furnishings
					Automobile(s)
					Recreational vehicles
					Boats
					Jewelry/furs
					Collections (art, coins, etc.)
					Hobby equipment
					Other (specify)
					Subtotal

Miscellaneous Assets

					Interest(s) in trust(s)
					Receivables
					Patents, copyrights, royalties
					Other (specify)
					Subtotal
					Totals of all columns

BUSINESS INTEREST

General Information

Full legal name   Phone
Address
Business now operates as   ☐ proprietorship   ☐ partnership   ☐ corporation   ☐ S corporation
When does the fiscal year end?
What accounting method is used?
What is the principal business activity?
In what year did this business begin operation?
If it began other than as a corporation, what is the date of incorporation?   state of incorporation?
Classes of stock   No. authorized shares   No. outstanding shares
What is your function in the business?
Do you have an employment contract?

Present Owners*

	Insurability Problem?		Form of Business		
			Corporation		Partnership
	Yes	No			
(A) _____ *Client* _____	☐	☐	owns _____ % common _____ % preferred	_____ % _____
(B) _____	☐	☐	owns _____ % common _____ % preferred	_____ % _____
(C) _____	☐	☐	owns _____ % common _____ % preferred	_____ % _____
(D) _____	☐	☐	owns _____ % common _____ % preferred	_____ % _____
(E) _____	☐	☐	owns _____ % common _____ % preferred	_____ % _____

*Indicate relationship to client by blood or marriage.

Key Employees (other than present owners)

	Insurability Problem			Insurability Problem	
	Yes	No		Yes	No
_____	☐	☐	_____	☐	☐
_____	☐	☐	_____	☐	☐
_____	☐	☐	_____	☐	☐
_____	☐	☐	_____	☐	☐

BUSINESS INTEREST (continued)

Disposition of Business Interest

Do you want your business interest retained or sold if you
retire? ☐ yes ☐ no   become disabled? ☐ yes ☐ no   die? ☐ yes ☐ no

IF RETAINED
Who will own your interest and how will the person(s) acquire it?

Who will replace you in your job?

IF SOLD
Who will buy your interest?

How is purchase price to be determined?

What is the funding arrangement?

Do you have a buy-sell agreement? ☐ yes ☐ no

If yes, is it a cross-purchase, entity-purchase, or "wait-and-see" type of agreement?

Where is it located?

Valuation of Business Interest

Estimate the lowest price for which the entire business might be sold as a going concern today.

What is the lowest price you would accept for your interest today?

If you were not an owner, what is your estimate of the highest price you would pay today for the entire business as a going concern?

What is the highest price you would pay to buy the interest of your coowners today?

Has an impartial valuation of the business been made? ☐ yes ☐ no   If yes, when?
What valuation method was used?   What value was established?

What is the average business indebtedness?

Estimate the highest it has ever been.   Estimate the lowest it has ever been.

Are there patents, special processes, or leased equipment/real property used by but not owned by the business? ☐ yes ☐ no
If yes, who owns what, and under what terms is each used or leased?

What are prospects for growth, sale, merger, or going public?

Survivor Control (letters in parentheses refer to owners named above on page 12)

IF (A) DIES	IF (B) DIES	IF (C) DIES	IF (D) DIES	IF (E) DIES
B wants _____ % control	A wants _____ %	A wants _____ %	A wants _____ %	A wants _____ %
C wants _____ % control	C wants _____ %	B wants _____ %	B wants _____ %	B wants _____ %
D wants _____ % control	D wants _____ %	D wants _____ %	C wants _____ %	C wants _____ %
E wants _____ % control	E wants _____ %	E wants _____ %	E wants _____ %	D wants _____ %
_____ wants _____ % control	_____ wants _____ %	_____ wants _____ %	_____ wants _____ %	_____ wants _____ %

EMPLOYEE CENSUS DATA*

	Sex	Marital Status	Name			Date of Birth			Date Employed†			Full-time‡	Hourly	Salaried	Earnings		Member of Collective Bargain Unit?	Occupation or Job Title
			Last	First	M.I.	Month	Day	Year	Month	Day	Year				Annual Salary or Wage	Additional Compensation		
1																		
2																		
3																		
4																		
5																		
6																		
7																		
8																		
9																		
10																		
11																		
12																		
13																		
14																		
15																		
16																		
17																		
18																		
19																		
20																		
21																		
22																		
23																		
24																		
25																		

*It is suggested that the client request this data directly from bookkeeper or other appropriate person.
†The date of its incorporation is also the date of employment of former proprietors or partners of a business.
‡A full-time employee is one who works 1,000 or more hours per year.

INVENTORY OF LIABILITIES

Outstanding Obligations of Client or Spouse	Original Amount	Maximum Credit Available	Present Balance	Monthly/ Annual Repayment	Effective Interest Rate	Payments Remaining/ Maturity Date	Secured?	Insured?
Retail charge accounts								
Credit cards								
Family/personal loans								
Securities margin loans								
Investment liabilities								
Bank loans								
Life insurance policy loans								
Income tax liability								
Federal								
State								
Local								
Property taxes								
Mortgage(s)								
Family member support								
Child support/alimony								
Other (specify)								
Total								

Are there any other liabilities your estate might be called upon to pay? ☐ yes ☐ no
If yes, explain.

Do you foresee any future liabilities (business expansion, new home, etc.)? ☐ yes ☐ no
If yes, explain.

LIFE INSURANCE BENEFITS*

Item	Policy 1	Policy 2	Policy 3
Policy number			
Name of insurance company			
Issue age			
Insured			
Owner of policy			
Type of policy			
Annual premium			
Net annual outlay by client			
Current cash value			
Extra benefits (e.g. waiver of premium, accidental death, etc.)			
Amount of base policy			
Dividends (value & option)			
Term rider(s)			
Loan outstanding			
Net amount payable at death			
Primary beneficiary and settlement option elected			
Secondary beneficiary and settlement option elected			

Item	Policy 4	Policy 5	Policy 6
Policy number			
Name of insurance company			
Issue age			
Insured			
Owner of policy			
Type of policy			
Annual premium			
Net annual outlay by client			
Current cash value			
Extra benefits (e.g., waiver of premium, accidental death, etc.)			
Amount of base policy			
Dividends (value & option)			
Term rider(s)			
Loan outstanding			
Net amount payable at death			
Primary beneficiary and settlement option elected			
Secondary beneficiary and settlement option elected			

*Policies and most recent policy anniversary premium notices should be examined for the information recorded on this page.

HEALTH INSURANCE BENEFITS*

Medical/Dental Benefits

	Policy 1	Policy 2	Policy 3	Policy 4
Type of policy				
Policy number				
Name of insurance company or other provider				
Insured				
Annual cost to client				
Type of continuance or renewal provision				
Deductible				
Percentage participation				
Stop-loss limit				
Inside limits				
Overall maximum				

Disability Income Benefits

Policy number				
Name of insurance company or other provider				
Insured				
Annual cost to client				
Type of continuance or renewal provision				
Definition of disability				
Monthly disability income				
Accident				
Sickness				
Partial disability provision				
Waiting period				
Accident				
Sickness				
Benefit period				
Accident				
Sickness				

*Policies should be examined for the information recorded on this page.

PROPERTY AND LIABILITY INSURANCE COVERAGE*

Homeowners Insurance

	Principal Residence	Seasonal Residence	Other Property
Policy number			
Name of insurance company			
Address of property			
HO form # (or other type of policy)			
Coverage on dwelling			
Replacement cost of dwelling			
Replacement cost of contents			
Liability limits			
Endorsements			
Deductibles			
Annual cost			

Automobile Insurance

	Auto #1	Auto #2	Auto #3 (or other vehicles, trailers)
Policy number			
Name of insurance company			
Automobile make/year			
Liability limits			
No-fault/medical benefits			
Uninsured motorist			
Collision/deductible			
Comprehensive/deductible			
Annual cost			

Other Property/Liability Insurance

	Policy 1	Policy 2	Policy 3
Type of policy			
Policy number			
Name of insurance company			
Property covered			
Limits			
Annual cost			

Umbrella Liability Insurance

Policy number	
Name of insurance company	
Liability limits	
Retention	
Annual cost	

*Policies should be examined for the information recorded on this page.

EMPLOYMENT-RELATED BENEFITS CHECKLIST

Name and address of client's employer_____

Name and address of spouse's employer_____

Who can provide detailed information on employee benefits for you and your spouse?

Client	*Spouse*
Name_____	Name_____
Title_____	Title_____
Department_____	Department_____
Phone_____	Phone_____

	Benefit now provided for client?		Benefit now provided for spouse?		Information/Comments
Life and Health Insurance	Yes	No	Yes	No	
Death benefits	☐	☐	☐	☐	_____
Accidental death/dismemberment	☐	☐	☐	☐	_____
Travel accident	☐	☐	☐	☐	_____
Medical expense benefits	☐	☐	☐	☐	_____
Short-term disability income (sick pay)	☐	☐	☐	☐	_____
Long-term disability income	☐	☐	☐	☐	_____
Retirement Benefits/ Deferred Compensation*					
Qualified pension plan	☐	☐	☐	☐	_____
Qualified profit-sharing plan	☐	☐	☐	☐	_____
Nonqualified deferred-compensation plan	☐	☐	☐	☐	_____
Salary reduction plan (401k)	☐	☐	☐	☐	_____
Simplified employee pension (SEP)	☐	☐	☐	☐	_____
Stock bonus plan	☐	☐	☐	☐	_____
Employee stock-ownership plan (ESOP)	☐	☐	☐	☐	_____
Employee stock-purchase plan	☐	☐	☐	☐	_____
Incentive stock-option plan [§422A]	☐	☐	☐	☐	_____
Restricted stock plan [§83(b)]	☐	☐	☐	☐	_____
Phantom stock plan [§83(a)]	☐	☐	☐	☐	_____
Tax-deferred annuity plan	☐	☐	☐	☐	_____
Salary continuation after death	☐	☐	☐	☐	_____
Other (specify)	☐	☐	☐	☐	_____
Miscellaneous Benefits					
Excess medical reimbursement plan	☐	☐	☐	☐	_____
Split-dollar life insurance	☐	☐	☐	☐	_____
Auto/homeowners	☐	☐	☐	☐	_____
Legal expense	☐	☐	☐	☐	_____
Company car	☐	☐	☐	☐	_____
Educational reimbursement	☐	☐	☐	☐	_____
Club membership	☐	☐	☐	☐	_____
Other (specify)	☐	☐	☐	☐	_____

*Describe appropriate benefits on page 20.

EMPLOYMENT-RELATED
RETIREMENT BENEFITS/DEFERRED COMPENSATION

| Type | Employee's Annual Contribution | Benefits to Client | | | Benefits to Survivors | | | |
| | | Lump-sum Pmts. | Monthly Income | | Beneficiary | Lump-sum Pmts. | Monthly Income | |
			Amount	Beginning/ Ending			Amount	Beginning/ Ending
Qualified pension plan								
Qualified profit-sharing plan								
Nonqualified deferred-compensation plan								
Salary reduction plan (401k)								
Stock bonus plan								
Employee stock-ownership plan (ESOP)								
Employee stock-purchase plan								
Incentive stock-option plan [§422A]								
Restricted stock plan [§83(b)]								
Phantom stock plan [§83(a)]								
Tax-deferred annuity plan								
Salary continuation after death								
Other (specify)								
Other (specify)								

Explain and describe pertinent details for planning purposes here (e.g., anticipated benefits not yet in place; client's views on relevance, need, and feasibility of these benefits; problems associated with implementing benefits; etc.).

Social Security Benefits

What are the estimated retirement benefits (in current dollars)?
client only: client and spouse:

What are the estimated disability benefits the client is eligible for if disabled today?
client only: client and family:

What are the estimated survivors' benefits payable to the client's family if death should occur today?

RISK/RETURN PROFILE

On a scale from 0 to 5, with 5 representing a strong preference and 0 representing an aversion, indicate your preference for the following instruments of savings and investment by circling the appropriate number.

Savings account	0	1	2	3	4	5
Money-market fund	0	1	2	3	4	5
U.S. government bond	0	1	2	3	4	5
Corporate bond	0	1	2	3	4	5
Mutual fund (growth)	0	1	2	3	4	5
Common stock (growth)	0	1	2	3	4	5
Mutual fund (income)	0	1	2	3	4	5
Municipal bond	0	1	2	3	4	5
Real estate (direct ownership)	0	1	2	3	4	5
Variable annuity	0	1	2	3	4	5
Limited partnership unit (real estate, oil and gas, cattle, equipment leasing)	0	1	2	3	4	5
Commodities, gold, collectibles	0	1	2	3	4	5

On a scale from 0 to 5, circle the number to the right of each of the items below that most accurately reflects your own financial concerns; 5 indicates a very strong concern and 0 indicates no concern.

Liquidity	0	1	2	3	4	5
Safety of principal	0	1	2	3	4	5
Capital appreciation	0	1	2	3	4	5
Current income	0	1	2	3	4	5
Inflation protection	0	1	2	3	4	5
Future income	0	1	2	3	4	5
Tax reduction/deferral	0	1	2	3	4	5

Planner's comments and observations

INCOME AND LUMP-SUM NEEDS FOR DISABILITY, RETIREMENT, AND DEATH

	Client	Spouse/Children
Disability Income Needs		
Monthly income needed in current dollars	$_____	$_____
Retirement Income Needs		
Monthly income needed in current dollars	$_____	$_____
Survivors' Income Needs*		
Monthly income needed in current dollars for surviving family members during the following periods after death:		
Adjustment period (adjustment of standard of living in a transitional period, as needed)	$_____	$_____
Until youngest child is self-supporting (number of years_____)	$_____	$_____
After youngest child is self-supporting	$_____	$_____
Survivors' Lump-sum Needs*		
Last expenses (final illness and funeral)	$_____	$_____
Emergency fund	$_____	$_____
Mortgage cancellation fund (if appropriate)	$_____	$_____
Notes and loans payable	$_____	$_____
Accrued taxes (income, real estate, etc., if not withheld)	$_____	$_____
Children's education (if not already funded)	$_____	$_____
Estate settlement costs and taxes (if not provided by liquidity)	$_____	$_____
Other (specify)	$_____	$_____
Total lump-sum needs in current dollars	$_____	$_____

*Some survivors' needs may be met by either periodic income or lump-sum payments or by some combination of the two approaches. Double counting in both categories should be avoided.

Notes

AUTHORIZATION FOR INFORMATION

TO: _____

_____

_____

Please provide any information that is in your possession and that is asked for in connection with a survey of my/our financial affairs to

_____

_____
(client's signature)

_____
(spouse's signature)

_____
(date)

TO: _____
(company)

Please provide any information that is in your possession and that is requested by _____

_____ concerning the following policies of which I am the owner:

_____   _____

_____   _____

_____   _____

Policyowner's
Authorization   _____
(signature of policyowner)

_____
(date)

Notes

RECEIPT FOR DOCUMENTS

Insurance Policies: Life, Health, Property and Liability

Company	Policy Number	☑	Company	Policy Number	☑
_____	_____	☐	_____	_____	☐
_____	_____	☐	_____	_____	☐
_____	_____	☐	_____	_____	☐
_____	_____	☐	_____	_____	☐
_____	_____	☐	_____	_____	☐

Original policies checked ☑ above have been received for review and analysis; they will be returned upon completion of analysis or client request.

_____
(planner)

_____
(address)

_____
(phone)

_____
(date)

All original policies and documents checked in this receipt have been returned to me.

_____
(client)

_____
(date)

Personal/Family Documents (copies)	**Date**	**Business Documents (copies)**	**Date**
☐ Tax returns (3–5 years)	_____	☐ Tax returns (3–5 years)	_____
☐ Wills (client and spouse)	_____	☐ Financial statements (3–5 years)	_____
☐ Trust instruments	_____	☐ Deferred-compensation plan	_____
☐ Financial statements	_____	☐ HR-10 plan (Keogh)	_____
☐ Personal/family budgets	_____	☐ Individual retirement account (IRA)	_____
☐ Sale/purchase contract	_____	☐ Simplified employee pension (SEP)	_____
☐ Current insurance offers	_____	☐ Pension/profit-sharing plan	_____
☐ Current investment offers	_____	☐ Tax-deferred annuity	_____
☐ Deeds, mortgages, land contracts	_____	☐ Stock-option/purchase agreement	_____
☐ Guardian nominations	_____	☐ Buy-sell agreements	_____
☐ Leases (as lessor or lessee)	_____	☐ Employment agreement	_____
☐ Notices of awards, elections	_____	☐ Employee benefits booklet	_____
☐ Power of attorney/appointment	_____	☐ Articles of incorporation	_____
☐ Separation/divorce/nuptial	_____	☐ Merger/acquisition agreement	_____
☐ Patents/copyrights/royalties	_____	☐ Partnership agreement	_____
☐ Employee benefits statement	_____	☐ Company patents	_____
☐ Other (specify)	_____	☐ Equipment leasing agreement(s)	_____
☐ Other (specify)	_____	☐ Other (specify)	_____

OBSERVATIONS FROM COUNSELING SESSIONS

As soon after counseling sessions as possible the financial planner should record impressions and observations about the client in terms of the following:

Personal appearance_____

Appearance of office or home_____

Personal interests (sports, hobbies, music, etc.)_____

_____

Civic-mindedness_____

Political awareness_____

Financial sophistication_____

College ties_____

Decision-making ability_____

Level of personal goals_____

Consistency of verbal and nonverbal behaviors_____

Condition of health_____

Mental/emotional maturity_____

Attitude toward spouse_____parents_____

    children_____other family members_____

Financial risk-taking propensity_____

Attitude toward financial counseling/planning_____

Investment decisions client has made and why_____

Client's financial status (self-made or inherited)_____

Concern with taking care of self during retirement_____

Concern with family after own death_____

Concern with self and family during disability_____

Concern with self right now_____

Concern with self and family right now_____

_____

Other pertinent observations, particularly concerning spouse:

TAX-PLANNING CHECKLIST*

Individual Planning

	At Present Yes	No	Advisable Yes	No
1. Does the client itemize rather than utilize the standard deduction?	☐	☐	☐	☐
2. Are all personal and dependency exemptions being taken (children, parents, foster children, etc.)? [§§151, 152]	☐	☐	☐	☐
3. Are maximum deductions for all expenses related to the production of income being taken?	☐	☐	☐	☐
4. a. Is optimum utilization being made of retirement plans for tax advantage?	☐	☐	☐	☐
b. Has the appropriate type(s) of plan been chosen?	☐	☐	☐	☐
5. Are contributions to charitable and other tax-exempt organizations being used as fully as the client is disposed to use them? [§170]	☐	☐	☐	☐
6. Are the client's real property investments being fully used for tax advantages?	☐	☐	☐	☐
7. Is the impact of the alternative minimum tax being considered for transactions involving tax-preference items? [§55]	☐	☐	☐	☐
8. Are income and deductions being directed to specific years to avoid drastic fluctuation by				
a. accelerating income	☐	☐	☐	☐
b. postponing deductions	☐	☐	☐	☐
c. postponing income	☐	☐	☐	☐
d. accelerating deductions	☐	☐	☐	☐
e. avoiding constructive receipt	☐	☐	☐	☐
9. To reduce estate taxes				
a. have incidents of life insurance ownership been assigned?	☐	☐	☐	☐
b. is a life insurance trust being used? [§§2035, 2042]	☐	☐	☐	☐
10. Have installment sales of investments, residences, or other property been arranged to minimize tax? [§453]	☐	☐	☐	☐
11. Is investment in tax-exempt instruments being used?	☐	☐	☐	☐
12. Is income being shifted to lower-bracket taxpayers through outright gifts or other lifetime transfers such as family partnerships or irrevocable trusts?	☐	☐	☐	☐
13. Is a qualified minors [2503(c)] trust being used effectively for income shifting or other tax advantage?	☐	☐	☐	☐
14. Have gifts been made under the Uniform Gifts to Minors Act (UGMA) or the Uniform Transfers to Minors Act (UTMA)?	☐	☐	☐	☐
15. Are gift/sale leasebacks being used?	☐	☐	☐	☐

*All code section references are to the Internal Revenue Code of 1986 as amended.

Individual Planning (continued)

	At Present Yes	No	Advisable Yes	No
16. Have alternative distribution methods for qualified plans been analyzed for tax consequences?	☐	☐	☐	☐
17. Are capital-loss offsets being used to reduce total income subject to tax?	☐	☐	☐	☐
18. Are qualified plan distributions, rollovers to another qualified plan, or IRAs advisable for the client in the near future?	☐	☐	☐	☐
19. Are contributions to a new or existing IRA advisable if a. the client can make deductible contributions?	☐	☐	☐	☐
b. the client can make only nondeductible contributions?	☐	☐	☐	☐
20. Have like-kind exchanges of property been compared with sale and repurchase and utilized when more advantageous? [§1031]	☐	☐	☐	☐
21. Is the client paying substantial amounts of nondeductible loan interest that should be consolidated under deductible home equity loans? [§163]	☐	☐	☐	☐
22. Have returns of capital on investment been distinguished from taxable income? (For example, has the client's basis in the investment been ascertained and any special tax treatment to which that investment is entitled determined?)	☐	☐	☐	☐
23. Is the client suited for tax-advantaged investments?	☐	☐	☐	☐
24. Indicate any situation unique to this client that does not appear above.				

TAX-PLANNING CHECKLIST (continued)

Business Planning

	At Present Yes	No	Advisable Yes	No
1. Are maximum allowable deductions for all expenses being taken?	☐	☐	☐	☐
2. Are expiring carryovers of credits, net operating losses, and charitable contributions being effectively used through timing of income and deductions? [§§38, 39, 46, 170, 172]	☐	☐	☐	☐
3. a. Is optimum use being made of retirement plans for tax advantage?	☐	☐	☐	☐
b. Has the appropriate type(s) of plan been chosen?	☐	☐	☐	☐
4. Are contributions to charitable and other tax-exempt organizations being used as fully as the client is disposed to use them? [§§170, 501]	☐	☐	☐	☐
5. a. Is the form of client's business or investment being fully utilized to maximize personal deductions and credits (e.g., corporation, partnership, trust, S corp.)?	☐	☐	☐	☐
b. Are the business's investments being fully used to maximize deductions and credits to the shareholder(s)?	☐	☐	☐	☐
6. Are income and deductions being directed to specific years to avoid drastic fluctuation by				
a. accelerating income	☐	☐	☐	☐
b. postponing deductions	☐	☐	☐	☐
c. postponing income	☐	☐	☐	☐
d. accelerating deductions	☐	☐	☐	☐
e. avoiding constructive receipt	☐	☐	☐	☐
7. Is the full range of deductible employment fringe benefits being explored and used within the client's limits?	☐	☐	☐	☐
8. Are gift/sale leasebacks appropriate for this client?	☐	☐	☐	☐
9. Have alternative distribution methods for qualified plans been analyzed for tax consequences?	☐	☐	☐	☐
10. Is sale-or-exchange treatment possible for redemption of equity in a closely held corporation? [§§301, 302, 303, 318]	☐	☐	☐	☐
11. Have nonqualified retirement or deferred-compensation plans been considered? [§83]	☐	☐	☐	☐
12. Are stock options possible and advantageous? [§422A]	☐	☐	☐	☐
13. Have simplified employee pensions (SEPs) been compared with other forms of deferred compensation?	☐	☐	☐	☐
14. Are qualified plans designed for maximum employee advantage during employment as well as at retirement? (For example, do they permit loans and rollovers from other plans, etc.?)	☐	☐	☐	☐

Business Planning (continued)

	At Present Yes	No	Advisable Yes	No
15. a. Have buy-sell plans to take effect at death been developed and formalized by legal agreements?	☐	☐	☐	☐
b. If yes, have they been appropriately funded?	☐	☐	☐	☐
16. Have lifetime transfer methods been considered to facilitate the orderly continuation of the business, for example, in case of disability?	☐	☐	☐	☐
17. Are employment contracts being used effectively to support the reasonableness of executive compensation?	☐	☐	☐	☐

18. Indicate any situation unique to this client that does not appear above.

Estate Planning

	At Present		Advisable	
	Yes	No	Yes	No
1. Have the client and spouse considered electing not to fully use the marital deduction if such an election is tax advantageous to their cumulative estates? [§2056]	☐	☐	☐	☐
2. Have life insurance policies been properly positioned to minimize estate taxes?	☐	☐	☐	☐
3. Does the estate appear to have sufficient liquidity to fund postmortem expenses and estate/inheritance tax liabilities?	☐	☐	☐	☐
4. Has optimum use been made of generation-skipping transfer exemptions? [§§2601-2663]	☐	☐	☐	☐
5. Have testamentary charitable dispositions and their advantages been explored? [§2055]	☐	☐	☐	☐
6. Are lifetime gifting programs being used to shift ownership of assets from the client's estate? [§2503(b), 2503(c)]	☐	☐	☐	☐
7. a. Is the client's will current?	☐	☐	☐	☐
b. Does the will dispose of estate assets in accordance with the client's wishes?	☐	☐	☐	☐
8. Has the value of each estate asset been explored in order to obtain an estimate of potential estate tax liability?	☐	☐	☐	☐
9. Has it been determined that the client can qualify for estate tax deferral? [§6166]	☐	☐	☐	☐
10. If the client qualifies for the requisite percentage of ownership in a corporation, can §303 be utilized to assure sale-or-exchange treatment for stock redeemed to pay administration expenses and estate taxes?	☐	☐	☐	☐
11. Have the client's personal planning objectives, feelings, and thoughts been given equal weight with tax planning?	☐	☐	☐	☐
12. Has an existing estate plan been evaluated as to the impact of the current unified credit, marital deduction, and gift tax exclusion? [§§2010, 2056, 2503, 2523]	☐	☐	☐	☐
13. Has consideration been given to the potential consequence of certain transfers made within 3 years of death? [§2035]	☐	☐	☐	☐
14. Have rules on valuation of certain property (e.g., family farms and real property used in a closely held business) been considered? [§2032A]	☐	☐	☐	☐
15. a. Is there any reversionary interest or power of appointment not on the client's balance sheet?	☐	☐	☐	☐
b. If so, has it been examined for its potential tax impact? [§§2037, 2041]	☐	☐	☐	☐
16. Indicate any situation unique to this client that does not appear above.				

FINANCIAL POSITION STATEMENT

Assets

Cash, Near-Cash Equivalents	Current Value	Projections for Subsequent Years			
		Assumptions	19_____	19_____	19_____
Checking accounts/cash					
Savings accounts					
Money-market funds					
Treasury bills					
Commercial paper					
Short-term CDs					
Life insurance, cash value					
Life insurance, accumulated dividends					
Savings bonds					
Other (specify)					
Subtotal					

Other Financial Assets

U.S. government bonds					
Municipal bonds					
Corporate bonds					
Preferred stock					
Common stock					
Nonmarketable securities					
Warrants and options					
Mutual funds					
Investment real estate					
Long-term CDs					
Vested retirement benefits					
Annuities					
HR-10 plan (Keogh)					
Individual retirement acct. (IRA)					
Mortgages owned					
Land contracts					
Limited partnership units					
Interest(s) in trust(s)					
Receivables					
Patents, copyrights, royalties					
Value of business interest					
Other (specify)					
Subtotal					

35

Assets (continued)

Personal Assets	Current Value	Projections for Subsequent Years			
		Assumptions	19_____	19_____	19_____
Personal residence					
Seasonal residence					
Automobile(s)					
Recreation vehicles					
Household furnishings					
Boats					
Jewelry/furs					
Collections					
Hobby equipment					
Other (specify)					
Subtotal					
Total assets					

Liabilities

Charge accts./credit cards					
Family/personal loans					
Margin/bank/life ins. loans					
Income taxes (fed., state, local)					
Property taxes					
Investment liabilities					
Mortgage(s)					
Child support					
Alimony					
Other (specify)					
Other (specify)					
Other (specify)					
Other (specify)					
Total liabilities					

Net Worth

Total assets minus total liabilities					

INCOME AND LUMP-SUM RESOURCES FOR DISABILITY, RETIREMENT, AND DEATH

Sources of Funds	For Disability			For Retirement			For Death		
	Lump-sum Pmts.	Monthly Income		Lump-sum Pmts.	Monthly Income		Lump-sum Pmts.	Monthly Income	
		Amount	Beginning/ Ending		Amount	Beginning/ Ending		Amount	Beginning/ Ending
Continuing income (p. 6)*									
Income of spouse									
Social security benefits									
Pension plan									
Profit-sharing plan									
HR-10 plan (Keogh)									
Individual retirement account (IRA)									
Nonqualified deferred compensation									
Other retirement benefits/ deferred compensation									
Group life insurance									
Personal life insurance									
Annuities									
Group short-term disability income									
Group long-term disability income									
Personal disability income insurance									
Asset liquidation									
Proceeds of sale of business interest									
Other (specify)									
Other (specify)									
Other (specify)									
Totals									

*Be sure to adjust for income sources from p. 6 of the Fact Finder that will terminate or decrease if client or spouse dies, retires, or is disabled.

CHECKLIST FOR FINANCIAL PLANNING REVIEW

Change in	Has Occurred	Is Expected		Has Occurred	Is Expected
1. Marital status			**9. Property ownership**		
Marriage	☐	☐	Purchase in joint ownership	☐	☐
Separation	☐	☐	Purchase, client owned	☐	☐
Divorce	☐	☐	Purchase, spouse owned	☐	☐
Remarriage	☐	☐	Purchase, dependent owned	☐	☐
			Transfer to joint ownership	☐	☐
2. Number of dependents			Transfer to client	☐	☐
Increase	☐	☐	Transfer to spouse	☐	☐
Decrease	☐	☐	Transfer to dependent	☐	☐
			Transfer to trustee	☐	☐
3. Health status					
Client	☐	☐	**10. Liabilities**		
Spouse	☐	☐	Leases executed	☐	☐
Dependent	☐	☐	Mortgage increase	☐	☐
			Lawsuit against	☐	☐
4. Residence	☐	☐	Judgment against	☐	☐
			Unsecured borrowing	☐	☐
5. Occupation			Cosigning of notes	☐	☐
Client	☐	☐			
Spouse	☐	☐	**11. Business ownership**		
Dependent	☐	☐	New business formation	☐	☐
			Interest purchase	☐	☐
6. Family financial status			Sale of interest	☐	☐
Borrowing	☐	☐	Transfer of interest	☐	☐
Lending	☐	☐	Reorganization among owners	☐	☐
Gifts over $1,000 received	☐	☐	Liquidation	☐	☐
Gifts over $1,000 made	☐	☐	Change of carrier	☐	☐
Purchase of property	☐	☐	Termination or lapse	☐	☐
Sale of property	☐	☐	Surrender	☐	☐
Investments	☐	☐			
Inheritance	☐	☐	**12. Legal document status**		
Deferred income	☐	☐	Change in last will	☐	☐
Pension plan	☐	☐	Change in trust	☐	☐
Tax-deferred annuity	☐	☐	Buy-sell agreement	☐	☐
Dependent's income	☐	☐	Agreement to defer income	☐	☐
7. Sources of income			**13. Insurance status**		
As employee	☐	☐	Life insurance	☐	☐
From self-employment	☐	☐	Health insurance	☐	☐
From tax-exempt employer	☐	☐	Group insurance	☐	☐
From investments	☐	☐	Other employer plan	☐	☐
Inventions, patents, copyrights	☐	☐	Property insurance	☐	☐
Hobbies, avocations	☐	☐	Liability insurance	☐	☐
			Change of plan	☐	☐
8. Income tax status					
From single to joint return	☐	☐	**14. Attitudes toward others**		
From joint to single return	☐	☐	In family	☐	☐
Capital gains	☐	☐	In business	☐	☐
Capital losses	☐	☐	In accepting professional		
Substantial contributions	☐	☐	advice	☐	☐
Unreimbursed casualty loss	☐	☐			
Sick pay received	☐	☐	**15. Interest in**		
Unreimbursed medical			Idea previously discussed	☐	☐
expenses	☐	☐	Plans seen or heard about	☐	☐
Tax-impact investment(s)	☐	☐			

Before financial services professionals can fully develop an estate plan, they must familiarize themselves with the property of clients. This includes information about the extent of the client's ownership interests as well as the form in which various assets are held. The term *property*, as used here, encompasses anything capable of being owned. It includes actual outright ownership of material objects as well as a right to possess, enjoy, use, consume, or transfer something. The limited ability to direct who will enjoy or possess some object may also be considered a property right. One may own property or something of value whether there is present possession or merely the right to come into possession at some designated time in the future. One can own the entire property or a limited portion of it in conjunction with others. Property can be owned absolutely with no restrictions. It can also be owned subject to a variety of conditions or limitations—such as time duration or use restrictions—whether future or present. Within the parameters imposed by law, one's imagination sets the bounds of the intricacies of ownership rights. The more common types of property ownership will be discussed herein.

REAL PROPERTY

All property falls within two broad categories. It is either real or personal. Real property is land and anything on the land that has been permanently attached or affixed to it. Land refers to the ground and everything attached or growing on it, or otherwise intended to be regarded as going with the ground, such as trees, shrubs, and growing crops. Real property includes buildings and fixtures that are permanently attached to and go with the land. However, it does not include such things as a mobile home if it is left in a readily moveable condition. For example, a mobile home with unremoved wheels will generally be regarded as personal property. In short, real property is all property other than personal property.

PERSONAL PROPERTY

All property other than real property is personal property. Personal property is further characterized as either tangible or intangible.

Tangible Personal Property

Tangible personal property is easy to identify. Stated simply, tangible personal property is anything that can be touched, seen, and felt. The property actually represents itself and is the actual object. For example, a chair has the look, feel, substance, and function of a chair. Tangible personal property has intrinsic value.

Intangible Personal Property

Other forms of personal property are known as intangibles. Intangible personal property has no intrinsic value in itself. The real value of intangibles is in excess of the value of the physical object that represents the property. The representation can be touched and felt, but it is not the thing itself. Some examples are stock certificates, leases, mortgages, bonds, and other such representations of property ownership.

MAJOR TYPES OF OWNERSHIP INTERESTS

At common law, the term *estate* historically referred to all manner of interests in real property only. An estate is defined in the Restatement of Property as an interest in land that "is or may become possessory" or "ownership measured in terms of duration." Today, estates in property refer to personal property as well as real property. It is possible to have absolute ownership of property without any limitations. It is also possible to own or have the right to use or possess something for a specified time, such as "use of my vacation house for 10 years." One can also receive an interest in property that will take effect only after a period of time, such as after 10 years, or after the person presently in possession dies. An individual who owns property subject to time limitations possesses an ownership right that is not perpetual or infinite. While these rights are subject to limitations, the property owner may enforce them to the extent of this individual's ownership rights. Although restricted, these rights can be presently valued by taking the limitations into consideration. For example, it is possible to use actuarial tables to place a present value on the absolute right to receive a property interest at a specified future time or when the present owner's interest ends.

Fee Simple Estates

The largest, most complete interest in real estate that one can own is referred to as a *fee simple estate* or *estate in fee simple absolute*. It is an interest that belongs absolutely to an individual. It is potentially infinite in time. Most individually owned property falls into this category. Someone who owns land, a farm, or a house outright possesses a fee simple estate in that property. The owner has the absolute right to keep it during lifetime and pass it on to his or her heirs (or anyone else) at the owner's death. If the owner wishes, he or she can sell the property or give it away during lifetime. Most property ownership falls into the category of the fee simple estate. Generally people who own their residences possess a fee simple interest in the real estate.

Although the fee simple absolute form of ownership provides the most complete interest in property to the owner, it is incorrect to assume that no restrictions exist as to the property rights. Virtually all property interests in modern society are subject to restrictions. For example, zoning laws limit the use of property to specific functions. Also a property owner cannot use the property for illegal purposes or to create a public nuisance. Finally, all property is subject to being taken by the government, with just compensation to the owner, by the constitutional powers of eminent domain.

Split-Ownership Interests

Life Estates

A more limited, but common, form of property ownership is a life estate in the property. A life estate can be measured by the life tenant's life or by the term of someone else's life, if another person's life has been designated as the measuring life. A life estate gives the owner the absolute right to possess, enjoy, or derive income from the property for the span of the measuring life, at which time the interest terminates.

> *Example:* Under his father's will, Alan Abel has been given the exclusive use and possession of his father's residence for Alan's lifetime. When Alan dies, the residence will be transferred to the beneficiary named under his father's will. Alan can live in the house until he dies, allow others to live in it, or rent it. He can also sell his interest. But his interest (or his buyer's interest) in the property will end at his death. The duration of this type of possessory interest is limited by the life of the life tenant (Alan).

> *Example:* Alan's father's will could have given Alan the exclusive use, possession, and enjoyment of the property for the life of Alan's brother, Bob. This type of transfer would still be a life estate in the property but it would be measured by the life of a person other than Alan, the life tenant. Alan's interest in the property would end when the individual who was the measuring life (Bob) died.

In contrast to an owner in fee simple, the owner of a life estate for his or her own life has no interest in the property to transfer at death. However, if the life estate is for the life of another (not the life tenant), the estate continues until the end of the measuring life and that interest can be transferred.

Although the holder of a life estate has the current rights to income from the property, the life tenant has certain duties to the remainderperson. The life tenant is bound not to waste the property. Examples of waste include (1) failure to pay property taxes, (2) failure to insure the property against foreseeable losses, and (3) destruction of the property's income-providing source. The waste of the property creates a legal right of action by the remainderpersons against the life tenant.

Estate for Term of Years

Another type of estate that may or may not outlast a life estate is one created for a definite, limited period of time. An interest in property established for a specific duration is called an estate for a term of years. The period of time involved may be as short as one month or last for many years. It may extend beyond the lifetime of the tenant. The important thing to remember is that it is a right to possess and enjoy property as an owner for a definite period of time.

> *Example:* Instead of receiving a life estate, suppose Alan (in the prior examples) was given exclusive rights to the residence for 10 years, after which the property would go to Bob. Thus Alan would possess an estate for a specified time period or a term of years, instead of a life estate.

If the tenant dies before the end of the term of years, the right to possess the property for the remainder of the term will be determined by the tenant's will or the laws of intestacy. However, the tenant in possession of an estate for a term of years does not have the right to transfer the property at the end of the term of his or her property interest. This is because someone else has retained or has been granted an interest in the property that will commence when the estate for years expires. Perhaps the most common modern example of an estate for a term of years is a leasehold; however, leaseholds may contain certain restrictions (for example, on assignability) that were not part of these estates at common law.

OTHER TYPES OF PROPERTY OWNERSHIP

Other types of property interests that can have significance for estate planners are future interests in property. The term *future interest* may be misleading because a future interest is a present right to possess or enjoy property in the future. Some examples of future interests are remainder interests and reversionary interests.

Remainder Interests

A remainder interest in property is a present right to future enjoyment as distinguished from a present interest in property that gives an absolute, immediate right to use and enjoy the property. The remainder interest must take effect immediately upon the expiration of another estate. Remainder interests may be vested, which means that the right to receive the property in the future is presently fixed and absolute. In contrast, the remainder interest may be a contingent one, which means that it may or may not come into effect at some future date, depending on the occurrence or nonoccurrence of a condition. If a remainder interest is vested and the remainderperson (the person who possesses a remainder interest) dies before the remainder has become effective, that person has an ownership right belonging to either his or her estate or a named beneficiary. As we shall see later, those limitations may affect whether that property will be included in the interim holder's estate at death. One must take remainders into consideration when valuing an estate, particularly because possession of a vested remainder may evoke unanticipated and undesirable federal estate tax consequences.

As has been previously noted, a remainder interest is a present interest, although it will only come into possession or enjoyment in the future. It may ripen or take effect at a designated future time or on the occurrence of an event, such as the death of the present life tenant.

> *Example:* Don is given property for his life. After that, it passes to Tom absolutely. Don possesses a life estate and Tom is the remainderperson. Tom's right to the use and possession of the property will begin when Don's interest expires. In this situation, Tom has a present absolute right to take possession of the property at Don's death.

Vested or Contingent Remainders

To further complicate this type of ownership right, remainders may be either vested or contingent. A vested interest in property is an absolute and presently fixed right to possess and enjoy the property either now or in the future. Postponement of actual possession to a future time does not prevent the interest from being presently vested. When an individual's remainder interest is vested, he or she owns a present legally enforceable right to possess and enjoy that property when the interest comes into being. Note that it is a presently determined right although enjoyment may not occur until a future date. A vested absolute right to receive the entire property at some future time after the present interest ceases is known as an *indefeasibly vested remainder*. Should the remainderperson die before that time, the vested remainder interest he or she possessed at death will become enforceable by the estate or heirs at the moment the present interest ceases.

On the other hand, a contingent property right is a more uncertain one. It may never become a possessory interest. A contingency is usually dependent on the occurrence or nonoccurrence of an event or condition. Only time will tell if the necessary contingencies occur that determine whether the right to possess and enjoy the property will actually be obtained. If the contingency does not occur, the anticipated property right dependent on the happening would not become a possessory one. On the other hand, if all conditions are met, the interest would vest and become absolute.

> *Example:* Suppose Tom (in the prior example) will receive his interest in property only by surviving Don, who has a life estate. But if Tom dies before Don, the property will go to Ed at Don's death. Tom is a remainderperson but, in this case, he is a contingent rather than a vested remainderperson. The contingency is whether Tom will survive beyond Don's interest in the property. Ed's interest is also a contingent remainder because he will inherit the property only if Tom predeceases Don.

Reversionary Interests

Another kind of interest in property is called a *reversion* or *reversionary interest.* This type of interest occurs when the owner of an estate transfers a lesser estate to another. A reversionary interest gives the owner (grantor) the right to have all or part of the property that he or she had originally owned and then transferred returned to the owner or the owner's estate.

The fact that the grantor has retained a reversionary interest by transferring less than the total estate does not mean that the grantor retained a present right to possess and enjoy the property concurrently with the present estate owner. In fact, a reversion is only a present *retained* right to future enjoyment. Reversions are always vested.

> *Example:* James owns Blackacre in fee simple absolute. He conveys Blackacre to Ellen for her life. Ellen has a life estate in Blackacre. But since James has conveyed less than his total interest, he has retained a reversionary interest in Blackacre. Because of the reversionary interest, at Ellen's death Blackacre will revert to James, if he is living, or to his estate.

The method for determining whether a reversionary interest has been retained can be ascertained by applying the following formula: If the estate transferred is less than the estate owned, then a reversionary interest exists.

Both remainder and reversionary interests are fraught with income and estate tax consequences that may create tax traps for the unwary. Essentially these are incomplete transfers that may cause the property transferred or the income generated to be taxed to the original grantor or the grantor's estate as if the grantor still was an owner in possession. It is essential to have property transfers structured so that the desired tax consequences will be achieved.

LEGAL OR EQUITABLE OWNERSHIP

It is possible to have different types of rights in the same property held by different parties. One may be the legal owner without the right to the beneficial enjoyment from the property, and vice versa.

The legal owner is the one who holds legal title to the property. As a rule, the legal owner is the absolute owner and has all the rights and obligations connected with property ownership. The person with legal title is generally the one in possession. He or she has the full rights of use, enjoyment, and control over the property. Technically an absolute owner holds both legal and equitable title.

There are certain circumstances, however, in which legal and equitable ownership are split between different parties. A common example of this division of title occurs when property is held in trust. By definition, under our trust laws, legal and equitable title are separated between parties. The trustee is the party who holds legal title. According to the terms of the trust, the trustee must invest and manage the property under the fiduciary standards established by state law. However, the income generated by the trustee's efforts is then distributed to or held for the benefit of others (the beneficiaries) who hold equitable title.

The person with equitable title to property is the one who is entitled to all the benefits from the property. This refers to such benefits as the right to use, possess, or enjoy the property, as well as the right to have income from the property. Equitable ownership and beneficial ownership mean the same thing and are sometimes used interchangeably. The equitable owner of a trust is the beneficiary of a trust for whose benefit the property is being managed. As long as the trust continues, the trustee will hold legal title (with all the attendant fiduciary responsibilities), and the beneficiaries will be the equitable or beneficial owners only. Upon termination of the trust and final distribution of the trust property to the ultimate beneficiaries, both titles will be united in the beneficiaries who will become absolute owners.

SITUS

Situs refers to the place where property is located or kept. Because each state has an interest in the welfare of its residents as well as the protection of property located within its borders, all transfers of real and personal property are subject to state law. Under both state statute and local ordinances, state and local governmental authorities regulate and tax all real estate within their jurisdiction. The state has this power over real property within its borders, irrespective of where the property owner actually lives. The situs or location of real property is particularly important to the estate planner because all real property as well as tangible personal property is subject to the laws and taxing powers of the jurisdiction in which it is located.

DOMICILE

Another important factor to consider when developing an estate plan is the domicile of an individual. Domicile is the place that individuals consider to be their permanent residence and to which they intend to return if they have temporarily left. Individuals may have personal residences in more than one state. While it was once thought that people could only have one domicile, the U.S. Supreme Court has decided otherwise as shown later in this reading under the heading "Possibility of Multiple Taxation." Generally a husband and wife are presumed to have the same domicile.

When a person dies, the estate is usually probated, distributed, and taxed under the laws of the state in which he or she is domiciled. One's domicile becomes significant because there is great variation among state death tax laws. Simply put, inheritance and estate tax laws imposed by different states are not uniform. A state has an interest in claiming that an individual is domiciled within its borders in order to subject this individual to taxation there.

Depending on the nature of a person's property, it may be taxed (1) by the state of domicile, (2) by the state of location, or (3) by both. Specific types of property are discussed below.

Real Estate

Real estate is taxed solely by the state where the property is located. This results from the principle that one state does not have jurisdiction to take action on real property located in another state. Courts have consistently followed this principle and prevented states from taxing real property located in other states. Another example of this principle is that succession of real property is also determined by the laws of the situs state.

> *Example:* Ted was domiciled in state X at the time of death but owned real property in state Y. Ted's will is invalid under the laws of state X but valid under the laws of Y. The real property in Y passes under the provisions of Ted's will, but Ted's other property passes under the intestate succession laws of X.

Tangible Personal Property

While it is simple to determine the situs of real estate, tangible personal property may be another matter since it is transportable. Generally, tangible personal property is taxed by the state where the property is kept. Depending on the local law, it may be taxed also by the state of domicile. The situs of tangible personal property is the place where its use is fixed for a reasonable time for ordinary and customary use purposes. Under the theory that all property belonging to a domiciliary is taxable by the state of domicile, that state may also attempt to tax tangible personal property of a decedent located elsewhere.

Intangible Personal Property

In some instances, local jurisdictions also have an interest in the taxation of the intangible personal property of their residents as well as nonresidents. Intangibles are generally taxed by the state of domicile, regardless of their location or connection with another state. It makes no difference where intangibles are kept. Any state with a reasonable connection or nexus to the property may impose a tax on its value.

> *Example:* If an individual is a resident of Pennsylvania but owns stock in a corporation in Delaware, the state of the corporate domicile (in this case, Delaware) can impose a tax on the transfer of shares of a nonresident stockholder, if its laws so provide. Some states, such as Pennsylvania, exempt intangible personal property of nonresidents from taxation when the property is transferred at death. However, many states (such as Pennsylvania) will tax the intangibles of a resident although the property is situated outside the state.

Establishing Domicile

There are a number of things an individual can do to establish domicile in a particular state.

Some actions that indicate intent to establish domicile are voter registration, automobile registration, location of bank accounts and safe-deposit boxes, situs of principal residence, and payment of property as well as income taxes. The place where financial and legal advisers are located will assist in determining which state is the state of domicile.

While an individual ideally should sever ties with a former state of domicile, many individuals (particularly those who spend winter months in a warmer climate) may retain residences and other connections in their former states. If so, care should be taken to reside in the state of intended domicile for more than one-half of the year. An individual may also establish memberships in social clubs and religious organizations in a particular state to indicate intent of domicile.

Possibility of Multiple Taxation

Since each state has its own revenue laws and public policy, state death taxation is locally determined. There is no simple way to predict the likelihood of double taxation of property passing at death. It is conceivable that more than one state will attempt to tax the same property. In a well-known Supreme Court case, *in re Dorrence Estate*, the Supreme Court held that it was legal for more than one state to have an interest in the property of an individual. The statutes of the states involved should be carefully researched when an individual owns property in more than one state, which would subject the property to taxation under that state's jurisdiction. If the courts of two different states have each made a lawful finding of domicile, there is no constitutional barrier to taxation by both states.

Individuals who split their residences between two states should take a definitive position as to the state where they wish their property to be taxed at death. Knowledge of state death tax laws is critical for proper premortem planning. In some instances, the only death taxes due will be state taxes since the federal estate tax deductions and the increased unified credit will eliminate estate taxation at the federal level for all but larger estates.

CONCURRENT OWNERSHIP—OWNERSHIP BY MORE THAN ONE INDIVIDUAL OR ENTITY

Property can be owned entirely by one individual, thereby making that individual the sole owner. A person may also own a portion of the property. Partial interests may either be segregated and delineated or may consist of an undivided interest in the entire property.

> *Example:* One can own an undivided one-third interest in real estate. Likewise, one can own 50 percent of the stock of corporation X. In both cases, the value of the interest owned is measured as a percentage of the whole.

There are several ways to own property in conjunction with other individuals. Following is a discussion of the more common types of co-ownership:

In most common-law states, there are generally three possible ways to own property in conjunction with others. They are (1) tenancies in common, (2) joint tenancies with right of survivorship, and (3) tenancies by the entirety. Each of these categories has distinguishing features. The rights of the co-owners vary depending on the forms of co-ownership that exist. Each form of concurrent ownership is governed by local law. In addition, there may be federal, estate, gift, or income tax consequences flowing from the transfer of a co-owner's interest either during lifetime or at death.

Understanding and properly structuring ownership of property interests is critical to the establishment of a carefully designed estate plan for an individual client. At best, there is both mystery and misunderstanding regarding the rights as well as limitations of various forms of co-ownership.

Tenancies in Common

Property owned concurrently by two or more persons who may be but are not necessarily related is generally called a tenancy in common. There may be any number of owners who hold property as tenants in common. Each tenant's share is an undivided part of the entire property. However, each tenant need not own an equal share with the other cotenants—ownership interests may or may not be equally divided. Each tenant's share may be based on an allocation that was agreed on by the cotenants. A common method for division of shares may be the percentage contribution that each tenant in common made to the purchase price of the property.

Unless restricted by contract or agreement with the other co-owners, each tenant is free to sell or dispose of his or her interest in the property to whomever the tenant wishes. The tenant does not require the consent or even the knowledge of the other cotenants. In other words, each cotenant is free to be divested of his or her property interest by sale, gift, or will. If the cotenant holds an interest in a tenancy in common and dies without a will, that individual's interest will be distributed to his or her heirs under the intestate laws of the state in which the cotenant resides. In legal parlance, a tenant in common's interest as described above is said to be freely alienable, descendible, and devisable.

A cotenant is generally treated as a separate owner of his or her share of the property for income tax purposes. Each cotenant is entitled to his or her share of any income generated by the property. If the cotenant's interest is sold, gain or loss will be realized as though the cotenant had owned the property individually. A tenant in common will have a certain basis in the property depending on his or her proportionate interest in and contribution to the property.

To the extent that one tenant has received a greater proportionate interest than his or her contribution to the tenancy, a gift has been made from the cotenant who contributed a greater proportionate amount to the cotenancy at its creation. A gift may also occur if the property is sold and a cotenant receives a greater share of the proceeds than his or her contribution represents.

Generally all tenants are obligated to pay expenses for maintaining or operating the property in proportion to their respective interests. In addition, state law may provide that the cotenant not in possession may be entitled to receive a proportionate amount of rent from the cotenant in possession of the property.

One of the most important characteristics of the tenancy in common is that there are no survivorship rights. Each tenant's interest in the property may be left to the tenant's heirs, and at death, the tenant's gross estate will include the fair market value of his or her proportionate interest.

When a cotenant sells or otherwise disposes of his or her interest in a tenancy in common, the new owner will become a tenant in common with the remaining cotenants. At the time of sale, the cotenant will realize gain or loss on his or her share that will be treated as if it was separate property. If a property is indivisible, a tenant in common may cause the entire property to be sold by a partition sale under local law. In that case, the sale proceeds will be distributed in accordance with the respective interests owned by each cotenant. Use of a forced sale to partition the property at auction will probably not generate a price equal to the true market value of the property potentially obtainable in a private sale.

A tenancy in common may also be created by operation of law when a joint tenancy is severed by agreement of the parties, by divorce of the joint tenants, or by the sale of a joint tenant's interest.

Joint Tenancies with Right of Survivorship

Individuals are often intrigued by ownership as joint tenants with right of survivorship because they have heard that joint tenancies are nonprobate property. There is a common belief that no tax consequences stem from such jointly held property. Some people think that the elimination of probate fees, including executor commissions and lawyer's fees, outweighs other considerations. In truth, there are some positive aspects of joint ownership with survivorship rights, especially convenience. In addition, some married couples may derive a sense of unity and partnership from owning some or all of their property in this form of joint ownership. However, as will be seen, joint ownership with survivorship rights also involves giving up some rights in the property and forgoing much flexibility in estate planning.

Joint tenancy with right of survivorship is similar to tenancies in common in that there may be two or more joint tenants. Joint tenants may or may not be related to each other. Each joint tenant is considered to be an owner of the entire property subject to the rights of the other joint owners. Therefore all joint tenants with right of survivorship must have equal rights and obligations with respect to the property. Unlike tenancies in common there cannot be disproportionate ownership: that is, one joint tenant with right of survivorship cannot have a two-thirds interest while another has a one-third interest.

During lifetime, each joint tenant may sell his or her interest in the property without the other joint tenants joining in the conveyance, but such a transaction will sever the joint tenancy with right of survivorship. One joint tenant may also sell his or her interest in the property to the other joint owners. On severance, the form of ownership may change to another form of joint ownership—generally tenants in common—or the property itself may be divided among the joint tenants. If the property is equitably divisible, a joint owner may receive his or her share of the property free of the other joint owners by physically partitioning the property. However, if the property is not equitably divisible, it must be sold and the proceeds divided.

The primary difference between tenancies in common and jointly held property with right of survivorship is that jointly held property will pass to the surviving joint tenants at the death of one of the joint owners. When there are more than two joint tenants, the property will ultimately pass to the last surviving joint tenant who, as sole surviving owner, has all rights in the property. The last surviving joint tenant is free to hold or dispose of it in whatever way desirable. If the last surviving joint tenant owns it at death, the full value will be included in his or her gross estate. Jointly held property is not transferred by will. It passes to the surviving joint tenants by operation of law outside of the will. That is what is meant by the phrase *right of survivorship*. Beneficiaries of a deceased joint tenant other than the surviving joint tenant(s) have no rights in the property. An advantage of a joint tenancy with right of survivorship is that the property will pass free of probate in many states. If so, the expenses connected with probate, such as executor's commissions or attorney's fees, may be eliminated. Jointly held property will be includible in the gross estate of the deceased joint tenant for federal estate tax purposes to the extent of that tenant's contribution to or interest in the property. In some states, the joint tenant's interest may be taxable for state death tax purposes as well, whereas there are those states that exempt a joint tenant's interest from state death taxes where the joint tenants were married.

Sometimes it is difficult to determine whether a co-ownership of property is a tenancy in common or a joint tenancy with right of survivorship. Local law generally favors tenancies in common over joint tenancies with right of survivorship. Any ambiguity in the form of ownership will be construed as a tenancy in common rather than as a joint tenancy. A jointly owned tenancy should include in the title the phrase *with right of survivorship* to make the intent clear. When a married couple is divorced, their jointly held property will generally be converted to a tenancy in common, unless they decide, by agreement, to hold the property as joint tenants with right of survivorship on a nonrelated basis.

When a joint tenancy is created and one of the joint tenants contributes more than his or her share of personal funds to acquire the jointly held property, that joint tenant has made a gift to the other joint tenant. Also, if one of the joint owners pays more than his or her share of either mortgage payments or the cost of maintenance and operation of the property, that joint owner is making a gift to the other joint tenants. This is true only if the contributing joint tenant cannot regain the property without the other joint tenant participating in the transfer. If the contributing joint tenant has full right of unilateral withdrawal, such as from a joint bank account, no gift is made at the creation of such a joint tenancy. It is only when the donee-joint tenant withdraws the jointly held property that a gift is made.

> *Example:* If Ms. Jones deposits money in a joint savings account that she opens in the names of herself and her son, she has not made a gift until her son withdraws some of the money for his own use. The donee-joint tenant must receive some benefit from the property before a completed gift is made.

Bank Accounts

Each state has its own laws with regard to the legal relationship between joint tenants with right of survivorship who own bank accounts, savings bonds, or securities. If a joint bank account is created, each joint owner will own a proportionate part of the account balance and be entitled to receive one-half of the interest income on which he or she will be taxable (unless it is tax-exempt income). Of course, if the account is owned by spouses who file a joint return, there will not be any income-splitting advantages. With other types of accounts, the interest should be reportable by each joint tenant in proportion to the amount the joint tenant contributed to the account. Banks usually report the income as taxable to the joint tenant whose social security number is on the account. There is no gift if a person uses personal funds to open a joint bank account. A gift is considered made only when the other joint owner (the donee) makes withdrawals.

Government Savings Bonds

When a Series E (EE) or Series H (HH) government savings bond is held in joint ownership, there is no gift when the bond is purchased because the joint owner who contributed the funds can cash in the bond at any time and get his or her money back. As with joint bank accounts, a gift occurs when the donee-joint tenant redeems the bond and retains a greater share of the proceeds than he or she had contributed to the purchase price. At that time, a gift has been made from the contributing joint tenant to the donee-joint tenant equal to the redemption value of the bond reduced by the percentage contribution to the purchase price that the donee-joint tenant had made.

When a safe-deposit box is held in joint ownership, both joint tenants have access to the contents of the box. This does not mean that the contents of the box would be considered owned in equal shares by each joint tenant. The contents of the box remain the property of the joint tenant who deposited them. Joint tenants of a safe-deposit box must comply with the joint-ownership requirements of local law with regard to the ownership of the box contents. Depending on the nature of the contents, there should be a written document specifying that a legal transfer from the sole owner to the other joint lessee of the box has occurred if they intend to own the contents equally as joint owners. If true joint ownership with right of survivorship is created, the income and gift tax consequences will depend on the type of property that has been thus transferred in writing.

Basically the above types of joint ownership (bank accounts and government savings bonds) are revocable creations that do not invoke gift tax ramifications at the inception of the joint tenancy. However, the treatment for joint ownership of securities is different, because there is a formal agreement between the joint owners of securities and the broker.

If the securities are registered in the names of the co-owners as joint tenants with right of survivorship and not as tenants in common, a gift occurs from the contributing joint tenant to the donee-joint tenant when the securities are transferred to the account or purchased for the account. However, the result is not the same if the account has been registered in street name. There is an IRS ruling that holds that no gift occurs on the creation of a joint street name account when one of the joint tenants has furnished more than one-half of the consideration. A gift occurs only when the other party withdraws from the account more than his or her proportionate contribution to the account, because securities registered in individuals' names as joint tenants require the signature of both to sell the securities. However, the signatures of both are not required when the account is in street name.

As to income tax consequences, if securities are registered in joint names, each joint tenant is entitled to a proportionate share of the interest income under local law. Again, if the joint tenants are husband and wife, it is likely that they will file a joint return that would make allocation of income irrelevant.

To summarize, the financial services professional should keep in mind that joint tenancies may have gift tax ramifications depending on the nature of the property held as joint tenants with right of survivorship, when there has been a disproportionate contribution to the property by one of the joint owners. No gift will occur if the contributing tenant can, at any time, withdraw the property contributed and regain sole possession of it, because the transfer is incomplete as long as the contributing joint tenant retains dominion and control over the property. A gift will occur when the noncontributing or donee-joint tenant withdraws from the joint tenancy a greater proportion than the amount contributed. At that time, the gift becomes irrevocable and complete. However, in the case of joint tenancies that require both signatures to sell or transfer property, a gift will be made at the time the property is transferred to a joint tenancy. If the joint tenants are husband and wife, there will be no gift tax liability, although one spouse may have contributed more than one-half of the property to the joint tenancy. This is so because since ERTA in 1981, the law now considers a married couple a single economic unit. Although a *gift* has been made from one spouse to another, the unlimited gift tax marital deduction applies so that there will be no tax to pay. Furthermore, no gift tax return is required for transfers from one spouse to a joint-ownership arrangement with the other spouse.

Tenancies by the Entirety

A tenancy by the entirety is similar to a joint tenancy with right of survivorship although it is more restrictive. It is limited to co-ownership of property held by a husband and wife. By definition, a tenancy by the entirety exists only during marriage and will be terminated upon divorce of the spouses. Local law will determine some of the features of a tenancy by the entirety. For example, each tenant is entitled to one-half of the income from the property in most states. However, in those states still governed by common law, the husband may be entitled to all the net income from the property.

The primary difference between a tenancy by the entirety and jointly held property with right of survivorship is that neither spouse may unilaterally terminate the tenancy by conveying his or her interest to a third party during lifetime. In contrast to the types of ownership previously described, a tenancy by the entirety cannot be severed by selling either party's undivided interest without the consent of the other tenant. Husband and wife must join in a sale or other conveyance to third parties.

Because there are variations under local law with regard to each of these forms of co-ownership, the financial services professional must review the local law before advising clients regarding the rights and obligations of each form of co-ownership. Generally it will be presumed that the form of ownership is a tenancy in common if co-owners are not married. However, if they are a married couple, a tenancy by the entirety may be presumed. Some jurisdictions insist that the words *right of survivorship* are necessary in order to construe the co-ownership as a joint tenancy or tenancy by the entirety. In many states today, tenancies by the entirety are limited to co-ownership of real estate by a husband and wife. Some states have completely abolished the tenancy-by-the-entirety form of ownership.

Advantages and Disadvantages of Joint Tenancies with Right of Survivorship and Tenancies by the Entirety

There are both advantages and disadvantages to these forms of property ownership beyond the tax considerations. Advantages of these forms of joint ownership include the following:

- Under most state laws, property owned as tenants by the entirety usually cannot be reached by creditors of one of the tenants. Such property can only be reached by joint creditors.
- These forms of ownership are convenient for certain types of assets, such as bank accounts, because either tenant has access to the account.
- Joint tenancies and tenancy by the entirety may give one or both of the tenants a feeling of security. This is especially true when the owners are spouses and one spouse has contributed most of the funds.
- When one tenant dies, the property passes directly to the surviving joint tenant. There are no probate delays. There may be little or no administrative and transfer costs. The property will remain fully accessible to the surviving owner.

2.15

- In many states, these forms of property ownership between spouses pass free of state death taxes.
- Since such property passes by operation of law and not under will, it is a private arrangement and not open for public scrutiny.

While these forms of ownership may be both convenient and psychologically comforting, they may not constitute the best estate plan for all persons and may severely impair an appropriate estate plan when used improperly. As an individual's estate increases, a review and analysis of such property should be made to determine if it is the best form of ownership for the individual's needs.

There are also disadvantages inherent in these jointly held property arrangements, which include the following:

- There are potential gift taxes at the creation of some of these property ownership interests.
- There may be additional federal estate taxation. The entire value of property held jointly with right of survivorship, except that held solely by spouses, may be taxed in the estate of the first joint owner to die. The entire property will then be owned by the surviving tenant and will be fully subject to estate taxation again at the survivor's death.
- The surviving tenant will gain full control over the property and may ultimately dispose of it in any way desired. The loss of control by the decedent-tenant is one of the major disadvantages of these types of ownership. The decedent's will, trust, or other dispositive documents will have no effect on the disposition of the jointly held property.
- The decedent's estate may be faced with a liquidity problem. Property passing directly to the surviving tenant may not be made available to the decedent's estate for the payment of taxes, debts, or expenses.
- Under most state laws, property owned as joint tenants with right of survivorship can be reached by creditors of an individual joint tenant.

It has been stressed that there are both tax and nontax reasons for the creation of different forms of property ownership when held by more than one individual concurrently. There is no one answer with regard to arrangements of property. Generally a combination of different ownership arrangements will provide the best results in good estate planning. One important factor to examine is the size of the relative estates of potential co-owners of property.

COMMUNITY PROPERTY

Another form of co-ownership limited to interests held between husband and wife that has particular significance today because of our mobile society is community property. Only 9 of the 50 states are community-property states, yet close to 25 percent of the American population resides in those states for all or some part of their married lives. Thus they are affected by community-property laws. The laws of the particular community-property state in which a married couple resides must be examined to determine accurately the specific effect on a married couple's property ownership. Each state has developed its own special variations that make it difficult to generalize about community-property laws for all nine states. The nine community-property states are as follows:

- Arizona
- California
- Idaho
- Louisiana (further complicated by the Napoleonic Code)
- Nevada
- New Mexico
- Texas
- Washington
- Wisconsin*

The nature and tax treatment of community property is discussed in detail in reading 3.

*Wisconsin recently adopted a form of the Uniform Marital Property Act and is now treated for federal tax purposes as a community-property state.

COMMUNITY PROPERTY AT A GLANCE

Rory R. Olsen*

THE PROBLEM

Assume that you have begun a professional relationship with a man in his early 50s who has been married to the same woman for 30 years. Your inventory discloses the following major assets, all titled in his name:

Bank accounts	$ 43,000
Securities	198,000
Life insurance	300,000
Real estate	159,000
Stock in closely held corporation	1,300,000
Total	$2,000,000

Before you can prepare an estate plan for this client, you must first ascertain how large his estate is for federal estate tax purposes.

In most states, you could assume that the entire value of the assets listed above——$2 million——would be includible in this client's gross estate. However, this is not true in all cases. If the client lived in a community-property state, only one-half of the community property would be includible in the gross estate. Just as in non-community-property states you could assume that the hypothetical client's gross estate was $2 million, so in community-property states could you assume that only one-half of the property, $1 million, was in the client's gross estate.

Unfortunately, these assumptions can prove dangerous if you do not know more about the client.

The problem with making these assumptions is that they ignore the well-known social phenomenon of mobility. Americans like to move from house to house and from state to state. Our hypothetical client may have acquired all the assets listed above in Texas, a community-property state, and then may have moved to Tennessee, a non-community-property state. If a Tennessee estate planner were to apply the usual assumptions as to the ownership of the assets described above, the estate planner would be wrong.

*Rory R. Olsen, MBA, JD, LLM, is a member of the North Carolina, Tennessee, and Texas bars; he has his own law firm in Houston, Texas.

Conversely, if our hypothetical client had stayed in Texas, an estate planner could not automatically assume that all the assets listed above were community property. Many or all of them could have been inherited, which, as will be discussed later, would make them separate (noncommunity) property.

Therefore the estate planner, whether residing in Texas, Tennessee, or anywhere else, should be conscious of the existence of the community-property system and know where it holds sway and where it does not.

Since there are only nine community-property states, it is much easier to remember these states than the non-community-property ones. All community-property states are located either partly or wholly west of the Mississippi.

Although there are only nine community-property states at the present time, it should be noted that earlier in this century a number of states— Hawaii, Michigan, Nebraska, Oklahoma, Oregon, and Pennsylvania—adopted the community-property system as a way of reducing income taxes for married couples. This proved to be an early forerunner of recent efforts to reduce the so-called marriage penalty. The Revenue Act of 1948 added income splitting between spouses to the Internal Revenue Code, thereby obviating the need for these states to adopt community property. Although all these states have now abandoned the community-property system, aftereffects remain. Many older couples lived in these states while they were community-property states and acquired assets that were and still remain community assets. An estate planner dealing with a couple who lived in any of these *temporary community-property states* would be well advised to review their situations closely.

WHAT IS COMMUNITY PROPERTY?

Historical Origins of Community Property in the United States

When the European settlers arrived in North America, they brought their culture and traditions with them, including their legal systems. The English, who settled on the Atlantic Coast, brought with them the English common-law system. The French, who settled in what is now Louisiana, and the Spanish, who settled in present-day Texas, New Mexico, Arizona, and California, brought with them the civil law. When those states originally settled by the French or Spanish joined the Union, they brought legal systems with them that, to varying degrees, attempted to blend the civil law into the American legal system, which was firmly and deeply rooted in the English common-law legal system. Later Washington and Idaho adopted a legal system based on that of California.

One of the central features of the law in these nine states, which is directly attributable to their early settlers and the civil law, is the existence of community property.

Community Property—A Definition

In discussing community property, two terms—*separate property* and *community property*—must be remembered. Between spouses, what is not separate property is community property, so in that sense community property is a negative concept.

Separate property is defined as either property owned before marriage by either spouse or property acquired after marriage by gift or inheritance. Property acquired during marriage by either spouse, if not defined as separate property, is treated as community property.

The essence of community property is the treatment of a marriage as a de facto partnership between the spouses. Each spouse receives an equal interest in property acquired by the other spouse during marriage. Unfortunately, there are substantial differences among the nine community-property states. The next section will describe in more detail some of the workings and problem areas of the community system and will of necessity be general in nature. It is important for the estate planner to consult the laws of the particular community-property state involved before attempting to resolve a particular problem.

Income from Separate Property

If a man or woman brings property into a marriage or inherits or receives property as a gift after the marriage, that property is separate property by definition. What about the income from that separate property—is it separate or community property?

The community-property states can be divided into two distinct groups with reference to this issue. One group—typified by California—holds that income from separate property retains its separate-property status.[1] This rule is a departure from the traditional civil-law rule.

Three other states—Texas, Louisiana, and Idaho—have retained to some extent the civil-law rule that all income earned during marriage is community property.

For example, Sec. 5.01(a) of the Texas Family Code defines a spouse's separate property as (1) property owned before marriage; (2) property acquired by the spouse during marriage by gift, devise, or descent; or (3) recovery for personal injuries (except for loss of earning capacity). Sec. 5.01(b) defines all other property earned during marriage as community property. Case law in Texas has long supported the proposition that income from separate property is community property.[2]

Notwithstanding this long-established rule in Texas, it is now possible for spouses or prospective spouses in Texas to agree to keep income from separate property as separate property. This change was brought about through an amendment to Article XVI, Section 15 of the Texas Constitution, passed in the 1980 general election.

3.3

In analyzing a client's estate, the estate planner should note not only where the spouses resided during marriage, but also the existence of any prenuptial or postnuptial agreements or other documents that may have kept income from separate property separate.

Presumptions concerning Community Property

Anyone who has ever acted as an executor or administrator of a decedent's estate or has attempted to bring order to his or her own records in preparation for filing an income tax return will readily agree that most people fail to keep complete, accurate, and orderly records of their personal financial affairs. Quite often financial details disappear rapidly into a record-keeping morass, never to be found again.

When a marriage in a community-property state is dissolved, either by divorce or by death, someone—the judge, attorney, accountant, or personal representative—will be forced to try to characterize assets as either community or separate property. There is a presumption in the community-property system that assets on hand at the dissolution of marriage are community property, unless proven to the contrary. For example, Sec. 5.02 of the Texas Family Code dictates that "property possessed by either spouse during or on dissolution of marriage is presumed to be community property."

Life Insurance

Life insurance is treated differently by different community-property states. There are three rules, typified by California, Texas, and Arizona.

The first rule (which holds sway in California) is called the *apportionment rule*, and works as follows: Assume that a policyholder buys a level-premium, whole life policy while he and his spouse live in a common-law state. Assume further that the first five annual premiums are paid out of the policyholder's separate property. Assume that after the fifth annual premium is paid, they move to a community-property state and that the next 5 years' premiums are paid out of community funds. If the policyholder dies at the end of the 10th year, 50 percent of the policy death benefit proceeds will be separate property and the other 50 percent will be community property.[3]

Texas follows what is known as the *inception-of-title doctrine*, which holds that a policy acquired with community funds after marriage is a community asset.[4] If a life insurance policy was purchased in Texas either before or after marriage, but with separate funds, the policy would be separate property, with the surviving spouse retaining a right of reimbursement for that spouse's half of the community funds used for premium payments. This right of reimbursement would only come into action if the policy beneficiary is the surviving spouse.

The final rule (exemplified by Arizona) looks toward the source of the final premium payment. If the final premium was paid from community funds, the policy is a community asset.[5]

Unlike many other areas of community-property law, this one is both complex and unsettled. Therefore only tentative generalizations, which may or may not be valid tomorrow, can be given. Care must be taken to ascertain the current status of the community-property laws of any given state before attempting to create or analyze an estate plan subject to those laws. While true in all areas, this caveat is particularly true regarding the status of life insurance.

Joint Tenancy

In common-law states, spouses often hold various types of property as joint tenants with right of survivorship or through a tenancy by the entirety, which is a form of joint tenancy between spouses. The essential element of a joint tenancy is that the surviving joint tenant, upon the death of a deceased joint tenant, acquires the deceased joint tenant's interest in the property by operation of law.

Joint tenancy or tenancy by the entirety is a very common way for spouses to hold property in common-law states. The obvious advantage of such an arrangement is that the survivor acquires the decedent's interest in the property automatically, free of the probate process. While joint tenancy may be the norm in common-law states, it is alien to community-property states and has met with varying degrees of hostility.

For example, assume that Harry, who lives in Texas with Wanda, places an order to buy 500 shares of stock in Dry Hole, Inc. When taking the order, Broker, Harry's account representative, will undoubtedly ask how he wants the shares titled—either in Harry's name alone or as a joint tenant with Wanda.

If Harry had the 500 shares of Dry Hole titled "Harry and Wanda, joint tenants with right of survivorship," did Harry create an enforceable joint tenancy? Probably not, despite the words on the face of the stock certificate.

In Texas, there is a statutory presumption against joint tenancy and in favor of tenancy in common. The presumption against joint tenancy can only be overcome through the existence of a written document indicating that joint ownership was the intent of the parties. No such agreement may be inferred from the mere fact that the parties took title as joint owners.[6] If the parties are husband and wife, taking title as joint tenants is insufficient by itself to change community property into property held under joint tenancy.[7]

In dealing with property of a husband and wife who live or have lived in a community-property state, the planner is urged to exercise great care. Deeds, securities, bank passbooks, or other indicia of ownership that appear to indicate the existence of a joint tenancy may be misleading. The law of that jurisdiction must be checked to see whether or not it recognizes joint tenancy between spouses and, if so, whether all the procedural requirements have been met.

3.5

Improvements to Separate Property

It should be evident by now that the faces of deeds, passbooks, and other indicia of ownership are not reliable guides for determining whether a given asset is community property. Here is another variation on the same theme.

Assume that Bob Smith, a budding young entrepreneur who is interested in starting a trucking company, meets, falls in love with, and marries Sally Jones, CLU, a prosperous insurance specialist. At the time of their wedding, Bob owns a tract of raw real estate in his name that would be ideal for use in his planned trucking company. On their honeymoon, Bob and Sally agree that she will let Bob use and invest part of her commissions in Bob's trucking venture.

Over the next 10 years, Sally's commission income is very large, and increases annually. Each year she turns over a good part of it to Bob, who constructs over time a massive warehouse and other buildings on the tract of raw realty that he had owned when they were married.

If the bonds of matrimony are severed after 11 years, either through death or divorce, what rights to Bob's real estate do Sally's heirs (in the case of death) or Sally herself (if there was a divorce) have?

In most community-property states, Sally or her heirs would not have legal title to the real estate. This land was Bob's when he met Sally and will be Bob's after they part. What Sally or her heirs have is a right of reimbursement for one-half of the community funds expended on the property. This right to reimbursement does not give title to Sally or her heirs but is in the nature of a charge or lien against the property.[8]

To Whom Is This Purchase to Be Credited?

A very similar problem arises where assets are acquired on credit. Again, the name on the dotted line may or may not control the legal results of the transaction.

For example, if Harry borrows money to buy a piece of real estate, is that real estate his separate property or is it a community asset? The answer to that question depends on the status of the borrowed funds. Are they the result of his separate credit or of the credit of the community? No hard-and-fast rule can be given here. At best, credit must be judged on the facts and circumstances of the transaction. In other words, what was the understanding of the parties as to the source of the credit and the funds to repay?[9]

If it is found that an asset was acquired partially with a spouse's separate funds and partially with funds obtained through community credit, the other spouse may have an enforceable right in the property, notwithstanding the fact that the first spouse was the only one whose name appeared on the deed or certificate of title.

Classification of Assets—A Closing Thought

The foregoing discussion of some of the variations and problems of community-property law is not intended to be a full or complete discussion of the community-property system. Such a discussion would require a voluminous treatise, rather than a short reading. What the foregoing discussion is intended to do is to illustrate to the reader that community property is indeed a different form of ownership of property between spouses. The assumptions and rules of law applicable to estate planning in a common-law context are not applicable in toto where community property is involved.

Because each of the nine current community-property states has its own history, traditions, courts, and legislature, it is also dangerous to rely on generalizations as to how the community-property system functions. What may be true in California may not be true in Texas. What is an enforceable right of a spouse in Louisiana may be unheard of in Idaho. Before a case dealing with the community-property laws of any state can be answered, the specific laws of that state must be consulted. Failure to verify the law of that particular state may lead to error, an unhappy client (or heirs), and/or litigation.

TRANSFER-TAX IMPLICATIONS

Under IRC Sec. 2033, a decedent's gross estate includes the value of all property of the decedent to the extent of the decedent's interest at the time of death. Since the determination of property rights is a matter of state law, the courts have looked to the laws of the various states before applying the estate and gift tax provisions of the IRC to particular situations.[10] Although not explicitly recognized by IRC Sec. 2033, the courts have long recognized that a decedent's gross estate does not include the surviving spouse's interest in their community property.[11]

Because of the inclusion of only one-half of the decedent's community property in the decedent's gross estate, a decedent dying while owning community property will have a smaller gross estate than will a decedent having identical assets, none of which is community property. For example, if Bob dies having assets worth $2 million all titled solely in his name, none of which was community property, his gross estate would include the full $2 million. On the other hand, if all of Bob's assets were community assets, he would have a gross estate of only $1 million. Community-property laws, in effect, tend to equalize the gross estates of the spouses.

As a practical matter, does the characterization of a decedent's assets as community assets have any practical tax effect? Since ERTA's unlimited marital deduction for both the estate and gift tax took effect on January 1, 1982, there is very little difference as to whether property passing to a surviving spouse is characterized as community property or as noncommunity property. Compare the following two hypothetical situations in which two men die and leave their entire property to their surviving spouses:

If Abe dies owning noncommunity assets of $2 million, the numbers would look like this:

Gross estate	$2,000,000
Less: Marital deduction	(2,000,000)
Taxable estate	-0-

If Ben dies owning only community assets of $2 million, the numbers would come out the same:

Gross estate	$1,000,000
Less: Marital deduction	(1,000,000)
Taxable estate	-0-

If the surviving spouse is not the sole recipient of the property of the deceased spouse, there may be a significant difference in the treatment of community and noncommunity assets.

In many instances, a testator (typically, although not exclusively, the husband) creates one trust to administer the property owned by the testator at the time of death. Quite often such a trust provides for a life income interest to the surviving spouse, with the principal to be distributed to other persons on the surviving spouse's death. If the decedent attempts to fund such a trust with community assets, the survivor must decide whether to take the community one-half outright or to take the benefits conferred under the will. Such a device is known as a *widow's election*. The widow's election is a creation of the community-property laws.

The tax effects of the widow's election are somewhat unusual. Independent of the estate tax consequences to the decedent's estate of this transfer by the decedent, which did not qualify for the marital deduction under pre-ERTA law, the surviving spouse was also deemed to have made a taxable gift of the remainder interest of the trust reduced by the surviving spouse's life income interest in the decedent's half of the community assets placed in trust.[12]

The other major peculiarity relating to transfers to third parties at death relates to life insurance. According to Treasury regulations, if the insured purchased a life insurance policy on his or her life with community funds and designated someone other than the spouse as the beneficiary—the decedent's secretary, ex-spouse, or spendthrift nephew, for example—the surviving spouse would be deemed to have made a gift of one-half of the policy proceeds to the beneficiary.[13]

An exception to this general rule was created by the Fifth Circuit Court of Appeals. In the *Kaufman* case, the husband made his wife beneficiary of $175,000 of community life insurance proceeds, and their daughters received $72,000. The IRS asserted that one-half of the $72,000 received by the daughters—$36,000—was a gift from the widow. The Fifth Circuit disagreed with the position of the Treasury regulations and distinguished one of its prior decisions. The court held that if the surviving spouse received her community share of the proceeds or more, the balance given to third parties would not be deemed to be a gift, unless there was some other evidence of an intent to make a gift.[14]

ESTATE PLANNING FOR THE MIGRANT CLIENT

The couple who moves from a common-law state to a community-property state, from a community-property state to a common-law state, or from one community-property state to another community-property state most probably will not realize that in changing addresses they are also creating potential legal problems for themselves. These problems may not become apparent until their marriage is dissolved by either death or divorce. At the time of the dissolution of the marriage, the true legal rights of the parties may be unintentionally disregarded because of the difficulty of separating community from noncommunity property. This difficulty is usually attributable to two causes.

The first cause of the difficulty in separating the community from the noncommunity property of the migrant spouses is a direct result of the passage of time. Unless the couple was unusually orderly and meticulous in their record keeping, it may be impossible to ascertain the character of their assets after a number of years. Records and receipts will vanish, making it impossible to trace the source of the funds used to acquire any specific asset. In community-property states, the application of the presumption in favor of community property discussed earlier may become impossible to refute because of an absence of records or other proof to the contrary. Conversely, if the couple moved from a community-property state to a common-law state, it may become impossible to prove the community nature of assets acquired with community funds because of an absence of records or other proof.

The second cause of the difficulty in separating the community and noncommunity assets of the migrant spouses is that often judges and lawyers in a state having one system will be unfamiliar with the legal status of assets acquired under the other system. That is, a lawyer or a probate judge in Delaware looking at a probate or a divorce case will not apply the same initial assumptions or presuppositions as would a lawyer or judge in Texas, although the couple may have acquired many of their assets in Texas. Unless the couple takes adequate steps to preserve the identity of assets acquired under the other system, it may be impossible for lawyers and judges familiar with one system to adequately treat assets acquired under the other system.

Several things can and should be done to protect the migrant couple. First, they should review their current situation with the help of an attorney in their state. Together they should attempt to ascertain the character of their property as it stands currently. The couple and the attorney should try to identify which of their assets are separate, community, mixed, or owned in a form not found in the new state.

The next step will be for the couple to adopt a plan or strategy designed to protect the character of their current holdings as well as to provide for an orderly transfer of their assets upon death or divorce. They will need to have the attorney review their current wills, living trusts, and other estate planning documents and revise them as required. If the laws of their new state allow postnuptial agreements, they should discuss the desirability of such an agreement with their attorney. In the community-property states that recognize such agreements it may be possible for the spouses to contractually change the applicability of the state's community-property rules, much as a person may draw up a will that takes precedence over the scheme of distribution provided by law in the event of intestacy.

Finally, the couple should create a system of books and records that will allow them to trace what they do with their property in the new state. The system need not be overly elaborate; rather, it should show the initial status of their assets and what use was made of the proceeds when and if the assets were sold.

An easy way to keep their bookkeeping system from becoming unmanageable (and then discarded) would be for the couple to use multiple bank accounts to assist in the process. For example, if a couple having separate property moves to a community-property state, they should open three different bank accounts—one for her separate property, one for his separate property, and the third for their community property. In later years, it will be much easier to ascertain how much of a life insurance policy is community property (for example, by seeing out of which bank account the monthly debit was drawn). The canceled checks, deposit slips, and check registers will form a major part of the overall bookkeeping system. If this three-account system is used, very little additional record keeping will be required.

CONCLUSION

A good professional estate planner should recognize that in this country there are two different legal systems affecting the rights of spouses to property. Irrespective of the system under which the estate planner lives, he or she should recognize that clients who have acquired property under the other system may have to be dealt with. While it is beyond the scope of this reading to fully explore in depth all the aspects of community-property law, it is hoped that this discussion has illustrated a few of the problems and difficulties of life under the community-property system, especially for those living in the 41 non-community-property states.

Before attempting to plan the estate of a couple who has moved from another state, the estate planner should be alert to potential problems caused by the differences between the laws of their current state and previous states of residence. No one can be expected to keep abreast of the laws of 50 states. However, the estate planner should be alert to the problems of migrant clients. If the estate planner is dealing with clients who have moved, he or she should ask for help from someone familiar with the laws of their former residence. If the estate planner does not exercise caution and get help when needed, there may be avoidable trouble created for both the clients and the estate planner.

NOTES

1. California Civil Code, §§ 5107, 5108, and 5118.

2. *King v. Bruce*, 201 S.W.2d 803 (Tex. 1947).

3. *Modern Woodmen of America v. Gray*, 299 Pac. 754 (1931).

4. *Parsons v. U.S.*, 460 F.2d 288 (5th Cir. 1972).

5. *Travelers Insurance Co. v. Johnson*, 544 p.2d 471 (1975); *Phillips v. Wellborn*, 552 p.ed 471 (1975); *Gaethge v. Gaethge*, 442 p.2d 870 (1968).

6. Texas Probate Code §46.

7. *Hilley v. Hilley*, 327 S.W.2d 467 (Civ. App. 1959), aff'd 342 S.W.2d 565 (1961).

8. *Dakan v. Dakan*, 83 S.W.2d 620 (1935); *Henry v. Reinle*, 245 S.W.2d 743 (Civ. App. 1952), reh. den., err. ref. n.r.e.; *Wheeland v. Rogers*, 124 p.2d 816 (1942).

9. *Edsall v. Edsall*, 240 S.W.2d 424 (Civ. App. 1952), reh. dem.; *Ford v. Ford* 276 Cal. App. 2d 9 (1969).

10. *Est. of Bosch*, 387 U.S. 456 (1967).

11. *Est. of Rowan*, 54 T.C. 633 (1970).

12. *Vardell's Estate v. Commissioner*, 307 F.2d 688, n. 3 (5th Cir. 1962); *Est. of Sparling*, 60 T.C. 330 (1973).

13. Treas. Reg. § 25.2511-1(h)(9) (1972).

14. *Kaufman v. U.S.*, 462 F.2d 439 (5th Cir. 1972).

LIFETIME TRANSFERS BY GIFT—AN OVERVIEW

Stephan R. Leimberg*

This reading is being presented in two parts to enable the student to better understand all aspects and elements of gratuitous lifetime transfers before studying the unified system of gift and estate taxation in a later assignment. The first part of the reading discusses the reasons (other than tax advantages) for making gifts, what constitutes a gift, various types of gifts, how to distinguish between gifts and other gratuitous transfers that are not gifts, gifts that are exempt, requirements for a completed gift, and valuation of gifts for gift tax purposes. The second part of the reading, presented in a later assignment, will review federal gift taxation and its relationship to the federal income and estate tax systems.

NONTAX ADVANTAGES OF LIFETIME GIFTS

Individuals give property away during their lifetimes for many reasons. Although a detailed discussion of the nontax motivations for lifetime giving is beyond the scope of this reading, some of the reasons include (1) privacy that would be impossible to obtain through a testamentary gift, (2) potential reduction of probate and administrative costs, (3) protection from the claims of creditors, (4) the vicarious enjoyment of seeing the donee use and enjoy the gift, (5) an opportunity for the donor to see how well—or how poorly—the donee manages business or other property, and (6) provision for the education, support, and financial well-being of the donee.

TECHNICAL DEFINITION OF A GIFT

Elements of a Gift

Under common law a gift is defined simply as a voluntary transfer without any consideration. But for tax law purposes neither the Code nor the Regulations specifically define what is meant by the term *gift*.

However, the regulations dealing with the valuation of gifts provide that in cases where property is transferred for less than adequate and full consideration in money or money's worth, the

---

*Stephan R. Leimberg, JD, CLU, is professor of estate planning and taxation at The American College. This reading has been updated due to recent tax law changes and portions of it have been substantially revised by the editor.

Value of property transferred
minus
Consideration received
equals
Gift.

Note that this definition focuses on whether the property was transferred for adequate and full consideration in money or the equivalent of money, rather than whether the transferor intended to make a gift. This is because Congress did not want to force the IRS to prove something as intangible and subjective as the transferor's state of mind. In fact, the regulations state that donative intent is not an essential element of the transfer for *gift tax* purposes. However, donative intent is required for a gift to be tax exempt for *income tax* purposes. As will be discussed later, the IRS may show the lack of donative intent to establish that a transfer was in the ordinary course of business and not, in fact, a gift. For gift tax purposes, the key factors are (1) the objective facts of the transfer (adequacy of consideration) and (2) the circumstances surrounding the transfer, not the subjective state of mind of the transferor. The donative intent may become important in the investigation of the circumstances of the transfer.

The courts examine certain factors to determine if a taxable gift was made:

- Was the donor (maker of the gift) competent to make a gift?
- Was the donee (person to whom the gift is made) capable of accepting the gift?
- Was there a clear and unmistakable intention on the part of the donor to absolutely, irrevocably, and currently be divested of dominion and control over the gift property?

Assuming that these three objective criteria are met, three other elements must be present. There must be

- an irrevocable transfer of the present legal title to the donee so that the donor no longer has dominion and control over the property in question
- a delivery to the donee of the gift (or the most effective way to command dominion and control of the gift)
- acceptance of the gift by the donee

All these requirements must be met before a gift is subject to tax. The essence of these tests can be distilled into the following factors (state law is examined to determine the presence or absence of these elements):

- There must be a transfer of property for less-than-adequate consideration.
- The donor must deliver the subject matter of the gift.
- The donee must accept the gift.

Adequate and Full Consideration in Money or Money's Worth Defined

Sufficiency-of-Consideration Test

Since the measure of a gift is the difference between the value of the property transferred and the consideration received by the transferor, a $100,000 building that is transferred from a mother to her daughter for $100,000 in cash clearly does not constitute a gift. However, the mere fact that consideration has been given does not pull a transaction out of the gift tax realm. To be exempt from tax, the consideration received by the transferor must be equal in value to the property transferred. This is known as the *sufficiency-of-consideration test*. If the daughter in the example above had paid $60,000, the excess value of the building—$40,000—would be within the scope of the gift tax. To escape the gift tax there must be *adequate and full consideration* equal in value to that of the property transferred.

Effect of Moral, Past, or Nonbeneficial Consideration

Consideration is not *in money or money's worth* when the consideration is moral consideration, past consideration, or consideration in the form of a detriment to the transferee that does not benefit the transferor. The classic example is a man who transferred $100,000 to a widow when she promised to marry him. (Upon remarriage she would forfeit a $100,000 interest in a trust established for her by her deceased husband; the $100,000 from her fiancé was to compensate her for the loss.) The Supreme Court held that the widow's promise to marry her fiancé was not sufficient consideration because it was incapable of being valued in money or money's worth. Nor was her forfeiture of $100,000 in the trust sufficient consideration, since the benefit of that value did not go to the transferor, her fiancé, although the widow did in fact give up something of value.

Consideration in Marital Rights and Support Rights Situations

Two issues often arise in connection with the consideration question: (1) Does the relinquishment of marital rights constitute consideration in money or money's worth? (2) Does the relinquishment of support rights constitute consideration in money or money's worth?

The Code is specific in the case of certain property settlements. IRC Sec. 2516 provides that transfers of property or property interests made under the terms of a written agreement between spouses in settlement of marital or property rights are deemed to be for an adequate and full consideration. Such transfers are therefore exempt from the gift tax—whether or not the agreement is approved by or incorporated into a divorce decree—if the divorce occurs within a 3-year period beginning one year before entering into such an agreement. For example, if a husband agrees to give his wife $100,000 as a lump-sum settlement in exchange for her release of all marital rights that she may have in his estate, the $100,000 transfer is not subject to the gift tax if the requirements stated above are met. But even in a case where the 2-year requirement (applicable under prior law) was not met, a taxpayer has successfully argued that the transfer was not made voluntarily and was therefore not a gift.

A spouse's relinquishment of the right to support constitutes consideration that can be measured in money or money's worth. Likewise, a transfer in satisfaction of the right to support of the transferor's minor children is made for money's worth. (But most transfers to or for the benefit of adult children are generally treated as gifts, unless state law requires the transferor to support that child for some reason.)

Transfers Pursuant to Compromises or Court Orders

Consideration is an important factor when a transfer is made pursuant to compromises of bona fide disputes or court orders. Such transfers are not considered taxable gifts because they are deemed to be made for adequate and full consideration. For example, if a mother and daughter are in litigation and the daughter is claiming a large sum of money, a compromise payment by the mother to the daughter is not a gift. However, in an intrafamily situation in which the court is not convinced that there was a bona fide arm's-length adversary proceeding, the gift tax will be imposed. For example, in a case where a widow *settled* with a son who threatened to *break* his father's will, the gift tax was levied.

Likewise, the gift tax can be applied even in the case of a transfer made pursuant to (or approved by) a court decree if there is not an adversary proceeding. For example, when an incompetent's property was transferred by the incompetent's guardian to another, the transfer has been held to be a gift even though it was approved or mandated by a court decree, assuming the incompetent had no legal duty to transfer the property. (Note, however, that if one who has been declared incompetent in appropriate legal proceedings attempts to personally give away property (that is, without the guardian's consent), a gift may not result if the local law requires legal capacity as an essential element of a valid gift.)

Types of Gifts

Direct Gifts

Cash or tangible personal property is the subject of most transfers affected by the gift tax law. Delivery of the property itself generally effectuates the gift. Real property is typically given by the delivery of an executed deed. If a person purchases a U.S. savings bond but has the bond registered in someone else's name and delivers the bond to that person, a gift has been made. (If the bonds are titled jointly between the purchaser and another, no gift occurs until the other person cashes in the bond or has the bond reissued in his or her name only.)

Income that will be earned in the future can constitute a gift presently subject to tax. For example, an author can give a right to future royalties to a daughter or son. Such a gift is valued according to its present value; that is, the gift is not considered to be a series of year-by-year gifts valued as the income is paid, but rather a single gift valued on the date the right to future income is assigned. Current valuation will be made even if, for some reason, the payments are reduced substantially or they cease. No adjustment is required—or allowed—if the actual income paid to the donee is more or less than the valuation.

Forgiving a debt constitutes a gift in nonbusiness situations. For example, if a father lends his son $100,000 and later cancels the note, the forgiveness constitutes a $100,000 gift.

Some forgiveness of indebtedness, however, constitutes income to the benefited party. If a creditor tore up a debtor's note in return for services rendered by the debtor, the result would be the same as if the creditor compensated the debtor for the services rendered and the debtor then used the cash to satisfy the debt. The debtor realizes income and does not receive a gift.

Payments in excess of obligations can be gifts. Clearly a person does not make a gift when he or she pays the bills. Therefore when a person pays bills or purchases food or clothing for a spouse or minor children, that person is not making gifts. Courts have allowed considerable latitude in this area. But if a father gives his minor daughter a $50,000 ring, the IRS may claim the transfer goes beyond his obligation of support. Payments made on behalf of adult children are often considered gifts. For example, if a mother pays her adult son's living expenses and mortgage payments or gives an adult child a monthly allowance, the transfer is a gift subject to tax.

In another situation the taxpayer, pursuant to an agreement incorporated in a divorce decree, created two trusts for the support of his minor children. He put a substantial amount of money in the trusts, which provided that after the children reached age 21 they were to receive the corpus. The court measured the economic value of the father's support obligation and held that the excess of the trust corpus over that value was a taxable gift. Only the portion of the transfer required to support the children during their minority was not subject to the gift tax.

Indirect Gifts

Indirect gifts, such as the payment of another's expenses, are subject to the gift tax. For instance, if a father makes payments on an adult son's car or pays premiums on a life insurance policy his wife owns on his life, such payments are gifts.

The shifting of property rights alone can trigger gift tax consequences. In one case an employee gave up his vested rights to employer contributions in a profit-sharing plan. He was deemed to have made a gift to the remaining participants in the plan. Similarly, an employee who has a vested right to an annuity is making a gift if the choice is made to take—irrevocably—a lesser annuity coupled with an agreement that payments will be continued to the designated beneficiary. No gift occurs until the time that the employee's selection of the survivor annuity becomes irrevocable.

4.5

Third-party transfers may be the medium for a taxable gift. For example, if a father gives his son $100,000 in consideration of his son's promise to provide a lifetime income to the father's sister, the father has made an indirect gift to his sister. Furthermore, if the cost of providing a lifetime annuity for the sister is less than $100,000, the father also has made a gift to his son.

The creation of a family partnership may involve an indirect gift. The mere creation or existence of a family partnership (which is often useful in shifting and spreading income among family members and in reducing estate taxes) does not, per se, mean a gift has been made. But if the value of a family member's services is nil or minimal and earnings are primarily due to assets other than those contributed by the partners in question, the creation of the partnership (or another partner's contribution of assets) may constitute a gift.

At the other extreme, if new partners are to contribute valuable services in exchange for their share of the partnership's earnings and the business does not own a significant amount of capital assets, the formation of a family partnership does not constitute a gift.

Transfers by and to corporations are often forms of indirect gifts. Technically the gift tax is not imposed upon corporations, but transfers by or to a corporation are often considered to be made by or to corporate shareholders. The regulations state that if a corporation makes a transfer to an individual for inadequate consideration, the difference between the value of the money or other property transferred and the consideration paid is a gift to the transferee from the corporation's stockholders. For example, a gratuitous transfer of property by a family-owned corporation to the father of the shareholders of a corporation could be treated as a gift from the children to their father.

Generally a transfer to a corporation for inadequate consideration is a gift from the transferor to the corporation's other shareholders. For example, a transfer by a mother to a corporation that she and her children own is treated as a gift from the mother to the children. (The amount of such a gift is computed after subtracting the percentage of the gift equal to the percentage of the transferor's ownership.)

A double danger lies in corporate gifts. The IRS may argue that (1) in reality the corporation made a distribution taxable as a dividend to its stockholders and (2) the shareholders in turn made a gift to the recipient of the transfer. Since any distribution from a corporation to a shareholder generally constitutes a dividend to the extent of corporate earnings and profits, the IRS could claim that a transfer was first a constructive dividend to the shareholders and then a constructive gift by them to the donee. For example, if a family-owned corporation sold property with a fair market value of $450,000 for $350,000 to the son of its shareholders, the transaction could be considered a $100,000 constructive dividend to the shareholder-parents, followed by a $100,000 constructive gift by them to their son.

There are exceptions to the general rule that transfers to or from corporations are contraindicated: a transfer may be deemed to be a charitable contribution from the corporation, not from the shareholders, and a contribution to a corporation for inadequate consideration may be deemed to be a contribution to capital rather than a gift. For example, a corporation may make a contribution to the Boy Scouts of America and take a deduction of up to 10 percent of its taxable income (with certain adjustments) (IRC Sec. 170(b)(2)). Furthermore, if there is a legitimate business motive, the transfer may not be a gift even if adequate consideration is lacking. Generally gift tax problems arise only when the corporation is family owned and closely held.

Life insurance—or life insurance premiums—can be the subject of an indirect gift in three types of situations: (1) the purchase of a policy for another person's benefit, (2) the assignment of an existing policy, and (3) payment of premiums. (The first two situations are discussed directly below. Premium payments are discussed later.)

If an insured purchases a policy on his or her life and

- names a beneficiary or beneficiaries other than his or her estate; and
- does not retain the right to regain the policy or the proceeds or revest the economic benefits of the policy (that is, retains no reversionary interest in himself or herself or the estate); and
- does not retain the power to change the beneficiaries or their proportionate interests (that is, makes the beneficiary designation irrevocable),

the insured has made a gift measurable by the cost of the policy. All three of these requirements must be met, however, before the insured will be deemed to have made a taxable gift.

If an insured makes an absolute assignment of a policy or in some other way relinquishes all rights and powers in a previously issued policy, a gift is made. It is measurable by its replacement cost (which in the case of a whole life policy is equal to the interpolated terminal reserve plus the unearned premium at the date of the gift).

This can lead to an insidious tax trap. Assume a wife owns a policy on the life of her husband. She names her children as revocable beneficiaries. At her husband's death, the IRS could argue that the wife has made a constructive gift to the children equal to the entire amount of the death proceeds. It is as if the wife received the proceeds to which she was entitled and then gave that money to her children. An extension of this reasoning, which was actually (and successfully) applied by the IRS, is a case where the owner of policies on the life of her husband placed the policies in trust for the benefit of her children. Because she reserved the right to revoke the trust at any time before her husband died, she had not made a completed gift—until his death. It was not until his death that she relinquished all her powers over the policy. When her husband died the trust became irrevocable, and the gift therefore became complete. The value of the gift was the full value of the death proceeds rather than the replacement value of the policy when it was placed in trust.

GRATUITOUS TRANSFERS THAT ARE NOT GIFTS

A number of common situations do not incur the gift tax because they do not involve gifts in the tax sense. These situations fall into three basic categories: (1) property or an interest in property that has not been transferred, (2) certain transfers in the ordinary course of business, and (3) sham gifts.

The Requirement That Property or an Interest in Property Be Transferred

Gratuitous Services Rendered

The gift tax is imposed only on the transfer of *property* or *an interest in property*. Although the term *property* is given the broadest possible meaning, it does not include services that are rendered gratuitously. Regardless of how valuable the services are that one person renders for the benefit of another person, those services do not constitute the transfer of property rights and therefore do not fall within the scope of the gift tax (Rev. Rul. 56-472, 1956-2 C.B. 21).

Difficult questions often arise in this area. For example, if an executor performs the multiplicity of services required in the course of administering a large and complex estate, the services are clearly of economic benefit to the estate's beneficiaries. Yet, since services are just that, they do not constitute a transfer of property rights. If the executor formally waives the fee (within 6 months of appointment as executor) or fails to claim the fees or commissions by the time of filing and indicates through action (or inaction) that he or she intends to serve without charge, no property has been transferred. Conversely, once fees are taken (or if the fees are deducted on an estate, inheritance, or income tax return), the executor has received taxable income. If the executor then chooses not to (or neglects to) actually receive that money and it goes to the estate's beneficiaries, an indirect (and possibly taxable) gift is made to those individuals.

Disclaimers (Renunciations)

Generally a potential donee is deemed to have accepted a valuable gift unless it is expressly refused. But in some cases an intended donee may decide (for whatever reason) that he or she does not want or does not need the gift. If the donee disclaims the right to the gift (that is, refuses to take it), it will usually go to someone else as the result of that renunciation.

By disclaiming, the intended transferee is in effect making a transfer to the new recipient that is subject to the gift tax—unless the disclaimer meets certain requirements.

A disclaimer that does meet those requirements is called a *qualified disclaimer* and is treated for gift tax purposes as if the property interest went directly from the original transferor to the person who receives it because of the disclaimer. In other words, the disclaimant is treated as if no transfer of property or an interest in property was made to the person to whom the interest passes because of the disclaimer. The property is treated as though it passed directly from the original donor to the eventual recipient. This makes the qualified disclaimer an important estate planning tool.

There are a number of requirements for a qualified disclaimer of gifted property:

- The refusal must be in writing.
- The writing must be received by the transferor, the transferor's legal representative, or the holder of the legal title to the property no later than 9 months after the later of (1) the date on which the transfer creating the interest is made (date of death) or (2) the date the person disclaiming is 21.
- The person disclaiming must not have accepted the interest or any of its benefits.
- Because of the refusal, someone other than the person disclaiming must receive the property interest. The person making the disclaimer cannot in any way influence who is to be the recipient of the disclaimed property.

The Promise to Make a Gift

Although income that will be earned in the future can be the subject of a gift, the Tax Court has held that the promise to make a gift in the future is not taxable—even if the promise is enforceable. This is because a mere promise to make a transfer in the future is not itself a transfer. The IRS agrees—as long as the gift cannot be valued. But if the promise is enforceable under state law, the IRS will attempt to subject it to the gift tax when it becomes capable of valuation.

Transfers in the Ordinary Course of Business

Compensation for Personal Services

Situations often arise in business settings that purport to be gifts from corporate employers to individuals. The IRS often claims that such transfers are, in fact, compensation for personal services rather than gifts and argues that the property transfer constitutes income to the transferee rather than a gift by the transferor. In these cases the focus is on the effect to the transferee; has the transferee received taxable income or a tax-free gift?

A payment may be taken out of the normal gift tax rules (and thus be considered taxable income to the recipient) by the regulations, which state that "the gift tax is not applicable to . . . ordinary business transactions." An ordinary business transaction, defined as a sale, exchange, or other transfer of property (a transaction that is bona fide, at arm's length, and free from donative intent) made in the ordinary course of business, will be considered as if made for an adequate and full consideration in money or money's worth.

A situation will be considered an ordinary business transaction and not be classified as a tax-free gift to the recipient if it is "free from donative intent." This means that donative intent becomes quite important. The taxpayer-recipient, of course, would like to have the transaction considered an income tax-free gift, while the IRS would reap larger revenues if the transfer was considered compensation and therefore was taxable income. A payment will be considered a tax-free gift (to the recipient—the donor must still pay any gift taxes), rather than taxable income, if the donor's dominant reason for making the transfer was detached and disinterested generosity, rather than consideration for past, present, or future services (an example is an employer who makes flood relief payments to employees because of a feeling of affection, charity, or similar impulses). It is not a gift if the primary impetus for the payment is (1) the constraining force of any legal or moral duty or (2) an anticipated economic benefit.

Among the factors typically studied in examining the donor's intent are

- the length and value of the employee's services
- the manner in which the employer determined the amount of the reputed gift
- the way the employer treated the payment in the corporate books and on tax returns; that is, whether the payment was deducted as a business expense. (The corporation's characterization of payment is often persuasive when the corporation makes a payment or series of payments to the widow or widower of a deceased employee. The employer generally prefers to have such payments taxed as compensation to the employee's survivors so that the corporation can deduct payments as compensation for the employee's past services.)

In one case, a business friend gave a taxpayer a car after the taxpayer had furnished him with the names of potential customers. The car was not a gift but was intended as payment for past services as well as an inducement for the taxpayer to supply additional names in the future. In another case, however, an employer had made a payment of $20,000 to a retiring executive when he resigned. After examining the employer's esteem and kindness as well as the appreciation of the retiring officer, the court stated that the transfer was a gift and not taxable income. In a similar case another court came to the same conclusion when it found payments were made "from generosity or charity rather than from the incentive of anticipated economic benefit."

This type of issue—whether the transfer was a gift or compensation—is settled on a case-by-case basis after an analysis of the circumstances evidencing motive or intent. Generally the intrafamily transfer will be considered a gift even if the recipient rendered past services, while transfers to persons outside the family will usually be considered compensation.

Bad Bargains

A bad bargain is another *ordinary-course-of-business* situation. A sale, exchange, or other property transfer made in the ordinary course of business is treated as if it was made in return for adequate and full consideration in money or money's worth. This assumes the transaction is bona fide, at arm's length, and not donative in intent.

There are a number of court-decided examples of *bad bargains* that have not resulted in gift tax treatment. In one case, certain senior executive shareholders sold stock to junior executives at less than fair market value, as part of a plan to give the younger executives a larger stake in business profits. The court noted that the transfers were for less-than-adequate consideration but stated that "the pertinent inquiry for gift tax purposes is whether the transaction is a genuine business transaction, as distinguished, for example, from the marital or family type of transaction." Bad bargains (transfers for less-than-adequate money's worth) are made every day in the business world for one reason or another, but no one would think for a minute that any gift is involved, even in the broadest sense of the term *gift*.

Another example of a *no-gift* situation would be if a group of business people conveyed real estate to an unrelated business corporation with the expectation of doing business with that corporation in the future.

But the *ordinary-course-of-business* exception has its limits; there would be no protection from the gift tax law if the transferor's motive was to pass on the family fortune to the following generation. In one case, a father transferred property to his children at a price below the fair market value. In return he received non-interest-bearing notes rather than cash, and continued to make certain payments on the children's behalf with respect to the property. The court ruled that these actions showed that, in reality, he was not dealing with his children at arm's length. That same result could occur if the father employed the son at a wage of $50,000 a year, but the son rendered services worth only $20,000 a year. The IRS could claim that the $30,000 difference constituted a gift.

Sham Gifts

It is often advantageous—for income or estate tax purposes—to characterize a transaction as a gift. The taxpayer's goal is to shift the burden of income taxes from a high- to a relatively low-bracket taxpayer and yet keep the income within the same family unit. But if the transfer has no real economic significance other than the hoped-for tax savings, it will be disregarded for tax purposes; that is, if the transaction does not have meaning—apart from its tax sense—it will not be considered a gift by the IRS or by the courts and will therefore not shift the incidence of taxation. For example, a well-known golfer contracted with a motion picture company to make a series of pictures depicting his form and golf style. In return the golfer was to receive a lump sum of $120,000, plus a 50 percent royalty on the earnings from the picture. But before any pictures were made he sold his father the right to his services for $1. The father, in turn, transferred the rights in the contract to a trust for his son's three children. The court held that the entire series of transactions had no tax effect and that the income was completely taxable to the golfer.

Assignment-of-income questions are among the most common and confusing in the tax law because they often involve inconsistent property, gift, and income tax results. For example, a mother could agree to give her son one-half of every dollar she earned in the following year. The agreement might be effective for property law purposes, and the son could have an enforceable legal right to one-half of his mother's income. Gift tax law might also recognize the transfer of a property right, and the present value of a mother's future income could be subject to the gift tax. Yet for income tax purposes, the mother would remain liable for taxes on the entire earnings.

A general agent for a life insurance company assigned renewal commissions to his wife. Although the wife had a property law right to the commissions and the present worth of the renewals the wife would receive was treated as a gift, the general agent was subject to income tax on the commissions as they were paid. In a similar case, a doctor transferred the right to accounts receivable from his practice to a trust for his daughter. Again, the court held that as the trustee received payments from the doctor's patients, those sums were taxable to the doctor even though he had made an irrevocable and taxable gift.

Gifts of income from property meet a similar fate. For example, if a woman assigns the right to next year's rent from a building to her daughter or next year's dividends from specified stock to her grandson, the transfers will be effective for property law purposes and will generate gift taxes, but the income will be taxable to the donor for income tax purposes.

Gifts of property, however, produce a more satisfactory result for donors; if the tree (property) is given away, the fruit (income) it bears will be taxable to the tree's new owner. Thus if the donor in the examples above had given both the building and the stock, gifts equal to the value of those properties would have been made. Thus the income produced by those assets would have been taxed to her daughter and grandson, respectively. Likewise, if stock that cost the donor $1,000 is transferred to a donee when it is worth $2,500 and is later sold by the donee for $3,500, the donee takes the donor's cost ($1,000) as basis (with adjustments for any gift taxes paid) and pays taxes on the gain ($2,500).

EXEMPT GIFTS

A few types of gratuitous transfers are statutorily exempted from the gift tax. A qualified disclaimer, described above, is a good example (IRC Sec. 2518(a)). Certain transfers of property between spouses upon divorce (IRC Sec. 2516) is another example.

Tuition paid to an educational institution for the education or training of an individual is exempt from the gift tax, regardless of the amount paid or the relationship of the parties (IRC Sec. 2503(e)). It is not required that the donor and donee be related for the gift to be exempt. This means parents, grandparents, or even friends can pay private school or college tuition for an individual without fear of incurring a gift tax.

Still another exempt transfer is the payment of medical care. A donor can pay for the medical care of a donee without making a gift. This allows children or other relatives—or friends—to pay the medical expenses of needy individuals (or anyone else) without worrying about incurring a gift tax (IRC Sec. 2503(e)).

Also transfers of money or other property to a political organization (as defined in IRC Sec. 527(e)(1)) are exempt from the gift tax if the transfer is for the use of the political organization (IRC Sec. 2501(a)(5)). But contributions to individuals do not come within the exemption.

REQUIREMENTS FOR A COMPLETED GIFT

A completed transfer is necessary before the gift tax can be applied. The phrase *completed transfer* implies that the subject of the gift has been put beyond the donor's recall; that is, the donor has irrevocably parted with dominion and control over the gift. There would be no completed gift if the donor had the power to change the disposition of the gift and thus alter the identity of the donee(s) or the amount of the gift. Technically stated, if the donor can revoke the gift (either alone or in conjunction with a party who does not have a substantial amount to lose by the revocation), it is not a completed gift.

Parting with dominion and control is a good test of completeness, but in a number of cases it is difficult to ascertain just when that event occurs. Some of the more common problem areas are (1) incomplete delivery situations, (2) cancellation of notes, and (3) incomplete transfers to trusts.

Incomplete Delivery

There is incomplete delivery when certain technical details have been omitted or a stage in the transfer process has been left uncompleted. For example, no gift is made at the moment the donor gives the donee a personal check or note; the transfer of a personal check is not complete and taxable until it is paid (or certified or accepted) by the drawee, or until it is negotiated for value to a third person. For instance, if a check is mailed in December, received in late December, but not cashed until January of the following year, no gift is made until that later year. This is because the maker of a check typically is under no legal obligation to honor the check until it is cashed (presented for payment or negotiated to a third person for value). Likewise, a gift of a negotiable note is not complete until it is paid.

An individual on his or her deathbed will sometimes make a gift in anticipation of imminent death from a specific illness, indicating that he or she wishes the donee to have the gifted property at the donor's death. Such a gift is called a gift *causa mortis*. It is a gift conditional upon the donor's dying as he or she anticipates. What happens if the donor recovers? Assuming that the facts indicate that the gift was indeed a gift *causa mortis* (that is, the transfer was made in anticipation of death from a specific illness and that the gift was contingent on the occurrence of the donor's death), neither the original conveyance nor the return of the property to the donor is subject to the gift tax if the transferor recovers and the transferee returns the property. A gift *causa mortis* is a conditional gift that becomes complete only at the donor's death, and is therefore incomplete as long as the donor is alive.

A gift of stock is completed on the date that properly endorsed stock certificates are delivered to the donee or the donee's agent by the donor. If the donor, instead, delivers the stock to his or her agent or broker or to the issuing corporation or its transfer agent for the purpose of having the stock certificates transferred into the name of the donee, the gift will be complete on the date the stock is transferred to the donee on the books of the corporation (Treas. Reg. 25.2511-2(h)).

Transfer of U.S. government bonds is governed by federal rather than state law. Even if state law requirements for a valid gift are met, for tax purposes no completed gift has been made until the registration is changed in accordance with federal regulations. For example, if a grandmother purchases a U.S. savings bond that is registered as payable to her and her two grandchildren as co-owners, no gift is made to the grandchildren until one of them surrenders the bond for cash.

The creation of a joint bank account (checking or savings) constitutes a common example of an incomplete transfer. Typically the person making a deposit can withdraw all the funds or any portion of them. Therefore the donor has retained a power to revoke the gift, and it is not complete. When the donee makes a withdrawal of funds from the account (and thereby eliminates the donor's dominion and control), a gift of the funds occurs.

A similar situation exists in the case of a joint brokerage account. The creation and contribution to a joint brokerage account held in *street name* is not a gift until the joint owner makes a withdrawal for personal benefit. At that time the donee acquires indefeasible rights, and the donor parts irrevocably with the funds. Conversely, if a person calls a broker and says, "Buy 100 shares of Texas Oil and Gas and title them in joint names—mine and my spouse's—with rights of survivorship," the purchase constitutes a gift to the spouse. The spouse has acquired rights that he or she did not have to a portion of the stock. (No gift tax would be due in this case owing to the unlimited gift tax marital deduction described in a later reading.)

Totten trusts (bank savings accounts in which the donor makes a deposit for the donee—"Joanne Q. Donor in trust for James P. Donee"—and retains possession of the savings book) are typical revocable transfers. Here again, because the donor can recover the entire amount deposited, no gift occurs until the donee makes a withdrawal of funds.

Some property cannot be delivered conveniently to the intended donee; farm property is a good example. When it would be difficult or impossible to make physical delivery of the gift, a gift will usually be considered completed when the delivery is as complete as possible. In one case, a father owned cattle he wished to give to his minor children. The court held that the gift was complete when he branded the livestock with each child's initials, even though he kept the cattle with others he owned. The court held that the father was acting as the natural guardian of the children and had done everything necessary to make a completed gift.

Real estate is transferred by executing a deed in favor of the donee. But if the donor retains the deed, does not record it, makes no attempt to inform the donee of the transfer, and continues to treat the property as his or her own, no transfer occurs.

Cancellation of Notes

In many cases, a transfer of property will be made and then the transferor will take back notes from the donee. The transaction will not be characterized as a sale until the transferee pays off the notes. But if the transferor forgives the notes, the forgiveness would be a gift.

Cancellation of notes is a frequently used technique for two reasons. First, it provides a simple means of giving to a number of donees certain property that is not readily divisible. Second, by forgiving the notes over a period of years, the donor could maximize the use of the $10,000 annual exclusion and unified credit discussed in a later reading. A good example is a donor who deeds real estate to her sons and takes back notes payable serially on an annual basis. Each son is required to pay his mother $10,000 per year. But when the notes come due, the donor marks the notes "canceled by." The gift would occur in the year each note was canceled—as long as there is no preestablished plan for the donor to forgive notes on a systematic basis in future years.

Incomplete Gifts in Trust

Donors will sometimes transfer property to a trust but retain the right to revoke the transfer. When property is transferred to such a revocable trust, that transfer is not a completed gift. Only when the donor relinquishes all retained control over the transferred property (that is, when the trust becomes irrevocable) is a completed gift made.

Tax liability is measured by the value at the moment the gift becomes complete rather than at the time of the transfer. This can have harsh tax consequences. For example, if the donor retains the power to alter the interests of the trust beneficiaries, even if no powers can be exercised for the donor's own benefit, the transfer is not complete. For instance, assume that a father transfers stock to a trust for his two children and three grandchildren. The income of the trust is payable to the donor's children for as long as they live, and then the remainder is payable to his grandchildren or their estates. If the donor retains the power to vary the amount of income his children will receive or reach into corpus to enhance their security, the gift is incomplete. But the gift will be complete when the donor relinquishes control. If that happens when the stock has substantially increased in value, as is often the case, the gift tax payable by the donor may also substantially increase.

VALUATION OF PROPERTY FOR GIFT TAX PURPOSES

Valuation is the first step in the computation of the gift tax. Only after the property is valued can the applicable annual exclusion and various deductions be applied in arriving at the amount of the taxable gift and the ultimate gift tax.

The amount of the gift is the fair market value of the property on the date the gift becomes complete. For gift tax purposes, value is defined as "the price at which the property would change hands between a willing buyer and a willing seller, neither being under any compulsion to buy or to sell, and both having reasonable knowledge of relevant facts."

Although the provisions of the gift tax law on valuation parallel the estate tax law in many respects, there is one major difference—property transferred during lifetime is valued for gift tax purposes on the date the gift is made. No alternate valuation date is allowed.

There are certain valuation problems unique to the gift tax law. These include problems associated with (1) indebtedness with respect to transferred property, (2) restrictions on the use or disposition of property, (3) transfers of large blocks of stock, (4) valuation of mutual fund shares, and (5) valuation of life insurance and annuity contracts.

Indebtedness with Respect to Transferred Property

Generally when the subject of a gift is encumbered or otherwise subject to an obligation, only the net value of the gift—the value of the property less the amount of the obligation—is subject to the gift tax. Under this rule, which assumes the donor is *not* personally liable for the debt, the amount of the gift is the donor's equity in the property.

However, if the donor is personally liable for the indebtedness—which is secured by a mortgage on the gift property—a different result occurs. In this case, the amount of the gift may be the entire value of the property, unreduced by the debt. The reason for the difference is that if a solvent donor makes a gift subject to a debt and the creditor proceeds against the pledged property, the donee is, in effect, paying the donor's personal debt. In some cases, this makes the donee a creditor of the donor. If the donee can then collect from the donor the amount paid to the donor's creditor, the donee has received the entire value of the gift rather than merely the equity.

For example, assume a donor transfers a $100,000 building subject to a $40,000 mortgage on which the donor is personally liable. If the donor's creditors collect the $40,000 by proceeding against the pledged building and the donee is subrogated to that creditor's rights against the donor-debtor (that is, the donee now stands in the shoes of the creditor), the donee can collect an additional $40,000 from the donor.

A third possibility is that the donor-debtor is personally liable for the indebtedness secured by a mortgage on the gifted property, but the donee has no right to step into the creditor's shoes and recover the debt from the donor. In this case, the amount of the gift is merely the amount of the donor's equity in the property. In the example above, that amount would be $60,000 ($100,000 fair market value minus $40,000 of indebtedness).

If the donee has no right to proceed against the donor and recover the debt, the actual facts must determine the result. If the donor in fact pays off the liability after transferring the mortgaged property to the donee, the donor is making an additional gift. But if the donee pays off the liability (or if the mortgagee forecloses), the gift was only the donor's equity.

One of the obligations that could be imposed upon a donee is a requirement that the donee pay the gift tax. The donor has the primary liability to pay the gift tax, and the donee is only secondarily liable. The donor could—expressly or by implication—require the donee to pay the donor's gift tax liability. If the donee is required to pay the gift tax imposed on the transfer (or if the tax is payable out of the transferred property), the value of the donated property must be reduced by the amount of the gift tax. But the gift tax computation is based on the value of the property transferred. Obviously, the two figures—the net amount transferred and the tax payable on the transfer—are interdependent. Fortunately there is a revenue ruling formula for making the computation when such interdependent variables are involved.

It is important to note that, for income tax purposes, there are cases that state that the donor must recognize gain if the donee pays the tax or if payment is made from the gifted property. Gain is realized by the donor for income tax purposes to the extent the gift tax paid by the donee exceeds the donor's basis for the property.

Restrictions on the Use or Disposition of Property

Value is affected by restrictions placed on the donee's use or ability to dispose of the property received. The general rule is that most restrictive agreements do not fix the value of such property but often have a persuasive effect on price. For example, a donor gives stock to his daughter subject to an agreement between the corporation and its shareholders. Under that agreement, the corporation is entitled to purchase those shares at their book value, $30 per share, upon the retirement or death of the stockholder. Does the existence of such an agreement fix the value of the shares at book value? After all, no buyer would pay more than $30 a share while the restriction is operative. But if the stock has *use values* other than sale values (for example, if the stock pays dividends of $10 a year), it may have a fair market value in excess of $30. On one hand, the corporation's option right to purchase the stock at $30 a share limits the fair market value; on the other hand, use values, such as the right to receive dividends, increase the fair market value. How much the use values increase the fair market value is largely dependent on how much time is likely to pass before the corporation has an opportunity to exercise its option and also on the probability that the corporation will exercise its option at that time.

In the example above, a court would probably state that the existence of a restrictive agreement would not fix the purchase price, since the circumstances requiring purchase (retirement or death) do not exist at the date of the gift. But the existence of the agreement itself is likely to have a depressing effect on the market value of the stock and result in a discounted gift tax value.

Transfers of Large Blocks of Stock

A principle that applies to the valuation of both lifetime gifts and testamentary transfers is the so-called blockage discount. This blockage rule may allow the taxpayer the benefit of a discount below the actual listed market value of transferred stock. The rule applies if the taxable transfer consists of a block of stock large enough to depress the market value of each share if the entire block was sold at once. The discount is allowed for the hypothetical reduction in value of the shares, assuming a sale of the entire block over a reasonable period of time. However, the transferor may diminish or remove the advantage of the blockage discount if the block of stock to be transferred is divided among several donees or the transfer is spread over a number of tax years.

Valuation of Mutual Fund Shares

Mutual fund shares are valued at their public redemption price per share.

Valuation of Life Insurance and Annuity Contracts

When a life insurance policy is the subject of a gift, the value is the policy's replacement value: the cost of similar or comparable policies issued by the same company.

If the policy is transferred immediately (within the first year) after its purchase, the gift is equal in value to the gross premium paid to the insurer.

If the policy is paid up at the time it is assigned (or is a single-premium policy), the amount of the gift is the amount of premium the issuing company would charge for the same type of single-premium policy of equal face amount on the insured's life, based on the insured's age at the transfer date. (The impaired health of the insured is not considered by the regulations, but the IRS might argue that the adverse health of the insured at the time of the gift affects evaluation.)

If the policy is in a premium-paying stage at the time it is transferred, the value of the gift is generally equal to (1) the interpolated terminal reserve plus (2) unearned premiums on the date of the gift.

Except in the early years of most contracts, the interpolated terminal reserve is roughly equivalent to the policy's cash value. In special conditions—such as when the interpolated terminal reserve does not approximate the policy's true value (for example, if the insured donor was terminally ill and had only one or 2 months to live)—the value of a premium-paying policy may be more than the sum of the interpolated terminal reserve plus unearned premiums as of the date of the gift. (Unearned premiums are defined as the proportionate part of the last premium paid that is attributable to the remainder of the period for which the premium was paid.)

Premiums paid by (or on behalf of) the donor after the transfer are also gifts. Therefore when an owner of a life insurance policy irrevocably assigns that policy to another person or a trust, each premium the owner pays subsequent to the transfer is considered a gift to the new policyowner (or the beneficial owner or owners of the trust's assets).

Usually the premium payer and the donor are the same. However, the IRS has stated that if an employee assigns his or her group life insurance policy to an irrevocable trust that had been established for the employee's family, a cash premium paid by the employer is deemed to be a gift in the amount of the premium. The deemed gift is from the employee to the beneficiaries of the trust. But a rather poorly considered and not widely accepted ruling has held that the assignment of the group term coverage itself was not a taxable gift because the coverage had no ascertainable value.

A *split-dollar policy* is often assigned to a trust. Here, an insured employee may assign the right to name the beneficiary of the proceeds in excess of the cash surrender value of a life insurance policy under an employer-pay-all plan to an irrevocable trust—a gift made annually. In this case, the employee's yearly gift tax liability is the greater of (1) the PS 58 cost of the insurance coverage or (2) the difference between the net premium and the annual increase in cash surrender values.

Perhaps the best-known and most widely used estate planning device is the trust. Trusts, like people, come in all shapes and sizes. That is to say, there are many types of trusts and they perform a variety of functions. The purpose for which a trust is created will usually influence the type used. Trusts may be designed to accomplish one or many goals. Within the parameters established by state law, the uses of trusts may be limited only by the imagination of the creator. The trust device can enable an individual to accomplish goals with respect to family and property that would be found difficult, if not impossible, to attain otherwise.

There are many types of trusts in existence today, and not all were created by natural persons. In addition to trusts created by individuals, there are corporate trusts, employee benefit trusts, government trusts, and others. Trusts may be created for personal, business, social, or charitable purposes. Basically, any group or organization (whether a business, charitable, or social group) that can legally own property can create a trust. Only living persons, however, can create a testamentary trust (a trust under a will), since wills are made solely by natural persons. This discussion will be limited to those trusts created by individuals for personal use. The rule against perpetuities and the subject of powers of appointment will also be examined. Testamentary trusts and pour-over trusts will be covered in the next reading.

No study of trusts would be comprehensible without an understanding of the role of trustees and other fiduciaries. Therefore this reading will begin with a discussion of the role of trustees and other fiduciaries as well as their appointment, duties, powers, and limitations. Some guidelines to consider in the selection of the most suitable fiduciaries will also be presented.

WHAT A FIDUCIARY IS

Under the common-law system predominant in English-speaking countries, a form of property ownership has evolved in which legal title to property is held by one person or entity separate from the beneficial or equitable ownership interest held by another person or entity. When this arrangement exists, the individual or institution who holds bare legal title has the duty to manage the property for the benefit of the equitable (beneficial) owner. The equitable owner (or beneficiary) is entitled to possess and enjoy the property as well as to receive income generated by the property. The person or institution who holds and manages property for the benefit of another is called a fiduciary.

Fiduciary is a broad term that applies to several types of relationships. By definition, a fiduciary is an individual or institution charged with the duty to act exclusively for the benefit of another party as to matters within the scope of the relationship between them. The relationship created between the one who manages the property and the other party (beneficiary) who receives the income as well as other benefits of ownership is called a fiduciary relationship.

All fiduciaries, whether individuals or institutions, are required to manage the property in their care according to strict fiduciary principles and standards established by state law. In accepting the responsibility for management of another's property, a fiduciary holds a special position of trust in relation to the beneficiaries. Because fiduciaries are entrusted with legal responsibility for the property of others, it is important to understand the role of fiduciaries as well as the scope of their duties and powers. The types of fiduciaries discussed in this reading are trustees, guardians, and personal representatives (executors and administrators) of estates.

Fiduciary relationships are created in different ways depending upon the type of fiduciary relationship involved. Differences and similarities among trustees, guardians, and personal representatives of estates exist as to the source of their powers, the duration of their position, and the nature and extent of their duties and responsibilities.

A person named to a fiduciary position does not have an obligation to accept the appointment. However, once the person accepts the position, he or she is under a legal duty to fulfill all the obligations inherent in the relationship until he or she is relieved of the fiduciary duties or resigns.

Sources of Powers

Fiduciaries receive their power from different sources. When an individual dies, the state has a particular interest in the orderly transfer of the decedent's property to the beneficiaries as well as in seeing that the estate will be settled and closed within a reasonably short time, usually no more than one to 2 years. It is in the best interest of the state that beneficiaries be self-sustaining during the administration of an estate and that the decedent's property is transferred as expediently as possible. Laws have been enacted that prescribe the procedures for settling estates and managing property during the period of estate administration or guardianship. Likewise, the state has an interest in the protection of the property of minors and incompetents.

Because of the state's concerns noted above, the personal representatives of estates (executors or administrators) and guardians of persons and/or properties all derive their powers from the statutory law. All these types of fiduciaries are appointed by the courts and must make an accounting to the court, either at regular intervals or in order to be discharged from their duties, or both. Upon satisfactory completion of their responsibilities, these fiduciaries may apply to the appropriate court to be discharged from their duties. The court that oversees these fiduciary relationships may be called a probate court, surrogate court, or orphans' court, depending upon the designation used by a particular jurisdiction.

On the other hand, a trust is not usually regulated by the court. Generally trusts are private arrangements established by a trust settlor (grantor) who appoints another person or entity to manage the individual's property for the benefit of others (possibly including the settlor). The trustee's powers therefore are generally derived from the trust instrument.

Duration of Fiduciary Powers and Duties

The average estate exists for a relatively short period, usually only one or 2 years and in any event no longer than the time that administration is completed and the decedent's property is transferred to the intended beneficiaries. An executor's (or administrator's) powers and duties generally terminate when the estate assets are distributed to the beneficiaries and the estate is closed. A trust, on the other hand, may last for many years. It is not unusual for a trust to be in existence for 20 or 30 years, or longer. The trustee's duties and powers will not terminate until the termination of the trust. After a guardian is appointed, the guardianship lasts until the legal disability of the ward, be it minority or incompetency, has terminated.

Both guardians and personal representatives are empowered to function as soon as they are appointed by the court. However, trustees do not assume their duties until property is actually transferred to the trust.

Accountability of Various Fiduciaries

A personal representative of an estate or a guardian will file an accounting with the court when his or her task is completed. If everything is in order, the estate will be closed or the guardianship terminated and the personal representative or guardian will be discharged. By contrast, a trustee is not required to make an accounting to the court. A trustee may, however, be required to account regularly to the beneficiaries. As noted earlier, the trustee is appointed by a grantor (creator of the trust) and receives powers and limitations under the terms of the trust instrument itself.

DUTIES OF A FIDUCIARY

The most fundamental duty owed by a fiduciary to the beneficiaries is the duty of undivided loyalty with regard to all matters within the scope of the relationship. A fiduciary can be held accountable to the beneficiaries if he or she does not conform with those standards.

A fundamental doctrine or statement of fiduciary principles has evolved that governs the conduct of all fiduciaries under the common law (now generally codified by state legislature). Recognized authorities on the law of trusts and trustees are generally in agreement regarding the basic principles common to all fiduciary relationships. They are as follows:

- The fiduciary has a duty to act for the benefit of the other party as to matters within the scope of the relationship.
- Fiduciary responsibilities are not to be delegated to others if they can be performed by the fiduciary.

5.3

- If the fiduciary enters into a personal transaction with the other party to the relationship, the fiduciary has a duty to make full disclosure of all facts known to him or her that may affect the transaction. If the transaction is unfair to the other party, the other party has the right to have it set aside. Generally speaking, a fiduciary is held to a higher standard of conduct than that standard acceptable in the business community.

The Restatement of the Law of Trusts[1] contains a list of the following fiduciary principles: Trustees must be loyal to the beneficiaries; they must not delegate their responsibilities to others if they can be performed by the trustees themselves; they must keep and render accounts of the trust or estate; they must furnish information to the beneficiaries (make full disclosure); and they must administer the trusts or estates with reasonable care, skill, and diligence in the fiduciary performance of their duties. If trustees are professionals, they will be held to higher standards than lay persons, and they will generally be held to the prudent-man standard with regard to investment and management of trust property (this standard will be discussed later). Trustees must also keep control of the property; preserve the property; enforce claims and defend actions against the property; keep the property separate and segregated from their own property and from the property of others; make the property productive; pay income to beneficiaries; and deal impartially with beneficiaries if more than one exists. Trustees have a duty to communicate with other trustees, if any, as well as to act in concert with them. The trust instrument may require the unanimous consent of all trustees (if more than one) or may stipulate that a majority vote of trustees is sufficient. The instrument may also state that a beneficiary-trustee may not take part in decisions involving his or her beneficial share.

Duty Not to Self-Deal

The fiduciary also has a duty not to self-deal or profit at the expense of the beneficiaries. This last duty actually concerns the duty of loyalty to the beneficiary. There are certain types of transactions that are considered improper for the fiduciary to engage in. The duty of loyalty would be violated if the trustee sold trust assets to himself or herself as an individual, even if they were acquired at fair market value. However, if the trustee made full disclosure of all the pertinent facts to all beneficiaries and they were competent to approve the transaction, it might be acceptable. Alternatively, if the appropriate court was made aware of the transaction and ordered or approved the sale, the trustee would be exculpated from liability for self-dealing. Certainly, a trustee should never sell trust assets to himself or herself at a bargain price, because the beneficiaries could hold the trustee accountable for the difference. The trustee should not permit self-interest to interfere with the duty of loyalty to the beneficiaries. Any sale of trust property to the trustee would be voidable (reversible) by the beneficiaries, unless they had been fully advised of all pertinent facts and had consented.

Some questions arise regarding the duty against self-dealing when the transaction would be profitable for the beneficiary. What if a trustee sold personal securities to the trust at fair market value or even at a better price than the marketplace offered? It might be to the financial advantage of the trust or estate to purchase these assets. If the securities are obtained by the trust at a good price and are a proper investment for trust assets, should a trustee be allowed to transact such a sale? Clearly, unless the trustee obtains the consent and approval of all beneficiaries who are of legal age and competent, the trustee's property should not be sold to the trust, and the trustee should not purchase trust property for himself or herself. If any of the beneficiaries are minors or legally incompetent, they would not have the capacity to consent to a sale; thus it would not be binding on them. If the sale was improper, a trustee would be held personally responsible to the beneficiaries for any loss incurred. On the other hand, if these same securities had been acquired from a stranger and then plummeted in value because the stock market declined, the trustee would have no obligation to restore the loss to the beneficiaries, provided the trustee had acted diligently and with reasonable care when purchasing the securities for the trust. Although there are times when it would be to the bona fide financial advantage of everyone concerned for the fiduciary to personally acquire trust property or sell property to the trust, it should not be attempted if there is any appearance of self-dealing or personal profit to be gained by the trustee through the transaction.

Duty to Preserve Property and Make It Productive

A fiduciary is also under a statutory duty to protect and preserve property as well as to make it productive. The fiduciary has a duty to keep trust property invested so that it produces income for the beneficiaries. Otherwise, the fiduciary may be personally surcharged for leaving money idle. In a recent case, an executor left cash in a checking account for almost 2 years at no interest and was personally surcharged and made to pay to the beneficiaries the amount of interest this money would have earned if invested at current rates.

Duty of Impartiality toward Beneficiaries

A trustee also has a duty to deal impartially with beneficiaries, which can be a difficult task if the income beneficiaries and remainderpersons are different. Investing in capital assets with high current yields but little chance of appreciation could increase the income beneficiary's share at the expense of the remainderperson. This is sometimes a difficult matter to resolve. Certainly, the trustee must try to act as impartially and objectively as possible regarding the interests of the various beneficiaries.

Other duties of trustees generally pertain to investing and managing the property prudently, taking care of trust administration expenses, paying all necessary taxes, keeping records and accounting to the beneficiaries when required to do so, and making payments of income and principal as required under the terms of the trust instrument. The trustee must follow all directions given in the trust instrument (except those that would be either illegal if fulfilled or impossible to fulfill), dealing impartially with beneficiaries and exercising discretion when applicable, according to instructions.

A fiduciary generally is said to be held to the standard of a person of ordinary prudence, care, and skill. A leading legal treatise states that the trustee must exercise that same degree of care and skill that a person of ordinary prudence would exercise in dealing with his or her own property. There is a different interpretation of this standard of conduct for the lay fiduciary than there is for the professional fiduciary. The professional fiduciary or the corporate trustee is held to a still higher standard since he or she is considered an expert.

Special Responsibilities of Corporate Trustees

The corporate fiduciary must be particularly careful not to profit or benefit from the relationship. Therefore, when a bank serves as trustee, the deposit of the trust funds into its own bank departments would be equivalent to making an unsecured loan from the trust to itself. There is conflicting authority regarding the deposit by a bank of fiduciary funds into its own banking department. This issue is covered by statute in some states. In other states, the issue has been resolved by the courts.

The Restatement of Trusts provides that a bank depositing trust funds into its own bank department commits a breach of trust, unless it is authorized to do so under the terms of the trust. National banks are not permitted to deposit trust funds in their bank departments, unless collateral security equal to the amount of the deposit is delivered to their trust department. In recent years with FDIC insurance increasing up to $100,000, this issue is not as significant as previously. As a general rule, a bank fiduciary is not disloyal to the beneficiaries of trusts if the bank is managing the trust funds in a prudent and reasonable way.

What about a corporate trustee who manages two trusts and sells the stock of one trust to the other? There would be a conflict of loyalty if the assets from one trust were sold to the other, even at a fair price. Neither should a corporate fiduciary sell property belonging to the estate or trust to any director, officer, employer, or affiliate of the institution by which he or she is employed. National banks are prohibited by regulation from participating in such transactions, except under certain circumstances that do not actually weaken this restriction.

Today most banks and trust companies do have authority to establish and operate common or collective investment funds for their trust accounts. This means that the assets of many small trusts, guardianships, and estates may be pooled, invested, and managed as a single fund, which is particularly important where small trusts are concerned. It permits the corporate trustee to make sound investments at reduced costs and gives the trust the advantage of expert advice as well as diversification that might not be possible if the trust were invested and managed separately. These commingled or collected investments have come to be known as common trust funds. They are allowed by the federal government without becoming taxable entities themselves. A bank or trust company may establish a common trust fund that is not subject to income taxes, provided that the trust is operated in accordance with the regulations promulgated by the federal reserve system and that such a fund is allowable

5.6

under state law. Common trust funds have been proven to provide good investment services for small trusts and guardianships at reduced administration expenses.

FIDUCIARY POWERS

Some common powers of fiduciaries include the power to retain or sell investments, mortgage property, borrow money, and mortgage or pledge property as collateral. There might be a power to register property in the name of a nominee. Other general powers include the power to compromise claims; employ attorneys, investment advisers, accountants, or other agents; and distribute property in cash or kind or both, and in divided interests at such values that an executor or trustee deems appropriate. Corporate trustees usually desire a power in the trust instrument allowing them to invest and reinvest in common trust funds, irrespective of any local law requiring diversification.

Other powers include leasing property and giving options to buy. Making loans from the trust to third parties is not often allowed under state law, even if secured, unless the instrument specifically authorizes them. Trust instruments may require the unanimous action of trustees, or alternatively, the majority vote to act on a specific matter. The trust instrument can also insulate trust or estate assets from the reach of the beneficiaries' creditors. It may also contain a clause that frees the trustee from all statutory restrictions in investments. A donor or testator generally has a wide latitude in the powers given to the trustee or executor.

Investment Powers

In the absence of investment provisions in the trust instrument, the source of investment restrictions on the trustee is the common law, the statutes, and the courts. States generally follow the prudent-man rule, or a legal list of qualified investments is prescribed.

Prudent-Man Rule

An often-quoted legal description of the prudent-man rule is as follows:

> In making investments of trust funds, the trustee is under a duty to the beneficiary (a) in the absence of provisions in the terms of the trust or a statute otherwise providing, to make such investments and only such investments as a prudent man would make of his own property having primarily in view the preservation of the estate and the amount and regularity of the income to be derived; (b) in the absences of provisions in the terms of the trust, to conform to statute, if any, governing investments by trustees; (c) to conform to the terms of the trust (except under certain specified conditions).

The statement of the prudent-man rule in the model statute is as follows:[2]

In inquiring, investing, reinvesting, exchanging, retaining, selling, and managing property for the benefit of another, a fiduciary shall exercise the judgment and care under the circumstances then prevailing, which men of prudence, discretion, and intelligence exercise in the management of their own affairs, not in regard to speculation but in regard to the permanent disposition of their funds, considering the probable income as well as the probable safety of their capital.

Legal-List States

Legal-list states prescribe the investments that fiduciaries must make, unless the terms of the instrument or relationship permit otherwise. Legal-list states are either mandatory or permissive. A legal-list state is said to be mandatory if there is a prescribed list of investments in which the fiduciary must invest. Any investments that the fiduciary makes outside the list would be considered a breach of trust, thus making the fiduciary liable to the beneficiaries for any loss suffered. In other words, any investment not specifically named in the list would be considered a nonlegal investment. Other legal-list states are said to be permissive. Those states print a list with prescribed investments or classes of investments in which the fiduciary may invest. If the fiduciary invests in a property named in the list, there will be no breach of duty to the trust. However, the fiduciary may invest in property not stated on the list, and take the chance of a beneficiary objecting to the investment. If any objection is made, it is the fiduciary's burden to show that the investment was proper.

Waiving Statutorily Imposed Limitations on Investment Powers

In addition to the standard of investment delineated under the law, there are authorizations and limitations for investments that are stated in the trust instrument. Most trust instruments expressly provide the powers of the trustee with regard to investments. If directed otherwise by the trust instrument, a trustee may invest outside the scope of the standards set by state statute or common law. Some trusts give the trustee broad discretion, not only with regard to the type of investments the trustee makes but also the manner as well as type of distribution that is made to the beneficiaries. One of the advantages of creating a trust is the flexibility that it can provide. But in order to obtain maximum flexibility, care should be taken that broad powers are given to the trustee to manage the trust according to the intentions of the grantor.

Breach of Fiduciary Duties

As already noted, the trustee is subject to statutory duties to protect and preserve trust property as well as to make that property productive. The trustee has a responsibility to keep the property invested and may be held liable for breach of that duty; for example, for leaving money idle. All fiduciaries are answerable to the beneficiaries for whom they act if they commit any breach of their responsibilities or duties as trustees, executors, or guardians. Occasionally, trustees who have been entrusted with large or small sums of money have been tempted to divert it to their personal use.

Example: A trustee borrowed trust assets for his personal use. He converted these funds and never repaid the trust. When this was later discovered, the beneficiaries had a right of action against him both civilly and criminally.

The foregoing was a clear case of a breach of duty. More frequently, the breach is not as evident.

Example: A trustee keeps funds in bank savings accounts secured by the Federal Deposit Insurance Corporation. These accounts are only earning 4 1/2 percent interest annually.

Since other liquid investments yield a higher return, is the trustee in the second example breaching fiduciary duty to keep the money invested properly? The trustee walks a fine line in this area. All decisions made by the trustee are fraught with some degree of potential liability. In addition, impartiality among different classes of beneficiaries as well as among beneficiaries of the same class must always be maintained. Can the trustee invest in assets that will increase the income to the income beneficiaries at the expense of safety of principal? The answer would be no. Sometimes the investment that produces the highest yield is also acquired at the greatest risk. But if there are two investments approximately equal in safety, the trustee has a duty to invest in the one that produces the higher yield.

Conflict between Trustee and Beneficiary

Not only must there be impartiality among different classes of beneficiaries, there must also be no conflicts of interest between the trustee and the beneficiary. The trustee cannot profit at the expense of the trust. For example, a corporate trustee may retain its own shares of stock in an account when its shares were held as an original investment by the grantor of the trust.

However, in dealing with its own stock, a corporate trustee must exhibit undivided loyalty to the trust. When a trust first comes into existence, there may be shares of the corporate trustee's own stock that had been investments originally owned by the settlor and are then transferred to the trust. In that case, a corporate trustee in a prudent-man state may retain its own shares of stock in the trust account. However, if the trust did not contain the corporate trustee's own stock, a corporate trustee would have a duty not to purchase this stock unless the trust instrument authorized or instructed it to do so. If the trustee was operating in a legal-list state, he or she might have to sell the corporate trustee's stock transferred to the trust within a reasonable time, if the stock did not qualify as a legal investment in that state. Of course, the trustee would have a duty to sell the stock at a fair price. Statutory authority generally does not encourage retention of original investments that might create a divided loyalty. The only time a trustee can retain stock owned by the creator of the trust, regardless of whether these stocks have been prudent investments or are qualified under the legal list of a state, is when the trust instrument specifically authorizes or directs the trustee to retain those investments.

The trustee has an obligation to look first to the trust instrument and then to the state's statute for guidance as to the trustee's responsibility. If the trust instrument contains a provision authorizing the trustee to retain original investments without liability to the trustee (except for loss or depreciation resulting from improper retention), the trustee may be permitted to do so without liability. However, in all cases regarding new investments, the trustee's duty is to invest trust assets in such a way that the intent of the trust is carried out and the interest of the beneficiary will be best served.

SELECTION OF A FIDUCIARY

What qualities are valuable in a fiduciary? In addition to the quality of loyalty, which is essential, a fiduciary should be honest, should have a high degree of integrity, and should be responsible and have an interest in the welfare of the beneficiaries. It is also important for a fiduciary to have experience in the management of property and the investment of assets. The fiduciary should be willing to serve and be available to make the appropriate investments as well as to devote sufficient time to the management of the trust. The fiduciary should also be available to communicate with the beneficiaries and should stay in contact with them as necessary, and should also be understanding to the beneficiaries and sympathetic to their needs.

Trustees

One of the most difficult decisions that grantors must make is the selection of appropriate trustees. Sometimes grantors will name themselves trustees. In other situations, grantors will name their spouses, siblings, trusted employees, or business associates as trustees. The problem that such a nomination presents is that if the grantor or a related or subordinate trustee is named, many (if not most or all) of the usual discretionary powers that create the flexibility in a trust must be forgone to achieve favorable tax consequences. On the other hand, much of the important flexibility inherent in a trust is lost if the grantor chooses not to forgo favorable tax benefits and to obtain them by providing substantial objective standards.

Flexibility is extremely important. Typically a grantor is primarily interested in the financial welfare of the life tenant (usually a spouse or other close relative) and is only secondarily interested in the security of the remainderpersons. Quite often a remainderperson is named in a trust merely to avoid the estate tax that would occur at the life tenant's death of an outright disposition to the life tenant's estate. However, trust law favors preservation of capital for the remainderpersons—even at the expense of the life tenant. For this reason, a trustee typically is hesitant to act in a way that might seem to unduly favor the income beneficiary. Without discretionary powers, the trustee is unable to serve the life tenant's best interests.

Would a related or subordinate trustee be deterred from liberally exercising discretionary powers, in spite of the existence of substantial objective standards? In other words, would the trustee go along with the suggestions of the grantor and the beneficiaries, even at the risk of assuming liabilities for the remainderpersons? Is the use of a related or subordinate trustee a way to achieve flexibility, while at the same time protecting the tax favorability of a trust?

There are at least five factors that ought to be considered in selecting trustees as well as in deciding between a corporate (and therefore independent) trustee and an individual (often related and/or subordinate) trustee.

- For tax reasons, if a beneficiary is also named as a trustee, that individual may not participate in any discretionary decision that may be personally beneficial. The income tax law will treat an individual who can spray the income among a class of which he or she is a member as being in constructive receipt of all such income, no matter how it is actually distributed. Likewise, if an individual, as trustee, can decide how corpus (principal) is to be distributed among a class of beneficiaries of which that individual is a member, that power over the corpus will cause the entire trust property to be part of the trustee's estate because the power to allocate corpus is considered the equivalent of a general power of appointment. Furthermore, if either of these powers is exercised in favor of others, the trustee-beneficiary may be treated as if he or she had made a transfer subject to the gift tax.
- Individuals can die or become incapacitated. Certainly, substantial physical changes are possible (and even likely) over the long period that most trusts run. If an individual trustee is about the same age as a mature grantor, it is likely that the benefits of having an individual trustee would be at best temporary.
- If an individual who is also a family member is selected as trustee, that person is often placed in an uncomfortable and perhaps untenable position. The possibility for a conflict of interest is great. Family discord and bitterness may arise when the trustee must refuse the request of one or more of the beneficiaries for what may be perfectly valid reasons. Most grantors would probably prefer not to place a son or daughter in the middle of such a family dispute.
- Regardless of the size of the trust fund, individual trustees will not be audited and consistently checked to the same degree as corporate fiduciaries. Temptations and pressures make individual trustees even more vulnerable to breaches of trust through arbitrary action, ignorance of obligations, or defalcations of agents. Unfortunately, law suits are generally meaningless, even where *temporary borrowing* of trust funds by individual trustees is discovered. Since their personal fortunes are usually not adequate to compensate the beneficiaries, judgments against them are worthless. Conversely, if an employee of a corporate trustee has made an error or is guilty of embezzlement, the bank will almost always have the financial ability to replace the loss.
- The incredible complexity of a rapidly changing tax law coupled with the investment, management, and other responsibilities of a trustee make that position a highly specialized and formidable task.

These five reasons all indicate that the use of an independent corporate trustee (often together with one or more individuals) is indicated where the

5.11

grantor desires favorable tax treatment as well as flexibility with regard to investment, management, and *beneficiary need*.

Executors

The only legal requirements in choosing an executor are that this person is a mentally competent adult. This individual also must not have been convicted of a felony and may have to furnish a bond. As already noted, this latter requirement can be waived by will. However, a court-appointed administrator or an out-of-state executor will be required to post a bond. In view of this requirement, it is prudent, if possible, to name at least one coexecutor who resides in the state where the will is being probated.

Choosing the right executor, however, requires some additional, careful consideration. In order to choose the best executor, one must look for qualities in an individual or institution that best carries out the task with which an executor is charged. At first blush, one may consider an individual who is closest to the family. Yet that individual may have no expertise either in managing assets or in dealing with the court system. Since an executor assumes his or her role at a time when a family may be under great stress after the decedent's death, it is wise to choose someone who is competent in managing property as well as honest and loyal; an executor must also be sensitive to the needs of the beneficiaries. Like other fiduciaries, the executor must adhere to fiduciary principles and exercise reasonable care, skill, diligence, and prudence in the exercise of his or her duties. When considering whom to name as an executor, one might ask some of the following questions:

- Does the prospective executor have the necessary business, financial, and administrative ability to assemble, conserve, and transfer the assets of an estate?
- Does the individual have the time and effort necessary to carry out an executor's duties, and will he or she be willing to devote energy to estate matters? Particularly when a business is a major estate asset, the executor may find that many more hours must be put in than anticipated when he or she accepted the responsibility.
- Does the individual have a knowledge of the testator's business, personal affairs, and family relationships?
- Is the individual likely to have a conflict of interest with other beneficiaries?

If one is writing a will, it is wise to designate a successor executor in the event the original executor is unavailable, unwilling, or unable to serve in that capacity when called upon. Another decision that must be made is whether to name an individual, a corporate fiduciary, or both as coexecutors. A corporate fiduciary will have expertise and experience in handling estate or trust property. Presumably, it would be objective and impartial in carrying out its responsibilities. A corporate institution affords a measure of continuity and financial responsibility. There would be no danger of a corporate trustee or executor dying or becoming incompetent. However, a corporate fiduciary may not have the same concern or personal interest in the beneficiaries. A corporate fiduciary also may not be as accessible to communicate with the beneficiaries on personal matters of concern to them. On the other hand, an individual executor might find the duties burdensome and unfamiliar. Without using professional services, an individual executor may also be incompetent. If all tasks are performed by the executor alone, including the filing of necessary tax returns, the best tax or financial results may not be achieved for the beneficiaries. The corporate executor always charges a fee that is printed on an established fee schedule and may be changed from time to time. An individual may also be allowed an executor fee for services; however, that fee might be voluntarily waived or reduced to a lesser amount if the executor is also a beneficiary under the will. Perhaps the best of both worlds would be to name a corporate executor (who takes primary responsibility for the investment and management of assets as well as the preparation of probate forms and tax returns) and an individual beneficiary (who might be consulted on matters of distribution and attend to personal needs of the beneficiaries). A combination of corporate and individual coexecutors offers checks and balances, thus ultimately providing greater service to beneficiaries. Another consideration is the size of an estate. A small, liquid estate would not require the same attention or expertise of a complex, large estate. In small estates, an individual executor might be a perfectly acceptable choice.

Guardians

A guardian is someone appointed by the court who is charged with the responsibility of caring for another. The individual who requires a guardian is either a minor or a person who is mentally or physically incompetent to care for his or her personal needs or property. The individual for whom the guardian is appointed is known as a ward. A guardian, unlike a trustee, does not have legal title to the property administered for the incompetent individual. Guardians are appointed by the court and must be discharged by the court when the term of the guardianship ends. The guardian's source of authority is the statutory and judicial law of the state in which he or she serves. This differs from the trustee, whose authority comes from both state law and from the trust instrument specifying the trustee's powers. Guardianship lasts only for the period of minority or incompetency. In actuality, a guardianship may last for the lifetime of the ward. In contrast, trustees may serve succeeding generations of beneficiaries. Like an executor, a guardian may be required to post a bond. Once the court is satisfied that the guardian is competent to serve, the court would issue letters of guardianship as evidence of the guardian's authority to take responsibility for the ward's property as well as to care for the ward personally. A guardian's duties may be as varied as those of a parent.

There are several types of guardianships. The most common are the guardian of the person or the property. When a guardianship pertains to the care and management of the ward's property, it is purely a business relationship for which the guardian receives a fee for services. A guardian of the person usually would be given funds from the guardian of the property to take care of the minor or incompetent. The guardian of the person might live with the incompetent and provide food, clothing, shelter, and education for the minor. Another type of guardian, called a guardian *ad litem*, is appointed by the court for a particular purpose, generally to defend a specific law suit or legal proceeding in which the minor is a party. This type of special guardian will be discharged by the court when the legal issue is resolved.

A parent may name a guardian of his or her minor children in a will. Unless there is good reason to override this choice, the court will usually honor the parent's choice and will appoint that person. This is called a testamentary guardian. The natural guardians of a child are the parents. However, courts in many states may not name the natural parent as guardian of the property of a minor. If the minor is old enough, a guardian may also be elected by the minor child. In some states a minor over the age of 14 or 15 may choose his or her own guardian who will be appointed, unless there are reasons not to do so. Occasionally a person assumes a guardianship of a minor or incompetent without seeking or obtaining court approval. This type of guardian is called a guardian *de son tort* (of his or her own wrong). Since this type of guardian has assumed these responsibilities, he or she will be held fully responsible for all acts performed as a guardian.

Since a guardian is a fiduciary, he or she is held to the same standards as trustees or executors. One should not accept a position as guardian unless one intends to devote the necessary attention as required by the scope of the relationship.

REMOVAL OF TRUSTEES

Authorities differ on whether to give trust beneficiaries the power to remove a corporate trustee and substitute a new one. There are valid arguments for giving the beneficiaries or other individuals such powers, as well as excellent reasons why such powers should not be given.

Among the reasons that powers should be provided to remove the trustee and substitute a new one are the following:

- The trust department personnel may change, and a beneficiary may not be able to *get along* with the new bank contact.
- It may be desirable to shift the situs of a trust from one jurisdiction to another because of changes in trust or local tax law.
- The residence of the beneficiary may change. If the beneficiaries have moved a substantial distance, it may be inconvenient and inefficient to have a trustee in one state manage the property of a beneficiary in another state. Personal interest may be lost due to lack of contact between the trust officer handling the account and the beneficiary.

Serious tax hazards exist if the beneficiary who has the power to remove a trustee can appoint himself or herself as successor. This might subject the property and the trust to inclusion in that beneficiary's estate. If the power to remove the trustee is desired, it generally should be specified that another corporate trustee must be designated as successor. For example, the adult income beneficiaries could be given the power to remove the corporate trustee and designate its successor provided "such successor must be another corporate trustee with paid-in capital and retained earnings of at least $_____" (insert dollar amount, for example, $100,000,000).

ORIGIN OF TRUSTS

The use of trusts originated in England during feudal times. At that time, there were many burdens associated with the legal ownership of property. By separating legal title from the benefits and use of property, a way was found to remove the burdens from the life tenant. In early times, the words *use* and *trust* were applied synonymously and interchangeably, although there were some differences between them. Both terms were first introduced into England shortly after the Norman conquest in 1066. The fiduciary relationship represented by the trust form of ownership was formalized in 1536 when the Statute of Uses was adopted in England.

In essence, the trust represents a split ownership of property. Legal title is held by one party while equitable ownership rests in another. Originally trusts were used principally

- to avoid the burdens of holding legal title to property, including being subject to the rights of creditors as well as the rights of dower and curtesy
- to allow religious houses to obtain profits from land, although they were prohibited under the law from owning land
- to provide greater freedom in conveying land during lifetime

In early times, trusts were unknown in countries that followed Roman or civil law. With time, however, substitutes for the trust form of ownership evolved. In recent years, the trust form of ownership has been adopted by statute in some civil-law countries.

PURPOSES OF TRUSTS

The purposes for which trusts are created are as varied as their creators. One of the primary reasons for setting up a trust is to obtain competent and professional management as well as investment of trust property. Another purpose is to protect the property for the beneficiaries, thereby providing them with income and asset security. A trust may supply a missing element or skill in the abilities of the settlor (grantor) or the beneficiaries. For example, the beneficiary may not have the necessary character, knowledge, skill, judgment, or business acumen to properly manage and invest the trust property. If a grantor is concerned that one or more of these characteristics are missing in the heirs, this individual may find that the creation of a trust is an ideal way to provide a substitute for the missing elements. Ultimately, the grantor wants to be assured that after his or her death, there is some way of achieving a measure of security and protection for the family as well as preserving the property that the grantor had worked so hard to accumulate during lifetime. Creating a trust may be an ideal solution that can relieve the grantor's concerns with the knowledge that care will be taken of his or her beneficiaries.

Another reason to use a trust may be to protect the interests of children of an earlier marriage. Also trust assets may be beyond the reach of a spouse's right of election at the grantor's death. The use of a living trust will help the grantor to leave property to whomever he or she wishes. Today marital problems are common. There are multiple parents and multiple children of more than one marriage with which to contend. Use of trusts can enable the grantor to arrange his or her property in such a way that it is channeled to the intended beneficiaries and protected from others.

A trust may also be established for the benefit of the grantor or for the grantor's spouse. If it is a living trust, it can free the grantor to do other things. There will be continuous management of the grantor's property during a trip or disability. A trust can protect one's assets from the reach of creditors if one is involved in a new business venture, particularly a risky one. A living trust will also give the grantor the opportunity to see the trust in operation while alive to make sure that it is being managed appropriately.

Although not directly stated, the trust can give the creator an opportunity to continue to manage after death. By specifying in the trust instrument the conditions and timing of distributions of income, principal, or both, the grantor may control the availability of assets for the beneficiaries after death. If the trust was an inter vivos trust that was in operation before the testator's death, the continuous management of the testator's assets forms a bridge between life and death.

A trust offers an excellent method of handling and consolidating accumulations of wealth. If it is an irrevocable trust, and the trust instrument provides for accumulation of income, the trust will function as a separate taxpayer possibly at a lower tax bracket than the grantor. If there are multiple beneficiaries or multiple trusts, substantial income tax savings may be obtained through allocation of income among the beneficiaries and the trust. For example, the trustee may be given discretionary powers with regard to sprinkling income and/or principal among one or more beneficiaries according to their needs. Or the trust instrument may be more restrictive by providing that income or principal is to be used to provide only such things as medical care, education, the purchase of a primary residence, or entry into a new business.

Trusts can also afford opportunities to save estate taxes. Any appreciation in the value of property transferred to an irrevocable trust will escape taxation in the grantor's estate provided that he or she does not retain certain powers. Should the property appreciate greatly in value after being transferred to the trust, considerable estate tax savings will result. Trusts can be structured so that the beneficiaries have broad access to both income and principal, and yet the trust principal will not be included in their estates for estate tax purposes. As noted earlier, the judicious use of trusts and their beneficiaries as multiple taxpayers also provides an opportunity to have trust income divided among more than one beneficiary in potentially lower tax brackets.

In addition, if a corporate trustee is used and the trust assets are invested in common trust funds, an individual with a relatively modest estate of $50,000 to $300,000 will benefit from the advantages of diversification and regular investment advice that otherwise would not be affordable.

In summary, trusts can be set up to provide management services, income and estate tax savings, and other benefits. However, the greatest benefit of many trusts is the flexibility they afford that enables beneficiaries to have the use of both trust income and principal to achieve the grantor's objectives.

FUNDAMENTALS OF A TRUST

What is this unique and versatile estate planning vehicle called a trust? By definition, a trust is a legal relationship in which one acts in a fiduciary capacity with respect to the property of another. Fiduciary capacity requires that a person (the fiduciary) receive and hold title to property that is held for the benefit of another person (a beneficiary) to whom the fiduciary owes the highest duty of good faith. When a fiduciary relationship exists, there is a legally enforceable obligation imposed on the person who holds legal title to the property to keep or use it as well as to deal with the property objectively and solely for the benefit of another. The holder of the legal title is called a trustee. The party for whom the property is managed is the equitable title holder and is known as the beneficiary. The trust is thus a fiduciary relationship concerned with certain persons and property to which are attached various rights and duties.

ELEMENTS OF A TRUST

There are five elements common to all trusts:

- the creator
- the trustee
- the property
- the beneficiaries
- the terms of the trust (generally contained in a written document)

Creator

The creator of the trust is the one who intentionally causes the trust to come into existence and is also variously known as the grantor, settlor, trustor, or testator (in the case of a testamentary trust). The creator of the trust is the individual who transfers his or her property to another—the trustee—who agrees to hold and manage the property for the benefit of yet another party, the beneficiary. Unless the grantor retains certain powers over the trust or serves as a cotrustee, his or her role in relation to the trust ceases once the transfers have been completed and the trust becomes operative. Of course, the grantor may continue to be involved with the trust as a beneficiary or trustee. Unless the grantor falls afoul of the grantor-trust rules (which are discussed later in this book and which would make trust income taxable to the grantor), the grantor's continuing relationship, if any, to the trust will generally be nominal.

Trustee

It was stated earlier that a trust is a fiduciary arrangement with respect to property. The fiduciary relationship exists between the trustee and the beneficiary, not between the grantor and the trustee. Also, after a trust is established, no fiduciary relationship exists between the grantor and the trust beneficiaries.

A trustee may be a living person or persons. The trustee may also be a corporate institution, such as a bank, or a combination of one or more individuals and a financial institution legally empowered to act in a fiduciary capacity. While every trust requires a trustee, the trust will not fail because the original trustee resigns, becomes incapacitated, or declines to serve. If no provision is made for designation of a successor trustee, the court of the jurisdiction where the trust is administered (the situs of the trust) may be petitioned to appoint a new trustee. If an interim period exists between appointment of trustees, the trust will remain temporarily inactive.

Despite the fact that a successor trustee can be appointed by a court of competent jurisdiction, the trust document should always designate at least one successor trustee. In the event that both the original trustee and the successor are individuals, it is a prudent idea to provide a corporate trustee as an ultimate successor if neither of the individual trustees can or will serve. This avoids the necessity for legal proceedings and costs.

It should be noted that a trust will be held invalid if the sole trustee is also the sole beneficiary under the common-law doctrine of merger. When legal and equitable (beneficial) title are merged in one individual, he or she is considered the outright owner and the trust ceases to exist. However, a trustee may also be a beneficiary provided that there are either cotrustees or other beneficiaries of the same trust.

Trust Property

The next essential element in the trust is the trust property. This is also called the trust corpus, res, or principal. Almost anything capable of legal ownership (real, personal, or even an enforceable contract right, such as is evidenced by the ownership of a life insurance policy) may be transferred to and held in a trust. This does not mean, however, that all property is suitable to be placed in a trust.

Beneficiaries

The fourth necessary element is the beneficiary. This is the person for whom the trust was created. Beneficiaries hold equitable or beneficial title to the property. The beneficiaries have legally enforceable rights that they may defend and protect in the event that the trust is managed improperly.

In addition to naming primary beneficiaries, contingent beneficiaries also may be named. The trust may also provide separately for beneficiaries who are to receive only income and for remainderpersons to whom the trust principal will be released when the trust terminates (or at an earlier time when distributions of principal are permitted). Note that beneficiaries must be legal persons (that is, persons or institutions who can enforce their rights in a court). This can be illustrated by the fact that trusts for the benefit of pets cannot be set up in the United States, although England has recently begun allowing them.

This result is different from a trust set up for a person who is legally incompetent, but who could have a guardian appointed who could enforce his or her rights.

Trust Terms

Trust-Term Provisions

The last element necessary for a trust is the terms of the trust. Usually, the trust terms are embodied in a written instrument called the trust instrument, deed of trust, or indenture of trust. The trust terms or powers are derived from those in the trust instrument as well as the law of jurisdiction in which the trust is situated and under which it is governed.

The trust terms include a set of powers, usually administrative, that may establish the scope of both the responsibilities and duties of the respective parties. The trust terms may also place limitations and restrictions upon the trustee's powers. The grantor may designate the types of investments permitted by the trustee, or the grantor may give the trustee broad discretion in making investments, limited only by the standard for investments by a fiduciary set forth by the local jurisdiction under which the trust is governed. Clearly, in constructing the trust, the grantor has the original power to give the trustee exclusive, discretionary, or limited powers with regard to the investment and management of the trust property as well as the distribution of property to the beneficiaries.

The trustee will be guided in the investment and management of trust property as well as in the administration of his or her duties by the above-mentioned sources—the terms of the trust instrument itself and governing state law. To the extent the trust instrument contains explicit directions and mandatory responsibilities, the trustee has an obligation to fulfill these acts with undivided loyalty for the beneficiary. The trustee must act in accordance with the grantor's directions but only as long as there is no impermissible conflict with state law. It may happen that the trust is silent with respect to certain administrative powers and duties. In that case, state law will control.

The trust may contain a spendthrift provision, which provides a restriction against attachment by creditors of trust assets, whether they are creditors of the beneficiary or the grantor. In this way, the trust protects beneficiaries from their own indiscretion and poor judgment. A trust may also contain a saving clause with respect to the rule against perpetuities. In effect, the provision may provide that, notwithstanding any other provision to the contrary, the trust will terminate within the time allowed under the rule against perpetuities. This will be discussed in more detail later.

Other standard provisions of a trust may provide instructions for appointment of a successor trustee in the event that the existing trustee resigns, is incapacitated, or fails to serve. Grounds for removal of a trustee and instructions for the replacement of a trustee may be found in the trust instrument. The trust may also contain a provision pertaining to the trustee's fee. Generally a corporate trustee will request that a provision be inserted in the trust stating that the institution be compensated in accordance with its standard schedule of fees in effect at any particular time.

Legal Limitations on Trust Duration

Rule against Perpetuities

There are two limitations pertaining to the duration of trusts that will affect the validity of the trust as well as the exercise of any power of appointment created by the trust or will. These limitations were enacted to prevent property from being held in trust indefinitely. The object of the law is that property should be alienable and should eventually take its place within the stream of commerce. (Alienation is the right to sell, give away, or dispose of property at will.) A perpetuity is any limitation or condition that takes away or suspends a person's power to alienate property for an extensive or infinite time period. The rule against perpetuities is a common-law rule providing that no interest in property is valid unless the interest must vest no later than 21 years plus 9 months (in the case of a posthumous child, the period of gestation) after some life or lives in being when the interest was created.

The date on which the interest is considered to be created is different for revocable and irrevocable trusts. If the trust is irrevocable when created, the date of creation of the trust starts the period within which the interest must vest. If the trust is revocable, the time period begins if and when the trust becomes irrevocable. If the interest is created by will, the date of the testator's death is the initial measuring point for a will or a testamentary trust, since the instrument does not become effective or irrevocable until then. The common-law rule against perpetuities has been enacted into law by statute in many states. Some state legislatures have also shortened the time period for vesting.

Before drafting a trust, the proposed distribution plan should be analyzed to determine that no interest will vest so remotely that the rule against perpetuities would be violated. In this analysis, it is crucial to remember the different dates of creation.

> *Example:* A direction in a trust specifies that it shall be held for the life of the grantor's wife and that on her death an equal share for each of the grantor's children shall be set aside and continued in trust for the child's life. At the death of the last of the grantor's children, the corpus is to be distributed to their children (the grantor's grandchildren) per stirpes. If the trust is a testamentary trust, there is no violation of the rule against perpetuities because the corpus beneficiaries (the grantor's grandchildren) will be ascertainable and the interests

will vest within a life or lives in being (the grantor's children) at the time the interest is created (the death of the grantor).

However, if the trust is an irrevocable inter vivos trust, it will violate the rule against perpetuities. This results because the interest comes into being at the time the trust is created, and it is possible that the last child of the grantor will not have been born at that time. (For purposes of the rule against perpetuities, the grantor and the grantor's spouse are presumed to be able to have children until they die.) Since distribution of the corpus is not to take place until the death of the last of the grantor's children, there is a chance that the interests will not vest within the prescribed period.

Note that generally the rule against perpetuities is violated if a *possibility* exists when the interest is created that the interest will not vest absolutely within the required time. This means that in most states, the operation of this rule does not wait to see what actually happens, but rather invalidates the interest prospectively. Draftsmen of trust instruments should be careful to see that shares for any individual not in being at the creation of the trust are made payable to such persons outright or held only during the lives of persons who are living when the trust is created.

A common testamentary scheme is to *skip* the tax on the primary beneficiary's death and to make a distribution of principal at that time. For example, an older brother may give his younger brother a life estate in property. At the younger brother's death, any of the brother's children surviving him will receive the corpus. If a child is deceased, that child's issue would take his or her parent's share. In this arrangement there are no problems with the rule against perpetuities, since all interests will vest indefeasibly at the expiration of a life in being at the creation of the interest. In other words, when the interest is created at the death of the older brother (the effective date of his testamentary disposition), all the interests must vest at the expiration of a life in being at the time the interest was created (the younger brother's). This result can be ascertained because at the death of the measuring life in being (the younger brother's) all his children will be ascertainable and the trust corpus under the terms of the example would belong to them absolutely if they are living. In the event a child of the younger brother is deceased, the deceased child's portion will belong absolutely to his or her issue.

The rule against perpetuities is extremely complex in application. Consequently most wills and trusts contain a perpetuities-saving clause to eliminate possible perpetuities problems. For testamentary trusts the following is a typical savings clause:

Notwithstanding the directions given my trustee above as to the distribution of income and principal, every trust established by this Will shall terminate, if it is not already terminated, 21 years after the death of the last survivor of my wife, my children, and any lineal descendant of mine alive *on the date of my death*. At

5.21

the termination of such trust or trusts, my trustee shall immediately transfer, convey, and pay over the principal of each of the trusts to the lineal descendants then living of the child of mine on whose account the trust was established, per stirpes. If there are no such individuals living, to my lineal descendants then living, per stirpes, and if none to The American Heart Association.

If the trust is an inter vivos trust, the underlined phrase should be replaced with a phrase such as "on the date of the creation of this trust."

Rule against Accumulations

There is another common-law rule, called the rule against accumulations, that states the period during which income may accumulate. It was enacted using the same principle as the rule against perpetuities, and in most cases the permissible period during which the interest must vest is the same as under the rule against perpetuities. There are a few states that have shortened the period for accumulations. Certain states permit accumulations today only for charitable purposes or during the time of a child's minority.

Trust Situs

Since a trust can be established anywhere, the grantor has some flexibility in establishing a situs for the trust. It need not be the grantor's domicile. A trust can generally be established subject to the laws of another state by stating that fact in the instrument. There may be tax or other advantages to setting up a trust outside of the grantor's domicile.

Flexibility through Trustee Discretion

Most modern trusts allow trustees broad latitude and discretion in their investment and management decisions. Trustees may also be given absolute discretion regarding distributions of income or principal to named beneficiaries. The trustee may have the power to distribute income or principal unequally among the beneficiaries, depending on their individual needs. Or there may be specific guidelines provided for allowing special expenditures for such things as undergraduate or postgraduate education, purchase of a principal residence, or investment in a new business. The more flexibility the trustee has, the better he or she may be able to serve and provide for the true needs of the beneficiaries as they arise, just as the grantor would have done if the grantor had retained control of his or her own property. Flexibility is especially important since within the general framework established by the grantor, the trustee generally is required to continue to carry out the grantor's objectives with regard to his or her property and loved ones long after the grantor is incapacitated or dead. In fact, a trust may continue to exist through several generations of beneficiaries. As will be seen later, however, there may be additional generation-skipping taxes with which to contend if the trust benefits more than one generation of income beneficiaries.

TYPES OF TRUSTS

The use of trusts for estate, gift, and income tax planning will be discussed at length later. At this time we will discuss some of the various types of trust arrangements commonly used today. The purpose of this discussion is to help the students become familiar with some basic types of trusts and their nontax characteristics.

Living Trusts

Revocable Trusts

A living (inter vivos) trust is created and operates before the death of the settlor. A *revocable* living trust is a trust created when the grantor transfers the trust property to the trustee but reserves the power to alter or terminate the arrangement and reclaim the trust property. As we will learn later, a transfer to a truly revocable trust does not change the federal estate, gift, and income tax picture of the grantor. Essentially the transfer is treated as an incomplete gift. Obviously there must be nontax reasons to create the revocable living trust. The advantages of this arrangement include the following:

- The grantor may not have the ability or time to manage the property to the maximum benefit of the beneficiaries.
- The grantor may be able to enjoy the psychological benefits of gifting property in trust for the trust beneficiaries while retaining the ability to reclaim the property.
- The grantor will have the ability to observe the operation of the trust under the current trustee. This also gives the trustee the opportunity to become familiar with the grantor's dispositive intentions before the trust becomes irrevocable.
- The revocable trust becomes irrevocable at the death of the grantor and passes by operation of law to the beneficiary. This will avoid the probate costs and provide for a transfer with less publicity.
- Ancillary jurisdiction for out-of-state property can be avoided if the grantor's out-of-state intangibles are transferred to revocable trusts in the grantor's state of domicile.
- A grantor who is a sole proprietor of, or partner in, an ongoing business may transfer the business to a revocable trust to avoid termination of the business at the grantor's death.

Irrevocable Trusts

A living trust may also be established as *irrevocable* by the grantor. In this case the property is transferred to the trust permanently, and the grantor cannot terminate the trust and reclaim the property before the trust terminates by its terms. As we will discuss later, a truly irrevocable trust is treated as a completed gift for gift, estate, and income tax purposes. Irrevocable trusts provide tax advantages, such as estate reduction and income shifting. Unfortunately, transfers to an irrevocable trust are completed gifts and may result in gift tax liability to the grantor.

Many grantors are reluctant to permanently lose possession and control over the trust property. Only extremely wealthly individuals with superfluous assets will typically feel comfortable with a permanent transfer of substantial assets to an irrevocable trust. However, besides the tax advantages mentioned above, there are several nontax objectives that are satisfied by the living irrevocable trust transfer. Among these objectives are the following:

- The grantor can establish the trust to manage property for a needy dependent. The trustee in this arrangement can provide a valuable service to the grantor. That is, the beneficiary will have to deal with the trustee rather than the grantor for the needed funds. This could prevent continuous undesirable conflicts between the grantor and the dependent.
- The trustee may provide investment and accumulation skills not held by the grantor for the management of the trust property.
- The trust property will avoid probate at the death of the grantor.
- The trust property will provide for the beneficiaries and will not be subject to claims of the grantor's creditors.
- The trust may be designed to shelter assets of the grantor from spousal election rights at the grantor's death. Therefore the grantor can be assured that children from a former marriage will be provided for at the grantor's death.

The terms of the trust should explicitly state if the trust is irrevocable. If revocable, the trust terms should indicate when it may be revoked and by whom. State law will determine this provision if the trust document is silent as to the revocability. Some states presume revocability, while others presume irrevocability. Since this provision has a significant impact on both federal and state taxation of the trust, it is always recommended that the trust provisions be clearly stated.

Testamentary Trusts

A testamentary trust is created under the will of a testator. As such, it is never irrevocable until the death or the permanent legal incapacity of the testator. Testamentary trusts will be discussed at length in the next assignment.

Charitable Trusts

Charitable trusts have a long history of development under the common law of England and are valid under the laws of all states of the United States. We will discuss in a later assignment the estate planning uses for specific types of charitable trusts. However, it is probably true that most gifts in trusts to charity are motivated by benevolent rather than tax-saving objectives.

Characteristics of Charitable Trusts

Charitable trusts have several elements in common with regular trusts. There is the normal requirement that the trust creator have an intention to create the trust and transfer the property to the trust. The legal title to the trust property is held by the trustee, who will administer the trust according to the trust terms.

The charitable trust is a type of public trust and has some special characteristics not existing in a truly private trust. First, the trust must be for a specific charitable purpose. Generally the objective of the charitable trust is to improve society in some manner. Charitable purposes include governmental improvement, advancement of religion, educational or scientific advancement, relief of poverty, and other purposes of community advancement. For tax purposes, the Internal Revenue Code is more specific as to the definition of a charitable purpose.

The terms of a charitable trust must not provide a benefit for a definite individual among the class of potential beneficiaries. However, the charitable trust must have a definite class of beneficiaries. For example, a charitable trust could be created to fund estate planning research at The American College. However, it would not be permissible to create a charitable trust to fund a travel budget for your favorite estate planning professor.

A charitable trust, as opposed to a private trust, may be created for an unlimited duration. We discussed the rule of perpetuities earlier, which provided that a trust could not have an indefinite life. This rule does not apply to a charitable trust and there is generally no legal time limit on the length of the trust. The trust will continue until it terminates by its terms or fails for some other reason. In fact, it is not necessary for a charitable trust to fail even when its intended purpose becomes impossible. A doctrine of law known as *cy pres* was developed in the law to prevent the failure of trusts that cannot be applied to their original charitable purpose. A court may enforce a trust that has a general charitable intent. When applying cy pres, the court will attempt to find another charitable purpose similar to the initial charitable intention of the trust settlor. Cy pres may be applied when the initial charitable trust does not provide enough property to meet its purpose, or when the trust purpose has already been accomplished or becomes impossible and additional funds remain in the trust.

A private trust is enforced in the courts by the intended beneficiary. This is one reason for the requirement that a private trust have specific beneficiaries. Since a charitable trust cannot have specific beneficiaries, there is no logical individual to enforce the terms. In general, the attorney general of the state is empowered to enforce charitable trusts.

POWERS OF APPOINTMENT

Basic Terminology

A power of appointment is an interest held in property by an individual known as the *donee* or *holder* of the power. The property interest is a right with respect to the property to designate the disposition of the property. The act of designating the property by the holder is known as the *exercise* of the power. The possible recipients of the property after the exercise of the power will depend on the terms of the power of appointment. Failure to exercise a power is known as *lapse* of the power. A power of appointment is created when the owner of the property, known as the *donor* of the power, creates the power in a donee to designate the property. The recipients of the property after the donee exercises the power are known as the *appointees*.

> *Example:* Tom Tuttle placed an apartment building he owns in trust under the following terms. The income from the trust is to be provided for Tom's wife, Tina, for life, and at her death Tina is given the power to appoint the property to any of Tom and Tina's children then living. In this case, Tom is the donor of the power and Tina is the donee. Any of their children living at Tina's death are possible appointees. If Tina designates in her will which of the children is to receive the property, the power will be exercised at her death. If Tina fails to make this provision, the power will lapse and the property will fall under these circumstances to Tom's heirs at law.

Types of Powers of Appointment

A power of appointment that gives the donee a right at any time to designate the property to an unrestricted class, including to the donee or the donee's estate or creditors, is known as a *general* power of appointment. The donee of a general power essentially has all rights to the property at the time the power becomes exercisable. We will learn later that the donee who possesses a general power at the time of death will have the property subject to the power included in his or her gross estate.

A *special* power of appointment is a power of appointment that restricts the donee's right to designate the property to a specific class of appointees. The power held by Tina Tuttle in the previous example is a special power since she may appoint the apartment building only to any of the children living at the time of her death.

The time that a power may be exercised may also be restricted by the donor. That is, the donee may be permitted to designate the property to an appointee at any time, or there may be only a specific time when the power can be exercised. One type of power that is important for estate planning is a testamentary power. This type of power is exercisable only at the death of the donee through the provisions of the donee's will. The power held by Tina Tuttle in the prior example is a testamentary special power of appointment.

Purposes of Powers of Appointment

There are some estate and gift tax consequences to planning powers of appointment. A discussion of these is reserved for future readings. However, the power of appointment is an obviously flexible and useful dispositive device for nontax reasons. The primary reason for using a power of appointment is to delegate a dispositive decision and/or postpone the time at which the dispositive decision must be made. The various types of powers, and the restrictions that can be imposed on the powers, create a flexible transfer mechanism. The donor of the power can retain some control over the property and the dispositive decision while delegating the actual decision to another. For example, the donor chooses the property made subject to the power. The donor can choose when the property will be transferred and restrict its ultimate receipt to a limited class.

The donor may have important reasons for delegating the dispositive powers to another. First, this removes the dispositive decision and any discontent resulting from the decision from the original owner of the property. For example, benevolent grandparents may want to transfer property to their grandchildren. By creating a power to be held by the grandchildren's parents, the grandparents place the decision in the hands of the parents, who best know the needs, worthiness, or goals of the grandchildren.

Furthermore, the donor may wish to postpone the time the transfer of property is to be made. For example, parents may not want to transfer property to their children until the children reach majority. To prepare for the contingency that the donor will not survive the period of postponement of the transfer, it is necessary to delegate the decision to another. A parent often will donate the power to the other parent to make the property transfer. Many powers are created by will for this purpose. By both delaying and delegating the ultimate transfer, the donor can take a wait-and-see approach for transferring property. By using this technique, the donee of the power will be able to exercise the power at the time the donor actually desired to transfer the property. The donee of the power can make the appropriate designation in light of the circumstances existing at that time.

NOTES

1. The Restatements are a series of treatises setting out general legal principles.

2. Model statutes are attempts by legal scholars to produce uniform laws and standards that will be adopted in all states.

Property is transferred at death by one of several methods. It can pass under the terms of a validly drawn will. Property may also be transferred or assigned by contract designation. Examples of this include life insurance policies and antenuptial and postnuptial agreements. Finally, property may pass by operation of law. Jointly owned property with right of survivorship falls into this category as does property passing by intestate succession.

TRANSFER BY WILL

A will is a personal declaration of one's intentions regarding the disposition of property at death. It describes matters to be taken care of after death. It becomes legally enforceable at death and is not operative until that time. Prior to one's death, a will may be amended, revoked, or destroyed by the maker at any time.

Much can be accomplished by writing a will. A properly drawn will can assure the orderly and sound distribution of an estate. It is a way to control disposition of one's property, especially when all property is held in an individual name. Since all property not transferred by contract or operation of law must be transferred through probate, the will becomes the complete estate plan for all probate property. Writing a will allows the decedent to name a personal representative of his or her choice who is called an *executor*. The decedent may direct that the executor be allowed to serve without posting a security bond if one is otherwise required by statute. The decedent also has the flexibility through the will to name a successor executor should the named executor be unable or unwilling to serve. Those matters can be attended to privately without court intervention.

A carefully drawn will contains positive directions and instructions to the executor. An executor is someone chosen by the decedent who is responsible for administering the estate. The executor should be an individual or corporate fiduciary who is competent to perform the required duties and whom the testator can trust. The testator can give the executor broad powers and discretion with respect to the management and distribution of the estate. It is as if the executor steps into the shoes of the decedent during the estate administration period. The executor is charged with the following duties:

- gathering the assets of the estate
- probating the will
- filing tax returns
- paying taxes and other debts of the estate

- providing interim support for the beneficiaries
- settling business interests of the decedent
- collecting benefits and income due to the estate
- filing an accounting with the probate court (also referred to as orphans' court or surrogate's court in some states)
- distributing property to intended beneficiaries
- closing the estate

Advantages of a Will

It is only by will that an executor of choice can be named. The will also may provide that an executor shall serve without posting a bond or other security in order to perform his or her duties. Under a will a decedent may transfer real estate, stock, or business interests as he or she wishes. The decedent can direct disposition of tangible personal property separately from the residue (the remaining part of the estate after all other gifts have been made). The decedent can also assure the maximum marital deduction desired for property passing to a spouse. The estate's share of the tax burden can be specified. In the absence of an instruction regarding payment of taxes, state statutes may provide that taxes shall be allocated among all beneficiaries in proportion to their respective inheritances. The beneficiaries may bear the tax burden proportionately. Alternatively, by inserting a tax clause in the will, the decedent would have had the power to direct the source of tax money. A direction may be given that taxes are to be paid from the residue of the estate, thus relieving the marital share or specific bequests of the tax burden.

A guardian may also be designated to care for minor children or other legally incompetent dependents. A will may contain trust provisions to protect the interests of beneficiaries from their creditors. Trusts under a will can be created to control the management and timing of the distribution of income and principal from the estate. Executors and trustees can be given broad powers to invest and manage property.

Wills give testators the ability to leave their property as they choose, not as the state dictates. Testators have the ability to name charitable beneficiaries in their wills. They can make gifts to anyone they choose, regardless of the relationship. In writing wills, testators may also disinherit someone who would otherwise take under the intestacy laws.

Testators can designate orders of survival of themselves and their spouses in the event of a common disaster. This would prevent the loss of the marital deduction and avoid potential additional taxation. Of course, it must be assumed that a will has been validly drawn and executed to obtain the above advantages.

Requirements of a Typical Will

While most wills are professionally drafted and executed under the guidance of an attorney, other types of wills may be acceptable as valid under state law if they conform to certain formalities and statutory requirements. These wills are *holographic* and *nuncupative* wills, and the requirements for

6.2

them are discussed later in this reading. A primary requirement of all written wills is that the instrument be signed at the end. All writing after the testator's signature or mark, other than the acknowledgment of witnesses or a self-proving provision, will not be recognized as part of the body of the will. In addition to the testator's signature, a will should be dated. Many states require witnessing the signing of the will by two or three competent witnesses. To prevent the possible voiding of an inheritance, a beneficiary with a financial interest should not be a witness to the signing of a will. Most, but not all, states require a will to be witnessed at the time of execution. However, all states require some attestation by witnesses when the will is admitted to probate. The attesting witnesses must swear that they are familiar with the signature of the testator and that the signature at the end of the document is the true signature of the testator.

Many states have passed laws that permit self-proving provisions at the end of wills. The existence of a self-proving provision eliminates the need to locate attesting witnesses at the time of probate. At the time of execution the witnesses sign a notarized acknowledgment that states that they saw the testator sign the will and that the testator was of sound mind as well as competent to execute a will at that time.

Testamentary Capacity

State laws strictly prescribe the conditions necessary for a valid will. The maker or testator (another name for the maker) must have the legal capacity to make a will. Legal capacity pertains to age and mental competence. In some states the person making a will must have reached the age of majority. In other states the age may be considerably younger. The testator must be of sound mind, which means that he or she understands what is being done. In other words, the testator knows that he or she is writing a will. The testator must have both recognition and knowledge of the property that he or she possesses and intends to dispose of by a will. The testator must recognize relatives and friends who are the natural objects of his or her love and affection. Lastly, the testator must understand how and to whom the property is being distributed. All these combined attributes, called *testamentary capacity*, are measured as of the time the will is written. The document will be upheld as valid if the testator understood what he or she was doing when it was written, despite the fact that the testator was mentally incompetent at the time of death.

Modes of Distribution under Will

There are two common forms of distribution for the property of a decedent. Distributions may be made *per stirpes,* which means "by roots or stock," or *per capita,* which means "by the heads." This distinction becomes particularly important when an individual has bequeathed property to children and one or more of those children have died survived by children.

Per stirpes distribution provides that members of a designated class, including deceased members, inherit as members of the class. Representatives (heirs) of a deceased member take the decedent's share by representation of the deceased ancestor, not as individuals. Per capita distribution provides that members of a class, including heirs of deceased members, share in the inheritance as individuals.

> *Example:* Suppose Adam had four children, three of whom were alive and one of whom was deceased but survived by four children. If distribution is to be made per stirpes, the estate would be divided equally into four parts. Each of the three living children would receive a one-quarter interest and the four surviving children of the deceased child would share that deceased child's one-fourth interest equally.

> On the other hand, if distribution is to be made on a strict per capita basis, each lineal descendant regardless of the degree of relationship to the decedent, will inherit the property. Thus the estate would be divided equally among the three living children and the four children of the deceased child. This would result in each of Adam's children and grandchildren taking one-seventh of the property.

The interpretation of the terms per stirpes and per capita differ under the various state laws. Also the absence of a specification in the will as to which method is applicable will be filled in by local law. The majority of states adopt per stirpes distribution in the absence of a clear intent by the testator to distribute per capita. The preferred method to avoid confusion and to guarantee that the intent of the testator is fulfilled is to provide for the desired distribution in the will. In this case the appropriate professional assistance should be secured and the testator's wishes should be clearly spelled out.

Contents of a Will

A will is a legal declaration of a person's intended disposition of property. The beginning usually includes a statement by the testator regarding the testator's intention of domicile. The statement usually reads, "I, John Jones of Marion County, Indiana, declare this to be my last will hereby revoking all former wills and codicils." Thus John Jones has declared himself to be a resident of the state of Indiana. The statement infers that he wishes his property to be governed by Indiana law. This statement is particularly important if the testator owns residential real estate in more than one state. A will should contain clear, positive directions. It is not the best place to make wishes. If the testator hopes but does not wish to direct absolutely that some of his or her wishes will be followed, it might be better to have a separate written document or letter expressing those desires. A will is usually looked to for guidance as if the testator were present directing the disposition of the property.

Under common law a husband was responsible for his wife's debts. Therefore a wife's will usually contained a provision directing the executor to pay all debts as well as expenses of her last illness and funeral from her estate. This permits these expenses to be borne by the estate rather than the surviving husband. On the other hand, a husband has always been held responsible for his own debts. Therefore a like provision in his will has been unnecessary. A final distribution of his estate could not be made without payment to his creditors. Today many states hold women responsible for their own obligations and debts. In such a state, the debt provision would not be necessary in the wife's will to relieve her surviving spouse of the responsibility for her sole debts. But such a provision may still be necessary to preserve estate tax deductions for these expenses for the wife's estate (Rev. Rul. 76-369, 1976-2, C.B. 281).

A will may contain directions regarding burial or cremation, perpetual care of a grave site, and payment for a tombstone or memorial plaque. If there are specific bequests, they are usually made early in the will. These may be bequests to individuals or charities in specific amounts or of specific objects. Bequests may be made in one of four ways:

- bequests of specific property
- bequests of cash
- bequests of cash to be paid from a special source
- bequests that are paid out of the residue or from what remains after all other legacies and expenses have been paid

Example: An unmarried individual with several friends may make many specific bequests of cherished objects, cash, and intangible personal property. The testator may then direct that the residue of the estate be given to several charities after payment of all expenses and taxes. In other words, the charities will get what is left in this particular case, rather than receiving specific gifts. A will could be written the other way with a specific gift to a charity made before the residue is distributed.

Also found in the early part of the will is a paragraph directing the disposition of the decedent's tangible personal property, including transfer of automobiles and automobile insurance. An executor is usually given a broad discretion either to dispose of tangible personal property that is not usable, or to allocate such property among the beneficiaries at the executor's sole discretion if agreement cannot be reached among them.

It may happen that the decedent does not have sufficient assets to make all the bequests provided for in the will. The state statute will provide the order in which bequests are to be abated or satisfied, if there are insufficient assets for all of them. In addition, if the decedent disposed of a particular piece of property that was the subject of a specific bequest, the issue of *ademption* arises. The legatees of that bequest will get nothing unless the will contains a provision to substitute other property.

After taking care of specific bequests and tangible personal property, the residue of the estate is distributed. This provision may or may not include the disposition of specific real estate or of a business interest that may be treated separately. If the residue of the estate is to be made payable to a trust, the direction is contained in the residuary clause.

The testator will also designate an executor, a successor executor, or coexecutors. A will usually also contains clauses giving the executor specific and general powers, such as the power to pay the taxes and debts of the decedent as well as the estate, the power to collect life insurance proceeds payable to the estate, and all other powers that an executor must have over the property to make the appropriate transfers and distributions. As noted earlier, it is usual for the will to contain a clause stating that the executor may serve without bond.

A will may also contain a clause stating that the testator either exercises or declines to exercise a power of appointment, if such a power has been granted to him or her. Carefully drafted powers of appointment often require that they be specifically exercised or waived within the donee's will. However, if a testator is the holder of a power of appointment, his or her wishes in regard to this power should be expressly set out in the will. This prevents an inadvertent exercise of the power if it is imperfectly drafted.

Another type of provision that is useful is one directing that the executor hold any assets for the benefit of minors or incompetents, or transfer these assets to the individuals responsible for caring for such disabled persons.

Types of Wills

Holographic Wills

Approximately one-third of the states will allow a will that is totally handwritten by the testator to be accepted for probate. This type of will is called a *holographic will*. It must be signed at the end but need not be witnessed. Some states require that the holographic will be dated by the testator, and at least one state requires that it be found among the valuable papers of the testator to be accepted as a valid will.

Nuncupative Wills

Nuncupative wills are oral wills made by the testator in the presence of witnesses during a final illness shortly before death when it is impossible to write a will. Where such wills are permitted, the witnesses must submit an affidavit declaring the testator's final wishes. Some states will allow nuncupative wills.

Joint and Mutual Wills

Joint and mutual wills are sometimes called love wills. Two related persons may decide to execute a single joint will if they have a common scheme for the disposition of their mutual property. Most often, a joint will is written by a husband and wife. As a practical matter, joint wills may create a problem upon probate. The original will for both parties will be admitted to probate at the death of the first party to die. Consequently, if the surviving party does not write a later will, it will be cumbersome and possibly costly to search for the original will that had been filed with the probate court and made part of the probate record of the first decedent. A question may also arise as to whether the living individual is, in some way, contractually bound when the original will is filed.

A joint will should be distinguished from a mutual will. A mutual will exists when two or more parties agree to have their property distributed in a particular fashion upon their death. They may execute separate wills that are reciprocal. Alternatively, a mutual will may be a single joint will. In a mutual will the parties have bound themselves, morally if not legally, to deal with their property according to a prearranged plan. After the death of one of the parties, it is questionable whether the second party is bound to the preexisting plan or is free to change the will. In many situations the courts have held that a binding contract existed between the parties that becomes irrevocable upon the death of the first party to a mutual will arrangement. Both joint and mutual types of will arrangements are cumbersome. They should not be entered into without objective advice regarding the ramifications. Many disputes among beneficiaries of contrary documents arise from writing such agreements. An example of an agreement to write a mutual will may be part of a property settlement agreement pursuant to a divorce.

> *Example:* Both parties may agree that no one but the offspring of their marriage will inherit any of their property. As part of the agreement, each party executes a reciprocal will leaving all their property to the children born of their marriage. There is some question of whether the parties can legally be contractually bound not to revise or revoke their wills. Such an agreement is contrary to the law of wills and the general principles providing that a will is a unilateral declaration that can be voluntarily altered, amended, or revoked at any time during the testator's life.

Living Wills

Modern medicine has developed artificial mechanisms for keeping persons technically alive, although they are not conscious and are basically nonfunctional. Life-sustaining procedures are used in cases of accident or terminal illness where death is imminent and recovery is unlikely. There have been cases in recent years where life has been sustained, much to the detriment and despair of the patient's loved ones. In response to these situations and the advancements of modern science, many individuals have begun to express the wish not to have their lives maintained solely through the use of sophisticated and extraordinary life-sustaining instruments and measures. By executing living wills, these individuals may request health care professionals to remove life-sustaining machines and allow them to die naturally, particularly if the chance of recovery is nil.

Several states have now addressed themselves to this issue. California was the first state to enact a statute pertaining to *living wills*. Many states have followed suit. Each of these statutes, while similar, contains variations with regard to the consent of one or more physicians as well as a statement by the physicians that death is, indeed, imminent. Individuals who execute a living will have made a decision not to prolong the dying process that may involve pain, suffering, and financial damage for them as well as their families if recovery or life as they know it is not possible. A definitional problem exists in this area with regard to what is considered a terminal condition that will result in death, regardless of the life-sustaining procedures used.

Living wills are of relatively recent origin. There are many serious questions regarding the legal effect of these provisions. It is important that the particular state law be examined. As noted, many states have not addressed themselves to this issue. One significant issue surrounding the right to die pertains to physicians or licensed health personnel who act according to the directive in the living will. Physicians also must be careful regarding their own criminal or civil liability. There may be a violation of professional ethics in this area where states have not enacted such statutes. The basic mandate of the physician is to do everything possible to continue and preserve life. Therefore it may be contrary to a physician's training and principles to be a party to the directive under a living will. Certainly, the law is still generally unclear in this area. Alternatively, a person might be forbidden from enacting a living will on religious or moral grounds. Any action taken by a state legislator would have an impact on whether a physician or other health personnel might chance following such a directive. In any event, more people who are concerned with the cost and emotional sacrifice to the family by artificially sustaining life are making decisions to enact a living will.

Amending or Revoking a Will

Wills are a unilateral declaration of intention and may be amended or revoked at any time. They are legally enforceable only if they meet the qualifications for validity and are still in effect at the time of death. Sometimes a will requires minor changes that may be made by writing a codicil. A codicil is a modification of the will. One or more paragraphs may be revoked or amended leaving the rest of the will intact. A codicil must be signed with the same requirements and formality as the original will.

A will may be revoked in its entirety in one of several ways. Most commonly, a more recent will is written declaring that all prior wills are revoked. Revocation can also occur by making a codicil that specifically invalidates the will. Not all subsequent wills or codicils have the effect of revoking a former will. To effect total revocation, a new will must state that it is intended to revoke the former document. In the absence of such a declaration, it is a matter for construction and interpretation by the courts as to whether the new will revokes the earlier one or merely modifies it. A modification may be accepted if there is a partial inconsistency. Making a later, valid will that is totally inconsistent with an earlier one can also constitute a revocation of the former will. Alternatively, a will can be revoked by the maker if he or she intentionally destroys it or mutilates it by tearing. However, inadvertent or unintentional destruction of an original will would not cause a revocation if there is some way of proving its existence and validity. A copy that is certified as the last will is usually accepted as such if it can be shown conclusively that the original was inadvertently destroyed.

In some states wills may also be totally or partially revoked by an act that would cause invalidation under state law. If a divorce occurs that is not contemplated in the will, the entire will would be revoked in some states. In other states only the provisions pertaining to the former spouse would be revoked by operation of law. When a testator marries subsequent to the writing of a will, the will may be revoked entirely, unless it specifically contemplates the marriage or the new spouse may be entitled to the equivalent of an intestate share. Similarly, afterborn or afteradopted children not contemplated in the will may cause the will to be revoked or they may be entitled to an intestate share unless the property in question would pass to a surviving spouse, or the omission of the adopted or afterborn child was intentional.

Furthermore, a murderer of the testator cannot inherit under the will. The state will not allow this individual to profit from such an act.

Spouse's Right of Election against the Will

A spouse who was legally married to the testator at the time of death cannot be totally disinherited under most state laws. Even though a will can disinherit a spouse totally, the spouse can generally assert a statutory right to claim a certain share of the estate (for example, a surviving spouse may have a right to 30 percent of the estate). In many states property subject to this right of election includes not only property owned by the testator at death but also certain property that the testator gave away during lifetime as long as he or she retained the right to the income or other use of the property until death. In some states life insurance paid to a named beneficiary avoids the right of election. The exercise of a right of election can be avoided by a valid antenuptial agreement.

Testamentary Trusts

A testamentary trust is one created within a will as a part of the will. It becomes both effective and irrevocable at the time of death. Because a testamentary trust is contained in the body of the will, it becomes a matter of public record when the will is probated. Thus it is open to public scrutiny. By definition, a testamentary trust becomes part of the probate estate. The trust is created under the will when the testator has used language indicating an intent to have some of the property held in trust. Frequently a trust under a will is a contingent trust. An example of such a provision is the testator who has bequeathed all the property outright to a surviving spouse. However, in the event that the spouse has predeceased the testator, he or she gives the property to the minor children in trust until they reach majority or other suitable age for distribution. The testamentary trust must contain the same elements as a living trust discussed in an earlier reading. There must be an intention to create the trust and trust property, as well as a method to determine beneficiaries.

A testamentary trust may be a trust that provides a lifetime income to the surviving spouse with the remainder passing to other beneficiaries at the spouse's death. If a testator has created this type of trust, the trustee will manage and invest property to provide income for the income beneficiary (surviving spouse). At the death of the income beneficiary, the trust principal will be distributed to the remainderperson in accordance with the terms of the trust. As with living trusts, the trustee holds legal title to the property with the beneficiaries holding equitable title. The testator may direct that principal be distributed either on the happening of an event, such as the death of an income beneficiary, or upon a remainder beneficiary reaching a stated age. A testator may also direct that the remainder beneficiary or beneficiaries receive partial distributions of principal at specific ages. It is also possible to accumulate income until the beneficiary attains a certain age, at which time it will be distributed. The testamentary trust may contain a power-of-appointment provision giving the donee of the power (for example, the surviving spouse) the ability to apportion assets among proposed remaindermen at some future time when distribution is to be made. This power provides flexibility in making sure that assets are distributed according to need as opposed to a fixed-share division determined when the trust is executed. As long as this power is limited so that the person who holds the power can only appoint to the remainderperson, it will not cause the testamentary trust to be included in the power holder's estate for estate tax purposes.

Since the testamentary trust is created under a will and becomes part of the probate estate, there is no saving in estate taxes or income taxes during the testator's lifetime. Moreover, there will be no protection from probate costs. A testamentary trust is frequently used when the testator does not wish to part with property during lifetime, but recognizes the need for a disposition in trust for one or more family members after his or her death. While there is no estate tax saving in the testator's estate, by creating a life estate for the first generation of beneficiaries, the property can be available to provide income and possible distributions of principal as needs arise during the beneficiaries' lives without passing through their estates at their death. Testamentary trusts can have built-in flexibility with discretion in the trustee to sprinkle income and possibly principal among various beneficiaries in different income and estate tax brackets whose needs may differ.

Tax savings may also be accomplished by the establishment of separate trusts. Trusts also can be divided into separate shares when the youngest or oldest remainder beneficiary attains a specific age, thereby creating additional tax-paying entities. The trustee may also be given discretionary powers to accumulate or pay out income, again taking into consideration the relative tax brackets of the beneficiaries as compared with the trust as well as their needs in any taxable year. Furthermore, the trustee may be given authority to purchase life insurance on the life of a life income beneficiary that will provide security for that beneficiary's family at the beneficiary's death. For example, a life income beneficiary who receives $50,000 of income per year from a trust would be a good illustration. At that individual's death, a substantial change in his or her family's living conditions may result when the income from the trust ends. The life insurance proceeds can be used to replace that income. Payment of life insurance premiums on the life of a beneficiary will not be taxable income to the beneficiary. Compared with the beneficiary purchasing his or her own life insurance with aftertax dollars, more tax savings can result if the trust is in a lower income tax bracket than the beneficiary.

To summarize, testamentary trusts function similarly to any other kind of trust after the testator's death. Because it is part of a will, the testamentary trust is revocable until death, at which time it becomes irrevocable. The trust can provide security and professional management for beneficiaries after the testator is gone. It also gives the testator some control even after death with regard to the intermediate and final distribution of property. While no estate taxes are saved at the testator's death, the trust may provide for life income beneficiaries so that assets escape taxation at the death of the income beneficiaries. Since the trust is irrevocable once it is operative, it can provide tax saving through income splitting and accumulation of income.

The testator may provide for any one or more of a variety of methods for distribution of principal from a testamentary trust. The principal may be distributable at the discretion of the trust beneficiary, which would amount to giving the trust beneficiary complete control over the trust principal. Another possibility would be to provide for trust principal to be distributed at the sole discretion of the trustee. This arrangement would give the beneficiary no control over when principal may be received. A variation of this arrangement would be to provide that trust principal would be distributed at the discretion of a designated third party, other than the trustee or the trust beneficiary. Under either of these last two methods, trust principal could be distributed at any time but would require the approval of someone other than the trust beneficiary. The testator may specify when trust principal is to be distributed. For example, the trust may provide that determined percentages of trust principal are to be distributed as one or more beneficiaries attain a specific age. Alternatively, there may be directions for a certain percentage of trust principal to be distributed each year or every second, third, or fourth year. A third possibility would be to provide for no distributions of trust principal until termination of the trust itself. Here, postponement of distribution of trust principal would be limited only by the rule against perpetuities. There are numerous choices available to the testator other than those previously mentioned. Generally a testator has complete flexibility to determine the method of distribution of trust principal, subject only to limitations on accumulations for an unreasonably long period of time.

The Pour-Over Trust

Pouring over refers to a dispositive device that has come into use in recent years. It simply means that property will be transferred or poured over from an estate or trust into a preexisting estate or trust. It may occur in one of several ways. An individual may create a living trust executed prior to a will that provides that, at the individual's death, the residue of his or her estate will be made payable to a preexisting trust to be administered with the other trust assets. Pour overs can also take place the opposite way. A preexisting, living trust may be poured into the estate and administered and distributed under the terms of the will as part of the residuary estate. By either means, the pour-over device can be used to consolidate the grantor's assets, thereby simplifying administration. Another benefit might be that administration costs will be reduced. If the pouring over is from a will into a living trust, a legal question arises concerning the preexistence of the trust. For example, a will cannot be made stating that assets are to be poured over into a trust that is not executed until the following year because the named trust was not in existence at the time the will was written. To have legal effect, pouring over must be done into existing instruments. Therefore the trust must be executed prior to a will if that is the type of pour-over arrangement in question. Also a question arises if the preexisting trust is amended or terminated after the will is executed. Since the amendment was not within the contemplation of the testator when the testator's will was written, does the pour-over device also refer to the amendment to the trust agreement? This problem has been resolved by statute in many states by authorizing the pouring over into an amendment trust agreement, if the original trust agreement was in existence at the time the will was executed. The financial services professional should consult the statutes of the jurisdictions in which a client resides to determine whether an amended trust will have validity for pouring over under a preexisting will. Otherwise, a new will should be drafted after the amendments to the trust are made. There is an act called the Uniform Testamentary Additions to Trust Act that has been adopted by a number of states. In those states that have adopted the act, amendments to a living trust enacted subsequent to the execution of a will from which assets will pour over to the trust will be deemed valid.

Contesting the Will

Disappointed heirs, entirely or partially overlooked in the will, may attempt to have the will set aside through legal channels. After a will is admitted to probate, any interested parties may file an action to contest the will's validity. An interested party is one who would stand to benefit if the will is overturned. There are six grounds on which a will may be contested. One or more of them may be alleged in an attempt to have the will invalidated.

- The first ground is improper execution. In other words, some ingredient essential to the valid execution of a will is missing, such as the fact that the requisite number of witnesses did not sign the declaration.
- It may be claimed that the testator was not legally competent to make a will at the time of execution.
- A third ground commonly alleged is that the testator was under duress or unduly influenced by another to make the will as he or she did. This has sinister implications. The accusation is that the testator was not functioning as a free agent in expressing personal intentions but was following the advice of another party (usually someone with a financial interest in the outcome).
- The fourth ground for contesting a will is fraud. Someone defrauded the decedent into making a particular will by outright lies or otherwise misleading him or her.
- The will is alleged to be a forgery. That means it is not the true will of the testator, and the testator did not sign it.
- A will may be contested on the ground that the one admitted to probate had been revoked by an act of the testator before death.

A will may also be wholly or partially revoked by operation of law. In other words, the provisions of the will were not legally enforceable in that the directions or bequests would not be legal if made.

Note that contesting a will is very different from a spouse's election to take against the will. Contesting a will is aimed at destroying the entire will's validity while the statutory election only gives a spouse a certain share of the estate while leaving the will otherwise intact.

TRANSFER BY CONTRACT

Property may also be transferred at death by contract. The most usual situation involves life insurance contracts. In addition, antenuptial and postnuptial agreements are becoming more common.

Life Insurance and Other Contracts

Life insurance proceeds payable to a named beneficiary pass outside the will to the beneficiary, be it an individual or a trust. Policy proceeds will always be distributed according to the beneficiary designation on the policy. Directions for distribution in the will have no effect, unless no designated beneficiary was named or the policy was made payable to the estate. Likewise, death benefits from retirement plans will pass to named beneficiaries outside the will unless they are made payable to the estate or the executor.

Antenuptial and Postnuptial Agreements

It is not uncommon today for persons to make prenuptial or antenuptial agreements with their intended spouse. An antenuptial or prenuptial (the terms are synonymous) agreement is a legally binding agreement between two parties in anticipation of marriage. The agreement provides for limitation on transfers of property between them in relinquishment of their marital rights to each other's property. These agreements can be very useful in situations where it is not a first marriage for one or both spouses. Either spouse may wish to protect property accumulated before the marriage for children of a prior marriage. An alternate way of preserving property for children is through the use of trusts. However, antenuptial agreements may serve a variety of purposes. The agreement may provide for certain transfers from one party to the other before the marriage as an inducement to enter the legal relationship. Antenuptial agreements may also substitute for statutory elections and other inheritance rights of a spouse at death. The agreement may provide that when one spouse dies, the other spouse will receive a fixed sum in full satisfaction of his or her rights to share in the deceased spouse's estate. The spouse who accepted the terms of an antenuptial agreement will receive that property on the death of the decedent in lieu of a statutory share that is the right of a surviving spouse. As stated earlier, the antenuptial agreement has the full force and effect of an arm's-length contract. Unless false information has been supplied or information has been hidden regarding the extent of assets and size of the estate of either party when the agreement was reached, a court of law will generally uphold its terms. Aside from trusts, the antenuptial agreement can provide full protection of one's estate for one's intended beneficiaries.

Postnuptial agreements may be entered into between spouses in settlement of marital rights and property usually pursuant to a divorce. Typically in such an agreement, each spouse will give up all rights in the other spouse's estate. These agreements may or may not provide for postdeath support benefits. To the extent that payments cease upon the death of either spouse, the other spouse has given up all rights as a creditor of the estate. However, if the benefits of a postnuptial or property settlement agreement survive death, the other party would have rights against the decedent's estate as a creditor.

TRANSFER BY OPERATION OF LAW

Property not passing by will or contract may pass by what is called *operation of law*. An example of property passing by operation of law is the transfer of jointly held property to the surviving joint tenant. In addition, certain property may pass to survivors under laws pertaining to family allowances and homestead allowances. Another type of transfer in this category is intestate succession.

Joint Tenants with Right of Survivorship

Property held jointly with right of survivorship (including tenancies by the entirety) will automatically pass to the surviving joint tenant. In addition, a bank account held in trust for a named individual will pass automatically to the beneficiary. This type of account is called a *Totten trust*. The decedent retains the right to control the assets in the account until death, at which time it passes automatically to the named beneficiary outside the will. The survivorship form of ownership will take precedence over provisions in a will.

Family Allowance

One of the first distributions from a decedent's estate permitted by many states is called a *family allowance*. It is a small, specified amount set aside for the interim support of a surviving spouse and minor children during the period of estate administration. The family allowance is property the family may keep. It is not considered part of the distributable estate and is usually exempt from state death taxation.

Homestead Allowance

Another amount set aside in many states is the homestead allowance or rights. Basically the homestead allowance is an exemption out of the reach of creditors for a specified amount of real property and, in some states, personal property of the decedent.

Intestacy

All property not passing by contract, will, or by operation of law passes under the laws of intestate succession (called *laws of descent and distribution* in some states). Intestate means "without making a will." A person who dies without a will or with a will that has been revoked, annulled, or in some other way declared invalid is said to die intestate. There are intestate laws of each jurisdiction that prescribe the way an intestate's (the word as used frequently signifies the decedent) property is to be distributed. The law of the state where the person is domiciled will control the distribution of all the person's property located within the state. The intestate distribution of real property or tangible personal property of the decedent located outside of the state of domicile will be made under the laws of the state where the property is located.

No distinction is usually made between real and personal property with respect to distribution under the laws of intestate descent. To provide for all property not otherwise transferred, each state has established laws of intestate succession. There is a prescribed order for disposition to the heirs of the deceased person. Intestate succession refers to the specified order of distribution by the state of the property of persons who have died without leaving a valid will.

There are variations among the states with respect to the descent and distribution of an intestate's property. In many states, the person given primary consideration is the surviving spouse. That is not to say that the surviving spouse takes all. Generally in these states, a surviving spouse will receive from one-third to one-half of the decedent's estate, if there are living children or parents of the decedent. One scheme of intestate succession first provides that a share be set aside for the surviving spouse. An example would be a provision for the first X dollars plus one-half of the estate to go to the surviving spouse. The remaining one-half would then be divided equally among all children of the decedent. If there is no surviving spouse, surviving children may inherit the entire estate in equal shares. Next in line of lineal descendants are parents of the decedent. If a spouse remains with no children, the parents will generally share the probate estate with the surviving spouse. Brothers and sisters usually come next in line, and so on. The order is a rigid one.

State intestacy statutes do not provide for inheritances for friends, business associates, or charities. Nor do they always make adequate provision for surviving spouses. Relatives of an individual who died intestate are frequently shocked, angered, and financially hurt by the controls put on the decedent's assets by the court. No amount of persuasion can alter the statutory scheme or convince the court that the decedent intended the property to pass to other persons.

If there are no living relatives, the property escheats to the state. Escheat means that property will revert to the state for lack of any individual competent to inherit the property. In other words, there would be no heirs or next of kin who exist to whom the property can pass by way of intestate succession. The state is the ultimate owner and taker of the estate and usually designates some state institution to receive the property.

Death is not always forewarned. It sometimes strikes suddenly and when it is least expected. The business affairs and personal obligations of an individual may be in order or, alternatively, when one's life is cut short, there may be many entanglements to unravel. After death, a process begins called estate administration. The purpose of estate administration is the resolution of all outstanding responsibilities, obligations, and rights of the decedent as well as the transfer of all property to intended beneficiaries. Before the final transfers can be accomplished, the decedent's unfinished business and personal obligations must be resolved. These include payment of debts and taxes, transfers of any business interests, and collection of all amounts owed to the decedent while living as well as amounts that would be payable to beneficiaries or the estate because of the individual's death, such as life insurance proceeds, veterans' or employee death benefits, and so forth. The funeral director must be paid as well as the medical and hospital bills resulting from the last illness. In addition, cash must be made available for the immediate living needs of the family and others to whom the decedent had some financial responsibility.

Basically, whether the decedent died testate (with a will) or intestate (without a will), the estate settlement process will be similar. There are several stages in the settlement process. They are as follows:

- initial responsibilities
- probating the will
- appointing an executor or administrator
- assembling property
- managing the estate
- paying debts and taxes
- distributing the estate

INITIAL RESPONSIBILITIES

Even before a personal representative is appointed, there are matters that require attention. They may involve arranging the funeral, notifying relatives as well as close friends, and making arrangements for distant relatives to come to the funeral. Action may be necessary to temporarily protect and preserve estate assets. If the decedent was a professional person, someone must temporarily assume these professional duties. If the decedent had been the owner of a closely held business or farm, responsibility for business activity may have to be delegated so that the business or farm may remain in operation. Once the funeral is over, a determination must be made as to the existence of a will.

PROBATING THE WILL

The probate process begins when the original will is deposited with the probate court of the county where the decedent resided. By definition, probate is the act or process of proving a will. To probate the will means to prove to the court that the instrument presented is the last valid will of the deceased person. The proof must be made before a duly authorized person that the document presented as the last will and testament of a deceased person is, in fact, the document it purports to be. The term *probate* has come to refer to all matters over which probate courts have jurisdiction, including settlement of decedents' estates, appointment and supervision of guardianships, and will contests. The jurisdiction of the probate, surrogate, or orphans' court extends to the probate assets of the decedent. Probate assets refer to the property that passes under and is subject to the terms of the will or, if no will exists, the property subject to administration by the court.

When a will is admitted to probate, the signature of the testator (decedent) must be verified. This is done by calling the subscribing witnesses (witnesses who were present at the signing of the will). If there were either no witnesses to the signing or the subscribing witnesses cannot be found, attesting witnesses must be summoned to verify the decedent's signature. These are persons who can attest to the fact that the signature on the will is the decedent's true signature and that they are familiar with the signature of the decedent as they have seen it written on various occasions. Fortunately, self-proving wills are now accepted in many states. Self-proving wills contain a notarized acknowledgment by the witnesses that they saw the testator, being of sound mind, voluntarily sign the will. A self-proving will can be admitted to probate without calling witnesses to the signing. The self-proving will saves the executor the time, expense, and inconvenience of locating subscribing witnesses.

Once the will is validated, the executor or administrator is sworn in and formally appointed. Letters testamentary or letters of administration (as they are called if an administrator is appointed) will then be issued.

Probate and Nonprobate Assets

A decedent's estate consists of all property owned outright, in conjunction with others, or in which the decedent possessed certain rights at the time of death. This property is characterized as either real estate or tangible and intangible personal property. Intangibles refer to such items as stock certificates, corporate or government bonds, bank accounts, bank certificates, mutual fund shares, or money market trust assets.

Other intangible assets and rights (such as social security benefits, veterans' benefits, proceeds of life insurance, benefits under private or government pension plans, benefits under state workers' compensation acts as well as survivor's interests in joint and survivor annuity contracts) may represent the substantial bulk of the estate assets. These amounts may be payable to a decedent's survivors by operation of law or under the terms of a contract. If these assets are payable to named beneficiaries, they pass directly to the beneficiary and not under the will. They are not subject to probate. Therefore they are nonprobate assets unless they are made payable to the estate. If payable to the estate, they would become probate property subject to estate administration.

While they pass outside the will, nonprobate assets may still be taxable, for either or both federal and state estate or inheritance tax purposes. An example of a nonprobate asset that may be taxable for state inheritance purposes is a bank account owned by the decedent but held in trust for a named individual, that is, a Totten trust. The proceeds of such an account will be transferred to the named beneficiary by operation of law. However, since this account was owned by the decedent alone but in trust for another (as opposed to joint ownership with rights of survivorship, which is exempt from *state* death taxes in some states), the account may be taxable under state law for estate or inheritance tax purposes. The administrator has a duty to include this property in the inventory submitted to the court and to pay any death taxes resulting from inclusion of such property in the estate. It should be remembered that the probate process is not an automatic one. Someone (either the executor named in the will or another interested party) must present the will for probate, if letters testamentary are to be granted to the executor.

Ancillary Probate

If property exists in other states, the executor has a duty to locate the property and make all necessary transfers, either by taking possession of the property or selling it on behalf of the estate. If a decedent possessed real estate in another state, ancillary administration may be necessary in that jurisdiction. If so, the court in the county where the property is situated will appoint an ancillary administrator to oversee the transfer of these assets. The role of this ancillary administrator will be coordinated with the executor in the state of domicile.

APPOINTMENT OF EXECUTOR OR ADMINISTRATOR

If the decedent had a will, an executor was probably named to whom authority was given for settlement of the estate. An executor is also known as the personal representative of an estate. Broadly speaking, a personal representative is the individual or institution charged with responsibility for management of the estate, including gathering all assets, collecting all amounts owed the decedent, paying debts, expenses, and taxes, and distributing assets to the beneficiaries. The position requires a high degree of responsibility and involves many duties. Although named in the will, an executor must petition the probate court for formal appointment to be recognized by all persons dealing with the estate as the estate's personal representative.

If a valid will is not found, a petition must be filed in the probate court of the county where the decedent resided to have an administrator appointed. Procedures for appointment of an executor or an administrator are prescribed by state statute and vary according to local law. If the decedent had not named an executor, state law will prescribe the order of persons entitled to be appointed as an administrator. This order is based on degree of relationship to the decedent. To qualify for the position of executor, one must be legally competent and of legal age, which in most states is 18 years. If a corporation is chosen, it must be one authorized to act as a fiduciary in that state. In some states, courts will not appoint an individual who is a nonresident. A court will usually be influenced by the wishes and recommendations of the family. As to the choice of a competent administrator, a family member who is eligible to be an administrator sometimes may not feel qualified to serve. The appointment may be renounced in favor of other persons or an institution better suited for the position. Also, the court may exercise its discretion in the appointment of an appropriate administrator so that, in its judgment, the estate will be settled properly. It is not bound to follow the order prescribed by state statute.

Posting Bond

Individuals may state in their wills that named executors may serve without posting a bond as security. The courts will honor this direction provided that an executor is competent to serve. If an individual administrator has been appointed by the court, a bond with surety (secured by cash or other collateral) will be required to protect the beneficiaries and creditors of the estate. In most states, if an institution is named as administrator, a bond may still be required but usually without surety. The amount of the bond will vary depending on the approximate size of the estate and the fee schedule prescribed by state statute. Generally bonds are posted in amounts up to twice the value of the probate estate. Since the exact size of the estate will be unknown at this early stage, it might be necessary to post an additional bond at a later date when the full value of the estate is determined.

Letters Testamentary

After the bond is obtained, letters testamentary or letters of administration are issued by the court. These letters are certifications by the court that the named personal representative has been granted authority to act on behalf of the estate during the administration period until he or she is discharged by the court, at which time the estate may be closed.

Advertising

The personal representative has an obligation to publicize the existence of the estate, thereby notifying all interested parties (including creditors and debtors) of the decedent that this personal representative has authority to act as the estate's representative for all purposes. This is done by advertising in a local newspaper of general circulation and in a legal periodical in the county in which the estate is being probated. Advertising provides notice to all creditors and debtors that the decedent has died and that they may settle their accounts with the personal representative. Advertising starts the statute of limitations running. If creditors do not notify the executor of their claim within a fixed period set by local law (generally 3 to 6 months but certainly within one year of the advertisement), they will be barred from collecting any amounts owed to them by the decedent.

ASSEMBLING THE ESTATE PROPERTY

One of the first tasks of the personal representative is to assemble the property belonging to the estate. All estate assets must be gathered, safeguarded, and managed during this interim period of estate administration. This task ranges from a relatively simple one to an extremely complex, time-consuming, and expensive project. Executors should make every reasonable effort to collect all accounts receivable due to decedents from their business or profession. They may find themselves involved in the sale or continued operation of a decedent's business.

Complications may arise if the decedent owned property or partial interests in property in conjunction with others, such as interests in limited partnerships. These may be based in states other than the state of domicile (where the will is usually probated), or abroad. The decedent may also have possessed assets or business interests in foreign countries. The decedent may have been the beneficiary of one or more trusts or the custodian of the assets of another. The estate may be entitled to death benefits under an employment contract. The decedent may have possessed retained or remainder interests in property. There are many involved property rights. The executor is the one with the responsibility to take possession of and make all appropriate transfers of a decedent's property. In addition to assembling the assets, the executor has a duty to make certain that valuables are safeguarded and insured, if necessary, during the administration period. This might involve the use of safe-deposit boxes and storage vaults. The executor may find that it is necessary to possess the instincts of a sleuth and the patience of a saint, if the estate was left in a disorganized condition. Whether simple or complex, it is the personal representative who has the legal responsibility to gather all estate property, wherever situated, making the transfers necessary to do so.

Safe-Deposit Boxes

One of the first places to look for information and valuable papers is the decedent's safe-deposit box. Once an individual passes away, a safe-deposit box titled in the decedent's own name will be closed, except for limited purposes. Usually a representative of the bank will be present when the box is opened for the first time after death. The will may be found in a safe-deposit box, which is not necessarily a good location for a will as one of the first things to find out is who has been named executor. A will has no integral value in itself. If possible, for simplicity's sake, it should be kept among the valuable papers of the decedent or with the decedent's attorney rather than in a safe-deposit box. The personal representative should make a diligent search for more than one safe-deposit box to assure that all safe-deposit boxes in the name of the decedent have been located. In some states the safe-deposit box cannot be opened except in the presence of a representative of the state taxing authority, in addition to a representative of the bank. If the box contains possessions belonging to someone other than the decedent, the personal representative should not surrender this property without obtaining a receipt from the person taking possession of the property.

Proceeds of Life Insurance and Qualified Plans

Life insurance policies should be located and a claim made for all life insurance benefits. The insurance company will provide the executor with Form 712, which is filed with the federal estate tax return. There are optional modes of payment of life insurance proceeds. These various settlement options should be discussed with the beneficiaries. An appropriate settlement option should be chosen, unless the insurance is made payable to the estate or to a trust, in which case the insurance is usually paid in a lump sum. If the decedent had a right to receive death benefits from pension or profit-sharing plans, these proceeds should be applied for. Here, again, there may be a choice of payment plan. The mode of payment may have significant income tax consequences and should be reviewed carefully. Surviving spouses may also apply for the lump-sum social security death benefits and any Veterans' Administration survivor benefits to which they are entitled.

MANAGING THE ESTATE

Once the estate has been assembled, the executor is obligated to properly manage the assets of the estate. This includes managing cash, securities, and business interests, valuing assets, and obtaining the necessary legal and accounting services.

Estate Accounts

Any cash belonging to the decedent should be deposited in an estate checking account as soon as assets are released to the estate. Checks should be ordered for payment of the estate's debts. Although funds necessary to pay bills should be kept in a checking account, the executor has an obligation to keep other reasonable sums of money-producing income during the estate administration period. Therefore a savings account or money market trust account in the name of the estate should be opened as well. If the decedent had a personal brokerage account, that account should be closed and the securities or cash should be transferred to an estate account, unless the decedent's will specifically directed the executor to keep that account open for a specific time or purpose.

Valuation of Assets

Besides locating and taking possession of the decedent's property, the executor must determine the value of all estate assets as of the date of death. These values will fix the value of assets in the estate for both estate and inheritance tax purposes. All banks in which the decedent had accounts must be contacted to obtain the date-of-death values, including all accrued interest for the short taxable year ending with the decedent's death. Real property and unique personal property of any special value (such as art objects or coins) may require appraisal by an independent appraiser. Copies of the decedent's income tax returns and canceled checks for the past 3 years should be obtained. They will provide a record of the time of financial transactions as well as their cost. It will also be necessary to learn of any valuable rights the decedent may have owned, such as patent rights, royalties, or contract rights, and to determine the fair market value of these rights on the date of death. If the decedent was a professional or a sole proprietor, the value of the decedent's business or profession must be appraised for estate tax purposes.

After all assets have been located and appraised, an inventory listing all the assets and their values is filed with the probate court.

Legal and Accounting Work

If the executor is inexperienced in financial, business, and tax matters, or if the estate is complicated, administrative duties may be delegated to others. For example, the executor may hire an attorney specializing in estate matters as well as an appraiser to obtain reasonable values for the estate property. The decedent's accountant may be consulted about the decedent's tax and business matters. An attorney specializing in estate planning may be called in by the executor to perform all legal work and assist with some of the financial matters as well. This is often the same attorney who drafted the will. Today, many banks, although not named as a fiduciary under the will, are willing to offer estate settlement services on a fee-for-service basis. The trust department of an estate handles these matters routinely. A trust department would have the capacity to perform all administrative tasks for the estate, including the preparation of all tax returns.

Management or Sale of Business

In addition to the foregoing responsibilities, an administrator or executor may have to sell assets of the estate by personal sale or auction to raise the necessary cash to pay the debts, taxes, and administration expenses of the estate. This may involve sale of a personal residence or all or part of a business interest. The executor must decide whether the business interest or professional practice of the decedent must be sold, or whether it can be maintained to provide a source of income for the family. The executor may become intimately involved in making decisions regarding the business until such time as it may be liquidated, sold, or transferred to the heirs. The executor is responsible for the interim management and investment of all assets of the estate.

PAYMENT OF DEBTS AND TAXES

It is the executor's responsibility to pay all bills and debts of the decedent and to keep records of all costs of administering the estate. The administrator or executor is also responsible for payment of any court costs, attorneys' fees, the fee of the administrator or executor as well as the fee for appraisals of property, and probate costs. Executors may also have some out-of-pocket expenses for which they may reimburse themselves.

Order of Payment of Claims

The executor will have to establish the validity of all claims against the estate. A creditor must present a claim within a statutory time period. As stated previously, this time varies from state to state and may be as much as one year, but in recent years the time period has been shortened by many states to 9 or 6 months. There is a prescribed order of priority for payment of claims. If there are insufficient assets to pay all the claims in full, then the primary classes are paid in full first, with lower priority claims remaining unpaid entirely. Within a class of claims, each debt must be paid pro rata. While each state establishes its own order of preference for payment of debts, the following is a typical order: (1) debts that have a special lien on property *secured creditors* not exceeding the value of the property; (2) funeral expenses; (3) taxes; (4) debts owed to the United States government and to the state; (5) judgments of any court of competent jurisdiction to the extent that they are a lien against the property of the decedent at death; (6) wages due to any domestic servant or mechanical or agricultural laborer for the year immediately prior to the decedent's death; (7) medical expenses and services provided during the year preceding the death; and (8) all other debts and claims.

Filing of Tax Returns and Payment of Taxes

Records of any federal gift tax returns must be obtained; gift tax returns for any taxable gifts made in the year of death must also be filed. If the gross estate plus adjusted taxable gifts exceed a statutory amount equal to the unified credit, the executor must file a federal estate tax return within 9 months after the decedent's death. Also, any elections or disclaimers must be made by the time the estate tax return is filed, including extensions.

In addition to payment of federal estate taxes, the estate may be liable for taxes on real property, personal property, and possibly intangible personal property located in the state. There will also be federal and state income taxes to be paid, both for the short taxable year prior to the decedent's death and the remaining period of that tax year after death. This may include filing a joint return with the surviving spouse for the year of death. State inheritance or estate taxes must be paid if any tax is due. If there is a discount for early payment of state inheritance tax, the executor must decide when to pay the inheritance tax and weigh the advantages or disadvantages of paying it early. Sometimes early payment is impossible because there are no liquid assets in the estate that can be used for this purpose. For example, the major asset of an estate may be real estate. Prior to the sale of such property, the estate will not have cash to pay many of its obligations. In that case, early payment of inheritance taxes is not possible and the discount would, of necessity, be lost. If a trust has been established, some taxes may be payable by the trust.

A determination will have to be made as to who the taxpayer is and how the taxes will be allocated among the estate, any trust, or the beneficiaries of each. Frequently a will contains a tax clause that directs the way taxes are to be apportioned. If there is no tax clause in the will, taxes will be allocated according to the state statutory scheme.

There are still other decisions that an executor should make with regard to payment of taxes. A choice will have to be made whether to have all assets valued on the date of death or the alternate valuation date, which is 6 months from the date of death. For decedents dying after July 18, 1984, the alternate valuation date can only be used if both the value of the gross estate and the amount of federal estate tax will decrease by using the alternate valuation date (IRC Sec. 2032(c)). An example of an estate that could still use the alternate valuation date is one that has substantial amounts of stocks and bonds whose prices have dropped significantly within the 6-month period between the date of death and the alternate valuation date. In that case the executor may select the alternate valuation date to reduce taxes. Also, if more than 35 percent of the adjusted gross estate consists of a closely held business or farm, the executor should consider the advisability of electing a 15-year payment of the estate tax attributable to the value of that closely held business or farm included in the estate. An extension of time to pay the tax may also be requested based on reasonable cause.

There is also a provision in the tax code for special valuation of a farm or business real estate. Any election to specially value these properties at their current use value rather than at their highest and best use must be made when the federal estate return is filed. If the estate contains qualified terminable interest property, the executor must also decide whether to elect to qualify this property for the marital deduction. There may be some credits or deductions that can be taken for taxes previously paid on the estate of a person whose property was inherited by the decedent within 10 years of the decedent's death. Also, the executor may be given discretion in the will to take deductions either in the federal estate tax return or in the decedent's income tax return to achieve the lowest tax liability. All the above decisions fall within the scope of the executor's discretion and responsibilities.

DISTRIBUTING THE ESTATE

As the estate administration process draws to a close, the executor will prepare an accounting for the court and the beneficiaries. This procedure varies from state to state. An accounting is filed in the county where the will was probated. It may be a formal proceeding with notice to interested parties, or it may be an informal proceeding. At this time, any interested parties have the right to object to the accounting and to have any matters at issue resolved by the judge with whom the accounting is filed.

If there is no objection to the accounting, the executor or administrator will then proceed to make final distribution of the estate assets. When the executor makes distributions, it is important that releases and receipts be obtained from the legatees to relieve the executor from further liability to each beneficiary because of the property transferred to them. When that has been accomplished, the administrator or executor may be discharged by the court, at which time the estate can be closed. If any property is found after that, it may be necessary to reopen the estate on a limited basis to have this property probated.

Disclaimers

The possibility may arise that a beneficiary does not wish to accept either a bequest under the decedent's will or an intestate share of the estate that he or she would be entitled to receive. A reason may be that the beneficiary's own estate is substantial. The beneficiary may not want to further burden his or her own estate with additional estate taxes. Alternatively, it may be a way of releasing an inheritance so that it will go to other beneficiaries in greater need than himself or herself. If a beneficiary does not wish to accept an inheritance, it is possible to refuse this legacy by making a qualified disclaimer. If the requirements of a qualified disclaimer are met, the property will be treated as if it had never passed to that individual. A disclaimer is a valid postmortem estate planning tool for insuring that the property comes to rest in the hands of the desired beneficiary. There is a section of the Internal Revenue Code that states four requirements to qualify a disclaimer for federal estate tax or gift tax purposes: (1) there must be an unqualified refusal by the beneficiary to accept the bequest or the gift; (2) this refusal must be written and received by the donor, the donor's legal representative, or the legal titleholder of the property within 9 months of the decedent's death or 9 months from the date of the gift or, if later, within 9 months after the beneficiary becomes 21 years of age; (3) the beneficiary must not have accepted the interest or any of its benefits; (4) the interest must then pass to someone other than the person making the disclaimer or to the spouse of the decedent without the beneficiary's direction.

All or part of an interest in property may be disclaimed. However, the disclaimed part must represent an undivided portion of the interest. The beneficiary of an estate has 9 months following the decedent's death in which to make this disclaimer. It must be received by the executor or administrator of the estate in writing. If a federal estate tax return is filed, a copy of the disclaimer must be filed with the return. It is also possible to disclaim a power of appointment over property if one meets the same four requirements stated above.

Once a beneficiary accepts a gift or bequest and then decides to disclaim this interest, the property cannot qualify as a valid disclaimer under federal law. The property would be treated as if it had been accepted by the beneficiary, after which time the beneficiary made a gift, possibly a taxable gift, to the subsequent recipient of the property. In the past, disclaimers that qualified under the federal gift tax statute were not necessarily recognized under state law. If a disclaimer was held invalid under state law, it would disqualify the disclaimer for federal estate and gift tax purposes. The law now provides that a disclaimer complying with the requirements of the federal tax statute will be considered to qualify for federal estate and gift tax purposes, regardless of qualification under local law. The new law provides equal treatment for all disclaimers, regardless of the vagaries of local law applicable only in determining the identity of the ultimate beneficiary. The new law will provide some uniformity in the application of the federal disclaimer statute, although state law may still hold the disclaimer to be ineffective to pass title directly to the later beneficiary without gift tax considerations.

Disclaimers can be useful estate planning devices when the surviving spouse received an inadequate share of the estate as well as when the person disclaiming the interest had substantial assets of his or her own. Conversely, a surviving spouse who possesses a substantial estate in his or her own right may wish to disclaim an inheritance that would increase the size of the surviving spouse's estate unnecessarily, thereby causing additional estate tax liability when that spouse dies. An increased share passing to the surviving spouse as the result of a qualified disclaimer made by another beneficiary will qualify that interest for the marital deduction.

Stephan R. Leimberg* and Ted Kurlowicz

PURPOSE, NATURE, AND SCOPE OF GIFT TAX LAW

Purpose

If an individual could give away his or her entire estate during lifetime without the imposition of any tax, a rational person would arrange his or her affairs so that at death nothing would be subject to the federal estate tax. Likewise, if a person could give income-producing securities or other property to members of his or her family, freely and without tax cost, the burden of income taxes could be shifted back and forth to lower brackets, and income taxes would be saved.

The federal gift tax was designed to equalize the transfer tax treatment between taxpayers who make inter vivos (lifetime) transfers and those who transfer their assets at death. The unified nature of the federal estate and gift tax system combines both tax systems and a common set of rates is applicable to both inter vivos and deathtime transfers.

Nature

The gift tax is an excise tax, which is not levied directly on the gift itself or on the right to receive the property, but rather on the right of an individual to transfer money or other property to another for less than full and adequate consideration. (The tax is imposed only on transfers by individuals, but certain transfers involving corporations are treated as indirect transfers by corporate stockholders.)

The gift tax is based on the value of the property transferred. It is computed on a progressive schedule based on cumulative lifetime gifts. In other words, the tax rates are applied to total lifetime taxable gifts (all gifts less the exclusions and deductions) rather than only to taxable gifts made in the current calendar year.

---

*Stephan R. Leimberg, JD, CLU, is professor of estate planning and taxation at The American College.

Scope

The Internal Revenue regulations summarize the comprehensive scope of the gift tax law by stating that "all transactions whereby property or interests are gratuitously passed or conferred upon another, regardless of the means or device employed, constitute gifts subject to tax." Almost any transfer or shifting of property or an interest in property can subject the donor (the person transferring the property or shifting the interest) to potential gift tax liability to the extent that the transfer is not supported by adequate and full consideration in money or money's worth—that is, to the extent that the transfer is gratuitous. Direct and indirect gifts, gifts made outright, and gifts in trust (of both real and personal property) can be the subject of a taxable gift. The gift tax is imposed on the shifting of property rights, regardless of whether the property is tangible or intangible. It can be applied even if the property transferred (such as a municipal bond) is exempt from federal income or other taxes.

This broad definition includes transfers of life insurance, partnership interests, royalty rights, and gifts, checks, or notes of third parties. Forgiving a note or cancelling a debt may also constitute a gift.

Almost any party can be the donee (recipient) of a gift subject to tax. The donee can be an individual, partnership, corporation, foundation, trust, or other "person." (A gift to a corporation is typically considered a gift to the other shareholders in proportion to their proprietary interests. Similarly, a gift to a trust is usually considered to be a gift to the beneficiary or beneficiaries in proportion to their interests.)

In fact, a gift can be subject to the tax (assuming the gift is complete) even if the identity of the donee is not known at the date of the transfer and cannot be ascertained.

TAX ADVANTAGES OF LIFETIME GIFTS

The 1976 unification of the estate and gift tax systems was an attempt to impose the same tax burden on transfers made during life as on those made at death. The disparity of treatment between lifetime and testamentary gifts is minimized through the adoption of a single unified estate and gift tax rate schedule. Both lifetime and testamentary gifts are subject to the same rate schedule and are taxed cumulatively, so that gifts made during a lifetime increase the rate at which gifts made at death will be taxed. Although at first glance it seemed that unification eliminated the advantage of inter vivos gifts, there are still some significant advantages.

First, an individual can give up to $10,000 gift tax free every year to each of an unlimited number of donees. This means that a father desiring to make a $10,000 gift to each of his four children and four grandchildren could give a total of $80,000 each year without gift tax liability. (This $10,000 annual gift tax exclusion is described in greater detail later.) Since an individual's spouse can also give, such gifts—up to $20,000 per year of money or other property, multiplied by an unlimited number of donees—can be transferred gift tax free.

8.2

In the example above, the donor and spouse together could give up to $160,000 annually on a gift-tax-free basis. In fact, one spouse can make the entire gift if the other spouse consents; the transaction can then be treated as if both spouses made gifts. This is known as *gift splitting*. Split-gift provisions are also covered in detail later.

A second tax incentive for making an inter vivos as opposed to a testamentary gift is that if a gift is made more than 3 years prior to a decedent's death, the amount of any gift tax paid on the transfer is not brought back into the computation of the gross estate. In the case of a sizable gift, avoidance of the *gross-up rule* can result in meaningful tax savings. The gross-up rule means that all gift tax payable on taxable gifts made within 3 years of death is included in calculating the value of the gross estate, even if the gift itself is not added back. For example, if an individual makes a $1 million taxable gift, the $345,800 gift tax payable on that transfer will not be brought back into the estate tax computation if the gift was made more than 3 years before the donor's death.

Third, when a gift is made during lifetime, any appreciation accruing between the time of the gift and the date of the donor's death escapes estate taxation. This may result in a considerable estate tax (as well as probate and inheritance tax) saving. If a father gives his daughter stock worth $100,000 and it appreciates to $600,000 by the date of the father's death 5 years later, only the $100,000 value of the stock at the time of the gift enters into the estate tax computation as an adjusted taxable gift. The $500,000 of appreciation does not enter into the computation as an *adjusted taxable gift* and thus does not increase the decedent's marginal estate tax bracket. An excellent example of both advantages is a gift of life insurance more than 3 years prior to the insured's death. A $1 million death benefit could be removed from a donor's estate at the cost of only the gift tax on the value of the policy at the time of the transfer (in the case of a whole life policy, usually roughly equivalent to the policy cash value, plus unearned premiums at the date of the gift). If the insured lives for more than 3 years after the transfer and the premiums are present-interest gifts of $10,000 a year or less, there would be no estate tax inclusion, and none of the *appreciation* (the difference between the death benefit payable and the adjusted taxable gift, if any, at the time the policy was transferred) would be in the insured's estate.

Fourth, there are often strong income tax incentives for making an inter vivos gift. This advantage derives from moving taxable income from a high-bracket donor to a lower-bracket donee. Of course, this advantage is limited by the tax rules related to unearned income of children under age 14.

Fifth, gifts of the proper type of assets may enable a decedent's estate to meet the mathematical tests for a Sec. 303 stock redemption, a Sec. 6166 installment payout of taxes, and the 2032A special-use valuation of farms and certain other business real property.

Sixth, no gift taxes will be paid until the transferor makes *taxable* gifts in excess of the unified credit in the year of the gift. (The *exemption equivalent* for 1984 was $325,000. It increased to $400,000 in 1985 and to $500,000 in 1986. For 1987 and later years it will be $600,000.) Only taxable gifts in excess of a donor's unused exemption equivalent will cause a loss of income and/or capital because of gift taxes paid.

COMPUTING THE TAX ON GIFTS

Gift tax rates are applied to a net figure—*taxable gifts.* Before the tax on a transfer is computed, certain reductions are allowed. These reductions may include

- gift splitting
- an annual exclusion
- a marital deduction
- a charitable deduction

Gift Splitting

The tax law permits a married donor—with the consent of the non-donor-spouse—to elect to treat a gift to a third party as though each spouse has made one-half of the gift. The election must be made on the applicable gift tax return of the donor-spouse.

Gift splitting is an artificial mechanism: even if one spouse makes the entire gift, the single transfer is treated for tax computation purposes as though each spouse made only one-half of the gift. This means that the rate of tax that each will pay is calculated separately by reference to each spouse's prior gifts.

Furthermore, if a non-donor-spouse has agreed to gift splitting, it will have a direct effect on the future gift tax and estate tax that the non-donor-spouse will eventually have to pay if the gift exceeds the annual exclusion. Even though the non-donor-spouse did not *actually* make one-half of the gift, it will—to the extent it exceeds the $10,000 annual exclusion—become an *adjusted taxable gift* to be added (1) to all other gifts deemed to have been made for purposes of calculating the future gift tax bracket and (2) to the taxable estate at the non-donor-spouse's death.*

Gift splitting, which applies only to gifts by a married donor to a third party and only with respect to noncommunity property, was introduced into the tax law to equate the tax treatment of common-law taxpayers with that of community-property residents. When one spouse earns a dollar in a community-property state, 50 cents is deemed to be owned by the other spouse automatically and immediately. Therefore if the couple gave that dollar to their daughter, each spouse would be treated as having given only 50 cents.

Gift splitting places the resident of a common-law state in the same position. For example, if a married individual in a common-law state gives her

---

*This would occur unless the gift has already been included as an adjusted taxable gift in computing the estate tax of the donor-spouse.

son a gift worth $20,000 and the requisite gift-splitting election is made, this individual is considered to have given only $10,000 for purposes of the gift tax computation. Her spouse is treated as if he had given the other $10,000—even if none of the gift was his property.

If the spouses elect to split gifts to third parties, all gifts made by either spouse during that reporting period must be split.

The privilege of gift splitting applies only to gifts made while the couple is married. Therefore gifts made by the couple before they were married may not be split, even if they were married later during the same calendar year. Likewise, gifts made after either the spouses are legally divorced or one spouse dies may not be split. But gifts made before one spouse dies may be split even if that spouse dies before signing the appropriate consent or election; the deceased spouse's executor can make the appropriate election or consent.

The Annual Exclusion

Purpose of the Exclusion

A *de minimis* rule is one that is instituted primarily to avoid the bother of administrative record keeping. The annual gift tax exclusion is a classic example of such a rule. It was instituted to eliminate the need for a taxpayer to keep an account of or report numerous small gifts. Congress intended that the amount of the annual exclusion be set large enough so that no reporting would be required in the case of wedding gifts or other occasional gifts of relatively small amounts.

Effect of Gift Splitting Coupled with Exclusion

Generally the annual exclusion allows the donor to make, tax-free, up to $10,000 worth of gifts (other than *future-interest gifts*, defined below) to any number of persons or parties each year. Since an exclusion of up to $10,000 is allowed per donee per year, the total maximum excludible amount is determined by multiplying the number of persons to whom gifts are made by $10,000. For example, if an unmarried man makes cash gifts this year of $2,000, $8,000, and $16,000 to his brother, father, and son, respectively, the $2,000 and the $8,000 gifts would be fully excludible, and $10,000 of the $16,000 gift to his son would be excludible.

If the same individual is married and his spouse consents to split the gift, each spouse is deemed to have made one-half of the gift. This means that both spouses can maximize the use of their annual exclusions. Assuming the non-donor-spouse made no gifts, the computation below shows that none of the $26,000 would be subject to tax.

Donee	Amount of Gift to Donee	Treated as if Donor Gave	Exclusion	Subject to Tax	Treated as if Non-Donor-Spouse Gave	Exclusion	Subject to Tax
Brother	$ 2,000	$ 1,000	$ 1,000	-	$ 1,000	$ 1,000	-
Father	8,000	4,000	4,000	-	4,000	4,000	-
Son	16,000	8,000	8,000	-	8,000	8,000	-
Totals	$26,000	$13,000	$13,000	$ -	$13,000	$13,000	$ -

Present versus Future Interest

An annual exclusion is allowed only for *present-interest gifts* and is denied to *gifts of future interest.* A present interest is one in which the donee's use, possession, or enjoyment begins at the time the gift is made. Stated technically, a present interest is an immediate, unfettered, and ascertainable right to use, possess, or enjoy the gift.

A future interest refers to any interest or estate in which the donee's possession or enjoyment will not commence until some period of time after the gift is made. Technically, "*future interest* is a legal term, and includes reversions, remainders, and other interests or estates, whether vested or contingent, and whether or not supported by a particular interest or estate, which are limited to commence in use, possession, or enjoyment at some future date or time."

Clearly the outright and unrestricted gift of property to a donee (even a minor) that passes legal and equitable title qualifies as a present-interest gift.

A single gift can be split into two parts: one is a present-interest that qualifies for the annual exclusion, and the other is a future interest that does not. For example, a widowed donor creates a trust this year and places income-producing property in the trust. The income is payable annually to the donor's son for life, and at the son's death the remainder is payable to the donor's grandson. The gift to the son of the right to receive income annually for life is a present-interest gift since he has an unrestricted right to its immediate use, possession, or enjoyment. If the son is 30 years old at the time of the gift and $100,000 is placed into the trust, the present value of that gift is $96,736 ($100,000 times .96736, which is the present value of an income stream payable for the life of a 30-year-old based on a principal amount of $100,000. The factor for the life interest (.96736) is based on the current (at the time of this writing) interest rate of 10.60 percent and current mortality. The valuation of life estates, term interests, and remainder interests is based on an interest rate adjusted monthly as mandated in I.R.C. Sec. 7520. The valuation methodology is further discussed in reading 11.) Since the annual exclusion is available for the gift of a life income interest, $10,000 of the $96,736 gift is excludible.

If the donor was married and the appropriate election and consent were filed, each spouse could claim a $10,000 exclusion even though only the donor placed property in the trust. No exclusion is allowed with respect to the ultimate gift of the corpus to the grandson, since his possession or enjoyment may not commence until sometime in the future.

If the donor had provided that her son was to receive income for 10 years and then the principal was to pass to her grandson, and the donor had placed only $1,000 in the trust, the exclusion for the gift of the income interest would be $634.87 ($1,000 times .63487, the value of a 10-year term interest at the current (at the time of this writing) interest rate of 10.60 percent). Gift splitting with a spouse would not increase the amount of the exclusion, and each spouse would be allowed a $317.43 exclusion. Again, no exclusion would be allowed for the gift of the future interest (remainder) that passes to the grandson at the end of 10 years, even though he has an interest that cannot be forfeited. This is because he does not have the right to immediate possession or enjoyment; any delay in the absolute and immediate right of use, possession, or enjoyment of the property or the income therefrom is fatal to the gift tax annual exclusion.

Note that if the trustee in either situation above had been given the power or discretion to accumulate the income, rather than distribute it, the donor's son would not have received the unfettered and immediate use of the income, and it would be impossible to ascertain the present value of the income interest. For example, assume the trustee is directed to pay the net income to the son for as long as the son lives, but is authorized to withhold payments of income during any period the trustee deems advisable and add such payments to corpus. In this case, even the income interest would be a gift of a future interest, and no annual exclusion would be allowed.

When a trustee is required by the trust agreement to accumulate income for a time (or until the occurrence of a specified event), the income interest is a future interest.

Gifts of Life Insurance. An outright no-strings-attached gift of life insurance will qualify for the annual exclusion. Life insurance (and annuity policies) are subject to the same basic test as any other type of property in ascertaining whether the interest created is present or future interest, even though the ultimate obligation under a life insurance policy—payment of the death benefit—is to be discharged in the future. It is not necessary that a policy have cash value at the time of the gift for the transfer to be one of a present interest. But the annual exclusion would be lost if the donor prevented the donee from surrendering the policy or borrowing its cash value, or limited the donee's right to policy cash values in any way.

Gifts of Life Insurance to Trusts. If the grantor transfers a life insurance policy to a trust, the present- versus future-interest rules discussed above will apply. That is, the annual exclusion will be available only if the donee-beneficiaries receive a present interest. Simply transferring life insurance to a trust will not typically create a present-interest gift. The life insurance trust usually pays no income, or the income will be used to provide premium payments and will not be currently available to donees. Qualifying as a present interest would be a significant hurdle for the life insurance trust if there were no exceptions to the general rule. Typically the initial cost of the life insurance policy transferred to the trust and the annual premiums that must be contributed to the trust by the grantor each year will be under $10,000. Therefore, if the annual exclusion applies, most irrevocable life insurance trusts will not incur gift tax liability. Fortunately it is possible to design an irrevocable life insurance trust that qualifies as a present-interest gift for annual-exclusion purposes.

Crummey Powers. The present-interest requirement for annual-exclusion purposes indicates that a gift in trust must currently provide the donees with an unfettered right to use, possess, and benefit from the trust. The benefit could be a current disposition of income or corpus, or the beneficiaries could be provided with current withdrawal rights or powers. Tax rules provide that if each trust beneficiary has, at a minimum, the so-called Crummey demand powers, the transfer to the trust will qualify as a present-interest gift for the beneficiaries. The demand powers held by the beneficiary should allow the beneficiary the noncumulative right to demand the lesser of (1) the annual addition to the trust, (2) $5,000, or (3) 5 percent of the trust corpus at the time the power is exercised. When there is more than one beneficiary, the Crummey powers should be given ratably to each. Since there is no chance that the beneficiaries can request an amount greater than the annual addition to corpus, the insurance policy will not be stripped by the beneficiaries. In actual practice, the beneficiaries cooperate since they realize that the long-term benefit of the trust is more important than the current demand rights. For the irrevocable life insurance trust with Crummey powers to qualify as a present-interest gift, each beneficiary must be notified of the right to exercise the powers by the trustee. This right must exist for a reasonable time each year (such as 30 days). If each beneficiary's demand power is limited to the amounts specified above, the annual lapse of this power will not be treated as a taxable gift by the lapsing beneficiaries.

Identity of Donees

The number and amount (or availability) of exclusions depend on the identity of the donee(s), the type of asset involved, and the restrictions, if any, placed on the asset. When a gift is made in trust, the beneficiaries of the trust (and not the trust itself) are considered the donees. For instance, if there are three life-income beneficiaries, up to three annual exclusions could be obtained. Conversely, if five trusts were established for the same beneficiary, only one exclusion is allowed. (Technically, the actuarial value of each gift in trust to that beneficiary would be totaled and added to direct gifts the donor made to that beneficiary to ascertain whether and to what extent an annual exclusion remains and is allowable for the present transfer.)

Transfers to two or more persons as joint tenants with right of survivorship, tenants by the entirety, or tenants in common are considered multiple gifts. Each tenant is deemed to receive an amount equal to the actuarial value of his or her interest in the tenancy. If, for example, one person has a one-half interest in a tenancy in common, a cash gift of $6,000 to the tenancy would be treated as a $3,000 gift to that person. This would be added to other gifts made directly by the same donor to determine how much of the exclusion will be allowed. (However, note that a tenancy by the entirety, in which neither spouse can sever an interest without the other's consent, will be considered a future-interest gift and will not qualify for the annual exclusion.) In all probability, gifts to partnerships should follow the same rules: a gift to a partnership should be treated as if made to each partner in proportion to his or her partnership interest.

Gifts to Minors

Outright gifts to minors pose no particular qualification problem. The IRS states in a revenue ruling that "an unqualified and unrestricted gift to a minor, with or without the appointment of a guardian, is a gift of a present interest." But there are, of course, practical problems involved, especially with larger gifts. Although minors can buy, sell, and deal with some limited types of property, such as U.S. savings bonds, gifts of other types of property create difficulties. For example, some states do not give minors the legal capacity to purchase their own property, care for it, or sell or transfer it. Some states forbid the registration of securities in a minor's name, and a broker may be reluctant to deal in securities titled in a minor's name. In many states, a minor has the legal ability to disaffirm a sale of stock sold at a low price that later rises in value. Furthermore, a buyer receives no assurance of permanent title when a minor signs a real estate deed. Legal guardianship of the minor is not a viable answer in many situations. Since guardianship laws are rigid, a guardian must generally post bond, and periodic and expensive court accounting is often required. Most important, a parent may not want to give a minor control over a large amount of cash or other property.

To minimize these and other practical problems involved with most large gifts to minors, such transfers are generally made in trust or under some type of guardianship or custodian arrangement. An incredible amount of litigation developed over whether such gifts qualified for the annual exclusion. Sec. 2503 of the Internal Revenue Code provides clear and precise methods of qualifying gifts to minors for the exclusion. There are three basic means of qualifying *cared-for gifts* to minors under Sec. 2503: (1) a Sec. 2503(b) trust, (2) a Sec. 2503(c) trust, or (3) the Uniform Gifts (Transfers) to Minors Act.

Sec. 2503(b) Trust. To obtain an annual exclusion for gifts to a trust, an individual can establish a trust that *requires* income to be distributed at least annually to (or for use of) the minor beneficiary. Income is the actual accounting income of the trust as determined by the trust agreement and state law. The trust agreement would state how income is to be used and would give the trustee no discretion as to its use. The minor would receive possession of the trust principal whenever the trust agreement specifies. A distribution does not have to be made by age 21; corpus may be held for as long as the beneficiary lives — or for any shorter period of time. In fact, the principal can actually bypass the income beneficiary and go directly to the individuals whom the grantor—or even the named beneficiary—has specified. The trust agreement can also control the dispositive scheme if the minor dies before receiving trust corpus. Trust assets do not have to be paid to the minor's estate or appointees.

Mandatory payment of income to (or in behalf of) beneficiaries seems onerous—especially while the beneficiary is a minor. But such income could be deposited in a custodial account and used for the minor's benefit or left to accumulate in a custodial account until the minor reaches majority (at which time the unexpended amount would be turned over to the beneficiary).

Although the entire amount of property placed in a 2503(b) trust would be considered a gift, for exclusion purposes it is split into two parts: income and principal. The value of the income—measured by multiplying the amount of the gift by a factor that considers both the duration over which the income interest will be paid and the discounted worth of $1 payable over the appropriate number of years—would be eligible for the annual exclusion. The balance of the gift would not qualify for the annual exclusion.

For example, assume a donor places $10,000 into a Sec. 2503(b) trust that is required to pay her 10-year-old daughter all income until she reaches age 25. The present value of the income the daughter would receive over those 15 years is $7,793.66. If the income were payable for her entire life, the present value would jump to $9,894.90.

It is important to note that, according to at least one revenue ruling, the annual exclusion would be denied for a 2503(b) trust that permits the principal to be invested in non-income-producing securities, real estate, or life insurance policies.

Sec. 2503(c) Trust. The Sec. 2503(b) trust described above has the advantage of not requiring distribution of principal when the minor reaches age 21, but it does require a current (annual) distribution of income. The Sec. 2503(c) trust requires that income and principal be distributed when the minor reaches age 21, but does not require the trustee to distribute income currently.

Certain requirements make it possible for a donor to obtain the exclusion by a gift to a minor under Sec. 2503(c): the trust must provide that (1) the income and principal are expended by or on behalf of the beneficiary, and (2) to the extent not so expended, income and principal will pass to the beneficiary at age 21, or (3) if the beneficiary dies prior to that time, income and principal will go to the beneficiary's estate or appointees under a general power of appointment. (The annual exclusion will not be lost merely because local law prevents a minor from exercising a general power of appointment.)

A substantial amount of flexibility can be built into the 2503(c) trust. Income that has been accumulated, as well as any principal in the trust, can be paid to the donee when the donee reaches age 21. This may be indicated if the sums involved are not substantial. But the donor may want the trust to continue to age 25 or some other age. It is possible to provide continued management of the trust assets and at the same time avoid forfeiting the annual exclusion by giving the donee, at age 21, a right for a limited period to require immediate distribution by giving written notice to the trustee. If the beneficiary fails to give written notice, the trust can continue automatically for whatever period the donor provided when the donor established the trust. Alternatively, some states have lowered the age of majority from 21 to 18, or some in-between age. A trust can provide that the distribution can be made between the age of majority and age 21 without jeopardizing the Sec. 2503(c) exclusion. (The rule is that 21 is the maximum rather than the minimum age at which the trust assets must be made available.)

A 2503(c) trust has a number of advantages over the type of custodianship found in the Uniform Gifts to Minors Act (UGMA) or Uniform Transfers to Minors Act (UTMA) arrangements described below, as shown in table 8-1.

Uniform Gifts (Transfers) to Minors Act. The Uniform Gifts (Transfers) to Minors Act (or comparable laws, such as the Model Gifts to Minors Act) provides an alternative to the Sec. 2503(c) trust. The Uniform Gifts to Minors and Uniform Transfers to Minors Acts are frequently utilized for smaller gifts because of their simplicity and because they offer the benefits of management, income and estate tax shifting, and the investment characteristics of a trust with little or none of the setup costs.

TABLE 8-1

Factor	Trust	UGMA or UTMA
Type of property	Donor can make gifts of almost any type of property	Type of property must be permitted by appropriate statute. Gift of real estate may not be permitted
Dispositive provisions	Donor can provide for disposition of trust assets if donee dies without having made disposition	Disposition must follow statutory guidelines
Investment powers	Trustee may be given broad, virtually unlimited investment powers	Custodian limited to investment powers specified by statute
Time of distribution of assets	Trust can continue automatically even after beneficiary reaches age 21. Trustee can make distribution between state law age of majority and age 21	Custodial assets must be paid to beneficiary upon reaching majority

The Uniform Gifts to Minors Act, a model statute that has been adopted by all states in some form, permits adults to make gifts of certain statutorily permissible property to minors with the property registered in the name of a custodian. ~~The custodian, who may be the donor, holds the property for the minor.~~ The initial forms of UGMA statutes included restrictive limits on the categories of investments permitted for a UGMA transfer. For example, a ~~UGMA transfer could not include real property.~~

Many states have amended their statutes to include broader investment powers, and approximately one-half of the states have adopted a new statute—the Uniform Transfers to Minors Act (UTMA). ~~The UTMA statutes generally permit any type of property transfer.~~

For example, in Pennsylvania the UGMA gift may be made as follows:

- if the subject of the gift is a security in registered form, by registering it in the name of the donor, other adult person, or trust company, followed in substance by the words "as custodian for _____

  Name of Minor

  under the Pennsylvania Uniform Gifts to Minors Act"
- if the subject of the gift is a security not in registered form, by delivering it to a guardian of the minor or a trust company, accompanied by a statement of gift in the following form or substance, signed by the donor and the person designated as custodian: "Gift under the Pennsylvania Uniform Gifts to Minors Act—I, _____, hereby deliver to _____ as custodian

  Name of Donor   Name of Custodian

  for _____ as custodian for the Pennsylvania Uniform Gifts

      Name of Minor

  to Minors Act," the following security(ies): (insert a description of the security or securities that is sufficient to identify it or them)

  _____

  (Signature of Donor)

- if the subject of the gift is money, by paying or delivering it to a broker or a bank, for credit to an account in the name of the donor, another adult person, an adult member of the minor's family, a guardian of the minor, or a bank with trust powers, followed in substance by the words "as custodian for _____ under the Pennsylvania Uniform

      Name of Minor

  Gifts to Minors Act"
- if the subject of the gift is a life or endowment insurance policy or an annuity contract, by causing the ownership of such policy or contract to be recorded on a form satisfactory to the insurance company or fraternal benefit society, in the name of the donor, another adult person, a guardian of the minor, or a bank with trust powers, followed in substance by the words, "as custodian for _____ under the

      Name of Minor

  Pennsylvania Uniform Gifts to Minors Act," and having the policy or contract delivered to the person in whose name it is thus registered as custodian

The type of asset given and the restrictions placed on that asset may prevent the donor from obtaining the annual exclusion.

Clearly, an outright gift of non-income-producing property will qualify for the gift tax exclusion. Will the same property qualify if placed in a trust? The IRS uses three arguments to disallow annual exclusions: (1) the right to income (which is the only current right given to a life beneficiary) from a gift of non-income-producing property is a future interest since its worth is contingent on the trustee's converting it to income-producing property; (2) it is impossible to ascertain the value of an income interest in property that is not income producing at the time of the gift; and (3) if a gift tax exclusion *is* allowable, the exclusion must be limited to the actual income produced by the property (or expected to be produced) multiplied by the number of years over which the income beneficiary is expected to receive the income—discounted to its present value according to tables in government regulations.

Non-dividend-paying stock is a good example of property that may not qualify for the gift tax exclusion. In a number of cases, the IRS has been successful in disallowing an exclusion for gifts in trust that consisted of stock in closely held corporations paying no dividends. Gifts in trust of life insurance policies pose the same problem: a mother assigns policies on her life to a trust created to provide financial protection for her daughter. The trust provisions do not provide the daughter with Crummey withdrawal powers. At the mother's death, the policy proceeds will be reinvested and the daughter will receive the net income of the trust for life. Will the mother be allowed the exclusion for the present value of her daughter's income interest? The regulations say no, since the daughter will not receive income payments until her mother dies.

Summary of Rules for Ascertaining the Amount and Availability of the Gift Tax Annual Exclusion

The rules regarding the annual exclusion can be summarized as follows:

- A gift in trust is a gift to a trust's beneficiaries and not to the trust in determining the number of annual exclusions to which a donor is entitled.
- The value of an income interest in a trust qualifies for the exclusion if the trustee is required to distribute trust income at least annually—even if the value of the remainder interest does not qualify.
- The gift of an interest that is contingent upon survivorship is a gift of a future interest. (If a gift in trust is made with income going to the grantor's son for life, and then to the grantor's daughter for life, the gift to the son will qualify but the daughter's interest will not.)
- A gift is one of a future interest if enjoyment depends on the exercise of a trustee's discretion. (The nature of the interest must be present as of the date of the gift and is not, for example, determined by what the trustee may subsequently do or not do in the exercise of a discretionary power.)

- A gift must have an ascertainable value to qualify for the exclusion. (The exclusion will be denied if the donor or anyone else can divert the income from the beneficiary.)

Exclusion of Transfers for Educational and Medical Expenses

For public policy reasons, Congress provided another exclusion for specific qualified transfers. A gratuitous transfer is excluded from taxable gifts if made on behalf of an individual (1) for tuition to an educational institution for the education or training of the individual or (2) to a provider of medical services for medical care received by the individual. This exclusion is not limited in amount and applies independently of the annual exclusion. However, it is important to note that the payments must be made directly to the provider of services to qualify for the exemption. Payments made directly to an individual as reimbursement for educational or medical expenses incurred are taxable gifts unless such gifts are eligible for an annual exclusion.

Gift Tax Marital Deduction

An individual who transfers property to a spouse is allowed an unlimited deduction (subject to certain conditions) known as the gift tax marital deduction. The purpose of the gift tax marital deduction is to enable spouses to be treated as an economic unit.

Requirements to Qualify for Gift Tax Marital Deduction

For a gift to qualify for the gift tax marital deduction, the following conditions must be satisfied: (1) The recipient of the gift must be the spouse of the donor at the time the gift is made. (2) The recipient-spouse must be a U.S. citizen. (3) The property transferred to the donee-spouse must not be a terminable interest that will disqualify the gift for the marital deduction.

Most of the qualifications above are self-explanatory. The terminable-interest rule for marital-deduction gifts is similar to the rule employed for estate tax purposes. The effect of these rules is that generally no marital deduction will be allowed if the donee-spouse's interest in the transferred property will terminate after a lapse of time or on the occurrence or nonoccurrence of a specified contingency at which time the donee-spouse's interest will pass to another person who received his or her interest in the property from the donor-spouse and who did not pay the donor full and adequate consideration for that interest. The exception is for a gift of *qualifying terminable interest in property* (QTIP) assets. (In the past, a gift or bequest of a terminable interest in property—one which could end at a spouse's death, for example, and therefore escape taxation—would not have been eligible for the gift or estate tax marital deduction.)

Current law provides that if a donor-spouse gives a donee-spouse a *qualifying income interest for life*, it will qualify for a gift (or estate) tax marital deduction. To qualify for QTIP treatment, (1) the surviving spouse must be entitled to all the income from the property (and it must be payable annually or more frequently); (2) no person can have a power to appoint any part of the property to any person other than the surviving spouse; and (3) the property must be taxable at the donee-spouse's death (in the case of a bequest, the first decedent's executor makes an irrevocable election that the property remaining at the surviving spouse's death is taxable in his or her estate).

Lifetime Gifts to an Alien-Spouse

The marital deduction is denied for gifts to a spouse who is not a U.S. citizen. Presumably, the purpose of this limitation is to prevent the avoidance of the federal estate and gift tax system by permitting deductible transfers to an alien-spouse, who could, conceivably, avoid the transfer tax system entirely by leaving the country with the gifted assets.

However, a special provision was enacted to permit significant nontaxable transfers to an alien-spouse as an exception to the rule above. Transfers to an alien-spouse will qualify for a special annual exclusion of $100,000 each year if

- the gift otherwise qualifies as an annual-exclusion gift
- the gift meets the requirements for a gift tax marital deduction (except for the requirement that the donee is a U.S. citizen)

The Gift Tax Charitable Deduction

A donor making a transfer of property to a qualified charity may receive a charitable deduction equal to the value of the gift (to the extent not already excluded by the annual exclusion). The net effect of the charitable deduction—together with the annual exclusion—is to avoid gift tax liability on gifts to qualified charities. There is no limit on the amount that can be passed gift tax free to a qualified charity.

The gift tax deduction is allowed for all gifts made during the calendar year by U.S. citizens or residents if the gift is to a qualified charity. A qualified charity is defined as (1) the United States, a state, territory, any political subdivision, or the District of Columbia, if the gift is to be used exclusively for public purposes; (2) certain religious, scientific, or charitable organizations; (3) certain fraternal societies, orders, or associations; and (4) certain veterans' associations, organizations, or societies.

Technically, the charitable deduction is limited and is allowable only to the extent that the gift is included in the total amount of gifts made during the year. The phrase *total amount of gifts* refers to gifts in excess of the annual exclusion. For example, this year a single client makes total gifts of $45,000: $20,000 to his daughter and $25,000 to The American College. After taking annual exclusions, the client's *gross* gifts would be $10,000 (the gift of $20,000 to the daughter, less a $10,000 exclusion) and $15,000 (the $25,000 gift to The American College, less the $10,000 annual exclusion). Therefore the client's charitable deduction would be limited to $15,000. The reason for the rule that the annual exclusion is taken first is obviously to prevent the allowance of a charitable deduction equal to the total amount of the gift, which, in turn, when added to the allowable annual exclusion, would result in an extra $10,000 exclusion.

In certain cases, a donor will transfer a remainder interest to a qualified charity. A personal beneficiary will be given all or part of the income interest in the transferred property, and the charity will receive the remainder at the termination of the income interest. Where a charitable remainder is given to a qualified charity, a gift tax deduction is allowable for the present value of that remainder interest only if at least one of the following four conditions is satisfied:

- the transferred property was either a personal residence or a farm
- the transfer was made to a charitable remainder annuity trust
- the transfer was made to a charitable remainder unitrust
- the transfer was made to a pooled-income fund

The terms *charitable remainder annuity trust*, *charitable remainder unitrust*, and *pooled-income fund* are defined in essentially the same manner as they are for estate and income tax purposes. These terms are further discussed in reading 17.

CALCULATING GIFT TAX PAYABLE

Computing the gift tax payable begins with ascertaining the amount of taxable gifts in the current reporting calendar year. To find the amount of taxable gifts, all gifts are valued first. If appropriate, the gift is then split, and annual exclusions as well as the marital and charitable deductions are applied. An example and computation format will illustrate the process.

Assume a single donor makes certain outright gifts in the last month of this year: $60,000 to his son, $2,500 to his daughter, $4,000 to his grandson, and $5,000 to The American College (a total of $71,500).

Computing Taxable Gifts

Step 1	*List* total gifts for year		$71,500
Step 2	*Subtract* one-half of gift deemed to be made by donor's spouse (split gifts)	$ 0	
	Gifts deemed to be made by donor		$71,500
Step 3	*Subtract* annual exclusion(s)	$21,500	
	Gifts after subtracting exclusion(s)		$50,000
Step 4	*Subtract* marital deduction	$ 0	
Step 5	*Subtract* charitable deduction	$ 0	
	Taxable gifts		$50,000

8.16

Note that, although there were four donees, the annual exclusion was $21,500 and did not total four times $10,000 or $40,000. This is because the annual exclusion is the lower of (1) $10,000 or (2) the actual net value of the property transferred. In this example, the annual exclusion for the $2,500, $4,000, and $5,000 gifts is limited to the actual value of each gift.

A slight change in the facts in the example above will illustrate the computation when the donor is married and his spouse consents to splitting their gifts to third parties. In this case, only one-half of the gifts made by the donor would be taxable to the donor (one-half of the gifts made by the donor's spouse to third parties would also be included in computing the donor's total gifts). A separate (but essentially identical) computation is made for the donor's spouse. That computation would show (a) the other half of the husband's gifts to third parties plus (b) one-half of the wife's actual gifts to third parties (since all gifts must be split, if any gifts are split).

Computing Taxable Gifts

Step 1	*List* total gifts for year		$71,500
Step 2	*Subtract* one-half of gift deemed to be made by donor's spouse (split gifts)	$35,750	
	Gifts deemed to be made by donor		$35,750
Step 3	*Subtract* annual exclusion(s)	$15,750	
	Gifts after subtracting exclusion(s)		$20,000
Step 4	*Subtract* marital deduction	$ 0	
Step 5	*Subtract* charitable deduction	$ 0	
	Taxable gifts		$20,000

(The calculation on the wife's return would parallel this return.)

Note that in this example the annual exclusions were computed *after* the split and each donor's exclusions would be

gift to son	$10,000
gift to daughter	1,250
gift to grandson	2,000
gift to The American College	2,500
	$15,750

If the married donor in this example had also made an outright gift of $120,000 to his wife, the computation would be as follows:

Computing Taxable Gifts

Step 1	*List* total gifts for year		$191,500
Step 2	*Subtract* one-half of gift deemed to be made by donor's spouse (split gifts)	$ 35,750	
	Gifts deemed to be made by donor		$155,750
Step 3	*Subtract* annual exclusion(s)	$ 25,750	
	Gifts after subtracting exclusion(s)		$130,000
Step 4	*Subtract* marital deduction	$110,000	
Step 5	*Subtract* charitable deduction	$ 0	
	Taxable gifts		$ 20,000

When the total value of taxable gifts for the reporting period is found, the actual tax payable is computed using the following method:

Computing Gift Tax Payable

Step 1	Compute gift tax on all *taxable* gifts regardless of when made (use unified rate schedule)	$_____
Step 2	Compute gift tax on all *taxable* gifts made prior to the present gift(s) (use unified rate schedule)	$_____
Step 3	Subtract step 2 result from step 1 result	$_____
Step 4	Enter gift tax credit remaining	$_____
Step 5	Subtract step 4 result from step 3 result to obtain *gift tax payable*	$_____

For instance, a widow gives $200,000 to her daughter and $25,000 to The American College in the last month of this year. Both transfers are present-interest gifts. If she had made no previous taxable gifts in prior years, the computation would be as follows:

Computing Taxable Gifts

Step 1	*List* total gifts for year		$225,000
Step 2	*Subtract* one-half of gift deemed to be made by donor's spouse (split gifts)	$ 0	

	Gifts deemed to be made by donor		$225,000
Step 3	*Subtract* annual exclusion(s)	$20,000	
	Gifts after subtracting exclusion(s)		$205,000
Step 4	*Subtract* marital deduction	$ 0	
Step 5	*Subtract* charitable deduction	$15,000	
	Taxable gifts		$190,000

To find the gift tax payable on this amount, the procedure would be as follows:

Computing Gift Tax Payable

Step 1	Compute gift tax on all *taxable* gifts regardless of when made	$ 51,600
Step 2	Compute gift tax on all *taxable* gifts made prior to the present gift(s)	$ 0
Step 3	Subtract step 2 result from step 1 result	$ 51,600
Step 4	Enter gift tax (unified) credit remaining (1987)	$192,800
Step 5	Subtract step 4 result from step 3 result to obtain *gift tax payable*	$ 0

The step 1 entry, $51,600, is found by using the unified rate schedule for estate and gift taxes, which shows that the tax on $150,000 is $38,800 and that there is a 32 percent tax on the remaining $40,000, which comes to $12,800. Note that the unified rate table is used regardless of when the gifts were made.

If the donor in the example above had made $100,000 of additional taxable gifts in prior years, the computation would be as follows:

Computing Gift Tax Payable

Step 1	Compute gift tax on all *taxable* gifts regardless of when made	$ 84,400
Step 2	Compute gift tax on all *taxable* gifts made prior to the present gift(s)	$ 23,800
Step 3	Subtract step 2 result from step 1 result	$ 60,600

Step 4	Enter gift tax credit remaining for 1987 ($192,800 − $23,800)	$169,000

Step 5	Subtract step 4 result from step 3 result to obtain gift tax payable	$ 0

This illustrates the cumulative nature of the gift tax (the $100,000 prior taxable gifts pushed the present $190,000 of taxable gifts into a higher bracket) and the progressive rate structure. The tax on $290,000 is $84,400, and the tax on $100,000 of prior taxable gifts is $23,800. The difference, $60,600, is the tax on the current gifts.

Credits

The Tax Reform Act of 1976 unified the gift and estate tax systems and created a unified credit against gifts made either during lifetime or at death. The gift tax credit, which provides a dollar-for-dollar reduction of the tax otherwise payable, is $96,300 in 1984, $121,800 in 1985, $155,800 in 1986, and $192,800 in 1987 and later years. In other words, each individual has available to him or her during lifetime or at death one unified credit against the gift or estate tax. If not exhausted by lifetime gifting, the unified credit remaining will be available to be taken against the estate tax after death.

REPORTING GIFTS AND PAYING TAX

Future-Interest Gifts

A gift tax return is required for a gift of a future interest regardless of the amount of the gift. For example, if a grantor transfers $100,000 to an irrevocable trust payable to the grantor's spouse for life and then to the grantor's son, a gift tax return would be required regardless of the value of the son's remainder interest. The term *future interest* is defined in the same manner as for annual exclusion purposes: a gift in which the donee does not have the unrestricted right to the immediate use, possession, or enjoyment of the property or the income from the property.

Present-Interest Gifts

No gift tax return is due because of the annual exclusion until present-interest gifts made to one individual exceed $10,000. At that point, a return must be filed on an annual basis when a gift to one person in one year exceeds $10,000, even if no gift tax would be due (such as when gift-splitting provisions eliminate the tax). For example, if a married woman gave $10,001 to her son, the transfer would be tax free. However, a gift tax return would be required, because it exceeded the annual-exclusion limit and because the gift was split. A return must be filed when a couple elects to split gifts.

A gift tax return must be filed and the gift tax, if any is due, must be paid by April 15 of the year following the year in which the taxable gifts were made. If an extension is granted for filing the income tax return, the time limit for filing the gift tax return is automatically extended also.

Gifts to a spouse that qualify for the marital deduction do not require the filing of a gift tax return.

Gifts to Charities

No return must be filed and no reporting is required for charitable contributions of $10,000 or less—except when a noncharitable gift is also made. In that case, the charitable transfer must be reported at the same time the noncharitable gift is noted on a gift tax return. If the value of the charitable transfer exceeds $10,000, the general rule is that the transfer must be reported on a gift tax return for that year.

If a split-interest gift is made to a charity (when there are charitable and noncharitable donees of the same gift), the donor will not be able to claim a charitable deduction for the entire value of the transfer. In this case, the donor must file and report the transfer subject to the filing requirements discussed above. For example, if an individual establishes a charitable remainder trust with the income payable to the individual's daughter for life and the remainder payable to charity at her death, a gift tax return must be filed.

Liability for Payment

The donor of the gift is primarily liable for the gift tax (Sec. 2502(c)). However, if the donor for any reason fails to pay the tax when it falls due, the donee becomes liable to the extent of the value of the gift (Sec. 6324(b)). This liability begins as soon as the donor fails to pay the tax when due.

Generally the tax must be paid at the time the return is filed. However, reasonable extensions of time for payment of the tax can be granted by the IRS—but only on a showing of *undue hardship*. This means more than inconvenience. It must appear that the party liable to pay the tax will suffer a *substantial financial loss* unless an extension is granted. (A forced sale of property at a sacrifice price would be an example of a substantial financial loss.)

RELATIONSHIP OF THE GIFT TAX SYSTEM TO THE INCOME TAX SYSTEM

When the gift tax law was written, one of its principal purposes was to complement the income tax law by discouraging taxpayers from making gifts to reduce their taxable income. It is true that to some extent the gift tax does supplement the income tax system and there is some overlap. However, it is important to note that the tax treatment accorded a given transaction when the two taxes are applied will not necessarily be consistent.

A lack of consistency between the gift and income tax systems forces the practitioner to examine three different issues:

- Is the transfer one on which the gift tax will be imposed?
- Will the transfer constitute a taxable exchange subject to the income tax?

- If the transfer was made in trust, will the income from the transferred property be taxable to the donor, or will the incidence of taxation be shifted to the recipient of the property (the trust or its beneficiaries)?

In summary, the treatment of a transaction for gift tax purposes is not necessarily consistent with the income tax consequences. Therefore it is important not to place undue reliance on the provisions and interpretations of the income tax law when determining probable results or potential interpretations of the gift tax system (or vice versa).

DETERMINATION OF THE BASIS OF GIFT PROPERTY

When property is transferred from a donor to a donee and the donee later disposes of the property through a sale or other taxable disposition, gain or loss depends on the donee's basis. In return, the donee's basis is *carried over* from the donor; that is, the donor's basis for the gift property immediately prior to the gift becomes the donee's basis for that property.

For example, if an individual has paid $10 a share for stock and transfers it when it is worth $20, and the donee sells it when it is worth $30, the donee's basis for that property is the donor's $10 cost. The gain therefore is the difference between the amount realized by the donee, $30, and the donee's adjusted basis, $10.

An addition to basis is allowed for a portion of any gift tax paid on the transfer from the donor to the donee. The basis addition is for that portion of the tax attributable to the appreciation in the gift property (the excess of the property's gift tax value over the donor's adjusted basis determined immediately before the gift). This increase in basis may be added to the donee's carryover basis for the property. Stated as a formula, the basis of gifted property is the donor's basis increased as follows:

$$\frac{\text{Net appreciation in value of gift}}{\text{Amount of gift}} \quad \text{x} \quad \text{gift tax paid}$$

This means that the basis carried over from the donor is increased only by the gift tax on the net appreciation in the value of the gift. For example, an individual bought stock worth $40,000 and gave it to his daughter when it was worth $100,000. If the donor paid $18,000 in gift taxes at the time of the gift, the daughter's basis would be as follows:

Donor's basis $40,000

plus

Gift tax on *net appreciation in value* (here, the difference between the $100,000 value of the gift at the time of transfer and the donor's cost, $40,000)

$$\frac{\$\ 60,000}{\$100,000} \ x\ \$18,000\ =\ \$10,800$$

equals

Daughter's basis $50,800

RELATIONSHIP OF THE GIFT TAX SYSTEM TO THE ESTATE TAX SYSTEM

The 1976 Tax Reform Act provided for a unified estate and gift tax system. The unification correlates the two laws in three essential ways:

- Lifetime gifts and testamentary transfers are taxed by using the same tax rates (so-called unified tax rates), rather than separate and different rates.
- There is a single unified tax credit that can be applied to lifetime and testamentary gifts. The unified tax credit replaces what was previously a specific estate tax exemption and a specific gift tax exemption.
- The estate tax imposed at death is found by adding gifts made during lifetime (after 1976) to the taxable estate (any gift tax paid on post-1976 transfers can be subtracted to arrive at the estate tax liability).

For these reasons there are many correlations between the two tax systems. Like the income tax law, however, the gift tax law is not always consistent with the estate tax law. When a gift is made, certain issues must be considered. In spite of the lifetime transfer, will the transferred property be included among the other assets in the donor's gross estate on the donor's death? Will the property a donor transfers during his or her lifetime be subjected first to a gift tax and later included in the donor's gross estate? For example, if the donor transfers property but retains a life interest, both gift and estate taxes will be payable. Although any gift tax paid (after the unified credit is exhausted) may be subtracted in arriving at the estate tax liability, because of the *time value* of money—that is, the donor's loss of the use of gift taxes paid—the net result is less favorable than a mere washout (that is, in essence, it is a prepayment of the death tax).

FACTORS TO CONSIDER IN SELECTING AN APPROPRIATE SUBJECT OF A GIFT

Gift tax strategy must be part of a well-planned and carefully coordinated estate planning effort. This, in turn, requires careful consideration as to the type of property to gift. There are a number of strategies and factors that must be examined in selecting the types of property that are appropriate for gifts. Some of the general considerations in planning gift tax property are as follows:

- Is the property likely to appreciate in value? Other things being equal, planners generally try to pick property that will appreciate substantially in value from the time of the transfer. Removal from the donor's estate of the appreciation in the property (as well as the income from the property) should save a meaningful amount of estate taxes. The best type of property will have a low gift tax value and a high estate

8.23

tax value. Life insurance, for example, is property with a low present value but a high appreciation potential. If held until the date the insured dies, its appreciation in value is guaranteed. Furthermore, since there are no carryover-basis problems, the proceeds will be exempt from income tax.

- Is the donee in a lower income tax bracket than the donor? Income splitting between the donor and the donee can be obtained by transferring high-income-producing property to a family member in a lower bracket. Naturally, high-income-producing property is best for this purpose. High-dividend participating preferred stock in a closely held business or stock in a successful S corporation is a good example of high-income-producing property. Conversely, if the donor is in a lower bracket than the donee (for instance, if the parent who is retired makes a gift to a financially successful middle-aged child), the use of low-yield, growth-type property may be indicated.

- Is the property subject to indebtedness? A gift of property subject to indebtedness that is greater than its cost to the donor may result in a taxable gain. A gift of such property causes the donor to realize capital gain on the excess of the debt over basis. For example, the gift of a building that cost the donor $10,000, appreciated to $100,000, and was mortgaged to $70,000 would result in an income tax gain to the donor on the difference between the debt outstanding at the time of the transfer and the donor's basis (assume $70,000 and the donor's basis of $10,000). In this example, the gain would be $60,000. It would be realized at the time the gift became complete.

- Is the gift property's basis above, below, or approximately the same as the property's fair market value? Income tax law forbids the recognition of a capital loss if the subject matter of the gift has a basis above the property's present fair market value. Neither the donor nor the donee can recognize a capital loss with respect to such property. Furthermore, if the gift property's basis is above present fair market value, there will be no gift tax addition to basis because that addition depends on appreciation at the time of the transfer. Since there is no appreciation, no gift tax addition would be allowed.

Conversely, if the donor's basis for income tax purposes is very low relative to the fair market value of the property, it might be advantageous to retain the property until death because of the *stepped-up-basis-at-death rules*. (This is especially true if inclusion of the property will generate little or no gift tax because it will pass to a surviving spouse and qualify for a marital deduction, or if the asset owner is *sheltered* by the unified credit.) The result of the stepped-up basis provision is that a portion of the future capital gain would be avoided in the event the property is later sold by the estate or heir. But if the property should be sold, it may pay to transfer it to a low-bracket family member by gift; that individual could then sell it and realize a lower capital-gains tax.

A third possibility is that the donor's basis is approximately the same as or only slightly below fair market value. Again, the rules providing for a gift tax addition to basis are of little help, since the addition to basis is limited to the gift tax allocable to appreciation in the property at the time of the gift. One further factor that should be considered is the likelihood that the ~~donee will want or need to sell the property in the foreseeable future~~. If this is not likely, the income tax basis (except for depreciable property) will be relatively meaningless.

INTRODUCTION

One primary objective of estate planning traditionally has been to obtain the maximum savings in federal and local death taxes as well as other transfer costs. Most clients desire to transfer their property to family members and other beneficiaries at a minimum cost with the least shrinkage to the estate. For many persons with medium-sized estates, the unified credit shelters the estate from tax.

In addition, there is now an unlimited maximum marital deduction that allows married individuals to pass their entire estate to their surviving spouses free of federal estate tax. In spite of these significantly liberalized benefits, the federal estate tax must be taken into consideration in planning an estate for the following reasons:

- The unified credit will only shelter up to $1.2 million per married couple from tax.
- The marital deduction is available only at the first death of a married couple (presuming the survivor doesn't remarry).
- Inflation will cause even modest estates to exceed the unified credit.
- The size of the federal deficit might cause Congress to look for increased revenue from the estate and gift tax system.

As a cautionary word, the financial planner must determine the unique objectives of a client in the estate planning process. Overall objectives must be planned. The effect of taxes on the estate is only one consideration in preparing an estate plan. While no plan should be implemented without an analysis of the tax consequences, federal estate taxes should not be the controlling factor, regardless of the size of the estate. The field of tax law, based on tax statutes as well as regulations and further supported by interpretations through case law and revenue rulings, is a dynamic and constantly shifting area of study. This reading and subsequent readings on the federal estate tax laws are limited to a review of general principles in the field that are sufficient to enable the financial planner both to understand and to explain the impact of federal estate taxation to a client. These readings, however, provide only an introduction to a complex, continually changing area of tax law.

THE FEDERAL ESTATE TAX

The federal estate tax is imposed on the transferor or the transferor's estate and is based on the privilege to transfer property. Congress recognized that a tax limited to property transferred at death would have been an open invitation to tax-avoidance schemes to dispose of property during lifetime. Therefore under the Tax Reform Act of 1976, a unified estate and gift tax system was enacted to prevent lifetime dispositions from escaping taxation or being taxed at lower rates. The act provided a unified, cumulative system for taxation of certain transfers by gift during lifetime and transfers at death at the same tax rates. Since January 1, 1977, these adjusted taxable gifts (as they are called) are taken into consideration and added to the taxable estate in computing any federal estate tax due at death.

Under certain sections of the federal estate tax law, Congress also addressed itself to those lifetime dispositions in which the donor retained certain interests or powers over the transferred property for life. Congress rightly perceived these incomplete lifetime dispositions as the substantial equivalent of testamentary transfers at death, since the donor still had some control over or enjoyment from the property during lifetime, or power over the property at death. These types of rights or powers, if held by a decedent at death, may be sufficient to bring the property within the gambit of federal estate taxation.

All property, either owned directly by the decedent at the time of death or subject to the decedent's control in a manner sufficient to cause that property to be included in the gross estate under one of the sections of the federal estate tax rules, is included in the estate for federal estate tax purposes. The federal estate tax applies to the entire estate and is imposed on the estate itself, which is primarily liable for payment of the tax. The form in which property was transferred is irrelevant in this regard. In other words, the property may have been transferred by will, intestacy, contract, or operation of law. To the extent that there are assets in the estate, the tax liability will fall on the estate. However, if the estate does not contain sufficient assets to pay the tax liability, beneficiaries of the estate may be charged with the tax liability to the extent of the value of property they inherit.

Estate Taxation of Residents, Citizens, and Nonresident Aliens

All property owned by citizens or residents of the United States at the time of their death is subject to the federal estate tax, regardless of where the property is located. The gross estate includes all property owned by a citizen or resident of the United States at death valued at its fair market value on the date of death or alternate valuation date (6 months after death). The tax is a progressive tax similar to the federal income tax. It is based on a graduated rate schedule that increases with the size of the estate.

The federal estate tax is applied differently to those who are considered nonresidents, noncitizens (nonresident aliens). Only the value of property located in the United States and owned by nonresidents, noncitizens at the time of their death is subject to federal estate tax. Note that the property owned by noncitizens may also be subject to foreign death taxes, as may foreign property held by U.S. citizens. The federal taxation of such individuals and their property will often depend on the terms of the estate tax treaty (if any) between the United States and the applicable foreign nation.

THE GROSS ESTATE—AN OVERVIEW

Keeping in mind that the federal estate tax is a tax on the privilege of transferring property, the logical place to begin is with an examination of those types of interests and transfers that constitute the gross estate. The gross estate of a U.S. citizen or resident is made up of the total value of all property owned by him or her at death. It makes no difference whether the property passes by will, intestacy (without a will), or by contract. Neither does it matter where any such property may be located. Items included in the gross estate are as follows:

- the value of any property interest of the decedent at the time of death to the extent of that interest (IRC Sec. 2033)
- dower and curtesy interests (IRC Sec. 2034)
- the value of certain gratuitous lifetime transfers made within 3 years of death and gift taxes paid within 3 years of death (IRC Sec. 2035)
- gratuitous lifetime transfers in which the decedent retained certain rights or powers for life, such as income from the property or control over the income (IRC Sec. 2036)
- certain gratuitous transfers taking effect at death. These are transfers in which possession or enjoyment of the property can be obtained only by surviving the decedent, and in which the decedent retained a reversionary interest in the property, and the value of such interest immediately before death was more than 5 percent of the value of the entire property. (IRC Sec. 2037)
- gratuitous lifetime transfers in which the decedent retained the power to alter, amend, revoke, or terminate the transfer. The value of this property will be included in the decedent's gross estate, although his or her powers can be exercised only in conjunction with others. (IRC Sec. 2038)
- annuities or similar payments under certain plans or contracts (other than life insurance) that were payable to the decedent if payments continue to another beneficiary for a period exceeding the decedent-annuitant's life (IRC Sec. 2039)
- jointly held property with right of survivorship (IRC Sec. 2040)
- the value of property subject to a general power of appointment that the decedent possessed at death (IRC Sec. 2041)
- proceeds of life insurance on the decedent's life, if the decedent possessed incidents of ownership in the policy or the proceeds were receivable by the estate or receivable by another for the benefit of the estate (IRC Sec. 2042)

Property includible under Secs. 2033–2038 will be discussed in this reading. Property includible under Secs. 2039–2042 is the subject of the next reading.

THE VALUE OF ALL PROPERTY INTERESTS IN WHICH THE DECEDENT HAD AN INTEREST (IRC SEC. 2033)

This section of the Internal Revenue Code states the general rule that the gross estate includes the value of all property interests, real or personal, tangible or intangible, of an individual on the date of death to the extent of his or her interest in the property.

In order to include a property or a property interest under this section, the decedent's interest must rise to the level of an *interest in property*. Who makes that decision? The general rule is that property rights are determined by state law; whether such rights are then subject to taxation by the federal government is a matter of federal law. This is essentially true. However, a federal court applying local (state) law will normally have the final word on what interest in property rises to the level of a property interest that would be includible under this section.

Types of Property Interests That Are Includible under Sec. 2033

The regulations are not particularly helpful in this regard as they say only that the property interest must be one that was a beneficial interest (Treas. Reg. § 20.2033-1(a)). That is to say that for purposes of IRC Sec. 2033, a mere legal interest—such as holding title purely as a fiduciary—would not be an interest that would rise to the level of a property interest in which the decedent had a beneficial interest and would not be includible in the decedent's gross estate.

Property and property interests that are includible under Sec. 2033 are those that most people would describe as "owned" by the decedent. While this ownership concept may provide a convenient shorthand way of describing the property interests includible in a decedent's gross estate under this Code section, it is not always precise. For example, some other limitations exist that may cause property or property interests owned by a decedent to be excluded from this section. Such property or property interests may be specifically included in the gross estate under other sections of the federal estate tax law.

For example, the right to borrow money against the cash value of an insurance policy may not be a property interest sufficient to include the policy proceeds in the decedent's gross estate under Sec. 2033, but the proceeds will be included because of another section that specifically requires their inclusion. Those types of interests in property that are specifically includible in the decedent's gross estate will be discussed later in this and the following reading.

Limitations on Property Interests Includible under Sec. 2033

The federal estate tax is levied on the right to transfer property at death. Therefore, if the decedent had no right to transfer property or a property interest to another at death, either by will or under the intestacy laws, the value of those property interests will not be includible in the gross estate under this section no matter how great the decedent's interests were during lifetime. An example of an interest in which the decedent possessed no right to pass the property at death is a life estate created by another. Any interest in property that was given to the decedent by another, the transfer of which the decedent cannot control and that ceases at the decedent's death, will not be included in his or her gross estate. As already noted, the federal estate tax is exacted on the transmission of property. Therefore only inheritable interests (interests that can be transmitted to another by the decedent at death) are subject to the tax.

There are three factors to be applied to all property in determining whether it will be includible in the decedent's gross estate under Sec. 2033. First, what types of property are includible under state or federal law? Second, was the decedent's interest in the property large enough to warrant its inclusion in the estate? Third, did the decedent possess this interest at the time of death and to what extent?

Specific Types of Property Includible under Sec. 2033

Under Sec. 2033 the decedent's estate will include any interest in real estate whether the property comes into the possession of the personal representative or passes directly to the heirs. The decedent's estate will also include cash or money equivalents whether kept in a bank, savings or checking account, certificates of deposit, money market funds, or a safe-deposit box. The gross estate will include any stocks, bonds (including tax-exempt bonds), notes, and mortgages owned by the decedent as well as the value of any outstanding loans the decedent had made to others. His or her estate also includes the value of income tax refunds not yet paid, patents, and copyrights.

Property subject to indebtedness is also includible in the decedent's gross estate. If the decedent is personally liable for the indebtedness, the full value of the property is included in the gross estate and the estate is allowed a deduction for the amount of the debt. If the decedent is not personally liable for the indebtedness (for example, a nonrecourse note), only the value of the equity in the property is included in the gross estate and no deduction is allowed for the debt.

Under Sec. 2033 the gross estate will also include any amount to which the decedent was entitled before he or she died. For example, a claim for damages for pain and suffering as a result of someone else's negligent act is includible in the decedent's estate since it could have been recovered by him or her before death. On the other hand, the proceeds of a wrongful death claim, although brought by the decedent's personal representative on behalf of his or her heirs, is not included in the gross estate because the decedent had no right of action or interest in the proceeds at any time before death. It is not relevant that the decedent's death was instrumental in someone else acquiring an interest in the property. The relevant test is whether there was anything the decedent had a right to own or receive while alive that could have been passed to another by reason of the decedent's death.

If the decedent was entitled to a refund because his or her income tax liability had been overpaid, this income tax refund is an asset includible in the gross estate under Sec. 2033. The same would be true if the decedent and the decedent's spouse had filed a joint return. In the case of a joint return in which an income tax refund is due, the amount includible in the decedent's gross estate would be the amount by which his or her contribution toward payment of the income tax exceeded the decedent's income tax liability. Any medical insurance reimbursements due to the decedent at the time of death will also be includible in the gross estate.

Also outstanding dividends declared and payable to the stockholders of record on or before the date of the decedent's death would be included in the decedent's gross estate (Treas. Reg. § 20.2033-1(b)). Thus, if a shareholder dies after the record date but before the dividend is paid, the dividend is the shareholder's property and is included in his or her gross estate. The critical date is the ownership on the record date of the dividend. If the decedent dies after the dividend is declared but before the record date, he or she will have not owned the right to the dividend at death. Therefore the value will not be included in the decedent's gross estate. Of course, if the dividend is declared after the date of death, it will not be included in the gross estate because the decedent's right to receive the dividend had not accrued while the decedent was alive.

Likewise, all rights to income accrued as of the date of death are includible. The term for accrued income items is *income in respect of a decedent.* Accrued dividends, unpaid interest earned and accrued to the date of death, rental income, postdeath partnership profits, salary, and rights to bonuses or commissions are examples of income in respect of a decedent. To the extent that estate tax liability results from the inclusion of income in respect of a decedent in the gross estate, there will be an income tax deduction allowed for that amount of tax to the one who receives and reports the income for income tax purposes. (IRC Sec. 691)

Also included in the decedent's estate is miscellaneous property, such as interests in partnerships and unincorporated businesses. These interests are listed in the estate tax return on a separate schedule from stock that a decedent might own in either a publicly held or a closely held corporation. All the decedent's tangible personal property—including furniture, jewelry, and household items—is includible in the gross estate. Frequently, however, household items and wedding gifts are considered as having been made to a wife when acquired at or near the time of the marriage. In such cases the value of these items would not be included; however, documentation may be necessary to successfully support the exclusion of such items.

Under Sec. 2033 the decedent's estate will also include any vested rights to receive property in the future. These future interests in property include reversionary interests as well as remainder interests and are includible at their values on the date of death computed actuarially according to IRS tables.

Example: If Stephen creates a trust for the benefit of his divorced wife, Betty, and gives Betty income for life with the property to revert to Stephen or his estate upon her death, his reversionary interest is an includible asset. Since the property will revert to Stephen if he survives her or his estate should he predecease her, ~~his estate and heirs have an absolute right to receive the trust property at some future time.~~ Therefore a value for this reversionary interest will be determined at Stephen's death.

~~Includible future rights also include fixed ascertainable rights to receive income from the property as well as remainder interests in the corpus either at some future time or upon the happening of some future event.~~ These future interests are also ~~includible~~. Examples include postdeath partnership profits. Entitlement to future income (such as renewal commissions) is another example of property rights owned outright by the decedent that must be includible in the gross estate. Property representing future income will, of course, be income taxable to the estate or beneficiaries when it is actually received. As already noted, to the extent that estate tax was attributable to the inclusion of these items in the estate, a special income tax deduction for the amount of estate tax allocated to these items will be allowed to the recipient in the year that the item is includible in income.

Sec. 2033 ~~will also include in the decedent's gross estate the value of his or her share of property held in conjunction with others.~~ Thus, if the decedent owns property ~~as a tenant in common with others, his or her share will be includible in the gross estate.~~ If disproportionate shares as tenants in common are ~~not specified~~, the interests will be ~~presumed to be equal~~. For example, if there are three tenants, they will each be presumed to own a one-third interest. The value of the decedent's ~~share of community property~~ will be included in the estate. As stated before, if the decedent's interests are limited to lifetime enjoyment and there is no property interest for him or her to pass at death (for example, a life estate conferred on the decedent by another), the value of that right will not be included in the gross estate. This results because the decedent never possessed rights in the property that could be transferred at death and the estate tax is levied on transfers of property. However, ~~an interest in property will be includible~~ in the gross estate although it is limited, contingent, or remote, provided that ~~it does not end with the decedent's death~~. Of course, ~~the contingency or remoteness of the interest will affect its valuation~~.

As already emphasized, ~~the estate tax imposed under Sec. 2033 is predicated upon the extent of the decedent's ownership interest at death.~~ This can raise difficult questions as to whether any property transferred by the decedent was void or voidable as well as whether the decedent disposed of any interest before death by a gift or sale. Transfers, sales, loans, partnership, or business ventures—especially those involving spouses and intrafamily arrangements where legal formalities have not been meticulously observed—present particularly difficult problems that must be resolved on an individual basis.

DOWER OR CURTESY INTERESTS (IRC SEC. 2034)

A dower right is property set aside for a widow under state law if it has been established that the decedent had an interest in the property. Curtesy pertains to the rights of a widower in his deceased wife's property. Some states have abolished dower and curtesy, replacing them with statutory rights of surviving spouses.

This section clarifies the fact that the amount of a property interest includible in a decedent's gross estate is not diminished by the fact that the property is subject to a dower or curtesy interest or a statutory interest created in lieu of dower or curtesy. Note, however, that if the property subject to dower or curtesy is transferred to the surviving spouse, the dower or curtesy interest may qualify for the marital deduction and thereby reduce the *taxable* estate.

CERTAIN GIFTS AND TRANSFERS MADE AND GIFT TAXES PAID WITHIN 3 YEARS OF DEATH (IRC SEC. 2035)

As a general rule gifts made within 3 years of death will not be included in the gross estates for decedents dying after December 31, 1981, except for certain limited purposes. The following are some exceptions to this rule:

- transfers with retained interests for life OR 2036
- transfers taking effect at death OR 2037
- transfers in which the decedent reserves the right to alter, amend, OR 2038 revoke, or terminate the transfer or the power to affect the beneficial interest in the transferred property
- transfers of life insurance policies by the insured OR 2042
- gift taxes paid

Note that Sec. 2035 does not cause inclusion of the transfers noted above if the decedent retains the interest until the time of death. Sec. 2035 deals only with a disposition of the interest by the decedent during the 3 years preceding death. A disposition may be a gift or the exercise or release of a right or power. Except for gifts of life insurance and gift taxes paid, the initial transfer need not be made within the 3-year period preceding the decedent's death, for it is the date of the disposition of the retained interest that is determinative.

Transfers with Retained Interests for Life

The first exception to the rule that lifetime gifts are no longer includible in the gross estate pertains to property transferred by the decedent during lifetime in which certain rights or powers were retained for his or her lifetime that would cause the property to be includible in the gross estate. Basically lifetime transfers in which the decedent reserved (1) the right to receive or determine who receives income from the property, or (2) the right to designate who is entitled to possession or enjoyment of the property (including himself or herself) either for (a) life or (b) for a period that did not actually end before death, or (c) that cannot be determined without reference to the decedent's death, will be includible in the decedent's gross estate unless he or she gave up these retained rights more than 3 years before death. Lifetime transfers in which the decedent reserved rights that will cause inclusion under this Code section include the use, possession, income, or other enjoyment of the transferred property for himself or herself, or the right to name other persons who may possess or enjoy the transferred property or income from the property. It makes no difference whether the decedent either retains this right alone or can exercise the right only in concert with another. Further, it is insignificant as to whether or not the person with whom the decedent had to act possessed an adverse interest in the property (meaning that the other person was a beneficiary or potential beneficiary of the property). More of the specific rules and some examples of transfers under this exception will be included later in a full discussion of IRC Sec. 2036.

Transfers Effective at Death

Other rights that cause the property to be includible in the gross estate are transfers that become effective at death. These are transfers to others that can be obtained only by surviving the decedent provided that the decedent retained a reversionary interest in the property and the reversionary interest exceeds 5 percent of the value of the property at the date of death. This type of transfer will be includible in the decedent's estate under Sec. 2035 if he or she either exercised the power or transferred it within the 3 years prior to death. If the decedent retained the power until death, the transferred property will be includible in the estate under IRC Sec. 2037.

Transfers in Which the Decedent Reserves the Right to Alter, Amend, Revoke, or Terminate the Transfer or the Power to Affect the Beneficial Interests in the Transferred Property

If a decedent disposes of any of the retained rights to alter, amend, revoke, or terminate the transfer, or to affect the beneficial interest in the transferred property within the 3 years preceding death, the value of the property will be includible in the decedent's gross estate under Sec. 2035. If the interests are retained until his or her death, the value of the transferred property will be includible under IRC Sec. 2038.

Gifts of Life Insurance within 3 Years of Death

The next type of inclusion under Sec. 2035 pertains to gratuitous transfers of life insurance made by the insured within 3 years of death. Gifts of life insurance policies made within 3 years of death are includible in the gross estate whether or not a gift tax return was required to be filed. There is no inclusion in the decedent's gross estate, however, for premiums paid or deemed paid by the decedent within 3 years of death to the extent these payments would not have caused the policy proceeds to be included in the gross estate under prior law. This exception is indicated in the Senate Committee Report on this rule. Life insurance is an unusual product because its value as a gift for gift tax purposes may easily fall below the level of the annual exclusion amount necessary to file a gift tax return or to make a taxable gift. Yet the value of the proceeds are undoubtedly much more substantial than any gift tax value. Therefore gratuitous transfers of life insurance made within 3 years of death are included in the gross estate at the full value of the proceeds.

Gift Taxes on Gifts within 3 Years of Death Includible

The gross estate of a decedent includes any gift taxes paid by either the decedent or the decedent's estate on any gift made by the decedent or the decedent's spouse within 3 years of the decedent's death. The amount of tax subject to this rule is the tax paid on gifts made after 1976, and within 3 years ending on the date of the donor's death. This *gross-up* rule also includes any taxes attributable to the decedent's consent to split a gift made by the decedent's spouse within 3 years of the decedent's death. The decedent's share of the gift tax on a gift split with a spouse is the amount of tax attributable to the decedent's share of the gift. Gift taxes paid by the spouse of the decedent on gifts split with the decedent are not includible in the gross estate of the decedent under this rule. The effect of this rule is to discourage deathbed gifts that would otherwise remove the amount of gift taxes paid from the donor's estate.

> *Example:* Suppose the decedent had made a taxable gift of $1,000,000 to an individual on which a gift tax of approximately $345,000 was payable, and the individual died 2 years later. The $1,000,000 would be excluded from his or her gross estate. (As discussed in another reading, it will be brought back as an adjusted taxable gift in computing the estate tax liability.) However, the amount of gift tax, approximately $345,000, would be includible under the gross-up rule of Sec. 2035.

Exceptions to the 3-Year Rule

Note that the law provides that no transfer made within 3 years of death need be included in the gross estate if no gift tax return was required to be filed. This refers to present-interest gifts worth less than the annual gift tax exclusion. Beginning in 1982, the annual exclusion increased to $10,000 of gifted present-interest property per donee per year. Therefore no gifts worth less than the amount of the annual exclusion will be included in the gross estate, since no gift tax return need be filed. The value of these transfers will be includible only for the limited purposes of determining qualification for the above tax benefits.

Also since ERTA, the value of *all* property effectively transferred within 3 years of death will be includible in the gross estate for the limited purpose of determining whether the estate qualifies for

- deferral of estate tax under Sec. 6166
- redemption of stock to pay administrative and funeral expenses and estate taxes under Sec. 303
- special-use valuation under Sec. 2032A
- determining the amount of property subject to federal estate tax liens

This exception has been added to the law to prevent a decedent from making deathbed transfers solely to facilitate qualification for the foregoing favorable tax benefits under Secs. 303 (special provision for capital gains for redemptions), 6166 (installment payment of estate taxes), or 2032A (special-use valuations). Otherwise, a decedent could easily gift nonbusiness or farm property, thus increasing the relative percentage value of the closely held business or farm in the estate so that the estate may qualify for special tax treatment. The same exception to the rule applies to gratuitous transfers made to a spouse within 3 years of death. Although no gift tax return is required to be filed because of the unlimited gift tax marital deduction, the law provides that the value of gifts between spouses made within 3 years of one spouse's death will be includible in the gross estate for the limited purpose of determining the qualification for the above-mentioned tax benefits.

TRANSFERS WITH RETENTION OF A LIFE INTEREST (IRC SEC. 2036)

A decedent's gross estate will include the value of all property transferred gratuitously by him or her during lifetime in which he or she has retained or reserved (1) the right to use, possess, or enjoy the property or the right to receive the income from the property; or, alternatively, (2) the right, either alone or in conjunction with any other person, to designate the persons who should possess or enjoy the property or the income from the property. In order for the property to be included in a decedent's gross estate under this Code section, the rights must be retained or reserved for

- the decedent's life, or
- for a period not ascertainable without reference to the decedent's death, or
- for any period that does not, in fact, end before the decedent's death.

Retention or reservation by the decedent of any of these rights or interests in the property will cause the entire value of the property transferred to be includible in the decedent's gross estate under this Code section. The value, however, will be reduced by the value of any income interest that is (1) not subject to the decedent's interest and power and (2) is actually being enjoyed by another person at the time of the decedent's death. Therefore, if the decedent retained income from only part of the property transferred, the amount includible in the gross estate will correspond proportionately to the value of the entire property.

> *Example:* Sheila Gordon transfers 1,000 shares of Exxon
> stock to her daughter but retains the right to receive income
> from one-half of the shares. The value of 500 shares at the
> time of Sheila's death will be includible in her gross estate, since
> she had reserved the right to receive the income from 500
> shares for her life.

Retention of Rights for the Benefit of the Transferor

A transfer with retained interests will be taxable in the gross estate when the transferor retains either the possession of, enjoyment of, or the right to the income from the transferred property for the indicated periods. It is not necessary that the transferor retain all rights.

9.11

> *Example:* If Michael makes a gift to Rachael of a Renoir painting, but reserves the right to keep the painting in his home for his lifetime, the value of the painting will be includible in his estate.

The retained life estate need not be legally enforceable as long as the donor has retained a substantial economic benefit.

> *Example:* If Michael conveys his personal residence to Rachael, but reserves the right (either expressly or by implication) to occupy the premises rent free during his lifetime, the value of the property at the time of his death will be includible in his gross estate.

Thus, in the above example, Michael actually did transfer the residence to Rachael by deed. She was the legal titleholder. However, there was an implied understanding that he was entitled to continue living there until his death, although he could not have legally enforced that understanding. The retained interest or powers that result in the inclusion of property in a decedent's gross estate need not be expressly provided for in the instrument of transfer, but may be inferred from the conduct of the parties.

Furthermore, a decedent will be considered to have retained the right to income to the extent that the income is to be used to discharge the decedent's legal obligations, such as the support of dependent children.

Another type of situation where property may be includible in the estate of the decedent is the following:

> *Example:* A decedent, Katherine, is the life income beneficiary of a testamentary trust created by someone else. She did not retain a life estate, because she had never possessed the original trust property. However, she is allowed to transfer additional property to the trust under the terms of the trust. During her lifetime, she adds $100,000 to the existing trust principal of $200,000. At her death, all trust property is passed to her heirs. Assuming that no other property is contributed to the trust, the proportionate share of the principal she contributed from which she received income for life will be treated as a retained interest and will be includible in her estate when she dies. Thus, if the trust was required to distribute all income currently, and the value of the principal passing at her death was $300,000, $100,000 (representing her contribution to the trust, from which she retained income for life) would be includible in her estate.

In a recent Tax Court case, a decedent transferred bonds to a trust for the benefit of her grandchildren. She did not retain any interest in the bonds. However, she detached the interest coupons and kept them as her own at the time of the creation of the trust. The value of the bonds was included in her gross estate because she indirectly kept control over and retained the income from the trust property.

Reciprocal Trusts. Another type of plan that is legally unenforceable but from which there is a course of conduct implying agreement to provide income for life involves the use of *reciprocal trusts.* If irrevocable reciprocal trusts are created (such as those created by a husband and wife for each other as life beneficiaries), the property of each trust will be includible in the life beneficiary's estate if the arrangement leaves both grantors in approximately the same economic circumstances in which they would have been had they created trusts naming themselves as life income beneficiaries.

Right to Vote Stock in a Closely Held Corporation. Another danger for the unwary planner may occur when an individual transfers stock of a controlled corporation but retains the right to vote the shares (either directly or indirectly). This retention of voting rights is considered a retention of the enjoyment of the transferred property. The value of the transferred stock will be included in the gross estate of the decedent. A controlled corporation is one in which the decedent directly or indirectly owned or had the right, either alone or with any other person, to vote stock having at least 20 percent of the total combined voting power of all classes of stock. In determining whether the corporation is a controlled corporation, the decedent would be considered to have owned stock actually held by family members.

This rule pertains to persons who have irrevocably transferred stock for less than full consideration after June 22, 1976. If the stock is not in a *controlled corporation,* it will not be includible in the decedent's gross estate although the decedent did hold the power to vote the transferred shares. In establishing whether the decedent had the right to vote stock possessing at least 20 percent of the total combined voting power of all classes of stock, the stock owned by the decedent's family—including his or her spouse, children, grandchildren, and parents—will be treated as owned by the decedent. These rules will also apply to stock owned by partnerships, estates, trusts, or corporations in which the decedent had an interest. The rationale behind the inclusion of the stock in the estate is that the decedent retained enjoyment of the transferred stock by his or her retention of the voting rights.

In another case, an individual transferred 19 shares of a closely held corporation's stock to a trust and gave the trustee sole authority to vote the shares. However, it was agreed at the time of the transfer that the trustee would consult with the grantor with respect to voting and that the trustee would vote only with the grantor's consent. It was held that the grantor-decedent indirectly retained the right to vote the transferred shares, although they were transferred to an irrevocable trust. The full value of the shares at the time of death was includible in the grantor's gross estate.

Retention or Reservation by the Decedent of Property for a Period Not Determinable without Reference to the Decedent's Death

This concept can be illustrated by the following:

Example: Mr. Harris transfers property to a trust with the provision that he receive quarterly installments of income. However, there is a condition that no part of the income accruing during the quarter in which he dies is to be paid to him or to his estate. Clearly, this would appear to be an attempt to thwart the rule regarding retained interests. Since the last payment could not be ascertained without reference to his death, the value of the trust property would be includible in his estate.

Retention or Reservation by the Decedent for a Period That Does Not, in Fact, End before the Decedent's Death

This concept can be illustrated by the following:

Example: Samantha Connors transfers Blackacre to her son, Henry, reserving the right to the income from the property for 10 years. Samantha dies in the eighth year. Based on these facts, the entire value of Blackacre is includible in Samantha's estate because she reserved an income interest not for her lifetime but for a period that did not, in fact, end before her death.

Right to Designate Who Shall Possess or Enjoy the Property

Although the decedent did not retain the right to enjoy or possess the property, Sec. 2036 requires that the gross estate also will include the value of all property over which the decedent retained the right to designate (alone or with any other person) who may enjoy or possess the property as well as the right to vary beneficial interests. Thus, if a grantor creates an irrevocable trust for beneficiaries other than himself or herself but is named as trustee and has the power to accumulate or distribute income, the value of the trust property will be included in the grantor's gross estate. The reason for inclusion is that the grantor had power to withhold income from the beneficiaries, thereby denying them possession and enjoyment of that income. This power to accumulate income is a retention of the right to designate who may enjoy the property. Retention of certain administrative and management powers over the trust also may cause the value of the trust property to be included in the grantor-trustee's estate.

In another case, the grantor created an irrevocable trust giving the trustee power to vary beneficial interests. She reserved in herself the right to fill vacancies for the position of trustee. There was no prohibition against the grantor appointing herself as trustee. The court held that the grantor in reserving this right had retained an interest sufficient to cause the trust property to be includible in her estate.

As a general rule, property placed in an irrevocable trust will not be included in the grantor's gross estate if the grantor merely retained the right to appoint a successor-trustee other than himself or herself upon resignation of the original trustee. However, in a 1979 revenue ruling, the IRS took the

9.14

position that if a grantor retains the ability to change corporate trustees without cause, the trust corpus will be includible in the grantor's gross estate. The IRS did issue a statement in 1981 that this ruling would not be applied retroactively to trusts created before 1979. This ruling is very problematic and places great restraints upon a grantor who, in effect, loses the ability to evaluate the performance of the corporate trustee during lifetime as well as to change trustees, if necessary or prudent.

Also the Internal Revenue Service has attempted to include trust property in situations where the grantor-trustee has retained only certain administrative and managerial powers over the trust but not the power to accumulate or distribute income. Most courts have held that the existence of these *boiler plate* powers does not give the decedent the right to designate persons who shall possess or enjoy the transferred property such that the property would be includible in their gross estate.

A frequently used estate planning device involves the irrevocable assignment of life insurance policies to a trust by the insured during the insured's lifetime. Proceeds of life insurance are not taxable in the insured's gross estate if the insured has totally been divested of all incidents of ownership in the policy more than 3 years prior to death and the proceeds are not payable to the estate. Under current law the result is not changed although the insured continues to pay premiums on the policy assigned. However, suppose that rather than continuing to pay the premiums directly, the insured funds the trust with income-producing property. Any income is to be applied first to the payment of premiums. The regulations under this section of the Internal Revenue Code provide that, if the income from property transferred by the decedent is required to be applied by the transferee for the decedent's pecuniary benefit, the decedent is considered to have retained the right to income or enjoyment of the transferred property. Whether payment of premiums by the trustee with trust income is a *pecuniary benefit* that requires the value of the property to be included in the decedent's gross estate depends on the irrevocability of the assignment.

If policies of life insurance are irrevocably assigned and the decedent is divested of all incidents of ownership in favor of the trust, the value of property transferred by the decedent to fund that trust should not be included in the decedent's estate merely because the income from the property has been used to pay premiums. It is the trust and the beneficiaries who have benefited from the premium payments, and not the decedent. Alternatively, if the decedent has retained any incidents of ownership in the policies, the payment of premiums from the trust income can certainly be regarded as having been for the decedent's pecuniary or economic benefit. Therefore the value of the policies will be includible in the decedent's gross estate.

If an individual transfers property to an insurance company in exchange for a commercial annuity, this section would have no application upon the transferor's death. The transfer is free and clear. It has been made for full and adequate consideration in money or money's worth, and the insurance company is obligated to pay the annuity without regard to the income or principal of the property transferred. Whether this section would have application in the case of a private annuity depends upon the transfer and the circumstances surrounding it. It has been held that a transfer of property by the decedent to an individual in return for a promise to make periodic payments to the decedent during lifetime was not an includible transfer, provided that the transferee was under an absolute obligation to make the payments and the amount of the payments was not determined by reference to the actual or estimated income from the property transferred.

> *Example:* Alex transfers property to Bruce in consideration of Bruce's promise to support Alex for the rest of Alex's life. If Bruce is free to use the property transferred in any manner that Bruce wishes and if Bruce discharges the obligation to support Alex irrespective of the amount of income from the transferred property, there is no inclusion. An opposite result was reached when a decedent transferred property to her children in return for their promise to pay her a stipulated amount of income for her life. At the time of the transfer, the estimated annual income from the property was equal to the amount of the annuity, but the income averaged less than the amount of the annuity after the transfer. Her children made no attempt to make up the difference. The Tax Court held that the value of the property was includible in the decedent's gross estate.

The Anti-Estate Freeze Rules—Sec. 2036(c)

The federal estate, gift estate, and gift tax system is often criticized for being somewhat "voluntary." Many wealthy individuals employ sophisticated estate planning techniques to pass their wealth on to the next generation while avoiding the sting of the federal transfer tax system. Quite often, by employing a combination of lifetime gifting and the restructuring of the form of property ownership, these individuals cause significant wealth to accrue to their heirs and avoid transfer tax, at least partially, by taking advantage of certain tax benefits in the system.

An estate freeze might be defined as any method designed to restrict to its current value an individual's eventual taxable estate. Following an estate freeze transaction, the appreciation in property subject to the freeze accrues to someone other than the original owner (presumably his or her heirs). However, an individual considering an estate freeze must also retain enough wealth to provide for his or her needs until death. Elaborate schemes have been employed to provide the transferor with an effective estate freeze through the transfer of appreciation rights in property to the next generation heirs, while leaving the transferor with enough strings attached to the property to provide a substantial current income stream. Thus an estate freeze can be distinguished from an outright gift by the fact that the transferor does not transfer all interests in the property during his or her lifetime.

Since substantial transfer-tax revenue is lost if the transaction is effective, the Treasury has always maintained a jaundiced view of estate freezes. The posttransfer appreciation in the property in a successful freeze escapes both estate and gift taxes. This tax savings is, of course, a goal of lifetime gifting.

The concern of both Congress and the IRS is that the typical estate freeze transaction differs from an outright gift of property because the transferor has not disposed of all interests in the property when the freeze is completed.

The preferred-stock recapitalization of a corporation was singled out by Congress as the classic estate freeze abuse mechanism.

> *Example 1:* Suppose parent P owns 100 percent of the stock in ABC corporation. If ABC recapitalizes by exchanging newly issued preferred stock for 90 percent of P's common stock, P now holds 90 percent of the value of ABC corporation in the form of preferred stock. Preferred stock generally yields fixed income rights (in the form of dividends and a fixed liquidation right) and does not generally share in any growth in the corporation. Thus, following the recapitalization, all of the growth in ABC corporation should accrue to the remaining common stock. In the classic estate freeze transaction, P would transfer, by sale or gift, the remaining common stock in ABC to P's children, C1 and C2. If the freeze is successful, all future appreciation following the transfer of the remaining common stock to the children will accrue their benefit. The preferred stock held by P until death will provide a substantial steady stream of income, but will possess a date-of-death value that is "frozen" (that is, no greater than its value at the time of the recapitalization). Thus P has retained a substantial current interest in ABC while effectively transferring all of the growth in ABC free of transfer tax to C1 and C2.

Expanded View of the Sec. 2036(a) Retained Life Estate

Despite its dislike for the transfer-tax revenue loss created by the estate freeze technique, the IRS has often been unsuccessful in attacking these techniques in court. In fact, the court had determined that the classic preferred-stock recapitalization did not result in a retained life estate (for Sec. 2036(a) purposes) by the preferred shareholder in any common stock he or she may have transferred in the recapitalization. Thus P in example 1 could enjoy the continued dividend income from ABC corporation without further enhancing the estate with growth in the corporation subsequent to the freeze.

Unable to close this loophole through previously existing law, the Treasury found a sympathetic ear in Congress and the anti-estate freeze statute was placed in the tax laws in 1987. This law has been further enhanced by changes in the Technical and Miscellaneous Revenue Act of 1988 (TAMRA '88).

Melting the Estate Freeze

Transfer of Disproportionate Appreciation Rights under Section 2036(c). The new statute amends Sec. 2036 so that the rights retained by a transferor in the classic estate freeze transaction can be considered as a retained life estate for Sec. 2036 purposes. Therefore if the estate freeze is transacted, the individual transferring the unfrozen interest in the property will be deemed to have retained a life estate in that transferred property as long as a frozen interest in the property is retained. This, of course, negates the effect of the freeze since the full growth of the property will be brought back to the transferor's gross estate.

It is necessary to examine the terms of the statute to determine those transactions that are affected by the statute and those that avoid its grasp. In general terms, the anti-estate freeze statute states that a transferor is deemed to have retained a lifetime interest in a property if

- the transferor holds, either directly or indirectly, a substantial interest in an *enterprise* (as defined below),
- "in effect" transfers property having a disproportionately large share of their potential appreciation in the enterprise, and
- the transferor retains a share of income, rights, or both in the enterprise.

Some special definitions apply to this portion of Sec. 2036, as follows:

- A *sale for full value to a family member* (defined as a spouse, parent, grandparent, or lineal decedent) is treated as an "in effect" transfer for the purposes of this law.
- A *substantial interest* is ownership (including indirect ownership with family attribution) of 10 percent or more of the voting power or income stream of an enterprise.
- An *enterprise* is undefined, but the congressional explanation refers to an enterprise generally as any non-personal-use property held by an individual for income or gain.
- A *disproportionately large share of the appreciation rights* means that the anticipated portion of appreciation in the property transferred by the grantor is greater than the anticipated portion of appreciation rights in the property retained by the grantor. The transfer is disproportionate with respect to appreciation rights if fraction (A), below, exceeds fraction (B), below:

(A)

$$\frac{\text{potential appreciation of the transferred property}}{\text{value of the transferred property}}$$

(B)

$$\frac{\text{potential appreciation of the retained property}}{\text{value of the retained property}}$$

Practical Results of the Statute. The intended result of this statute is to halt the loss of revenue to the transfer-tax system that results from the classic estate freeze situation. For example, if the recapitalization in example 1 had occurred subsequent to the effective date of the statute (December 17, 1987) the full value of the common stock transferred to C1 and C2 would have been included in P's estate at death at the full date-of-death value of the common stock. In addition, P's executor would also have had to include the value of the preferred stock held directly at death. The inclusion of the growth interest—the common stock transferred by P before death—results from the retention of income or rights in the enterprise (i.e., the preferred stock). For Sec. 2036 purposes this preferred stock is treated as a retained life estate in the *entire* enterprise. Therefore, in this scenario, P's estate is in no better position than it would have been if the freeze had never occurred. In fact, it may even be in an inferior position since a marital deduction may be unavailable for the inclusion of the growth interest transferred during P's lifetime.

A complete understanding of the anti-estate freeze statute will not be possible until further explanation is available of its application to many estate planning techniques used in the past. The statute has been criticized by both the Treasury and estate planning practitioners as being overbroad and confusing and may be repealed or revamped in the future.

Interpreting the Statute

The actual effect of the anti-estate freeze statute will depend directly on the meaning of several terms used in the law (e.g., enterprise, "in effect" transfers, spouses treated as one person, etc.). Many of the terms and phrases in the statute are undefined, and the problem is further exacerbated by the committee reports accompanying the statute, which either (1) contain no definition of key terms, or (2) contain definitions in vague or overbroad terms that only further obfuscate the material.

After the statute's original passage in 1987, there was hope that if not repealed, it would at least be clarified in succinct terms by TAMRA '88. Although the statute was clarified by the TAMRA revisions to some degree, much uncertainty still remains. The Treasury was empowered by the law to draft regulations explaining the statute. Thus far the IRS has responded with Notice 89-99, which has shed some light on the applicability of the statute.

From the key components of the statute it is clear that an enterprise (as interpreted below) must exist before the statute becomes effective. In addition, the decedent must have owned directly or indirectly (through family attribution) at least 10 percent of the voting power or income stream (or both) in such enterprise before the statute becomes effective. Since indirect ownership is included, the statute could be applicable to parents who transfer property that enhances the growth in an enterprise directly owned by their child. At least, it is clear that the statute is only applicable to situations where 10 percent or more of the enterprise is owned by the family unit.

An important issue raised by the statute is what is meant by *enterprise*. The broad definition indicated in the accompanying congressional reports includes virtually anything of value. Notice 89-99 provides that Sec. 2036(c) applies to all but personal use assets. Specifically exempted from the statute are life insurance policies and personal residences.

Another ambiguous issue is what constitutes an "in effect" transfer of the disproportionate growth interest. The legislative history indicates that Congress intended the statute to apply where the growth interest in an enterprise is somehow vested in a child through the actions of a parent who retains an interest in the income or rights of an enterprise. It is expected that this provision will be interpreted broadly to prevent loopholes from developing.

The Deemed Gift—Closing Loopholes in the Anti-Estate Freeze Statute

TAMRA's changes to the anti-estate freeze statute include a new concept called the *deemed gift*. Congress was concerned that individuals could avoid the anti-estate freeze statute by transferring the retained interest *more* than 3 years prior to death. Under traditional rules related to retained life estates, this type of transfer would result in avoiding the estate inclusion of the property. Thus, in example 1, P could have avoided the inclusion in the gross estate of the common stock gifted to C1 and C2 by transferring the preferred stock more than 3 years prior to death. Under the new provisions, the transfer of the retained interest will accelerate the transfer tax imposed on the transferor by assuming a deemed gift occurs at the time of such transfer. Thus if the anti-estate freeze statute is applicable, the transfer of the retained interest will result in an accelerated estate tax imposed on the full amount of the growth interest at its *current* value, along with the actual gift of the retained interest.

> *Example 2:* Assume the same facts as in example 1. Suppose P's common stock was transferred to C1 and C2 on September 1, 1989, when its value was $200,000. To the extent the gift exceeds the annual exclusion, P must either pay gift tax on this transfer or use unified credit to shelter the transfer from tax. P retains the preferred stock, worth $800,000, to provide a steady stream of income from the enterprise. In 1992, P retires and can live comfortably on the retirement income without needing the preferred stock dividend income. At this time, P transfers the preferred stock (still worth its frozen value—$800,000) to C1 and C2. This represents an additional taxable gift of $800,000. If the value of the common stock has grown to $750,000 at this time, the deemed-gift provisions of the anti-estate freeze statute will cause the post-transfer appreciation in the common stock ($550,000) to be treated as a taxable transfer that would cause estate tax as if P died at that moment.

A deemed gift will also occur if the appreciation interest is transferred by the original transferee. The value of the deemed gift at that time will be the appreciation in the growth interest since the time of the original freeze.

> *Example 3:* Assume the same facts as in the examples above. Suppose that in 1992 C1 and C2 decide to sell their common stock in ABC to a third party for its then-value of $750,000. At that time, P will have made a deemed taxable gift to C1 and C2 of the full appreciation—$550,000—which will be subject to estate tax as if P died at that moment.

Tax Apportionment Concerns

One concern brought out by the original anti-estate freeze statute was how the tax would be paid. This is of particular concern with a statute of this type because the transfer tax is imposed at the time of death on a property—i.e., the transferred appreciation rights—that is no longer in the hands of the estate. This problem would also occur in the case of a deemed gift, since the gift tax is imposed on property that has been transferred at an earlier date and is no longer in the hands of the donor.

The TAMRA changes to the anti-estate freeze law attempted to solve this problem by providing that the executor can recover the appropriate share of taxes (including penalties and interest) attributable to property included in the gross estate. That is, the tax liability will, in a sense, follow the gift into the hands of the younger generation heirs. The same recovery is permitted to the donor for the estate tax caused by a deemed gift. Of course, a client can provide through his or her will that the tax be provided otherwise. Tax apportionment clauses in wills drafted prior to the anti-estate freeze statute should be examined carefully should the client anticipate that his or her estate will be effected by the statute.

Marital-Deduction Concerns

One particular concern of the anti-estate freeze statute is that the marital deduction (discussed in more detail in reading 15) will be unavailable to the transferor in the estate freeze transaction. This concern results from the fact that the property subject to the inclusion—the appreciation interest— generally does not pass to the surviving spouse. If this occurs, estate planning will have to refocus on the possibility of first-death taxes when a family enterprise is involved. Very little explanation was included in the committee reports about the meaning of the phrase "the transferor and his or her spouse will be treated as one person for the purposes of this subsection." The IRS interpreted this phrase to mean that spouses would be treated as one person if the non-transferor-spouse received the retained property in a marital-deduction transfer. Thus the surviving spouse is subject to the Sec. 2036(c) rules if he or she inherits the retained interest. This would be consistent with the current estate tax philosophy that the second death of the two spouses generally creates the estate tax burden for the marital unit if the first spouse to die leaves all property to the surviving spouse in a manner qualifying for the marital deduction.

The Amount Includible in the Gross Estate

Under Sec. 2036 pertaining to retained interests for life, the amount that will be includible in the decedent's gross estate is not the value of the interest retained or controlled by him or her but the value of the entire property transferred valued on the date of death. The lifetime transfer is treated as if the decedent had retained the entire property and not just the right to income or beneficial enjoyment for life. It should be remembered that if retained rights are subject to a definite external standard, the property subject to the rights will not be includible.

The decedent's gross estate will include the value of property transferred by him or her for less than full and adequate consideration if the possession or enjoyment of the transferred property can be obtained only by the beneficiary surviving the decedent, *and* the decedent retained a reversionary interest (an ability to have the property returned to him or her) that was worth more than 5 percent of the value of the transferred property immediately before death.

Under the first condition, any beneficiary must survive the decedent in order to obtain possession or enjoyment of the property through ownership.

Example: Mr. Smith transfers property irrevocably in trust for the benefit of his wife, Barbara. Barbara is to receive income for life. The remainder is to go back to Mr. Smith, if living, at her death. If he is not living, the property will go to their children, Michael and Rachael. If Mr. Smith predeceases his wife, the interest to Michael and Rachael will be includible in Mr. Smith's gross estate, because it is contingent upon Mr. Smith's death. In this case Mr. Smith possessed a reversionary interest (assumed to be worth more than 5 percent of the value of the property transferred). The entire value of the transferred property subject to the reversion less the actuarial value of the outstanding income interest possessed by his wife is included.

Example: A decedent, Harvey, transferred property to a trust that was to pay income to his daughter for life. At his daughter's death, the trust will terminate and the property will pass to his daughter's surviving child or, if there is no surviving child, to the decedent or to his estate. Each beneficiary can possess or enjoy the property without surviving the decedent. Therefore the property will not be includible in the decedent's gross estate as a transfer taking effect at death no matter how great the value of the decedent's reversionary interest.

A reversionary interest includes the possibility that the transferred property either may return to the decedent or the decedent's estate, or may be subject to the decedent's power of disposition. It does not apply to the reservation of a life estate or to the possibility of receiving income solely from the transferred property only after the death of another individual. The term *reversionary interest* also does not include the possibility that the decedent may receive an interest in the transferred property by inheriting the property through the estate of another person.

Example: A transferor is not considered to retain a reversion in an outright gift to a spouse merely because of the possibility that the spouse will give the property back to the transferor or that the transferor will inherit the property back from his or her spouse by will. If some alternate event (such as the expiration of a term of years or the exercise of a power of appointment) triggers a transferee's possession or enjoyment of the property, such property generally will not be included in the decedent's gross estate. This is because the transferee could possibly obtain possession and enjoyment of the property while the transferor was still alive.

Caution should be exercised in the creation of irrevocable transfers to make certain that no interest or power with respect to income is retained. Although it appears that no reversionary interests exist, there may be an oversight if the grantor unintentionally neglects to provide for all contingencies. Under local law the result might be that the property would revert to the decedent or the decedent's estate if no designated beneficiary survives him or her (implied reversion). Included under this provision is the common situation of using a short-term trust to provide temporarily for the support of another individual.

> *Example:* A father creates an irrevocable trust for the benefit of his son. The son receives income for 11 years after which time the trust corpus is returned to the father, if living, otherwise to the father's issue. Should the father die before the expiration of the trust term, his reversionary interest in the property calculated actuarially will be includible in his estate.

The reversionary-interest requirement is met not only if the decedent or the decedent's estate might have reacquired the transferred property but also if there exists, immediately prior to death, a possibility that the property would be disposed of by the decedent.

> *Example:* If Anne transfers property in trust for Barbara during Anne's lifetime, with remainder to Carol, but if Carol dies without issue, Carol's estate is limited to a life interest and the property will pass to the individual(s) designated to inherit under Anne's will. Carol's interest is contingent upon surviving Anne. The property will be includible in Anne's estate, although it might not become known until well after Anne's death whether said power of disposition would actually come into effect.

For the value of the property subject to the reversionary interest to be includible in the decedent's estate, it must be worth more than 5 percent of the value of the property transferred as of the moment preceding the decedent's death. Furthermore, for the property to be included in the decedent's gross estate under this section, all three conditions described in this section must be met.

REVOCABLE TRANSFERS—POWER TO ALTER, AMEND, REVOKE, OR TERMINATE, OR TO AFFECT BENEFICIAL ENJOYMENT (IRC SEC. 2038)

If property transferred gratuitously by the decedent during lifetime is subject to any change through the exercise of a power to alter, amend, revoke, or terminate, or to affect beneficial enjoyment either by the decedent alone or in conjunction with any other person, and these powers exist at the decedent's death, the value of the property subject to the power is includible in the decedent's gross estate under Sec. 2038. This is true if the power is exercisable by the decedent alone or in conjunction with anyone (including beneficiaries who would have an adverse interest). The language is all-encompassing and will cause taxation in the decedent's estate. Thus, if a grantor-trustee has the power to distribute principal to an income beneficiary prior to the date the beneficiary is entitled to receive principal, the value of the property subject to the power will be includible in the grantor-trustee's estate. It does not matter that the prohibited power is not exercisable in favor of the decedent or is exercisable only in conjunction with persons having adverse interests, nor does it matter in what capacity the power is exercisable. Neither is it essential that the decedent did not retain the power but acquired it from another source. (IRC Sec. 2038(a)(1)) The critical factor is that the decedent possessed the power at the time of death.

Examples of the types of powers addressed by this section of the Internal Revenue Code include the power (1) to change the beneficiaries, (2) to hasten the time that the beneficiary can receive the property, or (3) to increase or decrease the amount of property allocated to any beneficiary.

As stated before, the decedent—either alone or with others—must have possessed one of the prohibited powers at the time of death to cause inclusion under this section. If, however, there was a condition beyond the decedent's control that limited the use of the power and that condition did not occur before the decedent died, the property will not be included in the decedent's gross estate as a transfer subject to the power to revoke.

It makes no difference in what capacity the decedent could have exercised this power. For example, if the decedent transferred property to a trust naming himself or herself trustee and then gave the trustee the power to revoke the trust, the property would be included in the decedent's estate. Similarly, if the decedent appointed another person as trustee, but retained the power to appoint a successor-trustee upon the resignation of the original trustee (including naming himself or herself as trustee), the property would also be included in the estate. Reservation of a power to remove a trustee at will and appoint another trustee will cause a similar result. However, if any rights to revoke, alter, amend, or terminate the trust or change trustees is given to another person and the decedent reserved no rights whatsoever with regard to these powers, the value of the property in the trust will not be included in the decedent's gross estate.

While the property would be included in the decedent's gross estate whether he or she had the power to change or terminate the property interest by himself or herself or together with others only, regardless of their capacity or interests, there are two exceptions to this rule: (1) if the decedent's power can be exercised only with the consent of *all* parties having an interest (either vested or contingent) in the transferred property, and (2) if this power added nothing to the rights of the parties under local law, the property will not be included in the decedent's estate. Note that this exception only applies if all parties must consent to the exercise of a power to change or end the property interest.

The following powers have been determined to be powers to alter, amend, revoke, or terminate that would cause the property subject to the power to be included in the decedent's gross estate. Note that only the part of the transferred property that is subject to the decedent's power as described above will be included in the gross estate under this provision of the Code.

Powers to alter, amend, revoke, or terminate include the following: (1) power to revoke or terminate a trust to which the property is transferred, whether this power results in a return of corpus to the grantor or acceleration of enjoyment by the beneficiaries; (2) power to control and manage the trust property, except where this power is limited to administrative or mechanical details only, such as designation of funds as income or principal, investment policy, issuance of voting proxies, or other matters that do not alter the rights or interests of the beneficiaries; (3) power to change beneficiaries or to vary the amounts distributable; (4) power to appoint by will or change shares of beneficiaries by will; (5) power to revoke, which exists by virtue of state law; (6) power to invade a trust created by another for whose benefit the decedent created a similar trust (reciprocal trusts); and (7) power to replace without cause the trustee with another.

The following powers have been determined *not* to constitute powers sufficient to cause taxation in the decedent's estate under Sec. 2038:

- power in others than the grantor to revoke the transfer or return part of it to the grantor (but such transfers may be taxed under another section discussed earlier as transfers intended to take effect at death)
- certain powers contingent on the happening of a particular event
- powers as to mechanics or details only, such as powers to direct issuance of voting proxies, to help determine investment policies, and to direct investment and reinvestment of funds
- power to add to corpus
- power over trusts created by others with funds not derived from the decedent and not supported by similar trusts created by others. An example of this last power is the power in the decedent as trustee over another's trust in which the decedent has no beneficial interest.

An example of retained powers under this section is the following situation:

> *Example:* The decedent, Mr. Jones, creates a trust that provides income to Mark for life with the remainder going to Sandra or her heirs. The decedent retains the power to invade principal for the benefit of Sandra during Mark's lifetime. The entire property will be included in the decedent's gross estate under this Code provision. The decedent, by exercise of his power to invade, can affect the time when Sandra receives enjoyment of the property as well as the amount of income Mark will receive. If, however, the decedent retained only the

power to accumulate income and add it to corpus, the only interest the decedent can affect is that of Mark, the income beneficiary. Therefore it is only the value of Mark's income interest that will be included in the decedent's gross estate under this provision.

It should be remembered that this provision sometimes overlaps and can operate in conjunction with the provision discussed earlier where the decedent retained powers to possess, enjoy, or receive income for life, or designate who is to receive or possess the property. That section (Sec. 2036) would bring the entire value of the property on the date of death into the decedent's gross estate. Sec. 2038 would include only the value of the interest in property subject to the powers to alter, amend, revoke, or terminate.

> *Example:* Ed Smith transfers property to a trust for the benefit of his 20-year-old son, Sandy. The trust provides that Sandy is entitled to all the income from the trust until he is 40 when he is to receive the corpus. Ed retains the right to terminate the trust at any time with corpus to be distributed to Sandy upon termination. Ed dies when Sandy is 30. The amount includible in Ed's estate under Sec. 2038 is the amount of the trust corpus *less* the value of the income interest (over which Ed had no power). The value of the income interest would be determined actuarially at the time of Ed's death.

Although the decedent possessed prohibited powers, the property interest subject to the powers will not be included in the decedent's gross estate if his or her power is subject to an *ascertainable standard*. This refers to an external standard imposed upon the decedent limiting the exercise of the power strictly to provide for the support, maintenance, health, or education of a beneficiary.

> *Example:* A decedent transfers property in trust to provide income to Ken for life, remainder to Don or his heirs. The decedent retains the power to invade corpus for Ken's benefit but only for his health, maintenance, support, or education. Since the decedent's power to invade corpus is subject to a standard that may be reviewed by the court, the situation is as if the decedent really holds no power at all. Note that if the decedent's power was not governed by an ascertainable standard, the fact that he or she could exercise this power only with the consent of the beneficiary whose interest would be adversely affected would not prevent the value of the property subject to this power from being included in the decedent's gross estate.

It is obvious from the discussion above that there are many potential problems to consider in planning gratuitous lifetime transfers of property in order to avoid inclusion of the property in a decedent's gross estate. Careful drafting of trust instruments can allow the decedent to retain some degree of control without triggering estate taxation under one of the Code sections. If the decedent wishes to retain some powers over property transferred during lifetime, he or she would be wise to consult a planner experienced in these areas. With good planning the decedent can accomplish his or her objectives, yet avoid inclusion of the property interests transferred in the gross estate.

ANNUITIES (IRC SEC. 2039)

With certain limited exceptions, a decedent's gross estate will include the present value of an annuity or other payment receivable by any beneficiary as a result of having survived the decedent. Included under this section are any agreements, commercial or private annuities, and employee retirement annuities (including all proceeds from qualified plans generally for decedents dying after December 31, 1984). Annuities or payments under certain contracts included in the gross estate are those that were payable to or receivable by the decedent

- for his or her lifetime
- for a period that did not, in fact, end before the decedent's death
- for a period that cannot be ascertained without referring to the decedent's death

A decedent's right to a payment is sufficient. He or she need not have actually received nor be receiving payments, nor must the time at which payments would commence have passed by the date of death. However, those annuities that end at the decedent's death and do not provide payments to any beneficiary afterward will not be subject to inclusion in the decedent's gross estate. Thus contracts under an annuity for life that provide payments to the decedent and end at his or her death are not included in the gross estate, because there is nothing that the decedent can transfer or pass on to another at death. In other words, nothing will be included in the decedent's gross estate because the decedent possessed no transferable interest.

Terms

The provision of the Internal Revenue Code concerning estate tax inclusion of annuities is a complicated one. It might be helpful to define some of the terms so that the student will understand the types of arrangements and rights to payment that may or may not cause their inclusion in the decedent's gross estate. As used under this Internal Revenue Code section, the term *annuity or other payment* refers to one or more payments extending over any period of time. That means that there may be several payments or a single lump-sum payment to be made to a beneficiary after the decedent's death. There is no requirement that these payments be equal, unconditional, or periodic. Stated differently, the amount as well as the timing of each payment may vary.

10.1

The meaning of the term *contract or agreement* is very broad and includes any arrangement, agreement, understanding, plan, or combination of these arising from the decedent's employment. An includible annuity may be a bona fide contract between the employer and the employee or it may be a plan for salary continuation, such as one that was established unilaterally by the decedent's employer. It may even include an unwritten arrangement for payments to an employee's beneficiary pursuant to a practice consistently followed by the employer.

The statutory term *was payable to the decedent* refers to annuity payments or other payments that the decedent was actually receiving at the time of death, regardless of whether he or she had an enforceable right to have these payments continued. Furthermore, an annuity is considered *receivable* by the decedent although it may be forfeitable on the occurrence or nonoccurrence of a particular event, such as the recipient's remarriage. However, if the annuity agreement contained a provision that certain occurrences or nonoccurrences would make it forfeitable, the possibility of forfeitability will have an effect on the value of the annuity in the gross estate. In addition, an annuity will be included in the gross estate if the decedent, immediately before death, had a right to receive payments in the future. In other words, as long as the decedent had an enforceable right to receive payments at some time, these payments need not have been immediately payable to him or her before death. As long as the decedent had been in compliance with his or her obligations under the contract or agreement up to the time of death, a decedent is considered to have had an enforceable right to receive future payments under a contract.

As stated earlier, the term *annuity* includes periodic payments for a specific time. There may be a single agreement or a combination of several agreements between the parties. Examples of contracts or agreements for payments that constitute annuities or other payments included in the gross estate are the following:

- a contract under which the decedent was receiving or was entitled to receive an annuity or other payment immediately before death and for the duration of his or her life. The contract provides that payments are to continue after the decedent's death to a beneficiary named by him or her if the beneficiary survives the decedent.
- a contract under which the decedent was receiving payments before death together with another person for their joint lives. Payments would continue to the survivor after the death of either individual. This type of contract is called a *joint and survivor annuity*.
- a contract or agreement between the decedent and his or her employer under which the decedent was receiving or entitled to receive an annuity or other stipulated payment after retirement for the duration of the decedent's life with payments to a designated beneficiary upon the decedent's death, if such beneficiaries survive the decedent. It makes no difference whether the payments to the survivor were fixed by contract or subject to any options or elections exercisable by the decedent.

10.2

- a contract or agreement between the decedent and the decedent's employer that provided for an annuity or other payments to a designated surviving beneficiary, if the decedent died prior to retirement or before the expiration of a specific time
- a contract or agreement under which the decedent, immediately before death, was receiving or entitled to receive an annuity or other payment for a specified time period with payments to continue to a named beneficiary in the event that the decedent died prior to the expiration of that time

As stated earlier, the value of an annuity contract will be includible in the decedent's gross estate although payments were not to begin until after the death of the purchaser and primary annuitant (generally the same individual). The key is whether the decedent had an enforceable right to receive payments from a plan or combination of plans during lifetime had he or she lived. For example, a right to receive disability income in the event of disability prior to retirement will cause a salary continuation plan to the employee's surviving spouse to be includible in the employee's gross estate if he or she dies before retirement. This is true even if the employee has never been disabled. In other words, the value of a surviving beneficiary's annuity or other payment is includible in the gross estate only if the contract or agreement (or combination) under which payments are to be made to the survivor also gave the decedent a payment or a right to payment. It is the right to the payment that controls inclusion in the gross estate, not whether the decedent actually received any amount under the annuity before death. Also any combination of arrangements or plans (except payments from qualified plans) arising out of the decedent's employment may be includible under this section. Such contributions are treated as if they were made by the decedent. Payments are includible whether they are paid to the estate or to a named beneficiary.

Amount Includible

The amount includible in the decedent's gross estate is the value of the payments to the surviving beneficiary that represents the proportionate part of the purchase price of the contract contributed by the decedent. This includes contributions made by the decedent's employer, if they were made by reason of his or her employment. However, to the extent that the surviving beneficiary or anyone other than the decedent furnished part of the original purchase price, that portion will not be included in the decedent's gross estate.

> *Example:* Tom Taylor purchased a joint and survivor annuity for himself and his wife, Ann. If he paid the total purchase price, the entire value of Ann's survivorship interest will be included in Tom's gross estate if he predeceases Ann. On the other hand, if Tom contributed 60 percent of the money to purchase the annuity and 40 percent of the contribution came from Ann's separate funds, only 60 percent of the value of the survivor's income interest would be includible in Tom's estate. It should be noted that if the decedent's employer or former employer contributed to the purchase price of the contract, the employer's contribution shall be treated as if it was made by the

decedent. Therefore, if Tom's employer purchased an annuity for him as a key employee and contributed the entire purchase price, the employer's contribution will be treated as if it was made by Tom, the decedent. Thus any survivorship interest will be fully includible in Tom's estate.

Specifically *excluded* from taxation under this Code section are all amounts paid "as insurance under policies on the life of the decedent." This is not to say that proceeds of life insurance will not be included in the decedent's gross estate. Proceeds of life insurance on the decedent's life are includible in the gross estate under another Code section (IRC Sec. 2042) if certain conditions exist. If a single contract contains or has contained both life insurance and annuity elements (as will probably be more common in the future), the amount includible, if any, under this section will be based on whether there was any insurance element in the contract at the moment of death.

Only those contracts that contained no life insurance elements will be includible under this Code section. The question of the amount of insurance a contract contains, if any, may be determined by the relationship of the policy's reserve value to the value of the death benefit at the time of the decedent's death. If the decedent dies before the reserve value equals the death benefit, an insurance element exists under the contract and the contract will be considered to be an insurance policy for estate tax purposes. Alternatively, if the decedent dies after the reserve value equals the death benefit, no insurance element exists any longer under the contract, and the agreement will be considered to be solely a contract for an annuity. Notwithstanding the above, if a death benefit under a contractual arrangement can never exceed the total premiums paid plus interest, there is no insurance element present (Treas. Reg. Sec. 20.2039-1(d)).

The following situation is adapted from the aforementioned IRS regulations section:

> *Example:* Under a nonqualified retirement plan, an employer, Marge, purchased a contract from a life insurance company that would provide her employee, Sam, with an annuity of $100 per month for life upon the employee's retirement at age 65. Under the contract a beneficiary named by the employee would receive a similar annuity for life upon the employee's death after retirement. In addition, the contract provided for a lump-sum payment of $20,000 to the designated beneficiary instead of the annuity described above if the employee died before he reached retirement age. Assume that the reserve value of the contract would be $20,000 when the employee reaches age 65. Thus, if the employee died after reaching retirement age, the death benefit to the beneficiary would be considered an annuity, includible in the employee's gross estate. On the other hand, if the employee dies before reaching age 65, the death benefit would constitute insurance under a policy on the life of the decedent because the reserve value would be less than the death benefit. Therefore the

includibility in the gross estate would be determined under the estate tax section dealing with insurance (IRC Sec. 2042) and not under this section.

Valuation

Commercial annuity contracts (those issued by companies regularly engaged in the sale of annuities) are valued differently from others. A commercial contract will be valued based on the cost of comparable contracts sold by the issuing company as of the date of the decedent's death. Therefore, in the earlier example, if Tom had purchased a commercial annuity for himself and Ann, the value in Tom's estate would be the cost of a single life annuity on Ann's life at the time of his death if he had contributed the entire purchase price (Treas. Reg. Sec. 20.2031-8(a)). If, however, the annuity was payable under a private contract, it would be valued for estate tax purposes according to the actuarial tables found in the federal estate and gift tax regulations (Treas. Reg. Secs. 20.2031-10; 25.2512-9).

Valuation Date

Date-of-Death Value

The value of benefits under an annuity contract is determined on the primary annuitant's date of death. Since an annuity is an asset that diminishes with mere lapse of time, the alternate valuation date is inapplicable to any annuity included in the gross estate (IRC Sec. 2032(a)(3)). Thus benefits under an annuity contract are always valued on the date of death. The benefits paid out during the 6-month period between the date of death or, if applicable, the alternate valuation date cannot be used to reduce the value of the annuity for estate tax purposes. Also, if the benefits are payable in a lump sum, the amount payable becomes the date-of-death value used on the estate tax return. However, as stated earlier, the amount included in the decedent's gross estate will be proportionately reduced if the entire cost of the contract is not considered to have been paid by the decedent.

Value of Annuity Reduced by Other Than Mere Lapse of Time

As stated earlier, the value of an annuity is always determined as of the decedent's death as opposed to the alternate valuation date. Date-of-death valuation applies to annuities and similar payments, although the estate qualifies for and elects the alternate valuation date (6 months from the date of death) for other assets. This is because the value of annuities (and other "wasting assets" such as mortgages and notes receivable) always diminishes with the mere passage of time.

It should be noted, however, that a different value may apply if a reduction in value occurs for a reason other than mere lapse of time.

> *Example:* Suppose a husband had purchased a joint and survivor annuity for himself and his wife. The husband dies, and after his death, his wife is entitled to receive payments for the

10.5

remainder of her life. Unfortunately, the wife dies 4 months after the husband. In this case an event other than mere lapse of time has occurred during the period between the date of death and the alternate valuation date that has reduced the value of the annuity to zero. In this case the only amount includible in the husband's estate would be the value, as of his death, of the payments received by his widow during the 4-month postdeath period. It is determined by finding the difference between the value of an annuity for her life determined as of the husband's death and the actual value of the annuity determined as of the date of her death.

Lump-Sum Payments

As will be seen later, lump-sum payments are included at full value. When payments are made in installments, whether for a fixed period, in a fixed amount, or for the life of the beneficiary, the valuation will be made on a commuted basis (the present value of the right to receive future income).

Annuities Receivable from Qualified Employee Retirement Plans

The Deficit Reduction Act of 1984 generally repealed all estate tax exclusion of qualified plan proceeds for decedents dying after December 31, 1984. There are two exceptions.

(1) A nonemployee-spouse's interest in qualified plan proceeds that arise solely as a result of the application of community-property laws will be totally excluded from his or her gross estate provided that the nonemployee-spouse predeceases the employee plan participant (IRC Sec. 2039(c)).

(2) If the proceeds of a qualified plan were in pay status on December 31, 1984, *and* prior to the date of enactment of the Deficit Reduction Act of 1984 (July 18, 1984) the participant had irrevocably elected a beneficiary designation that would have qualified the plan proceeds for estate tax exclusion, the $100,000 exclusion amount is still available (DRA Secs. 525(b)(2); (b)(3)).

JOINTLY HELD PROPERTY WITH RIGHT OF SURVIVORSHIP (IRC SEC. 2040)

Joint Tenancies Held by Married Couples

A second rule has been enacted that controls the estate taxation of joint property with right of survivorship held solely by husband and wife as well as property held as tenants by the entirety. The present rule with respect to spousal joint tenancies with right of survivorship is as follows: one-half of the value of such property, regardless of which spouse furnished all or part of the consideration, will be included in the gross estate of the first spouse to die. This is an automatic rule. The actual contribution of each spouse is irrelevant.

Percentage-of-Contribution (or Consideration-Furnished) Rule

All property held in joint tenancy with right of survivorship by joint tenants other than a husband and wife alone is treated under a different rule. The property is included in a deceased joint tenant's estate according to a percentage-of-contribution rule. Property held as joint tenants with right of survivorship by a decedent is included in the decedent's estate to the extent of his or her interest (the fractional share of the joint tenancy) at the time of death. However, any part of the decedent's interest in the joint tenancy will not be included in the decedent's gross estate if it can be proved that the joint tenancy originally belonged to a surviving joint tenant or was purchased by funds contributed by the surviving joint tenant. In addition, if it can be shown that the surviving joint tenant received his or her interest from the decedent for less than full and adequate consideration, that portion of the joint tenancy will be included in the decedent's estate. This rule is limited to the actual gift of the property or the direct funds to purchase the property held in joint tenancy. Thus, if one joint tenant gave income-producing property to another joint tenant and if the posttransfer income was contributed toward the purchase of jointly held property, the amounts attributable to such income will not be deemed to have been received from the other joint tenant.

> *Example:* Ted and Carol are siblings who hope to purchase a vacation home at the New Jersey shore. Since Ted is currently short on funds, Carol provides the entire purchase price. Ted dies tragically 3 years after the purchase of the property when the vacation home is worth $350,000. The general rule is that Ted's interest in the property, valued at $175,000 at the time of his death, is included in his gross estate. However, Ted's estate is capable of rebutting the general rule by proving that Carol provided all the original purchase price. If such evidence can be established, no amount of the joint tenancy will be included in Ted's estate at the time of his death.

Burden of Proof

Under the percentage-of-contribution rule the burden of proof to demonstrate that the surviving joint tenant had made some contribution to the acquisition of the joint tenancy remained upon the surviving joint tenant or the estate. If successful, that portion representing the percentage of contribution made by the surviving joint tenant was excluded from the gross estate.

Joint Property Acquired by Gift or Inheritance

Jointly held property that is acquired by gift, bequest, or inheritance is treated in a slightly different way. If the decedent and the decedent's spouse acquired the property by gift or inheritance, one-half of the value will be included in the decedent's estate. However, if the decedent acquires the property as joint tenants with right of survivorship as a gift or inheritance with persons other than a spouse, the value representing his or her fractional interest will be includible in the estate. To determine the decedent's fractional share, the value of the property will be divided by the number of joint tenants

10.7

with right of survivorship, the presumption being that each joint tenant owns an undivided interest in the entire property.

> *Example:* If a decedent, James, inherited a farm from his father in equal shares with his three sisters and a brother, and he was the first joint tenant to die, one-fifth of the value of the property would be included in his gross estate.

The Advisability of Joint Tenancies with Right of Survivorship between Husband and Wife

Advantages

There are still advantages in holding property jointly with right of survivorship by spouses. Jointly held property between spouses is generally nonprobate property. This means that the property will not be subject to estate administration. All benefits of ownership will remain available to the surviving joint tenant without interruption during the administration period. Because the property does not pass through probate, total administration expenses and attorney's fees will be smaller. One-half of the property attributed to the decedent's interest included in the decedent's gross estate will be entitled to the full benefit of the unlimited marital deduction. Therefore there will be no estate tax liability because of the property's inclusion. Another benefit of joint ownership is that it is comforting and creates a feeling of harmony and security between husband and wife.

Disadvantages

A disadvantage may be that the surviving joint tenant will obtain full control over the future disposition of the property. This may defeat a portion of the original estate plan of the first joint tenant to die. Should the survivor remarry, the property will become subject to a spouse's right of election by the second spouse.

In addition, only one-half of the property will receive a step-up in basis at the first joint tenant's death. As mentioned earlier, the saving in estate tax and probate costs may possibly be worth less than the potential savings in capital-gains tax had the property been fully included in the decedent's gross estate and acquired a fully stepped-up basis.

Alternatives

Alternate solutions involve keeping the property in sole ownership.

> *Example:* If a decedent-husband held the property in his name alone and left the property outright to his wife as a special bequest in his will, the entire property, although included in the gross estate, would also be eligible for the marital deduction. Therefore no estate tax would result from inclusion of the property in his estate. In addition, the basis in the hands of the surviving wife would become the fair market value on the date of the husband's death or alternate valuation date, if

applicable. Of course, the property would then be probate property, which may generate additional costs to the estate. There also may be a delay in formally transferring the property to the surviving spouse. Furthermore, if the husband retains ownership of the property with the intention of passing it to his surviving spouse using the unlimited marital deduction, and his wife predeceases him, he will have lost the benefit of the marital deduction for the property passing through his estate. However, when he dies, the entire property will receive a stepped-up basis in the hands of his beneficiaries. It should not be forgotten that, even if the husband had died first, at his spouse's death, the entire value of the property would be taxable for federal estate tax purposes in the second estate. In other words, to the extent the property is not disposed of by either spouse during their lifetimes, it will be included at full value in the estate of the second spouse to die. Of course, the next tier of beneficiaries will obtain another step-up in basis to fair market value at the time of the second death.

Other factors to consider when arranging property ownership are the size of the relative estates of the parties as well as the variation in their ages and other health factors. Likewise, the relationship of the parties is significant. Although no-fault divorce laws and equitable distribution statutes now apply to some extent in almost all states, jointly held personal property is freely accessible to either spouse whether together or separated. Possession by the donee may defeat the interest of the donor's spouse temporarily or permanently, to the extent the asset is converted or consumed.

Because of one or more of the above considerations, the estate planner may recommend the termination of a joint tenancy between spouses thereby transferring the entire interest to one of the spouses. Keep in mind that the unlimited marital deduction for gift tax purposes now makes it possible to transfer property back and forth between spouses without the gift tax ramifications that previously existed. For example, if the decedent's estate includes a closely held business for which special-use valuation may be applicable, or if an election to defer payment of estate taxes attributable to the closely held business or a Sec. 303 redemption is a possibility and the decedent owns the business in his or her own name, the value of the business in relation to the decedent's adjusted gross estate can be increased if he or she is willing to transfer some nonbusiness joint assets to his or her spouse as sole owner. The proportionate increase in the value of the business interest in relation to the decedent's estate may enable the estate to qualify for any of these potentially desirable tax benefits by meeting the percentage tests for eligibility. Alternatively, if the property under consideration is solely owned nonbusiness property, placing it in joint names will remove one-half of the date-of-death value from the decedent's estate, thereby easing the possibility of qualifying for Sec. 303 redemptions, Sec. 6166 deferral to pay estate tax, or special-use valuation under Sec. 2032A.

The following example illustrates how ownership of property in joint names as opposed to sole ownership will affect the ability to qualify for one of the tax benefits above where qualification is based on a percentage test:

> *Example:* Mr. Jones is the sole shareholder of a closely held business that has a fair market value of $600,000. His gross estate is valued at $2,000,000. He desires to leave approximately one-half of his estate to his second wife, with the net balance after payment of taxes and expenses to his two sons from a prior marriage who work with him in the business. Debts and expenses of the estate will probably be about $75,000. Under such a plan the estate would not qualify for the tax relief provided by either Sec. 6166 (providing for installment payment of estate tax over 14 years) or a Sec. 303 redemption (providing for a redemption of stock to pay estate taxes and funeral and administrative costs). This is because the value of the business interest equals only 31 percent of this adjusted gross estate—not the 35 percent required by Secs. 303 and 6166. Considering the division of property above, his sons would have difficulty meeting the estate tax liability payable from the residue unless the closely held business had significant amounts of cash.

> As an alternative plan, if Mr. Jones desires to maintain the flexibility to qualify for the tax benefits described, he can transfer approximately $900,000 of a nonbusiness property to joint ownership with his spouse. This would reduce his adjusted gross estate by $450,000. The reduced amount would enable the estate to qualify under the 35-percent-of-adjusted-gross-estate test under Sec. 6166 and Sec. 303. Bear in mind that if he does not survive more than 3 years after making the transfer to a joint tenancy with his spouse, the property transferred will be included in his estate for purposes of qualification for Sec. 6166 and Sec. 303 redemptions. However, the use of joint tenancies for this purpose has interesting potential for planning possibilities with regard to estate tax considerations.

POWERS OF APPOINTMENT (IRC SEC. 2041)

A power of appointment over property is a right that the holder of the power has to specify who will become the recipient or owner of the property. Depending on the type of power of appointment, the holder of the power may or may not be able to designate himself or herself as the property owner.

General Powers

The gross estate includes the value of all property subject to a general power of appointment possessed by the decedent at the time of death. A general power of appointment is a power over property so broad that it approaches actual ownership or control over the property subject to the power. If the decedent has been given a power by another person (called the donor of the power), and this power allows the decedent to appoint the property to himself or herself, his or her creditors, the estate, or the estate's creditors, it is considered a general power of appointment. Note that the decedent need not have the power to appoint property to all four categories. The power to appoint to one of the four is sufficient for a power to be a general power of appointment for estate tax purposes (*Estate of Edelman v. Comm'r*, 38 T.C. 972 (1976)). The person who possesses the power and has the right to exercise it is called the donee of the power.

As long as the decedent holds the power, it makes no difference whether the power is exercisable by him or her only during lifetime or only at death, or both during life and at death (*Snyder v. U.S.*, 203 F.Supp. 195 (W.D. Ky. 1962); *Jenkins v. U.S.*, 428 F.2d 538 (5th Cir. 1970)).

> *Example:* The decedent—a surviving spouse—has been given income from the property for life with the right to appoint or dispose of the property at death to his or her estate, creditors, or beneficiaries by will. Although the power to transfer the property did not include lifetime transfers in this case, the value of the property subject to the power would be included in the surviving spouse's estate because there was full power over the disposition of the property at death. The person who possesses the power and has the right to exercise it is called the donee of the power.

A general power includes the unlimited right of the decedent-donee to use the corpus of a trust for the decedent's own benefit.

> *Example:* If the decedent, Herman, was given the power in a trust to distribute or appoint trust principal to or among any of four beneficiaries not including himself, this would not be a general power of appointment. However, if the trust contained an additional power in the decedent to invade corpus without limitation for his own benefit at any time, the power would be a general power of appointment since he has the power to deplete corpus partially or totally for his own benefit, thereby defeating the rights of the other beneficiaries. It is immaterial for estate tax inclusion whether or not he exercises this power in favor of himself.

Special Powers

A general power of appointment is to be distinguished from a limited or special power. A special power is one in which the donor of the power limits the donee with respect to the persons to whom the donee may appoint the property. As already noted, a power of appointment will not qualify as a general power unless it is exercisable in favor of at least one of the following: the decedent, the decedent's estate, the decedent's creditors, or the creditors of the estate. If the power is exercisable only in favor of one or more persons (or all other persons) not including the decedent, the decedent's creditors, the estate, or the creditors of the estate—or if it is specifically not exercisable in favor of the decedent, the decedent's creditors, the estate, or the creditors of the estate—it will not qualify as a general power. Property over which the decedent has a special or limited power will not be includible in his or her gross estate. However, if the decedent had a power over property that he or she exercised in favor of someone else but the decedent retained an interest in the property for life, the value of the property will be includible in the decedent's gross estate.

> *Example:* A decedent, Franklin, was given a lifetime general power of appointment by his sister to designate who would receive a lakefront vacation home. The decedent exercised this power in favor of his daughter but retained for himself the right to use the property for his life. The right to use the property for life will bring the value of the property subject to the power into his gross estate, although he had previously exercised the power and disposed of the property.

Limited by Ascertainable Standard

If the decedent possesses the power to consume or invade for his or her own benefit but limited the power by an ascertainable standard (such that the property may be used or invaded only for reasons of the decedent's health, education, support, or maintenance), the power of appointment will be considered a special and not a general power. Support and maintenance will generally be construed in accordance with the standard of living to which the decedent was accustomed.

> *Example:* If Mr. Smith creates a trust and gives his son, Walter, the right to invade corpus for Walter's health, education, support, or maintenance, Walter has been given a special power of appointment that will not cause the corpus subject to the power to be included in his gross estate (IRC Sec. 2041(b)(1)(A)).

Powers Exercisable Only with the Consent of Others

A power of appointment that would otherwise cause the value of property subject to the power to be includible in the estate of the donee of the power may escape inclusion, wholly or partially, if the power can only be exercised with the consent of others.

Powers Exercisable Only with the Consent of the Donor of the Power

A power created after October 21, 1942, that can be exercised only with the consent or joinder of the creator (donor) of the power will not be considered a general power of appointment for federal estate tax purposes (IRC Sec. 2041(b)(1)(C)(i)).

A power created after October 21, 1942, that can be exercised only with the consent or joinder of a person having a substantial adverse interest will not be treated as a general power and the property subject to the power will not be includible in the estate of the donee (IRC Sec. 2041(b)(1)(C)(ii)).

> *Example:* Assume that Albert grants John and Betty the unrestricted power to appoint property to Betty during Betty's lifetime. In default of the appointment, the property will pass to John at Betty's death. At Betty's death, if the property has not been appointed to her, no portion of the value of the property will be includible in her gross estate because she is not deemed to have a general power of appointment since John had a substantial adverse interest.

If the consent of the person without an adverse interest is required, the value of the property subject to the power will be fully includible in the donee's estate.

> *Example:* Assume that Albert grants John and Betty the unrestricted power to appoint property in favor of Betty during Betty's lifetime. In default of appointment, the property will pass to Carol on Betty's death. When Betty predeceases John, Betty is deemed to possess a general power of appointment since John did not have a substantial adverse interest in the property subject to the power. In no event could John have been the beneficiary of the property. The entire value of the property subject to the power will be included in her gross estate at her death. This is so because Betty and John could have appointed the property to Betty during her lifetime and she was not limited to exercising the power only in conjunction with the creator of the power or someone having an adverse interest in the property.

Note that a trustee whose only powers are administrative ones exercisable in a fiduciary capacity is not a person who has an adverse interest in the property.

If a power created *before* October 21, 1942, is exercisable by the decedent only in conjunction with *any other person*, it will not be treated as a general power (IRC Sec. 2042(b)(1)(B)). Note that for general powers created before October 21, 1942, it is irrelevant that the party whose consent was required had no interest, adverse or otherwise, in the property. The mere requirement of the consent of another person is sufficient to defeat inclusion of property subject to such powers in the decedent-donee's estate.

Powers Exercisable Only with the Consent of Other in Whose Favor the Power Could Be Exercised

If a person is given a power that can only be exercised in conjunction with others in whose favor the power could be exercised, only a fractional part of the property will be includible in the donee's estate. The fractional portion is determined by dividing the value of the property by the number of persons in whose favor the power could be exercised (IRC Sec. 2041(b)(1)(C)(iii)).

> *Example:* Assume that Albert grants John and Betty the unrestricted right to appoint property to either of them (with the consent of the other) during their lifetimes. In default of an appointment, the property will pass to Myrna. At Betty's death, one-half of the value of the property would be includible in her gross estate.

Other Limitations on Powers

Although the decedent has been given what otherwise is a general power of appointment, it will not be included in his or her gross estate if the decedent's power is limited to a noncumulative right to withdraw the greater of $5,000 or 5 percent of the aggregate value of the property each year. This power is sometimes referred to as a *5-and-5 power.* Failure to withdraw the money each year would be said to be a lapse constituting a release of the power. If the decedent died possessing this power, the amount includible in his or her estate would be only the amount that the decedent could have appointed in favor of himself or herself in the year of death. To the extent that his or her power to appoint the property exceeds the greater of $5,000 or 5 percent of the value of the assets subject to the power, there is a taxable disposition by the decedent's failure to exercise his or her power of withdrawal. In other words, the decedent is deemed to have made a gift of the excess property that is not withdrawn each year to the remainderperson. The gift tax effect is exactly the same as if the decedent had appointed the property to himself or herself and gifted it to the remainder portion of the trust.

> *Example:* A trust established by Mr. Ford was funded with $500,000 worth of securities. His son, Frank, was to receive all income for life with the remainder to Frank's children. Frank was given a noncumulative right to withdraw $40,000 a year from the trust. Since this is a noncumulative right, he has released those funds in each year that he does not withdraw all or part of the $40,000. Releasing the excess of the greater of $5,000 or 5 percent of the trust corpus is treated as a taxable transfer (it is a gift to the trust). In this example, 5 percent of the trust corpus equals $25,000. The excess distribution equals $15,000 ($40,000 − $25,000). It is a taxable transfer with a reserved right to income from the portion remaining in the trust. Since he is the life income beneficiary, a portion of the trust valued at the date of his death will be included in his gross estate. The ratio for inclusion is determined by dividing the

excess distribution ($15,000) by the total current value of the trust ($500,000). In this case, 3/100 or 3 percent of the value of the trust corpus at Frank's death will be includible in his gross estate.

If failure to exercise a power of withdrawal occurs in more than one year, the proportionate amount of property over which the power lapses that is treated as a taxable disposition is determined separately for each year. It is the aggregate of all taxable portions for all years (not to exceed 100 percent) that will be includible in the decedent's gross estate. Remember that the value of the 5-and-5 power in the year of death will also be includible.

Disclaiming a Power

Under the federal disclaimer statute (IRC Sec. 2518) a qualified disclaimer exists when a refusal to accept the property has been made in writing and received by the transferor of the interest or the transferor's legal representative within 9 months after the later of the day on which the transfer creating the interest in the disclaimant was made or the day the disclaimant becomes 21 years of age. When a valid disclaimer is made, the disclaimant has no right to pass the property to someone else. The property must pass to another without any action or direction on the part of the disclaimant.

If a decedent refuses to accept a power of appointment given to him or her in a manner consistent with the requirements of a qualified disclaimer, the decedent will be considered to have disclaimed or renounced the power of appointment. Therefore nothing will be included in the decedent's gross estate although the power was a general power, because that power was never accepted by the decedent. A disclaimer is invalid once the power over the property has been accepted. Also a qualified disclaimer does not result in a taxable gift if the necessary federal requirements are met.

If the donee of a power does not wish it to be included in his or her gross estate, the donee must release or exercise the power during lifetime. Also the donee must not exercise the power and retain any rights or power over the property that would cause it to be included under IRC Secs. 2036, 2037, or 2038 (for example, the right to income for life) or the property will still be included in the donee's gross estate, unless he or she releases these impermissible retained rights more than 3 years prior to death (IRC Sec. 2041(a)(2)).

Time and Method of Creation of a Power

A power of appointment created by will is considered to be created on the date of the testator's death. A power of appointment created by deed or other instrument during the creator's lifetime is deemed to be created on the day the instrument becomes effective.

The use of the words *general power of appointment* is not essential. Determination of the existence of a power will be based on what it purports to accomplish rather than on either the wording used by the creator or local property law connotations. Therefore a right given to a person with a life estate in a trust to withdraw or consume the trust principal may rightly be considered a general power of appointment over the property.

Effect of Legal Competence to Exercise a Power

Property subject to a general power of appointment will be includible in the decedent's estate even though the decedent could not exercise the power because he was legally incompetent or a minor (Rev. Rul. 75-351, 1975-2 C.B. 368; Rev. Rul. 55-518, 1955-2 C.B. 384). Numerous U.S. Circuit Court of Appeals decisions support this conclusion and there no longer appears to be any doubt about this issue. (See *Estate of Gilchrist v. Comm'r,* 630 F.2d 340 (5th Cir. 1980); *Pennsylvania Bank & Trust Co. v. U.S.,* 597 F.2d 382 (3d Cir.), cert. denied, 444 US 930 (1979).)

It has even been held that the possession of a general power at death is sufficient to cause inclusion of the property subject to the power in the decedent's estate even though the decedent was not aware of the existence of the power (*Estate of Freeman v. Comm'r,* 67 T.C. 202 (1976)).

LIFE INSURANCE (IRC SEC. 2042)

Types of Contracts Included

Life insurance as used in this section refers to all types of policies. It includes whole life policies, term insurance, group life insurance, limited-payment life, endowment contracts (prior to being paid up), retired lives reserves insurance, and death benefits paid by fraternal societies operating under the lodge system. In addition, the proceeds of certain other types of insurance policies (such as accident insurance and flight insurance available at air terminals) are considered proceeds of life insurance for estate tax purposes. Likewise, proceeds of war-risk insurance and national service life insurance are included in the gross estate as well as insurance paid under double-indemnity clauses by reason of the accidental death of an insured. To be considered an insurance contract, there must be an element of risk that is an actuarially determined one on which the premium cost is based. There must be risk sharing between the insured and the insurer so that the insurer stands to sustain a loss, if the insured does not live for his or her intended life expectancy. Another element inherent in insurance policies is that the original purchaser must have an insurable interest in the policy.

Proceeds of life insurance on the decedent's life are included in the gross estate under this Code section if (1) the decedent possessed any incidents of ownership in the policy, (2) the proceeds are receivable by the estate, or (3) the proceeds are receivable by another for the benefit of the estate.

The term *incidents of ownership* refers to a number of rights of the insured or the insured's estate in the economic benefits of the policy. It is not limited to ownership in a technical sense. Rights that are considered incidents of ownership include the following:

- the power to name or change beneficiaries or beneficial interests
- the right to assign the policy
- the right to revoke an assignment
- the right to surrender or cancel the policy
- the right to pledge the policy for a loan
- the right to obtain a loan against the surrender value of the policy
- the power to change the beneficiary when the policy is owned by a closely-held corporation of which the decedent is a sole or controlling shareholder. (However, to the extent that proceeds are payable to the corporation or a third party for a valid business purpose, such as payment of a corporate debt, the corporate-owned policy on the life of the sole or controlling shareholder will not be attributed to the shareholder and will not be includible in his or her estate.)
- the right to prevent cancellation of an insurance policy owned by the decedent's employer by purchasing the policy for its cash surrender value
- the power to change the beneficial ownership in a policy or its proceeds, or to change the time or manner of enjoyment of the policy or its proceeds should the policy of life insurance on the insured's life be owned by a trust
- the reservation of rights to deal with the policy even if the policy is physically transferred to another
- the power to require the nominal owner of the policy to exercise an incident of ownership, thereby having control over the actions of the owner of record
- the right to a reversionary interest worth more than 5 percent of the value of the insurance policy immediately before the insured's death. (In other words, there must be more than a 5 percent chance based on the value of the policy immediately before the death of the insured that the right or rights will return to him or her.)

If the insured possesses any of the above rights, the full proceeds of life insurance will be included in his or her gross estate even if the insured cannot exercise these rights without the consent of some other person. Inclusion in the estate will occur, regardless of the decedent's ability to exercise the right at death. For example, the decedent might have been in flight or incompetent at the time of death. If the insured retains rights of ownership while acting in a fiduciary capacity, the policy proceeds will be included in the estate if he or she can exercise any of the rights of incidents of ownership for his or her personal benefit.

Decedent as Trustee

In general, if the decedent has no beneficial interest in the insurance policies while acting as a trustee, he or she is not considered to have powers equivalent to a testamentary disposition that would bring the proceeds of life insurance into the estate. There is at least one court case that has rejected this differentiation and has included proceeds in the decedent's estate if a mere incident of ownership was possessed, regardless of the manner in which the decedent acquired it and the capacity in which he or she possessed it (as trustee). In this case, the decedent-insured was the owner and beneficiary of

10.17

life insurance policies as sole trustee of three trusts created by his brother. As trustee, he had the power to change the time and manner of enjoyment of the policies and proceeds by his power to withdraw dividends, obtain loans, and convert the policies from whole life insurance to endowment life insurance (*Rose v. U.S.*, 511 F.2d 259 (5th Cir. 1975)).

In another situation the IRS has ruled that proceeds were includible in a decedent-insured's gross estate because he was the trustee of his wife's residuary trust for the benefit of their children. Powers that he possessed as trustee included the right to elect optional modes of settlement as well as the right to make an assignment of the policy or pledge it as collateral.

In another case decided in the same circuit as the case above, insurance proceeds were included in the estate of the decedent-insured who transferred the policy to a trust created by his wife. He was named as cotrustee and had the power to elect limited settlement options in a fiduciary capacity at his death. He was prohibited by the trust instrument from exercising incidents of ownership over the policy. His wife, not he, retained the right to amend or revoke the trust as well as to remove the fiduciary. The mere right to exercise these limited incidents of ownership at his death caused the policy proceeds to be included in his estate (*Terriberry v. U.S.*, 517 F.2d 286 (5th Cir. 1975); Cert. denied 424 U.S. 977 (1976).) See also Rev. Rul. 76-261, 1976-2 C.B. 276.

Of course, there have been other cases in which the decedent possessed similar rights that have reached a contrary result. Without question, a financial services professional should make a client aware that any meaningful rights in the policy held by the decedent may cause the entire proceeds to be includible in the decedent's gross estate. It is irrelevant how the decedent obtained these ownership attributes or whether exercise of these rights or powers would directly or indirectly benefit him or her. The distinguishing factor that will cause inclusion in the decedent's estate is whether the right was possessed at death, and not whether the decedent had the capacity or ability to exercise it.

Proceeds Payable to or Used for the Benefit of the Estate

Full proceeds of life insurance will also be included in the decedent's estate if they are "payable for the benefit of the estate." This phrase is operative if the life insurance is receivable by the estate, the executor, or any other person who has the power to act on behalf of the estate. It is immaterial that the policy was purchased and owned by someone other than the decedent and that the owner retained complete control over the policy during the insured-decedent's lifetime (IRC Sec. 2046(1)). Similarly, the proceeds will be included in the decedent's estate if they were made payable to a trust that is required to use the proceeds for the payment of death taxes, claims, and administrative expenses of the decedent or the estate. However, if the trustee is merely given a discretionary power to pay these expenses but is not required to use trust assets to satisfy estate obligations, the proceeds will not be included in the estate except to the extent they are actually used to satisfy estate obligations.

If proceeds have been used as collateral security for a loan held by a corporation, they are considered receivable for the benefit of the estate since the corporation is a creditor of the estate. However, the value of the unpaid balance at the date of the decedent's death with interest accrued will be deductible from the gross estate as a debt of the estate.

If the proceeds of life insurance made payable to the decedent's estate are community assets in community-property states, only one-half of the proceeds belongs to the decedent. Therefore only one-half will be included in the decedent's gross estate as proceeds receivable by or for the benefit of the estate (Treas. Reg. Sec. 20.2042-1(b)(2) *Estate of Madsen v. Comm'r*, 690 F.2d 164 (9th Cir. 1982)).

Proceeds Used to Pay Estate Taxes

As noted in the preceding example, insurance proceeds are also includible in the decedent's gross estate as insurance receivable by the personal representative when the proceeds are actually used to pay estate taxes. Also, if proceeds are receivable by an individual beneficiary but the beneficiary is legally obliged to pay taxes, debts, and other expenses of the estate, the proceeds will be includible in the estate to the extent of the beneficiary's obligation to use the proceeds for these purposes. Life insurance proceeds paid directly to a divorced spouse will be includible in the decedent's gross estate, if the decedent was required to name his or her former spouse as beneficiary of the insurance proceeds on his or her life and if the decedent was required to maintain the policies, unless the former spouse died or remarried. However, the above is an arm's-length, bargained-for agreement; as such, a deduction in the amount of the proceeds will be allowed from the gross estate as a debt of the estate.

Group Life Insurance

Group life insurance is treated similarly to other types of life insurance. A group life insurance policy taken out by an employer will be included in the decedent-employee's estate if the decedent had the right to change beneficiaries, terminate the policy, or prevent cancellation of the contract by purchasing the policy. However, if the employee's power to terminate the policy is limited to terminating employment, that is not an incident of ownership sufficient to bring the policy proceeds into the employee's gross estate. Also a right to convert the group policy to an individual policy when the decedent's employment ends is not a right sufficient to bring the policy proceeds into the estate, if this right is transferable and the decedent irrevocably assigns the policy as well as the conversion privilege to another. Thus the decedent had no control over the assignee's right to the proceeds and no incidents of ownership over the policy.

Proceeds from the Estate of Another

The terms *incidents of ownership* and *reversionary interest* do not apply to either a life insurance policy or to the proceeds a decedent received by inheritance through the estate of another person (such as a surviving spouse under a statutory right of election).

Insurance on the Life of Another

Policies of life insurance that the decedent owns on the life of another are not included under this section. However, the value of these policies would be included in the decedent's gross estate as property owned at death under Sec. 2033, the general inclusion section. If the decedent owns a policy on someone else's life, the amount includible in the decedent's estate will be determined as follows:

- If the policy is new, the gross premium paid would be the value.
- If the policy is a paid-up or a single-premium policy, its value is its replacement cost—that is, the single premium that the issuing company would have charged for a comparable contract of equal face value on the life of a person who was the insured's age (at the time the decedent-policyholder died).
- If the policy is a premium-paying whole life policy, the value is found by adding any unearned portion of the last premium to the interpolated terminal reserve.
- If the policy is a term policy, the value is the unused premium.

Relationship to Marital Deduction

If insurance is payable to the spouse or the spouse's estate in a lump sum or in the form of an annuity only if the spouse survives the decedent by up to 6 months, the proceeds will qualify for the marital deduction assuming they have been included in the gross estate. If proceeds are left at the interest option for the life of the surviving spouse, they will qualify for the marital deduction if they are payable to the spouse's estate or to persons to whom the spouse appoints the property at death. If the spouse fails to exercise this power of appointment over the proceeds, they may still qualify for the marital deduction if the proceeds are received by named contingent beneficiaries as a result of the spouse's failure to appoint them. Likewise, if proceeds are to be paid in installments for a definite period of time or if there is a refund feature, the proceeds will qualify if payments following the death of the surviving spouse are payable to those beneficiaries whom the surviving spouse has designated to receive the remaining payments. Proceeds will also qualify for the marital deduction if the spouse receives all the interest for life and proceeds pass to a trust or named beneficiary at the spouse's death under the qualified terminable interest rules. Note that if life insurance is payable to a surviving spouse but is not includible in the decedent's gross estate because he or she retains no incidents of ownership, the marital deduction will not apply.

Transfers of Life Insurance within 3 Years of Death

Any gratuitous transfer of a life insurance policy by an insured made after 1976 and within 3 years of a decedent's death will be includible in the decedent's gross estate as a transfer made within 3 years of death. In these circumstances, however, the proceeds are not reportable on the life insurance schedule as proceeds owned at death, but are reportable on the schedule provided for lifetime transfers. Motivation or intention in making the transfer is irrelevant. Although other completed gifts made within 3 years of death have been excluded from the gross estate by the Economic Recovery Tax Act of 1981 effective for decedents dying on or after January 1, 1982, there is a specific exception for gratuitous transfers by the insured of life insurance policies on the insured's life within 3 years of death. The full value of life insurance proceeds from policies on his or her life transferred by the decedent within 3 years of death will be included in the gross estate (IRC Sec. 2035(d)(2)).

All insurance on the decedent's life whether or not owned by him or her is reported on Schedule D of the federal estate return. If proceeds are received in a lump sum, the value reported is the net proceeds received but if policy proceeds are paid other than in a lump sum, the value listed is the value of proceeds as of the date of the decedent's death. Insurance proceeds on the life of a nonresident, noncitizen (nonresident alien) are not taxable for federal estate tax purposes and need not be reported. Along with the schedule on the estate tax return, the personal representative must file a Form 712 Life Insurance Statement for each life insurance policy listed in the schedule that is included in the gross estate. These statements may be obtained from the insurance company that issued the policy.

Life insurance taken out in a business context will not be discussed in this reading. However, the subject will be reviewed in a later reading that discusses the uses of life insurance in estate planning.

VALUATION OF ASSETS FOR FEDERAL ESTATE AND GIFT TAX PURPOSES

Stephan R. Leimberg* and Ted Kurlowicz

IMPORTANCE OF VALUING ASSETS

One of the most complex and uncertain aspects of the estate planning process is the valuation of property for federal estate and gift tax purposes. Frequently, the taxpayer's representative will value property at one amount; the IRS will attempt a second figure; and, if the issue cannot be settled between the taxpayer and the IRS, the courts will generally settle on some middle ground. Thus value is a variable upon which reasonable minds can and will differ. But value is not determined merely by flipping a coin. There are tools and techniques used to substantiate values. These devices include the use of careful and thorough appraisals by qualified experts, documentation of sales of similar property recently sold, and well-drawn, arm's-length restrictive agreements, such as buy-sell arrangements.

The life insurance professional must be keenly aware of the problems and costs associated with the lack of predeath valuation planning. There are a number of reasons why valuation is of particular importance in the estate planning process.

First, it is impossible to determine potential liquidity needs that an executor may experience unless values are placed on the various assets owned by the client. A hypothetical *probate* of the estate is impossible until values are assigned to various assets. Qualification for stock redemptions under IRC Sec. 303 or installment payments of taxes attributable to business interests under Sec. 6166 depend on the value of the decedent's stock relative to the value of the decedent's other assets. If the appropriate test(s) cannot be met, neither technique for paying estate taxes will be available. For planning purposes, this means that both the value of a client's stock and the worth of other assets must be *guesstimated* with reasonable accuracy.

In addition, many estate owners are thinking about establishing gift programs or have already done so. Because of the income and estate tax advantages still inherent in gifts, gratuitous transfers of property may be meaningful when they are subject to minimal gift tax costs. Furthermore, inter vivos gifts to charity can yield large, immediate income tax deductions. But to

---

*Stephan R. Leimberg, JD, CLU, is professor of estate planning and taxation at The American College.

properly consider the various ramifications and potential advantages involved in a lifetime transfer, a knowledge of valuation is essential.

The third reason that valuing assets is an important technique for the estate planner relates to the funding of buy-sell agreements. For example, if a client is one of several owners of a business, quite often a buy-sell agreement is advisable. The first step in arranging such an agreement is to arrive at a fair market value for the business. Obviously, it is impossible to assure each costockholder (or partner) that beneficiaries will receive an equitable price on death or disability unless the current worth of each person's business interest is ascertained.

WHY THE LOWEST VALUE IS NOT ALWAYS THE BEST

Because both federal estate and gift taxes are based on the value of property interest transferred, at first glance it would make sense to attempt to value property at the lowest reasonable figure. Yet achieving the lowest possible valuation for an asset is not always the most appropriate objective.

One example where a higher valuation might be advantageous is in the formula for a buy-sell agreement. Especially from the point of view of the decedent's survivors, where alternative liquidity funding is impractical, it may be better to set a formula in a buy-sell agreement that will put a higher value on the stock in a closely held business (and therefore provide more cash for the decedent's survivors) than to establish a formula that will provide a lower estate tax value (yielding a lower price for the decedent's business interest).

When closely held stock is valued high relative to other estate assets, the disadvantage of the additional tax payable due to the higher valuation may be more than offset by the advantages of qualifying for a Sec. 303 stock redemption or a Sec. 6166 election to pay federal estate taxes attributable to a business interest in installments. In a number of situations, a corporation often purchases key person life insurance to deliberately increase the relative value of the decedent-shareholder's stock and therefore make it more likely to qualify for one of the above liquidity devices.

DATE ASSETS ARE VALUED

Generally federal estate taxes are based either on the fair market value of the transferred property as of the date the decedent died or, if applicable, on the value of the property 6 months after the date of the decedent's death (alternate valuation date). Once selected for valuation purposes—whether date of death or alternate valuation date—such date applies to all assets in the estate, subject to the exceptions noted below.

If the alternate valuation date is selected and if the property is distributed, sold, exchanged, or otherwise disposed of within 6 months of the decedent's death, it will be valued as of the date of distribution, sale, exchange, or other disposition, not the 6-month date.

Certain types of property diminish in value as time goes on; for example, the present value of an annuity is reduced each time a payment is made. Any such property interest or estate whose value is affected by the mere passing of time is valued as of the date the decedent died.

GENERAL VALUATION RULES

There is very little in the Internal Revenue Code about how to value items for federal estate tax purposes. Although the value of the gross estate is mentioned in the Code, the word *value* is not defined. The estate and gift tax regulations provide that value is meant to be *fair market value*, which is defined as

> the price at which the property would change hands between a willing buyer and a willing seller, neither being under any compulsion to buy or to sell and both having reasonable knowledge of relevant facts.

By this definition, the value that may be placed on property can vary substantially, depending on who is valuing the item and what factors are used. The regulations state that it is not necessary to have either an established market for an item or a willing buyer and seller as mentioned above. In the absence of an actual sale, the value of an asset is based on a hypothetical sale.

Generally the following external factors are examined in deciding the extent to which sales price is indicative of value:

- the frequency of sales. (Courts tend to disregard isolated or sporadic sales.)
- the relationship between the seller and the buyer. (Sales between parents and children or employers and employees are seldom given great weight in the light of their almost definitional unequal bargaining position.)
- options to purchase or sell. (Offers as opposed to options present little evidence of value.)

Once all these value-affecting factors are considered, each factor must be given a relative weight.

SPECIFIC PROBLEMS IN VALUATION

Some items present minimal valuation problems. If there is an established market for identical property, value is basically a question of fact. But evidential proof—and often opinion—is necessary when the following occurs:

- There are different markets for the same property, such as in the case of a property with both wholesale and retail markets.
- The appraisal of worth must be made on the basis of comparison with somewhat similar property. (Which comparable property should be selected? How comparable is it?) In which case what is derived is at best an opinion based on fact.

11.3

- The property in question is unique, such as a patent or copyright, in which case the data must be analyzed (Is the examiner capable of making an adequate analysis?), and an opinion must be formulated as to how much the potential anticipated benefits are worth.

In practice, valuation problems are frequently viewed by the IRS and the courts as problems of negotiation and compromise. An appraiser's object is to derive a fair and sound value that, if litigated, most likely would be sustained in court.

VALUATION OF SPECIFIC PROPERTY

It is beyond the scope of this reading to examine the valuation process for all types of property. However, the valuation of real property as well as stocks of closely held corporations will provide a good example of the essential gift and estate tax valuation process.

Valuing Real Property

Land is unique. Therefore the value of any real property (land or property affixed to land) on a given date may be subject to widely differing opinions. If there is no market for such property, a controlling factor is the greater of (1) the highest price available or (2) the *salvage* value, which is the disposal value of the property at the end of its useful life. When there is a market for real property, the basic factors that affect valuation are

- the size, shape, and location of the property
- the nature and condition of the property, its physical qualities and defects, and the adequacy or inadequacy of its improvements
- the actual and potential use of the property and how the trends of development and economic conditions (such as population growth) affect it
- the suitability of the property for its actual or intended use
- zoning restrictions
- the age, size, and condition of the buildings (degree of deterioration and obsolescence)
- the market value of other properties in the area in which the property is located
- the value of net income received from the property. (Rentals are often capitalized at a rate of between 6 and 12 percent and then adjusted for depreciation; the same principle can be applied to gross rents after adjustment for operating cost.)
- prices at which comparable property in the same area was sold at a time near the applicable valuation date—providing the sale was an arm's-length transaction for the best price available
- the cost to duplicate the property after taking depreciation into account
- the value accepted by state probate courts for purposes of state death taxes, if based on appraisals made by qualified real estate experts
- unusual facts

In the event of a sale of real property within a reasonable period of time after the decedent's death in such a manner as to insure the highest possible price, the amount received will usually be accepted as its value. Unaccepted offers to purchase the property will also be considered. What about a sale at auction? Usually this price will be accepted only if it appears that there was no other method that would have obtained a higher price.

Land does not have to produce income or have an active market to attain substantial value. When land is in or adjacent to a settled community, owners frequently hold such land in anticipation of realizing its true value from future sales. For example, a home at the edge of an expanding shopping center might be worth far more to the shopping center developer than it would be to a potential buyer in the residential market.

Special-Use Valuation for Certain Real Property*

The test of fair market value described above is the *highest and best* price that would be agreed upon between a willing buyer and a willing seller. This has often caused farm or business real estate to be valued at the price at which it might have been valued if it was going to be used for residential or industrial development, rather than the price it is worth according to its current use. An executor (if certain conditions are met) can elect to use a *current-use valuation* approach. That is, the real estate will be valued taking into consideration how it is *currently* being utilized instead of how it *might* be used if placed in its best use.

The special valuation provided by this method cannot be used to reduce a decedent's gross estate by more than $750,000.

Requirements for Special-Use Valuation

The following conditions must be satisfied before current-use valuation will be allowed for estate tax purposes:

- The decedent must have been a U.S. citizen or resident.
- The farm or other closely held business must constitute at least 50 percent of the decedent's gross estate (after certain adjustments for mortgages and liens).
- The real property in question must pass to a *qualified heir* (essentially, a lineal descendant of the decedent's grandfather).
- Either the decedent or a family member must have owned the real property—and used it as a farm or in a closely held business—for at least 5 out of the 8 years immediately prior to the date the decedent died.
- Either the decedent or a member of the decedent's family must have materially participated in the operation of the farm or business for at least 5 out of the 8 years immediately prior to the decedent's death.

---

*IRC Sec. 2032A

11.5

A special tax lien is placed on all real property valued according to current use. The lien remains on the property until the potential liability to pay a recapture tax ceases, and the heirs remain personally liable to pay that tax.

Furthermore, a written agreement must be filed with the estate tax return. It must be signed by anyone who has an interest in the real property qualifying for special valuation. Each of these individuals must consent to the imposition of the recapture tax described below.

Special-Use Methods Available

There are a number of methods allowed for valuing real estate of closely held businesses or farms. An example of one way the farm method might work can be illustrated in the following example:

> *Example:* Farmer Jones owns 300 acres of farmland in Wildwood. Nearby farmland of about the same acreage produces an average annual gross rental of $20,000. Average annual state and local real estate taxes are $3,000. Assume the interest rate for loans from the Federal Land Bank is 9 percent.
>
> The average annual computations are made on the basis of the 5 most recent calendar years before the farmer's death.
>
> Under the *farm-method* formula, the farmer's land would be computed as follows:

$$(\$20,000 - \$3,000) \div .09 = \$188,888.88$$

This formula for valuing farmland would not be used if there is no comparable land from which the average rentals can be determined. An executor might elect to value the farmland in the same manner that closely held business real property would be valued (through a capitalization method, comparable sales prices, or any other factor that fairly values the farm or other closely held business).

Recapture of the Special-Use Tax Benefit

If the property is disposed of to nonfamily members within 10 years after the death of the decedent, there will be an additional estate tax or recaptured tax imposed on the qualified heir. If the heir or a member of the heir's family fails to participate materially in the business operation for 3 or more years during an 8-year period ending within 10 years after the decedent's death, it will be treated as a cessation of the qualified use, causing recapture.

Recapture of the difference in tax between the current-use and highest- and-best-use methods of valuation occurs when the real estate is sold, disposed of, or no longer used for the same qualified use within the 10-year period. Also the eligible qualified heir must be engaged in the active management of the farm or business during the recapture period. If during this period the heir is under age 21, disabled, a full-time student, or the surviving spouse, a fiduciary may qualify in providing active management for the heir.

There is a 2-year grace period following the decedent's death before the heir must commence the qualified use without risking recapture. If recapture occurs and results in additional estate taxes, the real estate will receive a new basis stepped up to what the basis would have been if special-use valuation had not been elected. Otherwise, the basis upon a subsequent sale of the property will be the current-use valuation. However, the increased basis obtained if recapture occurs will not include retroactive changes in depreciation, other deductions, or credits reflecting the increased basis.

Exceptions to the recapture rules are loss of the property through involuntary conversion or exchange of the real estate in a like-kind exchange. No recapture will be triggered generally under these circumstances. There are also special rules for woodlands and a limited right of judicial review.

Valuation of Household and Personal Effects

The general rule for valuing household property and personal effects, such as watches, rings, and so forth, can be called the *willing buyer-willing seller rule*. A room-by-room itemization is typical, especially when household goods include articles of artistic or intrinsic value, such as jewelry, furs, silverware, paintings, engravings, antiques, books, statuary, oriental rugs, and coin or stamp collections.

In other than community-property states, *household goods* and the like personally acquired by and used by husband and wife during marriage are generally presumed to be the property of the husband. Therefore, in the absence of sufficient evidence to rebut this presumption, household goods and personal effects would be includible in the husband's estate.

Valuation of Listed Stocks

Where a stock has an established market and quotations are available to value the stock as of the date in question, the fair market value (FMV) per share on the applicable valuation date governs for both gift and estate tax purposes.

The FMV is based on selling prices when there is a market for the stock or bond. This would be the mean between the highest and lowest quoted selling price on the valuation date. If there were no sales on the valuation date, but there were sales on dates within a reasonable period both before and after the valuation date, the FMV is determined by taking a weighted average of the means between the highest and lowest sales on the nearest date before and the nearest date after the valuation. The average is then weighted inversely by the respective number of trading days between the selling date and the valuation date.

When a large block of stock cannot be marketed in an orderly manner, the block might depress the market because it cannot be converted to cash as readily as could a few shares. Therefore selling prices and bid-and-asked prices may not reflect fair market value. Sometimes it may be necessary to value this type of stock as if it was closely held and not actively traded. If this can be established, a reasonable modification of the normal basis for determining FMV can be made. In some cases a *blockage discount* is determined by the effect that block would have had on the market if it was sold over a reasonable period of time and in a prudent manner. A similar situation occurs when sales at or near the date of death are either few or of a sporadic nature, and may not indicate a fair market value.

The converse of the blockage situation above is when the block of stock to be valued represents a controlling interest (either actual or effective) in a going business. Here, the price of normally traded shares may have little relation to the true value of the controlling lot. The large block can have the effect of increasing value because of its element of control.

Valuation of Corporate Bonds

Valuation of bonds is similar to that of listed common stock. The means of the selling prices on or near the applicable valuation date, or if there were no sales, the means of bona fide asked prices weighted inversely to the number of trading days from the valuation date, will determine the fair market value of the bonds.

In the absence of sales or bid-and-asked prices, the value must be determined by

- ascertaining the soundness of the security
- comparing the interest on the bond in question to yields on similar bonds
- examining the date of maturity
- comparing prices for listed bonds of corporations engaged in similar types of business
- checking the extent to which the bond is secured
- weighing all other relevant factors, including the opinion of experts, the goodwill of the business, the industry's economic outlook, and the company's position in the industry as well as its management

Valuation of U.S. Government Bonds

Series E (EE) bonds are valued at their redemption price (market value) as of the date of death since they are neither negotiable nor transferable, and the only definitely ascertainable value is the amount at which the Treasury will redeem them.

Certain U.S. Treasury bonds (so-called flower bonds) owned by a decedent at the date of death and forming part of the gross estate may be redeemed at par value if used to pay federal estate taxes. These bonds are valued at the higher of the market price or par value.

Even if such bonds are not used to pay estate taxes, the courts have often held that when the bonds could be used for the payment of estate taxes, they will be valued at the higher of market or par value. When the bonds could not be applied to pay the estate tax, their value is market (the mean quoted selling price).

Valuation of Life Insurance

Proceeds of life insurance on the life of the decedent receivable by or for the benefit of the decedent's estate will be taxed in the insured-decedent's estate. In addition, when the decedent held incidents of ownership, such ownership will invoke taxation. The amount includible is the amount receivable by the beneficiary. This includes dividends and premium refunds. In determining how much is includible, no distinction is made between an ordinary life policy, a term policy, group insurance, or an accidental death benefit.

If a settlement option is elected, the amount that would have been payable as a lump sum is the amount includible. If the policy did not provide for a lump-sum payment, the amount includible is the commuted amount used by the insurance company to compute the settlement option payments.

The value of an unmatured policy owned by a decedent on the life of another is included in the policyowner's gross estate (when the policyowner predeceases the insured) according to the following:

- If a new policy is involved, the gross premium paid would be the value.
- If the policy is a paid-up or a single-premium policy, its value is its replacement cost—that is, the single premium that company would have charged for a comparable contract of equal face value on the life of a person who was the insured's age (at the time the decedent-policyholder died).
- If the policy is a premium-paying whole life policy, the value is found by adding any unearned portion of the last premium to the interpolated terminal reserve.
- If the policy is a term policy, the value is the unused premium.

Valuation of Stock of Closely Held Corporations

The valuation of closely held corporate stock is often one of the most difficult and time-consuming problems faced by the executor of a decedent's estate. By definition, closely held stock is incapable of valuation solely by recourse to an established market (that is, closely held stock is seldom traded). In fact, the criteria used to define closely held stock include (1) a limited number of stockholders, (2) restrictions imposed upon a shareholder's ability to transfer the stock, (3) the absence of an exchange listing or regular quotation in the over-the-counter market, and (4) an irregular and limited history of sales or exchanges.

There is no formula provided by the Internal Revenue Code or the regulations that will be applicable to every closely held stock valuation

11.9

situation. However, there are guidelines that should be considered in every valuation case. The key IRS ruling on point, Rev. Rul. 59-60, suggests that the following factors be considered:

- the nature of the business and the entire history of the enterprise
- the economic outlook in general as well as the condition and outlook of the specific industry
- the book value of the stock and the financial condition of the business. (The Tax Court considers this factor in almost every case.)
- the company's earning capacity. (For many businesses—especially those that do depend heavily on capital to produce profits—this will be the most important valuation factor.)
- the company's dividend-paying capacity
- the existence of *goodwill*. Goodwill can be defined as the economic advantage or benefit that is acquired by a business *beyond* the mere value of the capital invested in it, because of the patronage it receives from constant or habitual customers, its local position, its reputation for skill or punctuality, other accidental circumstances or necessities, or public partialities or prejudices. In short, goodwill is a broad term implying that a company has a purchase value exceeding the worth of its tangible assets. (It is important to note that a business may have goodwill value even if no amount for goodwill is shown on its accounting statements.)
- stock sales and size of the block of stock to be valued
- fair market value of stock of comparable corporations engaged in the same or similar type of business where the stock is actively traded in an established market

Rev. Rul. 59-60 reaffirms that no fixed formula of valuation can be devised that is applicable to all situations and that, ultimately, the fair market value of closely held stock must be determined on an individual basis.

When faced with a gift or estate tax valuation question, courts sift through innumerable elements—besides the eight basic factors mentioned in Rev. Rul. 59-60. Some of the valuation factors used by the courts (but given varying weight depending on the circumstances) are

- the values accepted by the IRS when other estates held the same stock
- the price for the stock in the decedent's will
- the values as determined by expert witnesses
- the relationships between prices, earnings, and book values
- the degree of control of the business represented by the block of stock to be valued
- the value of the services of the key individual who has died

Valuation Methods Used by the IRS

Although the Internal Revenue Service incorporates many factors into most valuations of closely held businesses, the two methods consistently used as starting points are (1) adjusted book value and (2) capitalization of adjusted earnings.

Adjusted Book Value. Book value (stated assets less liabilities divided by the number of outstanding shares) is particularly applicable in the following instances:

- when the business in question is primarily an asset-holding company, such as an investment company
- when the company is in the real estate development business and assets, rather than earnings, are the key to valuation
- when the company is a one-person corporation, which is generally worth only its liquidation value
- if the corporation is being liquidated at the valuation date or it is likely that it will be liquidated in the near future. (It is important also to consider the impact of sacrifice sales and capital-gains taxation, since the true value of a liquidating corporation is the amount that is actually available to the shareholders after the liquidation.)
- when the industry is highly competitive but the business is only marginally profitable. (Adjusted book value is particularly useful in these cases, because past earnings are probably an unreliable tool in the measurement of potential future profits.)

The adjusted-book-value method involves adjusting the asset components of a business to an approximate fair market value for each such component. An adjustment is necessary, since most accounting statements carry assets at some figure other than fair market value. Adjustments are necessary to reflect the difference between true market value and book figures when

- assets are valued at cost. (Most accounting statements carry land, for example, on the balance sheet of a company at an amount far less than what it is worth on the open market. The result is a book value bearing little or no relationship to present worth.)
- assets have been depreciated at a rate in excess of their true decline in value. (For instance, equipment may have been purchased for $500,000 and depreciated to $200,000. Although it is carried on the firm's books at $200,000, the asset may really be worth a lot more or a lot less than its cost, or the $200,000 used on the balance sheet.)
- mention of items such as potential future lawsuits or unfavorable long-term leases has been omitted or not clearly noted in the footnotes or body of the firm's balance sheets
- assets have been completely written off even though they possess substantial value, resulting in a book value far below reality
- assets such as franchises and goodwill are shown on accounting statements at nominal cost or not shown at all
- there are difficulties in collecting accounts receivable
- a firm's inventory includes items that have become obsolete or are not readily marketable

There are still other factors that indicate the need for adjustment of pure book value. For instance, a downward adjustment from pure book value is indicated when the business's liquidity position is poor (the business has low current assets relative to its current liabilities); the firm is experiencing a shortage of adequate working capital; or it is burdened with sizable long-term debt. If large selling expenses and capital-gains taxes are likely in the event of liquidation, downward adjustments from book value are indicated.

Another factor that is difficult to ascertain but quite important is the need, if any, to adjust book value because of retained earnings. The book value of a business might appear to be high because of the retention of earnings over a number of years. This might be deceptive, since the company's current earnings may be low and the outlook for increased earnings in the future may be poor. Since valuation is an attempt to ascertain what a hypothetical *willing buyer* would pay, such a situation would indicate the need to reduce book value.

After these adjustments to book value are made, the adjusted book value is then divided by the number of shares outstanding to determine the per-share value of the stock.

Capitalization of Adjusted Earnings. The second of the two basic starting-point methods is the capitalization-of-adjusted-earnings approach. Here the IRS multiplies adjusted earnings by a factor appropriate for the specific industry at the predetermined valuation date. The capitalization rate will vary inversely with the degree of risk and the rate of return, as illustrated in table 11-1.

The investment return on capital invested in a well-established business with minimal risk is relatively low. Another way of stating this same principle is that it will take a long time to recover the capital invested in such a business. However, the low-risk factor coupled with a yield in excess of the amount possible from alternative investments encourages potential buyers to offer relatively high prices. Conversely, an individual investing in a business with a higher risk factor would demand a higher rate of return, would want to receive capital back more quickly, and therefore would be willing to pay less for the business. A comparison of two companies might be helpful in illustrating this point. Assume that both companies earn $100,000 a year after taxes.

> *Company A:* The Tools Company is relatively small and is in a highly competitive industry. It is likely that a buyer would desire a return of 20 percent per year on his or her money (in other words, for this level of risk, the buyer wants to recover capital fairly quickly) to warrant the risk of purchasing this company. So the less paid for the business, the faster the recovery of capital. A buyer who thought he or she could receive 20 percent per year on his or her money would be willing to pay no more than, for example, five times the annual aftertax earnings: $500,000 ($100,000 x 5). This is essentially the procedure the IRS uses to value the firm; it multiplies aftertax earnings by an appropriate capitalization rate.

TABLE 11-1

Risk	Categories	Rate of Return	Capital-ization Rate
Low to medium	Old, established businesses with large capital assets and established goodwill (Few businesses will fit into this category.)	8%	12
Medium to high	Established businesses of competitive character needing highly competitive management (such as factories manufacturing products under patents and trademarks)	10% to 15%	7 to 10
High	Businesses requiring skill in management, but no special or rare type of knowledge; earnings constantly present under highly competitive conditions; large capital not required to enter field	18% and above	6
High	Small businesses—highly competitive—requiring small capital	18% and above	5
High	Businesses depending on special skills of one person or a small group of individuals; highly competitive; small capital required; high mortality	18% and above	2 to 4
High	Personal businesses involving minute amount of capital and depending on the skill of one person	18% and above	1 to 2

Company B: Assume the Techniques Company is an older corporation with a proven record of profits; it has a strong management team, high profit potential, and a substantial average annual earnings growth rate. The same investor might be willing to settle for a much lower rate of return given this level of risk. Another way of stating this same point is that an investor would value the business at a higher amount because of its safety-of-principal factor—say, a total of $800,000 (8 years' aftertax earnings).

It is important to note that table 11-1 is only a guideline. The return a potential buyer would demand will vary from time to time depending on (1) the specified level of risk and (2) the earning rates of comparable alternative investments. There are no *correct* capitalization rates; different rates are used at different times and under different circumstances by the IRS and the courts.

11.13

Another factor that must be considered even before applying the capitalization rate to the aftertax earnings is that the earnings themselves must be adjusted in many cases. A realistic appraisal of the earning power of a company can sometimes be obtained only by first adjusting earnings by

- adding back bonuses paid to stockholders or their families
- adding back salaries that were excessive, or reducing earnings when salaries paid were inordinately low
- adding back excessive rents paid to stockholders, or subtracting nominal and unrealistically low rents paid to stockholders
- eliminating nonrecurring income items
- adjusting for excess depreciation
- adjusting earnings to take into consideration nonrecurring expenses, a major change in accounting procedures, widely fluctuating or cyclical profits, abnormally inflated or deflated earnings, or strong upward to downward earning trends. (Sometimes the IRS will average earnings over a 3- to 5-year period and then weight the average so that an upward earnings trend is given greater weight.)

The total capitalization result is then divided by the number of shares outstanding to ascertain the per-share value.

The reasonableness of the final result obtained by capitalization can be checked by a method once officially used (and still unofficially used) by many IRS agents. This is known as the A.R.M. (Appeals and Review Memorandum) 34 method. Basically under A.R.M. 34 a five-step process is used:

- Figure a reasonable rate of return on the tangible assets of the business.
- Subtract that return from the annual earnings figure used. The difference is the portion of earnings generated by intangibles.
- Capitalize profits generated by those intangibles to determine their value.
- Add the results of computation three to the net worth of tangibles. The total should be the value of the corporation.
- Divide the total value of the corporation by the number of shares outstanding. This will result in the per-share value of the corporation.

Effect of Minority or Controlling Interest

When the shares being valued represent a minority interest in a business, a reduction in value is often allowed. This minority-interest discount arises because, by definition, minority shares have no power to force dividends, compel liquidation, or control corporate policy. This makes the stock less appealing and narrows the potential market to the remaining (and usually controlling) shareholders. It therefore reduces the price at which each share might be purchased. Discounts of from 10 to 30 percent are often allowed.

The opposite result occurs when the shares in question represent a controlling interest. In this case the IRS will generally seek to substantiate a higher value. In other words, the size of the block of stock itself is a relevant factor. Although it is true that a minority interest in an unlisted corporation's stock is more difficult to sell than a similar block of listed stock, by the same token the controlling interest of a corporation represents an added element of value. It therefore justifies a higher valuation for a specific block of stock. More than 50 percent of the voting shares constitutes a controlling interest, while less than 50 percent constitutes a minority interest. Note that if a father leaves two shares to his son who already has 49 shares (assume only 100 shares are outstanding), the two shares represent in value more than a mere 1/50 of the value of the outstanding stock. Together with the interest that the son already owns, those two shares represent control of the corporation.

Use of Restrictive Agreements

Although a closely held corporation has a limited market by definition, most shareholders restrict the marketability of coshareholders' stock even further through *purchase options* or mandatory buy-sell agreements. If the terms of such an agreement definitely fix the value of the shares in question, it is not necessary to examine either book value or earnings. The price fixed in the restrictive agreement will generally serve as the fair market value of the shares if the agreement was formed by unrelated parties. However, to peg the value of the stock for federal estate tax purposes, three requirements must be met:

- The agreement as to per-share value must be made at arm's-length and must have been fair and adequate at the time the agreement was executed.
- The agreement must be binding during the lifetime of the stockholder; that is, he or she must be obligated to offer the stock to the corporation or other shareholders (a *first-offer commitment*) at the specified offer price before offering it to an outsider, if the stockholder wishes to dispose of the stock during lifetime.
- The agreement must be binding at death—the stockholder's executor must be legally obligated to sell the shares to the corporation at the price fixed by the agreement. Furthermore, the price stated in the agreement must either be fixed (that is, fixed-dollar price or book value on the repurchase date) or determinable according to a preset formula.

When the stock is family held, the rules of Sec. 2036(c) apply. The IRS generally would scrutinize the restrictions to determine whether the agreement is a bona fide arm's-length arrangement, rather than a device to pass the decedent's shares for less than an adequate consideration to the natural objects of the decedent's bounty. The rules of Sec. 2036(c) require that the purchase price be fair at the time of death to peg the estate tax value of the stock to the price set in the restrictive agreement if family members are involved.

The four types of restrictive agreements that have been successful in pegging the value of stock for federal estate tax purposes are

- reciprocal options among stockholders, during life and death. Under an option a specified person is given the right to purchase the stock at a designated price for a fixed period of time. Here, the buyer controls the event.

- options granted to one stockholder only (but the price must be fair and arrived at by arm's-length bargaining). Intrafamily arrangements in this category will be suspect.
- options granted to the corporation
- mandatory buy-sell (cross-purchase and stock-redemption) agreements under which the estate of a deceased stockholder must sell and the corporation (or other stockholders) must buy at a predetermined price or according to a predetermined formula. The obligation to sell at the agreed-upon price, however, must be binding not only upon the decedent's executor at the decedent's death but also upon the stockholder himself or herself during lifetime. The price at death will not control, if a shareholder is free during lifetime to realize a higher price. Restrictions effective during the decedent's lifetime only—but not at death—are equally ineffective. In a mandatory buy-sell agreement, neither party controls the event.

A mere right of first refusal, which requires that any shares offered for sale must first be offered to the corporation (or other shareholders) at the proposed transfer price, does not conclusively peg the value of the stock. However, a first-offer commitment may have the effect of depressing the value of the stock.

Restrictions on the transfer of closely held shares are never conclusive regarding value for gift tax purposes but are a factor to be considered in arriving at valuation.

Setting a Price in a Restrictive Agreement

In general, the first decision that must be made in establishing a buy-sell agreement is the establishment of a price. The problem is difficult and perplexing because so many factors (such as the time of death, the condition of the business on the date of the buy-out, and the influence of economic conditions) pose a multitude of variables that are not only unknown and unknowable but also interdependent. In spite of these problems, it is necessary to arrive at a price-of-valuation formula. Obviously there is no *right* method and every method has its problems.

There are essentially four methods that business individuals use as a price-setting mechanism in a buy-sell agreement. These price-setting mechanisms include

- fixed price
- formula-determined price
- appraisal-determined price
- combination of the above mechanisms

Fixed Price. Setting a price and stating it in the agreement has the advantage of being simple and clear. If Steve, Robert, and Lee are all parties to the agreement, each person knows exactly what his family would receive upon his death as well as what he would receive in the event of disability. For example, if they use a fixed price of $900,000 and each individual owns a one-third interest, each person's interest would be worth one-third of $900,000, or $300,000.

There are drawbacks to a fixed-price mechanism. The main disadvantage is that the fixed price is not likely to reflect accurately the current value of the business at the time an owner becomes disabled or dies. Generally the business is worth considerably more or considerably less than the fixed price set in the agreement. The mere passage of time and the fortunes of business, together with the effects of inflation, may substantially increase the value of the business or depress values far below what they were when the price was set. Although a fixed price may be fair (neither party knows in advance who will survive and who will predecease), it is at best a gamble because of the large number of uncertainties associated with the fixed-price mechanism.

Can the drawback of the fixed-price mechanism be alleviated by a requirement that the parties revalue the business each year and that the last value control? In theory, the solution seems sound. However, as a practical matter, the parties to a buy-sell agreement seldom actually make their intended annual revaluation. If the value of the business increases substantially from the time the fixed price is set, the survivors of the deceased business owner will be receiving an amount that does not accurately reflect the true value of the business. Likewise, if one of the business owners becomes ill, he or she will want to readjust the price upward to provide more cash for the family in return for the business owner's business interest. But the interest of the healthy business owners will be diametrically opposed to that of the sick colleague. The result is that the equal bargaining position contemplated by the agreement no longer exists.

It may make sense to set a fixed price (using one or more of the valuation methods discussed above that are used by the IRS and the courts) and then provide in the contract for yearly revaluations plus an additional provision that, if no revaluation has been made within X months of the date of death, then the price shall be the average of the valuations rendered by two qualified appraisers (or some similar technique).

Formula Mechanism. The main disadvantage of a fixed-price mechanism for valuing a business interest is definitional (that is, the price is fixed by agreement while the value of the business interest may fluctuate widely). What is indicated is a pricing mechanism based on a formula. The formula itself may take a number of factors into consideration. For example, the formula may be an adaptation of an A.R.M. 34 or some other method that considers various, easily ascertained, objective factors.

The most common formula approach uses some type of capitalization-of-earnings method. Often the parties will take other value-affecting factors into consideration by the multiple used. For example, one business may be valued at 10 times average earnings for the past 5 years, while another might be valued at three times average earnings for the past 8 years. Obviously the greater the risk and the lower the stability of a business, the lower the earnings multiple will be. Industry studies by statistical analysis companies can be used to discover the multiple for any given type of industry. Adjustments for specific facts or abnormalities with regard to a particular business may have to be made. Many of these adjustments are discussed above. The multiple itself may vary from time to time as economic conditions change. In some cases, the formula gives more weight to the earnings of those years immediately preceding the decedent-business owner's death than to the earnings of prior years.

Appraisal. Many authorities feel that the fairest means of ascertaining the value of a business is by stating, in the buy-sell agreement, that two appraisers should be employed. One appraiser would be hired by the surviving shareholders, while the other would represent the decedent's interest. The two appraisers would come to an agreement on an appropriate valuation, or in the absence of agreement, a third appraiser would be appointed by the first two to make a final binding determination of value.

The parties can give the appraisers carte blanche in their appraisal process, or they can instruct them to take into consideration certain factors and ignore others. For example, the buy-sell agreement might specify that the appraisers are to ignore goodwill or value it in a certain way.

Combination Mechanism. A fixed-price mechanism coupled with a reappraisal or a formula method, which begins with a fixed price as a floor and enhances that amount if earnings or book values have reached a certain level, are other ways to solve the difficult and perplexing problem of providing variable but realistic prices for a business owner's interest.

Valuation of Partial Nonconcurrent Property Interests

It is often necessary to value partial interests in property, such as annuities, term interests, and life estates, since these property rights are often transferred to heirs and will become subject to either estate or gift taxes. In addition, certain charitable transfer techniques, such as charitable remainder and lead trusts, must be valued to determine the estate, gift, and/or income tax deductions. Congress recently revamped the tax valuation methodology for such partial interests and has added additional complexity to the process in an effort to stamp out perceived abuses in the old methods.

Sec. 7520 of the Internal Revenue Code now mandates that the current mortality rates and the current interest rate (revised monthly) must be used to determine the actuarial present value of annuity, term, remainder, and life interests in property. The new mortality rates are based on 1980 census data and gender-neutral tables.[1] The interest rate used to discount the partial interests to present value is 120 percent of the applicable federal midterm rate (AFMR) for the month in which the valuation is made.[2] The actual factor used to determine the value of a partial nonconcurrent interest involves several calculations and will vary month-to-month according to changes in the AFMR.

The nature of the calculation for determining such valuations causes the need for a significant degree of mathematic acumen and creates a high possibility for error. As a result, most practitioners will rely on software for making such calculations.[3] An additional problem with using these new rules is the monthly variation in the interest rate. The tax value of such partial interests must be determined at a specific point in time. For example, gift tax calculations must be made at the time of the transfer. Thus the gift tax imposed on the inter vivos transfer of a partial nonconcurrent interest is based on the value of the interest using the applicable rate for the month in which a completed transfer is made. The same rule holds true when determining the income or gift tax deduction for a charitable remainder or lead interest donation. The applicable rate for the month in which the decedent dies is used to value the testamentary transfer of such partial interests. Therefore the tax benefits or detriments of the transfer of remainder, term, annuity, or life interests in property will depend on the month of the transfer.

Example: Suppose Donor (D) creates a charitable remainder trust by placing $1 million of marketable securities in the trust. D gifts the current interest to her son (S), aged 50, for his life with the remainder interest to The American College. The current interest pays 10.6 percent of the value of the trust assets (actually, this is a charitable remainder unitrust, which is discussed in reading 17). The trust is executed and irrevocably funded in May 1990 when the applicable Sec. 7520 rate is 10.6 percent. The tax valuations are as follows:

Remainder factor	.12173
Income and gift tax deduction	$121,730
Life interest factor at age 50	.87827
Taxable amount of gift to S	$878,270

NOTES

1. The actual tables are presented in the *Actuarial Tables Alpha* and *Actuarial Tables Beta* available by writing the Superintendent of Documents, United States Government Printing Office, Washington, DC 20404.

2. The applicable federal rates are published monthly in the *Internal Revenue Bulletin* and are reprinted in numerous loose-leaf services on tax and financial planning. The actual rate used for Sec. 7520 purposes is 120 percent of the AFMR rounded to the nearest two-tenths of 1 percent. For example, 10.54 percent is 10.6 percent for the purposes of valuing remainder, term, annuity, or life interests.

3. For a complete discussion of the calculation methodology and its planning implications, see Robert J. Doyle and Stephan R. Leimberg, "New IRS Valuation Rules: Impact on the Tools and Techniques of Estate and Financial Planning," *TAXES—The Tax Magazine*, May 1990.

HOW STATE DEATH TAXES AFFECT OVERALL ESTATE PLANNING*

Staff of J. K. Lasser Tax Institute

No estate planning can be adequate without careful consideration of the effect of state death taxes on the estate. This reading provides material necessary for a preliminary survey of state death tax liability. These taxes may be quite high when applied to the shares of certain beneficiaries. Recent changes in state laws indicate that various states are seeking increased revenues and speedier collections. Many states have changed from the inheritance type of tax on beneficiaries to the estate type of tax on estates of decedents—presumably for the additional revenue the latter type may yield. Although the impact of death taxes on the immediate family—especially the surviving spouse—has been eased in some cases, states have steadily increased the tax rates for other heirs and relatives. The need for state death tax planning is especially great if there is any chance that property will pass to persons other than the surviving spouse.

Another serious problem arises when a decedent owns a home or other property in more than one state, and each state claims the decedent as a resident and enforces its right to tax the estate. The District of Columbia, Puerto Rico, and every state impose estate or inheritance taxes.

With so many variables affecting tax liability, the only insurance against unnecessary tax erosion is informed counsel. Most important to counsel is a knowledge of the nature, location, past as well as future disposition of all property involved, and the client's domiciliary status. Because death taxes differ from state to state, it is particularly important both to know the differences and to understand how each state's laws will apply to a client who either moves from one state to another or owns property in several states.

It has long been recognized that states have authority to tax the transfer of property at death.[1] But with planning, there is no reason why state statutes should undermine the intent of the decedent.

As often happens, a client's surviving relatives, although they may be quite close to him or her personally, are classified as distant relatives by the states. Their personal exemptions are smaller and their tax rates higher than those paid on the shares of less distant relatives. The resulting discrimination against these relatives in the matter of exemptions and rate of taxation has been

---

*Reprinted with permission from J. K. Lasser's *Estate Tax Techniques*, published by Matthew Bender & Company.

upheld as constitutional by the Supreme Court.[2] Precautions taken to avoid such discrimination must be initiated as part of an overall estate plan.

Another hazard to an estate is the taxation of powers of appointment. The death tax laws of most states permit the taxing of powers of appointment. The Supreme Court has held that such powers are taxable to a resident even if they were created by a nonresident-donor, and the powers are over intangible personal property located in the nonresident's state of domicile.[3]

There are other important sources of vulnerability or advantage to an estate. They stem from the treatment in the various state death tax laws of such matters as dower, curtesy, and homestead; jointly owned property; community property; insurance; contingent estates and future interests; deductions; the liabilities of nonresident-decedents; and the property subject to tax.

STATE DEATH TAX

Important aspects of state death tax laws are described below as follows:

Type of Tax

There are three types of death tax.

- *State Inheritance Tax*—a tax on the right of a beneficiary to succeed to the ownership of property from the estate of the deceased. The tax is based on the value of the share received by each beneficiary. It is generally taxed at graduated rates, depending on the value of the taxable gift and the beneficiary's relationship to the decedent. Many states impose an inheritance tax, although the trend is toward an estate type tax or a credit estate tax.
- *State Estate Tax*—a tax imposed on the right of the deceased to leave property to his or her heirs. It is similar in form to the federal estate tax.
- *Credit Estate Tax*—a tax imposed by most states either as the sole death tax, or in addition to an inheritance or an estate tax. Its purpose is to bring the amount of the total tax up to the amount of state death tax credit allowed under federal law against the federal estate tax. A table of the maximum allowable federal credit follows.

Beneficiary Classes and Their Exemptions

In most states, persons entitled to share in the estate are divided into classes of beneficiaries. The largest exemptions and the lowest rates are given to the surviving spouse and closest relatives of the deceased. The first class of beneficiaries is usually called *Class A* or *Class 1* and is subject to the least tax. This class will sometimes include only the widow or widower but may also include children, parents, and grandchildren of the deceased. In some states, different relatives placed in the same class may be given larger or smaller exemptions within the class. But all members of a class are subject, nevertheless, to the same tax rate on their shares.

TABLE 12-1
Credit for State Death Taxes*

Adjusted taxable estate equal to or more than— (1)	Adjusted taxable estate less than— (2)	Credit on amount in column (1) (3)	Rate of credit on excess over amount in column (1) (4) (Percent)
0	$ 40,000	0	None
$ 40,000	90,000	0	0.8
90,000	140,000	$ 400	1.6
140,000	240,000	1,200	2.4
240,000	440,000	3,600	3.2
440,000	640,000	10,000	4.0
640,000	840,000	18,000	4.8
840,000	1,040,000	27,600	5.6
1,040,000	1,540,000	38,800	6.4
1,540,000	2,040,000	70,800	7.2
2,040,000	2,540,000	106,800	8.0
2,540,000	3,040,000	146,800	8.8
3,040,000	3,540,000	190,800	9.6
3,540,000	4,040,000	238,800	10.4
4,040,000	5,040,000	290,800	11.2
5,040,000	6,040,000	402,800	12.0
6,040,000	7,040,000	522,800	12.8
7,040,000	8,040,000	650,800	13.6
8,040,000	9,040,000	786,800	14.4
9,040,000	10,040,000	930,800	15.2
10,040,000		1,082,800	16.2

*Computation of maximum credit for state death taxes (based on federal adjusted taxable estate, which is the federal taxable estate reduced by $60,000)

Tax Rates

Be sure to use the rates applicable to the proper class of the beneficiary. And observe that, in some states, the exemption is deducted from the value of the share before applying the rates; in other states, the amount of the exemption is deducted from that part of the share that falls in the bottom tax bracket. In effect, the latter method gives a smaller tax saving as the exemption is taken off that part of the share that is taxed at the lowest rates.

Deducting the exemption at the rate of the lowest bracket also guarantees that the tax saving is equal for both large and small estates.

When Payment Is Due

The due date for payment varies. The tax may be due and payable at death, or a set number of months may be allowed after death or assessment. Interest begins to accrue if the tax is not paid within the time allowed after death. Good cause for delay may be shown to avoid delinquent penalty. Extensions for filing the return or paying the tax vary from state to state. Some states permit an automatic extension if an extension is granted for federal estate tax purposes.

Federal estate tax procedures require the estate tax return to be filed, and the tax paid, within 9 months from the date of death. Many states have adopted the same time limit.

Property Taxed

Although the estates of most decedents are generally taxed by only one state, certain situations arise when either the estate or the shares that the heirs receive are liable to the taxes of more than one state. The rights of the different states to levy a tax on the transfer of any property included in an estate depend very much on the kind of property involved.

To get a clear picture of the death tax liabilities of an estate, the property must be divided into the following three classes:

- *Real Estate*—land and permanent buildings. The courts have ruled and it has long been accepted that a state cannot tax real property outside its boundaries. It has been held that such taxation would violate the Constitution.[4] And it has been a principle of the common law that a state cannot tax land outside its borders.[5] Therefore the transfer of a decedent's real estate is generally liable to tax only by the state in which the property is situated.
- *Tangible Personal Property*—may include automobiles, yachts, household goods, cameras, art collections, goods, wares, and merchandise, etc. Tangible personal property is also taxable only in the state in which it has a taxable *situs*.[6] The location of the property must be definite and particular, and any removal from such a location must be only temporary.
- *Intangible Personal Property*—securities such as stocks, bonds, etc., and notes, mortgages, and other instruments evidencing debt. The value of the same intangible personal property in an estate may be taxed by several states [the tax may be applied by states with significant contacts with the property—Ed.] The Supreme Court has ruled that there is nothing in the Constitution that forbids this harassing situation.[7] This decision leaves the stocks and bonds of many estates subject to taxation by more than one state and overrules previous cases which held that the decedent's intangible property could only be taxed by his or her state of domicile.[8]

Domicile

If the decedent had residences in more than one state or if the state of domicile is not clearly established, two or more states may tax the same intangible property in his estate. The Supreme Court ruled in 1937 that there was nothing in the Constitution to bar the states of California and Massachusetts from taxing the intangibles in a decedent's estate.[9] The decedent had maintained residences in both states.

In a case where four states (Texas, New York, Florida, and Massachusetts) imposed inheritance taxes on the intangible property of one estate, the Supreme Court was moved to act because the taxes of all the states as well as the federal tax added together would have been greater than the estate. It was possible that one state in this instance would have been unable to collect its lawful tax. The Court ruled[10] that Texas, New York, and Florida could not impose their taxes, and that Massachusetts alone could tax the intangibles in the decedent's estate, as it was the decedent's only domicile.

However, where the decedent—a Massachusetts resident—had established a trust in Missouri, the stocks and bonds in the estate were taxed by both states. And as the property was sufficient to cover the claims of both states, the Supreme Court refused to accept the dispute.[11]

In Trust in Another State

If the deceased grantor of a trust resided in another state, both the state of residence and the state of trust *situs* may have the right to levy death taxes on the property in trust.

Where a woman who was a resident of Tennessee created a trust in Alabama, the Supreme Court ruled, "when taxpayer extends his activity with respect to his intangibles, by availing himself of the protection and benefit of the laws of another state, in such a way as to bring his person or property within reach of the tax-gatherer there, the reason for a single place of taxation no longer obtains. . . ."[12]

Thus securities may be taxed in a decedent's estate, either because the decedent had residence in a state or because the securities have *tax-situs* in the state where they are held by a trustee.

State of Incorporation

The Supreme Court has upheld the right of the state of incorporation to tax a corporation's stock in the estate of a nonresident-decedent. However, the danger from such taxation is now rare, because all but few states have adopted corrective amendments or additional statutes that wholly or contingently relinquish such rights. Many states provide a specific exemption for intangibles, such as corporate stock of a nonresident-decedent, and others offer a reciprocal exemption that is effective if its own residents are offered the same exemption by the decedent's state of domicile.

Business Situs of Intangibles

Intangible property that has acquired *business situs* in a state other than the resident state of the decedent is vulnerable to taxation by that state.

The Supreme Court has not rendered a definite decision on this matter. But from other decisions permitting more than one state to tax the intangibles of an estate, the danger from business situs must not be overlooked.

The danger is increased by the vagueness of the term *business situs*. It would be well to be careful of all business use of any intangible outside of the state of residence (for example, use as collateral for a business loan in another state).

The physical location of the intangibles in another state, however, has been ruled to be insufficient proof of business situs. Putting securities in a safe-deposit vault in another state does not at present place them in double-taxation peril[13] due to business situs of intangibles.

Life Insurance

Generally, life insurance proceeds payable to the insured's estate, executor, or administrator are taxable as part of the estate. But a few states exempt all or part of such proceeds. The exemption may depend on whether distribution is made by the estate to a surviving spouse or children, or whether the insurance proceeds are used to pay death taxes.

Many states do not tax life insurance proceeds paid to named beneficiaries other than the estate. Others tax proceeds payable to named beneficiaries, if the decedent possessed some incidents of ownership in them at his or her death. But most of such states provide exemptions in varying amounts. Since the laws defining "incidents of ownership" are not uniform throughout the states, it is imperative that the law of the taxing state be carefully examined.

Community-property life insurance also gets a wide range of tax treatment. In some states, one-half of the proceeds is exempt from tax. In others, life insurance may be wholly exempt if payable to a named beneficiary; or it may be wholly taxed if payable to a named beneficiary other than the surviving spouse. Also, community-property life insurance proceeds may be one-half exempt if payable to the surviving widow, but wholly exempt if payable to the surviving husband. Generally, if the community-property policy is on the life of the *surviving* spouse, one-half of the present value of the policy is taxed.

Nonresidents

Most states provide an outright or a reciprocal exemption for the intangibles of nonresident decedents.

Thus the danger of double or multiple taxation is greatly reduced except where there is uncertainty as to the state of domicile or there is a trust in

~~another state, or the intangibles owned by the decedent are used for business purposes outside the state of domicile.~~

Generally, taxable property in the estate of a nonresident-decedent is taxed in the same manner as in the case of a resident. But although the same rate tables may be used, ~~the exemptions and deductions permitted a nonresident's estate are often reduced.~~

Many states give a *full* exemption (equal to that given a resident) to the estates of nonresidents. Other states give only a *proportional* exemption to the estates of nonresidents. The proportional exemption is equal to a computed fraction of the full resident's exemption. The exemption is allowed only in the proportion that the property in the state bears to the entire estate.

> *Example:* The resident state of the decedent is state X. He owns real estate worth $10,000 in state Y, and his total estate amounts to $50,000. The property is to pass to the widow. In Y, the exemption given to a widow is $10,000. But as Y gives only a proportional exemption to the estates of nonresidents, the widow is only entitled to an exemption of $2,000.

$$\frac{\$10,000}{\$50,000} = 1/5 \quad 1/5 \times \$10,000 = \$2,000$$

In some states, nonresidents are not subject to the additional estate tax that absorbs the amount by which the maximum federal credit for state death taxes exceeds the inheritance taxes paid to the states.

NOTES

1. *Magoun v. Illinois Trust & Savings Bank,* 170 U.S. 283 (1898).

2. Ibid.

3. *Graves v. Schmidlapp,* 315 U.S. 657 (1942).

4. *Louisville and Jeffersonville Ferry v. Kentucky,* 188 U.S. 385.

5. 45 Harv. L. Rev. 777, 778.

6. *Frick v. Pennsylvania,* 268 U.S. 238; *Triechler v. Wisconsin,* 338 U.S. 251.

7. *Utah v. Aldrich,* 316 U.S. 174.

8. *Farmers Loan & Trust Co. v. Minnesota,* 280 U.S. 204; *Baldwin v. Missouri,* 281 U.S. 586.

9. *Worcester County Trust v. Riley,* 302 U.S. 292.

10. *Texas v. Florida,* 306 U.S. 398.

11. *Massachusetts v. Missouri,* 308 U.S. 1.

12. *Curry v. McCanless,* 307 U.S. 357.

13. *Buck v. Beach,* 206 U.S. 392; *Baldwin v. Missouri,* 281 U.S. 586.

COMPUTING GAIN OR LOSS

One cannot compute the amount of gain or loss on the sale of an asset without knowing its cost. In most cases the basis of an asset is the original price paid to acquire the property increased by certain adjustments (such as expenditures for improvements) and decreased by certain tax benefits (such as depreciation taken during the term of ownership).

Before an asset is transferred, four factors must be established. The first is the basis in the hands of the transferor; second, whether the asset is characterized as a capital or noncapital asset; third, the holding period in the hands of the transferor; and fourth, the fair market value of the asset at a relevant point in time.

Function of Basis

The main function of basis is to measure gain or loss when property is sold, exchanged, or transferred in a taxable transaction. A second function of basis is to serve as a departure point for depreciation and will not be discussed here. Basis becomes important when property changes hands. If the transaction is taxable, the transferor must establish the basis in order to calculate gain or loss on the transaction. The transferee's basis will determine gain or loss on a later transfer. The basis assumed by the transferee will vary, depending on the character of the transfer—that is, whether the transfer is a taxable sale or exchange, a nontaxable transfer by gift or inheritance, or a tax-free exchange. The transferee's basis will be used to determine gain or loss when the asset is sold.

Capital Assets

The Internal Revenue Code defines a capital asset as "property held by the taxpayer with specified exceptions." A major exception is inventory or property held primarily for sale to customers in the ordinary course of business.

Unless such property falls within the ambit of certain depreciable real property used in a trade or business (which receives special tax treatment), this property will be considered ordinary income property. All gain or loss on the sale of property other than capital assets is taxable as ordinary income. If the asset is treated as a capital asset, however, it will receive capital-gain tax treatment and the seller will be taxed only to the extent of gain.

13.1

Holding Period

The holding period is determinative with regard to whether the taxpayer will have long-term or short-term capital-gain or -loss treatment. Long-term capital gains or losses result from the sale of a capital asset held for more than 6 months.

Fair Market Value

The fourth element, the fair market value of an asset, may become important in determining basis for special situations involving gratuitous transfers at death. Fair market value may be defined as the price agreed upon by a willing buyer and a willing seller, neither being under compulsion either to buy or to sell.

BASIS OF PROPERTY TRANSFERRED AT DEATH

General Rule

The way property was acquired will influence its basis upon future disposition. There are special rules pertaining to the basis of property transferred at death. When property is acquired from a decedent, it will acquire a new basis equal to the value of the property either on the date of death, or the alternate valuation date (6 months after death) if the estate is eligible to use the alternate valuation date and an election is made by the executor to use it. When an individual dies, the original basis becomes irrelevant. Property included in the decedent's gross estate acquires a new basis, which is either increased or decreased to the fair market value of the asset on the date of death. In the past two or three decades, the fair market value of property has steadily increased as a result of our inflationary economy. These upward trends have caused the basis of property inherited from a decedent to be adjusted in an upward direction more often than not. This increased basis has become known as a stepped-up basis. The stepped-up basis can result in a windfall to the transferee of the property. The stepped-up-basis-at-death rule effectively eliminates the tax on all potential gain accrued to the date of death. In those cases where property has greatly appreciated in value, there is a substantial income tax advantage to the estate or beneficiaries. Actually the stepped-up-basis rule is a form of tax relief afforded to those people receiving property transferred at death.

Since the rule provides that basis will become the fair market value on the date of death, it may also be *stepped down* if the asset has declined in value from the time it was acquired by the decedent. Until now it has been more usual to find assets having a *stepped-up* rather than *stepped-down* basis. If the decedent possessed an asset that declined in value, he or she would have been wise to sell the asset while alive, thereby taking advantage of the loss on the sale. If a property that has declined in value was not sold during the decedent's lifetime, the cost basis to the beneficiary will become the fair market value at death. Any tax benefit from the unrealized loss would be gone forever.

At the present time, inflation appears to be slowing down. This factor, coupled with a recessionary economy, may reduce the benefit of this special basis rule in the future. More properties may be *stepped down* to their fair market value on the date of death than have been in recent decades. Lifetime estate planning judgments regarding the holding or disposition of assets should be made. Unquestionably, the basis rules should be factored into such decisions. The financial services professional has a responsibility to advise clients to take losses during lifetime if the property is not being held for sentimental value.

Property Subject to Power of Appointment

Also, if property passed to another because the decedent exercised a general power of appointment over the property under his or her will, that property will be treated as other property transferred by a decedent at death that is included in the decedent's gross estate. The property subject to the power will receive a new basis stepped up to its fair market value on the date of the decedent's death.

Retained Powers

There are also adjustments to basis for property included in the decedent's gross estate either as a retained lifetime interest or because the decedent possessed certain powers over the transferred property that were not released during the 3-year period prior to death. These powers include the right to revoke the transfer as well as the right to alter or control the beneficial enjoyment or the income from the property. The stepped-up-basis rules apply to these properties transferred during lifetime that were brought back into the gross estate for valuation purposes because of the retained powers.

> *Example:* If the decedent transferred real estate to a son but retained the right to use the property for life or the right to income from the property for life, the property would be included as a retained life income interest in the decedent's estate at its value on the day the decedent died. In that case the property would then receive a new basis equal to the fair market value for federal estate tax purposes. Thus, if highly appreciated property is given away, the donee may benefit from the inclusion of that property in the decedent's gross estate since the donee will receive a new stepped-up basis. When the property is subsequently sold, the new owner will have a smaller capital-gains tax to pay.

Effect of Step-Up in Basis on Jointly Held Property

The general rule that all property included in the gross estate will receive a stepped-up basis at death includes property held jointly with right of survivorship. In the case of nonspousal joint tenancies (under the consideration-furnished rule), whatever value is attributed to the property that represents the decedent's joint interest will receive a stepped-up basis to the date-of-death value in the hands of the surviving joint tenant or tenants.

13.3

Should the entire value of jointly held property be included in the decedent's gross estate, the property will receive a fully stepped-up basis equal to the value on the date-of-death or alternate valuation date, if applicable. This value will then become the new basis in the hands of the surviving joint tenant for later sale purposes.

This rule has a strange effect on joint tenancies between spouses. Since only one-half of the property can now be included in the gross estate of the decedent's spouse, the property will receive a stepped-up basis for the value of one-half of the property only. The original basis of the other half of the property will be retained by the surviving spouse. This will affect the amount of gain realized should the property be sold during the spouse's lifetime. If, however, the surviving spouse holds the property until death, the entire property will be included in the survivor's estate. The entire property will then acquire a fully stepped-up basis in the hands of the beneficiaries.

> *Example:* A decedent, Mary Beth, and her husband acquired real estate in 1965 for $50,000 and titled it in joint names with right of survivorship. The entire contribution had been made by the decedent. At the decedent's death in 1987 the fair market value of the property was appraised at $200,000. Under current law, only one-half of the value of the property (the one-half that is included in the decedent's gross estate) will receive a stepped-up basis. The new basis in the hands of the decedent's spouse will be computed as follows: the one-half included in his estate will receive a new basis of $100,000. The other half that is treated as contributed by the surviving spouse will be valued at its original basis of $25,000. If the surviving spouse later sells the property for fair market value, the combined basis will be $125,000 ($100,000 plus $25,000) and a taxable gain will occur. One way to avoid this additional gain is for the surviving spouse to hold the property until death, or, at the very least, to hold the property until age 55 when the rule pertaining to exclusion of the first $125,000 of gain on the sale of a principal residence applies.

To summarize, the current rule for estate tax inclusion with respect to jointly held property with right of survivorship is actually two separate rules depending on whether the property is held by the spouses alone or by the decedent and one or more persons. For all other joint tenancies other than spousal joint tenancies, the consideration-furnished rule applies. The rule pertaining to spousal joint tenancies has been amended in the Code to define a *qualified joint interest* as any interest held by the decedent and the decedent's spouse as joint tenants with right of survivorship or as tenants by the entirety, if they are the only joint tenants. All former requirements pertaining to qualified joint interests have been eliminated, including filing a gift tax return on the creation of the joint tenancy as well as making elections under the gift tax provisions to treat the creation as a gift.

Exceptions to General Stepped-Up-Basis Rule

Basis of Income in Respect of a Decedent (IRD)

The stepped-up-basis rules do not apply to income that is included in the decedent's gross estate as *income in respect of a decedent* (IRD). Income in respect of a decedent is any income that the decedent was entitled to (but did not receive) while alive. The income will be includible at full value for estate tax purposes. It will then also be taxed to the beneficiary of the income as ordinary income for income tax purposes. However, the beneficiary will be allowed an income tax deduction for the estate tax paid as a result of the IRD being included in the gross estate.

Receipt of Property in Kind

Also, if the beneficiary receives property instead of a cash bequest, the basis of the property in the beneficiary's hands will equal the amount of cash bequest that the property transferred satisfies.

> *Example:* Suppose the decedent leaves $20,000 to a cousin. Instead of paying the cousin $20,000, the executor transfers property worth $20,000 to the cousin. The cousin will acquire a basis of $20,000 for the property. If the fair market value of the property on the date of death was $17,000, the basis to the estate would be the date-of-death value, or $17,000. Since this property appreciated in value after the date of death and was distributed in lieu of $20,000 cash, the estate will realize a gain of $3,000.

Basis of Community Property

Residents of community-property states should take note that a special rule pertains to community property held by the decedent and the surviving spouse under the laws of a community-property state. If at least one-half of the community property was includible in the decedent's gross estate, and received a basis equal to the value of that one-half share on the date of death, the property that represents the surviving spouse's one-half share of community property held with the decedent will receive a new basis in the property adjusted to the fair market value of the property at the decedent's death.

Certain Property Acquired by Gift within One Year of Death

The stepped-up-basis-at-death rule will be ignored under a certain set of circumstances. The rule will not apply when appreciated property is acquired by the decedent by gift within one year before death if, upon death, the property then passes directly or indirectly back to the original donor or the original donor's spouse. This exception was carved out to eliminate schemes to obtain the stepped-up basis for certain property that, in actuality, did not belong to the decedent and was intended to return to the original owner at the decedent's death. This scheme involves a sham transfer made for the purpose of increasing the basis of the asset to the original owner. The nature of the bequest has no bearing on the application of this exception to the basis rules.

The following situation illustrates the type of scheme this new provision is designed to thwart:

> *Example:* Sam Summers owns 500 shares of IBM stock that he acquired 20 years ago for one-tenth of its present value. Martin Summers, his brother, is terminally ill and expected to die shortly. Sam transfers stock that cost him $100,000 to Martin when the shares are worth $1,000,000. Martin subsequently dies and, under the terms of his will, there is a specific bequest of the IBM stock to his brother, Sam. At the time of Martin's death, the stock has a fair market value of $1,000,000. Sam sells the stock 2 months later for $1,100,000. If he had never transferred the stock to his dying brother, Sam would have long-term capital gains of $1,000,000. If Sam were allowed to obtain a stepped-up basis as a result of this sham transfer, he would have avoided $900,000 of gain and would have received a stepped-up basis of $1,000,000 that would have provided him with a long-term gain of only $100,000.

To prevent this type of windfall, Congress enacted a rule that states that any property transferred by gift to the decedent within one year of death that reverts back to the original donor or the donor's spouse as a bequest from the decedent (either directly or indirectly) will not receive a stepped-up basis when the property is sold or exchanged. The property will retain the same basis in the hands of the donor-heir that it had in the hands of the decedent immediately before death. This rule applies to property acquired after August 13, 1981 (the date the law was signed), by decedents dying after December 31, 1981.

The stepped-up basis will be denied only to the extent that the donor-heir is entitled to receive the appreciated value. Thus if the heir only inherits a portion of the property that was transferred because it was used to satisfy debts or administrative expenses, the rule will apply on a pro rata basis. It should be noted that if the decedent lives more than one year after the original transfer, the general stepped-up-basis rule will be applicable. The general rule will also apply to transfers made by the decedent to someone other than the original donor or the donor's spouse, although the property was transferred to the decedent within one year of death. If, in the preceding illustration, the decedent, Martin Summers, had left the IBM stock to his brother's grandchildren rather than to his brother or his brother's wife, the stepped-up-basis rule would apply. This rule was enacted to prevent a windfall to an heir who transfers appreciated property to a terminally ill relative shortly before the relative's death with the knowledge that the heir will get the property back through inheritance after the relative's death occurs, thus receiving a new basis equal to the fair market value of the property on the date of death.

The stepped-up-basis provision offers excellent estate planning opportunities. Since there are relatively few ways to successfully avoid taxation of gain, the stepped-up-basis rules create an opportunity for elimination of potential gain when property has greatly appreciated in value acquisition. Any substantially appreciated property owned by the decedent will be passed on to the heirs with a higher basis. That increment of gain (from the time the property was obtained until the decedent's death) would be wiped out or eliminated when the property was subsequently sold. In effect, what exists is a loophole in the tax law because some gain will escape taxation entirely.

The estate owner can avoid potential tax by determining whether it would be more advantageous to hold the property for life, or whether he or she would derive a greater tax benefit if the property was disposed of during lifetime. Certainly the stepped-up-basis rule should be taken into consideration when a decision to hold or sell property is made by a mature estate owner. Again, the decision will vary depending on many factors, including the following: (1) whether property has substantially increased in value; (2) whether the basis is close to or greater than the fair market value when a transfer is contemplated; (3) whether there is the potential for future increase in value; and (4) what the relative impact of the estate and gift taxes is as compared with the income tax, if the property is sold.

There is yet another tax consideration when property is transferred at death, which pertains to the holding-period rules for long-term capital-gains treatment. The length of time property was held by the decedent prior to death and the holding period by the estate or beneficiary afterward are not determinative for long-term capital-gains treatment on a later sale. The general rule is that any person acquiring property from a decedent that was included in the gross estate and to which the stepped-up-basis rules apply will be considered to have held the property for more than 6 months. In other words, when an asset is transferred as a result of death, the transferee will receive long-term capital-gains treatment, regardless of the holding periods before and after death.

PROPERTY TRANSFERRED DURING LIFETIME BY GIFT (IRC SEC. 1015)

The stepped-up-basis rule for property passing at death does not apply to property transferred during lifetime by gift. A carryover- or substituted-basis rule applies to property transferred gratuitously during lifetime. When a gift is made after December 31, 1976, the donee acquires the donor's basis increased by any gift tax paid on the net appreciation at the time of the gift. The net appreciation is the amount by which the fair market value at the time of the gift exceeds the donor's adjusted basis. The amount of gift tax paid that can be added to the donee's basis is computed by taking the ratio that the net appreciation bears to the fair market value of the gift and applying that ratio to the total gift tax paid (IRC Sec. 1015(d)(6)).

Any appreciation in the property that might have resulted in capital gains if the property was sold is deferred until such later time as the donee disposes of the property. The increment of gain or appreciation in the value of the property between the date of the gift and the time it is transferred in a taxable exchange will not avoid taxation because the property was given away. It will merely be deferred until the time of sale. This is called the carryover- or substituted-basis rule. When a gift is made, the basis of the property in the hands of the donor is carried over and becomes the basis in the hands of the donee. This rule should not be confused with the stepped-up-basis rule for property passing at death, which effectively eliminates taxation of the potential gain from the time of acquisition by the decedent to the date of death. The following situation illustrates the basis rule for property transferred by gift:

> *Example:* A father who had acquired property for $30,000 made a taxable gift to his daughter in 1983 when the fair market value was $60,000. Because it is a taxable gift, it will be valued for gift tax purposes at $60,000. Assuming he has never made any other taxable gifts, his gift tax will be $13,200. The gift tax attributable to the net appreciation in the property from the time he had acquired it to the time of the gift is $6,500. Therefore the daughter's basis will become her father's basis of $30,000, plus that portion of the gift tax paid attributable to the net appreciation in the value of the gift (or $6,500). Thus the daughter's basis would become $36,500.

General Rule for Basis of Gifted Property

When property is acquired by gift, the basis to the donee will remain the same basis that the donor had in the property increased (but not above fair market value) by the portion of the gift tax paid attributable to the net appreciation in the value of the gift. To determine the net appreciation, the fair market value of the property at the time of the gift is reduced by the donor's adjusted basis.

The rule is different when the donor gives away property whose fair market value is less than the adjusted basis. For purposes of loss, the donee's basis will be the lesser of the donor's basis or the fair market value at the time of the gift.

> *Example:* Suppose James Jessup gives away property worth $25,000, which had cost him $50,000, to Sally Saraon. If Sally then sells the property for any price between $50,000 and $25,000, she will not realize either a gain or a loss on the sale.

Bargain Sales to Individuals

A gift between individuals is not always entirely gratuitous. A bargain sale, not an arm's-length transaction, occurs when the purchaser (donee) transfers less than fair market value for the property to the seller (donor). The transaction can be viewed as consisting of two components—part sale and part gift. In this circumstance, the seller cannot realize a loss on the sale if the proceeds received are less than the basis. However, a gain is realized if the proceeds received exceed the basis. The seller (donor) is deemed to make a gift of the excess of the fair market value over the amount received for the property.

Example: Sam sells property with a current fair market value of $100,000 to his son for $60,000. Sam had a basis in the property of $75,000. Sam has made a gift to his son of $40,000 ($100,000 − $60,000). Sam will realize no loss on the sale despite receiving proceeds less than his basis.

The basis rules for the purchaser (donee) in the bargain sale situation require careful study. The purchaser (donee) acquires a basis equal to the greater of (1) the amount paid for the property increased by the gift tax paid by the seller (donor) attributed to the appreciated portion of the property while held by the seller, or (2) the seller's (donor's) basis at the time of the transfer increased by the gift tax paid by the seller (donor) attributed to the appreciated portion of the property while held by the seller. However, the basis of the purchaser cannot exceed the fair market value of the property at the time of the original transfer for the purpose of determining loss on the part of the purchaser.

Example: Sam transfers property with a fair market value of $100,000 to his son for $60,000. Sam had a basis of $75,000 in the property and paid a gift tax of $10,000 on the transaction ($7,500 of the gift tax is attributable to the appreciation of the property in the hands of Sam). The son gets a basis in the property of $82,500.

Example: Same facts as above except the son pays $80,000 for the property. The son now has a basis in the property of $87,500.

Example: Sam transfers property with a fair market value of $75,000 to his son for $60,000. Sam had a basis of $100,000 in the property at the time of the transfer but paid no gift tax on the transfer. The basis of the property in the hands of the son is $100,000. However, if the son subsequently disposes of the property, the son's basis is limited to $75,000 (fair market value at the time of the original transfer) for the purpose of determining loss.

Bargain Sales to Charity

The transfer of property to a charity for less than fair market value has some advantages for planning purposes. However, the transaction creates some unique tax effects. For the purpose of determining the gain realized by the transferor, the transaction is fictionally divided into two components—part sale and part gift. The basis of the property sold must be allocated to the portion of the property deemed "sold" and to the portion deemed a "gift" to charity. The basis of the property allocated to the "sale" portion of the transaction is that portion of the total basis as the ratio of the amount realized on the sale bears to the fair market value of the property. The formula for determining the basis for the "sale" is as follows:

$$\frac{\underline{\text{Amount realized}}}{\text{Fair market value}} \text{ x } \text{ basis of property } = \text{ basis for sale}$$

The portion of the basis deemed "gifted" to the charity is determined by subtracting the basis allocated to the sale from the total basis held by the transferor.

After the gross estate is determined, the next step in calculating the taxable estate is to determine the adjusted gross estate* by deducting the following:

- funeral expenses
- administration expenses attributable to property subject to claims against the estate
- claims against the estate
- unpaid mortgages
- other administration expenses
- losses

The deductions above are described in this reading. It should be noted that as an alternative, some of these items may be deducted from other tax returns that must be filed (for example, the decedent's last income tax return or the income tax return for the estate). However, if a certain deduction is taken on the income tax return, that same deduction cannot be taken also on the estate tax return (except as noted later under the heading "Taxes").

This reading concludes with a discussion of the factors involved in determining where it might be best to take the deductions.

THE TAXABLE ESTATE

All the foregoing are allowable deductions from the gross estate to arrive at the adjusted gross estate. Two additional deductions are then permitted— the marital deduction and the charitable deduction, which will then result in arriving at the taxable estate. These deductions are treated in the next two readings.

---

*Editor's Note: The adjusted-gross-estate calculation is not a required calculation on Form 706 (Federal Estate Tax Return). However, this calculation is required for a variety of other reasons. For example, to determine if a Sec. 303 redemption is permissible; or where a formula marital deduction provision is used (for decedents who never amended the marital provisions since the enactment of the unlimited marital deduction); or where a closely held business is part of the gross estate, an adjusted-gross-estate calculation can help to ascertain whether installment payments of federal estate taxes are possible under Sec. 6166.

FUNERAL EXPENSES

Certain expenditures, such as funeral expenses limited to a *reasonable amount, are deductible for estate tax purposes only*. Such expenses include costs associated with internment, a burial lot or vault, a grave marker or monument, the perpetual care of the grave site, and transportation of the body to the place of burial. The traveling costs of relatives is generally not an allowable deduction.

ADMINISTRATION EXPENSES ATTRIBUTABLE TO PROPERTY SUBJECT TO CLAIMS AGAINST THE ESTATE

The costs of administering property includible in the decedent's gross estate are generally deductible from either the estate or the estate's income tax return. Deductible items include expenses incurred in the collection and preservation of probate assets, the payment of estate debts, and the distribution of probate assets to estate beneficiaries. Such expenses include court costs, executor's commissions, attorney's fees, accounting fees, and miscellaneous costs, such as the expenses incurred on the sale of estate property as well as the excise taxes included in these sales if a sale was necessary to settle the estate. Any expenses that were incurred for the benefit of the heirs individually are not deductible. The key question is whether the expenditure was essential to the proper settlement of the estate.

Medical Expenses

Medical expenses relating to the decedent's last illness may be deducted on either the estate tax return or the decedent's last income tax return. However, these expenses are deductible on the decedent's last income tax return only if the estate files a statement waiving the right to an estate tax deduction.

CLAIMS AGAINST THE ESTATE

All claims against the estate, including any bona fide debts that the decedent was validly obligated to pay while alive plus interest accrued to the date of death, are deductible from the gross estate only. These obligations must be based on a promise or agreement. They are deductible only to the extent that they are based on adequate and full consideration in money or money's worth and represent personal obligations of the decedent existing at the time of death, whether or not they have matured. The interest on the indebtedness is deductible but is limited to the amount accrued to the date of death, although the executor may choose the alternate valuation date. Also, liabilities imposed by law or arising out of torts are deductible. If the decedent has made a pledge or subscription that is evidenced by a promissory note or other proof, it may be deductible by the estate only to the extent that the liability was contracted for both bona fide and adequate consideration in cash or other property. Alternatively, if the pledge is a bequest and thus an allowable charitable deduction, it will be deductible under this section.

Taxes

Certain taxes are deductible on the estate tax return as claims against the estate. These include income taxes, unpaid gift taxes, and real property taxes accrued to the date of death. Federal income taxes owed to the date of death are deductible only on the federal estate tax return. However, state, local or foreign income taxes as well as property taxes may be deducted on either the federal estate tax return or the federal income tax return. Real estate taxes not accrued before death as well as local and foreign income taxes on estate income will be deductible on the income tax return of the estate. Any federal income taxes on estate income are not deductible either on the estate tax return or for income tax purposes. The general rule denying a double deduction has the following exception: taxes, interest, and business expenses accrued at the date of the decedent's death that are attributable to income in respect of a decedent are deductible on the decedent's final income tax return and are also deductible as administration expenses on the estate tax return.

MORTGAGE DEBT

A deduction will also be allowed from the gross estate for the full, unpaid balance of a mortgage or other indebtedness, including interest accrued to the date of death, if the following two conditions are met: (1) the full value of property that is not reduced by the mortgage amount or indebtedness must be included in the value of the gross estate; and (2) the decedent's estate must be liable for the amount of the mortgage or indebtedness.

OTHER ADMINISTRATION EXPENSES

Deductions allowed under this heading refer to expenses in administering property not subject to claims. Property that is not subject to claims usually refers to the nonprobate estate. Jointly held property and life insurance are typical nonprobate assets. Expenses for administering nonprobate assets that were included in the gross estate are deductible, provided that the expense is paid before the time for filing the federal estate tax return.

CASUALTY LOSSES

Casualty and theft losses are deductible expenses that are incurred during the estate settlement period but only to the extent that these losses are not compensated by insurance. Casualty and theft losses are deductible if the loss arose from fire, storm, shipwreck, or other casualty or theft. The loss must have occurred during the estate settlement process and before the estate was closed. The loss will be reduced to the extent that restitution was made through insurance or other compensation to offset the loss. Such a casualty loss to property permits a deduction from the gross estate for either estate tax purposes or estate income tax purposes. However, the estate may not claim both deductions.

DECISIONS TO BE MADE IN ORDER TO MINIMIZE TAXES

Deductions from Either the Gross Estate or the Income Tax Return

As previously mentioned, the executor has discretion regarding deduction of certain items from the federal estate tax return or on income tax returns. This choice does not apply to all debts and expenses. Some expenses are allowable on the federal estate tax return only. Some expenses may be allowed on either the estate tax return or the income tax return. The primary reason for concern about where to take a deduction is the minimization of taxes. Before any administration expenses or casualty losses may be deducted for income tax purposes, the executor must file a timely statement waiving the right to claim these expenses on the decedent's federal estate tax return. Unless the estate tax deduction is waived, deductions for administration expenses will not be allowed from the income of either the estate or the beneficiary for income tax purposes. The executor may file a waiver for a portion of the deductible items while the rest are allowed for estate tax purposes. Once the waiver is filed, it cannot be revoked. The waiver should be filed with the income tax return in the year that the expenses are taken as deductions for income tax purposes. This statement does not apply to deductible expenses that relate to income in respect of a decedent (IRD).

Splitting Deductions between Returns

Sometimes the best result is found by taking certain deductions on the estate tax return and other deductions on the income tax return. Income tax rates range from 15 percent to a maximum of 33 percent after 1987. The estate tax rates will have a maximum rate of 55 percent. The regulations permit splitting deductions between the income and estate tax returns. This allows the executor to deduct some administrative expenses on the estate tax return and other allowable expenses on the estate income tax return. In situations where distributions are made to beneficiaries, the relative estate and income tax brackets of the beneficiaries must be examined. If the beneficiary is in a low income tax bracket, tax savings may be achieved by splitting the deduction between the beneficiary's income and the estate's income. Also proper timing of distributions may allow additional tax savings, particularly if the estate has chosen a fiscal year different from the taxable year of the beneficiary.

Since the maximum income tax rate is 33 percent and the minimum estate tax rate (after the unified credit is applied) is 37 percent, the "optional" deductions are generally more valuable on the estate tax return. However, many estates will not be taxable due to the marital deduction and unified credit. In these cases the deductions may be more useful on the estate's income tax return. The executor often has to "wait and see" before making the appropriate choice. Quite often the executor will deduct the expenses on both returns and later amend one return by removing the deduction after this choice is finalized.

Executor Fees as Either Bequest or Income

Executors who are also named beneficiaries of the decedent may consider the desirability of waiving their executors' fees, since they will be receiving a bequest that is income tax free. If an executor's commission is deductible on the federal estate tax return, it will then be received as taxable income whether or not the executor is a beneficiary of the estate. However, if the commission or devise is considered a bequest, it will not be deductible by the estate for either estate or income tax purposes. Executors must act promptly to waive any commissions if they find that more tax would be saved by receiving the bequest income tax free than would be saved by characterizing the executor's commission as a deductible expense of the estate. The critical factor to evaluate is whether greater tax savings will result from a deduction on the federal estate tax return when the additional income tax incurred by the executor is taken into consideration.

THE MARITAL DEDUCTION

Stephan R. Leimberg*

Property included in a decedent's gross estate for federal estate tax purposes that is passing (or has passed) to a surviving spouse may qualify for a deduction from the adjusted gross estate in arriving at the taxable estate. No deduction is more important to the typical married individual's estate than this estate tax marital deduction. It is often possible, through judicious use of this deduction, to reduce or eliminate the estate tax on the death of the first spouse. But if used improperly, the marital-deduction transfer can result in an overall combined estate tax on the total estates of both spouses that is far greater than if no transfer to a surviving spouse was made.

For these reasons, and because the rules in the Internal Revenue Code for qualifying for the marital deduction are strictly construed, a member of the estate planning team must have a thorough knowledge of the marital-deduction requirements.

BACKGROUND

Married residents of nine states (Arizona, California, Idaho, Louisiana, Nevada, New Mexico, Texas, Washington, and Wisconsin) operate under a community-property system. Essentially this means that all property acquired (other than by gift, devise, bequest, or inheritance) by husband and wife during marriage while living in one of these states belongs to the *community*; that is, each spouse automatically and from the inception of ownership owns one-half of the property. Upon death, a decedent can only dispose of his or her share of the community property by will. Because of this state property law concept, only one-half of the community property is includible in the estate of whichever spouse dies first.

> *Example:* Assume Herb and his wife, Roz, are living in California. Herb's salary is large enough to allow him to save $50,000 a year. One-half of that, $25,000, is deemed to be Roz's property. Therefore only one-half of the $50,000 would be includible in Herb's estate if he died first. Likewise, if Roz died first, $25,000 would be includible in her estate even though Herb earned the entire $50,000.

---

*Stephan R. Leimberg, JD, CLU, is professor of estate planning and taxation at The American College.

This tax advantage has been reflected in the income and gift taxation of community-property residents as well as in the estate taxation. As a result, residents of common-law states grew indignant, recognizing that their community-property neighbors were taxed more favorably under a state property law system that treated one-half of the earnings of either spouse as automatically belonging to the other.

Some traditionally common-law states (such as Pennsylvania, Michigan, Hawaii, and Nebraska) sought to achieve tax parity by converting to what was in effect a community-property system. Great interstate resentment and confusion about the disparities that developed prompted Congress to aim for tax parity by making a federal estate tax marital deduction available to married residents of common-law states.

This Code provision allows a deduction for the value of any qualifying property interests includible in the decedent's gross estate that passed from the decedent to the surviving spouse.

THE AMOUNT OF THE MARITAL DEDUCTION—COMMON-LAW STATES

A federal estate tax-free interspousal transfer is now allowed either during lifetime or at death. In other words, the law now allows a deduction for unlimited assets passing from one spouse to another. Even residents of community-property states can take advantage of this unlimited marital deduction, because community property now qualifies for the marital deduction to the extent that it is includible in the decedent-spouse's estate. Conceivably this means that Charlie Plotnick could leave his entire $10 million estate to his wife, Diane, and not pay any federal estate tax. However, the deduction cannot exceed the net value of the *qualifying interests* (defined below) passing to the surviving spouse.

QUALIFICATIONS ON THE AMOUNT OF THE MARITAL DEDUCTION

The estate tax marital deduction is allowed on the net value of a qualifying interest passing to a decedent's surviving spouse. Therefore it is necessary to define the term *net value*.

Net value refers to the gross estate tax value of a property interest—that is, its date-of-death value or, if applicable, its value as of the alternate valuation date, minus any charges against that interest.

This means that the gross value of a property interest passing to the surviving spouse must be reduced by (1) taxes payable out of the interest, (2) mortgages or liens against the interest, and (3) administration expenses payable out of the interest.

Taxes payable out of the interest would include any federal estate tax or state death tax. The word *payable* is important because in order to reduce the marital deduction, it is not necessary that the taxes actually be paid out of the marital share—only that they be *payable*.

15.2

Example: If Lara's will authorizes her executor to pay death taxes out of Lara's husband's share of her $300,000 estate, the value of the interest passing to the husband will be reduced for purposes of computing the marital deduction, even if, in fact, Lara's executor uses other funds to pay the tax.

If the surviving spouse takes an interest subject to a mortgage or a lien, the gross value of the interest will be reduced by the amount of that obligation. For instance, if Lara left her husband a $100,000 boat on which she owed $20,000, only $80,000 of qualifying property would be passing. However, if Lara's will (or state law) required the debt to be discharged before the title to the boat was transferred to her husband, the gross value of the boat would be used in the marital-deduction computation; the amount of the lien would not reduce the marital deduction.

When administration expenses are chargeable (under a decedent's will or under state law) against the surviving spouse's share of the estate, the amount of those expenses reduces the allowable marital deduction.

These reductions are usually avoided by requiring in the decedent's will that expenses, debts, and taxes be paid out of the share of the estate passing to beneficiaries other than the spouse.

TRANSFERS QUALIFYING FOR THE MARITAL DEDUCTION

A number of very strictly construed technical requirements must be met before property will qualify for the marital deduction, and there are certain qualifications and limitations that must be considered:

- the citizenship requirement for the surviving spouse
- the requirement that property be included
- the requirement that property must *pass or have passed*
- the marital-status requirement
- the *terminable interest rule*

Citizenship Requirement for the Surviving Spouse

The marital deduction is generally allowed only for transfers to a spouse who was, at the date of the decedent's death, a U.S. citizen. The marital deduction can be preserved if the surviving spouse becomes a citizen before the decedent's estate tax return is filed. Reading 16 discusses in detail marital-deduction planning for the resident-alien-spouse.

Requirement That Property Be Included

A transfer will not qualify for the marital deduction unless the property interest is included in the decedent's gross estate for federal estate tax purposes. For example, no marital deduction is allowed when a wife purchases a life insurance policy on the life of her husband with her own funds and is the owner and beneficiary of such a policy. Since the proceeds of the policy will not be includible in the husband's gross estate in the first place, they will not qualify for a marital deduction. However, if for any reason the life insurance proceeds *are* includible in the decedent's gross estate, they can qualify for the marital deduction.

Requirement That Property Must Pass or Have Passed

The *passed-or-have-passed requirement* has two implications:

- An interest owned by the decedent must pass from the decedent to a surviving spouse; that is, the surviving spouse must receive the property by means of a transfer from the decedent, as opposed to a transfer from someone else.
- The surviving spouse must receive the interest as beneficial owner rather than as trustee or agent for someone else.

An interest can be transferred from the decedent to a surviving spouse in a number of ways that will qualify for the marital deduction. These include transfers from the decedent

- by will, intestacy, or similar law
- by election against the will. In many states, a decedent cannot disinherit a surviving spouse since the survivor can elect to receive the amount that would have been received had the decedent died intestate—that is, without a will. The amount received as a result of the election will be *property passing.*
- by transfer to a spouse made by the decedent during lifetime and for some reason includible in the estate (for example, a transfer the decedent made when a life estate was retained)
- in the form of life insurance death proceeds. This assumes the decedent retained incidents of ownership in the policy.
- by survivorship (for example, when the surviving spouse was a joint tenant with rights of survivorship). Note that, in this case, the marital deduction is allowed only to the extent the jointly held property is includible in the decedent's estate for federal estate tax purposes. Since only 50 percent of all spouse-owned jointly held property is includible, only the value of that portion will be counted in computing the actual marital deduction even though the survivor receives title to the entire property.
- by power of appointment. For example, the surviving spouse could have been the appointee of a general power that the decedent, as donee, exercised, or a *taker in default* when the decedent failed to exercise a general power.

If the decedent leaves a bequest to a surviving spouse and the spouse *disclaims* (in other words, states in a timely disclaimer that "I renounce all my rights to the property"), the interest disclaimed will be treated as if it never had passed to the surviving spouse. Therefore it will not qualify. But if the bequest was first accepted by the surviving spouse and then transferred to a child, the property will be considered to have passed from the decedent to the surviving spouse. (The spouse may be subject to gift tax on the value of the transfer to the child.)

15.4

Example: Frank named his wife, Mary Jo, primary beneficiary of a $100,000 life insurance policy he owned on his life. He named his daughter, Julia, secondary beneficiary. At Frank's death, Mary Jo could have taken the proceeds in a lump sum. Instead she directed the insurance company to hold the proceeds at interest. In this case an includible interest (the $100,000 in proceeds) is considered to have passed from the decedent to the surviving spouse. Her disposal of the property after that point will not affect the marital deduction. But if Mary Jo had made a timely disclaimer, she would have been treated as if she had never received the proceeds, and therefore no marital deduction would have been allowed.

There is another way a disclaimer (also called a *renunciation*) can affect the marital deduction. Sometimes a decedent's will leaves the entire estate to a son or daughter. If the child makes a timely disclaimer, the result is the same as if no interest had ever passed to the child. If the child's refusal to accept the property causes all or a portion of it to pass to the surviving spouse, it will qualify as property passing from the decedent to a surviving spouse. In other words, if the effect of a disclaimer by a third party is to increase the amount of property passing from the decedent to the surviving spouse (in any one of the methods listed above), the result may be to increase the marital deduction.

Estate tax law is specific on what must be done for a disclaimer to be effective:

- It must be an irrevocable and unqualified refusal to accept an interest in property.
- It must be in writing.
- It must be received by the transferor of the interest (or his or her legal representative or holder of the legal title to the property) within 9 months of the day (1) on which the transfer creating the interest is made, (2) the grantor died, or (3) the person disclaiming attains age 21.
- It must be made before any part of the interest or its benefits are accepted.

Furthermore, the interest must pass to a person other than the person making the disclaimer, and the disclaiming person cannot direct the transfer of the property to another person.

The result of making a qualified disclaimer is that federal estate and gift tax provisions apply with respect to the disclaimed property interest as if the interest had never been transferred to or received by the person disclaiming.

There is a second implication to the passed-or-have-passed requirement. Regardless of whether the surviving spouse receives property outright or in trust for his or her benefit, the interest must be as an equitable owner in order to qualify; if the spouse is merely made a trustee for somebody else or is bound by agreement to transfer the property to another person, it is not considered to pass to the surviving spouse. So a bequest in a will providing

15.5

that "my land in Wildwood is to go to my wife, Lynne, for the benefit of my invalid son, Marvin," will not qualify.

Marital-Status Requirement

Appropriate marital status is an essential element. The decedent must have been (1) married at the date of death and (2) survived by the spouse receiving the property in question.

Obviously the words *surviving* and *spouse* present difficult questions in two situations: (1) when there has been a divorce or separation and (2) when the order of deaths of the decedent and the spouse cannot be established by proof.

The status of the surviving spouse is determined as of the date of a decedent's death. A legal separation or interlocutory (temporary and not yet final) decree of divorce that has not ended the marital relationship by the date of the decedent's death does not change the surviving spouse's status. So a bequest to a spouse when the decedent was legally separated will still qualify for the federal estate tax marital deduction.

However, if, for example, a property interest passes from the decedent to a former wife who is not married to him at the date of his death, even though she may survive him, the interest does not pass to a *surviving spouse*.

If the decedent transferred property to someone, who at the time of the transfer was not his or her spouse but who was his or her spouse on the date of death, the transfer will be considered made to a surviving spouse. If for any reason that transfer must be included in the decedent's estate, it will qualify for the marital deduction. For instance, if Mary gives IBM stock to Pat but retains the right to the dividends that it produces, the stock would be includible in her estate. If Mary has married Pat (either before or after the gift) and they are still married at the time of Mary's death, a marital deduction will be allowed with respect to the stock.

The survivorship requirement is generally not difficult to meet in most cases. But problems do occur when deaths result from a common accident and the order of deaths cannot be determined.

At the time an estate is planned, a conflict of interest can develop. On one hand, the marital deduction may be desirable only if it is likely that the surviving spouse will be able to use and enjoy the marital property for a relatively long period of time. If the surviving spouse should die immediately or shortly after receiving the marital share, that property (1) will be subject to a second probate and its consequent costs, (2) may be subject to federal estate taxation, and (3) will be subject to a second round of state inheritance tax in states that have neither a marital deduction nor a credit for previously paid taxes. Furthermore, the original decedent's property may pass to his or her spouse's heirs—a result the decedent may not have desired and would have taken steps to prevent had it been known that his or her spouse would only live a short period of time.

15.6

Conversely, there are situations where the use of the marital deduction makes good planning sense, even if the surviving spouse will probably not enjoy the property for long. One such case is when the original decedent has a large estate and the spouse has a small estate. The present value of the tax dollar saved through the use of the marital deduction at the first death, together with the availability of a second estate tax unified credit, can be a sizable advantage.

Will the marital deduction be allowed if there is no evidence as to the order of deaths? The regulations provide that when it is impossible to ascertain which spouse died first, any presumption—whether established by the decedent in a will, by state law, or otherwise—will be recognized. This means that, to the extent the presumption results in the inclusion of a bequest in the gross estate of the spouse deemed to have survived, a marital deduction will be allowed.

This presumption is generally made in a will or life insurance settlement option in the form of a *presumption-of-survivorship clause*. A typical clause might read as follows:

> In the event my wife and I die under such circumstances that there is no sufficient evidence to establish who survived the other, I hereby declare that my wife shall be deemed to have survived me, and this will and all its provisions shall be construed upon that assumption and basis.

The importance of a presumption-of-survivorship clause in a decedent's will or life insurance settlement should not be underestimated. Assume a husband owns property in his own name worth $800,000 and the wife's assets are nominal. The husband leaves his entire estate to his wife. He has made no taxable lifetime gifts. If the wife either actually survives or, because of a presumption clause in a will or life insurance settlement option, is deemed to survive, the difference can be sizable, as the illustrations below show. (Assume funeral and administrative expenses of $40,000 as well as debts and taxes of $10,000.)

If the marital deduction is lost, the difference in cost in this hypothetical example (computed before credits) is $248,000, the difference between the tentative tax when no marital deduction is allowable ($248,000) and the tentative tax if the marital deduction is obtained ($0).

What happens if there is a common disaster in which both spouses die and no presumption-of-survivorship clause has been inserted in a will or life insurance settlement option? As mentioned above, state laws will govern.

With the Marital Deduction

Gross estate		$800,000
Funeral and administration costs	$ 40,000	
Debts and taxes	10,000	
		50,000
Adjusted gross estate		750,000
Marital deduction		750,000
Taxable estate		---
Adjusted taxable gifts		---
Tentative tax base		---

Without the Marital Deduction

Gross estate		$800,000
Funeral and administration costs	$ 40,000	
Debts and taxes	10,000	
		50,000
Adjusted gross estate		750,000
Marital deduction		0
Taxable estate		750,000
Adjusted taxable gifts		---
Tentative tax base		750,000
Tentative tax		$248,000

Practically all states have adopted the Uniform Simultaneous Death Act. This act provides that if the order of deaths of the spouses cannot be determined and there is no presumption-of-survivorship clause in the will and/or life insurance contract, each decedent's estate will be distributed as though he or she were the survivor. In other words, in the probate of the husband's will, it will be assumed that he survived his wife. In the probate of the wife's will, it will be presumed that she survived her husband. This results in a tax tragedy—the loss of the marital deduction, which, in the example above, would be quite costly to their heirs.

15.8

Terminable-Interest Rule

The term *qualifying interest* is frequently used in discussions of the marital deduction; the implication is that some transfers may not qualify for the marital deduction because of the nature of the property interest itself.

Why are some interests deductible and others nondeductible? Obviously, if the transfer does not meet the tests discussed, it will be nondeductible. But there is a further roadblock to deductibility known as the *terminable-interest rule.*

To understand how the terminable-interest rule operates—and when exceptions will apply—it is necessary to review briefly tax history and philosophy.

The principal purpose of the marital deduction is to create tax parity after death between residents of common-law and community-property states—assuming, of course, equal estates. Given the same size estates and general dispository schemes, the federal tax consequences should be substantially equal, regardless of the decedent's domicile.

This thrust toward equalization grew out of the fact that in a community-property state, one-half of what one spouse acquired through earnings or as income from community property during the marriage was automatically considered the property of the other spouse. If the wife survived, she owned the property outright. She could give it away (and it would be subject to gift taxes), or she could keep it until death (and it would be subject to estate taxes). Regardless of whether she made a lifetime gift or a testamentary gift, the IRS had its proverbial bite of the tax apple.

The marital deduction was designed to give residents of common-law states the same federal estate tax treatment—but no more. In other words, since the share of a community-property decedent's surviving spouse has to be included in the surviving spouse's gross estate (the one-half portion that is not taxed at the decedent's death because community-property law deems it to be the surviving spouse's), it is only fair that when the surviving spouse of a decedent in a common-law state dies, the share of the decedent's estate that escaped estate taxation at the decedent's death by virtue of the marital deduction should be taxed at the surviving spouse's death. The marital deduction is therefore not a tax-avoidance device; it merely defers taxation until the death of the second spouse.

This is the general theory and goal of the terminable-interest rule—to allow the marital deduction only when the nature of the interest passing to the spouse is such that, if retained until death, it will be taxed in the spouse's estate.

Emphasis should be placed on the words *general, theory,* and *goal.* Generally speaking, the *intent* of the law is to deny a deduction for any interest acquired by a surviving spouse that would not be includible in the surviving spouse's estate for federal estate tax purposes if held until death.

15.9

For example, if a wife in her will gives her husband the right to land in Wildwood for life, with the remainder going to their children at his death, no part of the value of the land would be includible in the husband's estate. To allow a marital deduction for such a devise would favor common-law over community-property residents.

If an interest will be includible in a surviving spouse's estate if held to his or her death, does the converse of the general rule make it deductible? The answer is no. There can be situations in which an interest will be nondeductible, even though it will cause estate tax liability at the surviving spouse's death.

The *includible-in-the-surviving-spouse's-estate* rule should be remembered therefore only to review the basic intent of the law. But to understand how the terminable-interest rule is actually applied and when exceptions will be operative, it is more fruitful to examine the rule—and its exceptions—directly.

Actually there are two terminable-interest rules. The first provides that property will be considered a nondeductible terminable interest if all the following conditions exist:

- *It is a terminable interest,* that is, if it is an interest in property that will terminate or fail upon the lapse of time or upon the occurrence or nonoccurrence of some contingency. Life estates, annuities, and copyrights are good examples of this rule. Upon the death of a life beneficiary, a life estate or life annuity ends. Likewise, a patent will expire at the end of a given period of time. Other terminable interests include an estate for a term of years, such as "to my wife for 10 years," and a widow's support allowance that—under state law—ends when the widow dies or remarries. If Ed left Joyce property in Wildwood in the following manner, "to my wife, Joyce, during the time until she remarries," her interest would terminate at that event. If Ed had said, "to my wife, Joyce, absolutely but if she does not survive my father, then the property is to go to my sister," again Joyce's interest is terminable. Note that it is not necessary that the contingency or event actually occur—or fail to occur—in order that the interest be considered *terminable;* all that is required is that the surviving spouse's interest could terminate.
- *Another interest in the same property passed from the decedent to some person other than the surviving spouse or the spouse's estate.* For example, if the decedent gave her husband a life estate and provided that at his death their children would receive the remainder, such remainder interest would be *another interest in the same property,* and it would be passing from the decedent to someone other than the surviving spouse or his estate.
- *The interest passes or has passed to the "other person" for less than adequate and full consideration in money or money's worth.* In the example discussed above, the remainder interest would pass to the children without payment by them in money or money's worth. However, if the children had purchased the remainder interest for its

fair market value and the proceeds were given to the decedent's estate, this provision would not be met (and therefore would qualify for the marital deduction).

- *Because of its passing, the "other person(s)" or his or her heirs could possess or enjoy any part of the property when the surviving spouse's interest terminated.* Note that if a decedent left property "to my daughter, Pat, for life, then to my wife, Lynne, absolutely," the present value of the wife's interest (that is, the value after subtracting the daughter's life interest) would not be disqualified for the marital deduction, since no one can possess or enjoy any part of the property when the wife dies. In fact, the wife's interest is not terminable.

So generally a terminable interest—such as a life estate—will only be disqualified if it falls within all of the latter three categories. Therefore a transfer "to my wife for life, then to her estate" will qualify for the marital deduction. This lifetime bequest to the surviving spouse qualifies, since the decedent designated his surviving spouse's estate (rather than their children) as the remainderperson; hence, no interest passes to someone other than the surviving spouse or her estate.

There is a second type of terminable interest that will not qualify for the marital deduction—even though no person other than the surviving spouse acquires an interest in the property. This is a situation in which the decedent in his or her will has directed the executor (or a trustee) to take assets ostensibly available to the surviving spouse and purchase a terminable interest with them. For example, if Al leaves $100,000 to his wife, Leslie, in a specific bequest in his will but directs his executor to use the $100,000 as the purchase price for a nonrefund life annuity for her, the $100,000 bequest will not qualify for the marital deduction. Likewise, if Al's executor was directed to use the $100,000 to purchase a patent, copyright, or other terminable interest for Leslie, such a bequest will not qualify.

Exceptions to the Terminable-Interest Rules

There are four important exceptions to the terminable-interest rules. The four exceptions are listed directly below and are then discussed in the paragraphs that follow.

- An interest will still qualify for the marital deduction (it will not be considered a nondeductible terminable interest solely because it will terminate or fail upon the surviving spouse's death) if the bequest to the surviving spouse was conditional upon his or her surviving for up to 6 months after the decedent's death—as long as the surviving spouse does, in fact, survive for the specified period. (For example, an interest will not be disqualified for the marital deduction merely because it states "if my husband fails to survive me by 6 months, this will and all its provisions shall be construed as if he predeceased me.") However, if the specified termination does occur, the marital deduction will be lost.
- A bequest of a life estate can qualify for the marital deduction if it is coupled with a general power of appointment.

- A life insurance policy payable to the surviving spouse for life can qualify if the spouse has a general power of appointment over the proceeds.
- A qualified terminable-interest property election can also qualify.

The first exception to the terminable-interest rule provides that an interest passing to a surviving spouse will not be considered nondeductible merely because it will terminate or fail upon the surviving spouse's death within a period of not more than 6 months of the decedent's death. (This type of provision is sometimes used to prevent *double probate* and *double state death taxation* when the death of one spouse occurs within a short time of the other spouse's death.)

> *Example:* Ike leaves his wife, Tina, a life estate in his land in Stone Harbor. The remainder is payable to Tina's estate. But Ike's will provides that Tina will receive no interest in the land if she does not survive Ike for 6 months. If Tina in fact survives the 6-month period, a marital deduction will be allowed in Ike's estate. If Tina does not survive Ike by the required period of time, no deduction will be allowed.

If Ike required Tina to survive him by some period in excess of 6 months (such as survival by one year or survival "until my estate is closed"), the transfer would not qualify because it did—or could—exceed the 6-month permissible period. If Ike's will provided "my land is to go to Tina, my wife, for life, and the remainder, at her death, is to go to my son, Sophocles, but for my wife to receive her interest, she must survive me by 3 months," the interest would not qualify for the marital deduction even if Tina did survive the 3-month period. This is because the failure of a contingency to occur cannot convert what is otherwise a nonqualifying terminable interest (the life estate to the wife and remainder to the son) into a qualifying interest.

A second part of this exception deals with common-disaster provisions. Assume Ike's will stated, "I leave my entire estate to my wife, Tina, but if she and I die in a common disaster, my estate goes instead to my son, Sophocles." Assume also that state law defines a common disaster as an event in which both spouses die within 30 days from injuries attributable to a common accident. If Tina survives for 2 months and then dies, she would have received Ike's estate. Since the terminating contingency—the deaths of both spouses in a common disaster as defined by state law—did not occur, the marital deduction would be allowed in Ike's estate. But if Tina died 3 weeks after the accident, no marital deduction would be allowed because the terminating contingency did, in fact, occur.

The second exception to the terminable-interest rule is that the interest will not be disqualified if it meets all the following five conditions:

- The surviving spouse is entitled to all the income from the interest in question.
- The income is payable annually or more frequently. (The marital trust is the receptacle into which probate assets qualifying for the marital

deduction are placed. If the marital trust has a specific provision either authorizing investment in non-income-producing assets or allowing the trustee to retain unproductive assets (non-income-producing), this requirement may not be satisfied. This militates against the purchase of life insurance by the marital trust or leaving closely held stock that has never paid a significant dividend or unproductive land, unless the surviving spouse has an unqualified right to demand that trust assets be sold and converted into income-producing property.)

- The surviving spouse has the power to appoint the interest to herself or her estate.
- The power must be exercisable by her alone and in all events. It can be a lifetime power or power exercisable by her only at her death— that is, by will, or a power exercisable in either event.
- No person other than the surviving spouse has a power to appoint any part of the interest to anyone other than the surviving spouse.

This second exception makes the *power-of-appointment trust* the most widely used method of qualifying property in trust for the marital deduction. Essentially the power-of-appointment trust is, as its name implies, a trust designed to hold assets for the surviving spouse and to qualify for the marital deduction by providing the surviving spouse with a general power of appointment over the corpus. The primary purpose of such a trust arrangement is to require the surviving spouse to take affirmative action to direct the corpus at death from the original estate owner's planned disposition.

Generally the testator's will sets up two trusts: a marital (spouse's) trust and a nonmarital (family) trust. The marital trust is designed to hold assets that qualify for the marital deduction, while the nonmarital trust is intended to provide management for assets that are taxable at the testator's death.

If it is drafted properly, the nonmarital (family) trust will provide the spouse with additional income and even limited amounts of principal without causing an inclusion of principal in his or her gross estate. In a sense this trust is a *bypass trust*, since it provides security for the spouse but bypasses taxation in his or her estate when the spouse dies. Quite often this trust is called a *credit-equivalent bypass trust* (CEBT) since—ideally, at least—it should be funded with assets equivalent to the testator's unified credit equivalent.

> *Example:* Assume Joan McFadden's adjusted gross estate was worth $1 million. If she died in 1987, the formula in her will for determining how assets are to be divided might provide that an amount equal to the credit equivalent ($600,000) go to the CEBT and the balance of his estate to her surviving spouse. The federal estate tax on the $600,000 that goes into the CEBT would be eliminated by the credit (the $600,000 of assets would generate $192,800 of estate tax, which would be wiped out by the $192,800 credit). The $400,000 that passes to her husband (either directly or in trust) would qualify for the unlimited marital deduction and therefore escape federal estate tax.

The advantage of *carving out* a credit-equivalent bypass trust before determining the marital deduction is that when the spouse dies, at least $600,000—the amount in the CEBT—escapes taxation in his estate. Through a more effective use of his wife's unified credit (and the avoidance of *stacking* assets into the husband's estate), significant estate tax savings can be realized. (The results are even more dramatic if there is a substantial increase in asset values between the first and second deaths.) For instance, in the example above assume that the surviving spouse had no estate of his own. At his death, examine the following:

	If husband received only $400,000	If husband received $1,000,000
Tentative tax base	$400,000	$1,000,000
Tentative tax	121,800	345,800
Unified credit	192,800	192,800
Tax		$ 153,000

The same result is often obtained by establishing an inter vivos trust during the grantor's lifetime, and then *pouring over* probate assets by will into this trust and naming the trust direct beneficiary of death benefits from life insurance proceeds and employee benefit plans. At the grantor's death, the trust would be split into two trusts or two portions—a marital and nonmarital—with the same functions as the testamentary trusts described above. When the surviving spouse is given a general power of appointment over assets in the marital trust, it is known as a *power-of-appointment trust*.

The intended result can be accomplished by giving the surviving spouse a power to withdraw the property in the marital trust anytime during his or her life or to direct by will at his or her death that the property is to become part of his or her estate or be used to satisfy creditors.

The surviving spouse can be restricted to a power exercisable only by will; the trust will qualify for the marital deduction even if the spouse has no power to withdraw the corpus during his or her lifetime.

In addition to the power-of-appointment trust, the *estate trust* is also a viable method of obtaining a marital deduction. An estate trust is one in which the surviving spouse is given an interest for life, with the remainder payable to his or her estate. In effect, this gives the surviving spouse the equivalent of a general power of appointment by will, since he or she can *transfer* (or more correctly, shift) property subject to the power to anyone he or she chooses.

The estate trust does not run afoul of the nondeductible terminable-interest rule for another reason: no interest will pass to anyone other than the surviving spouse *or his or her estate*.

An estate trust is a useful alternative to the power-of-appointment trust for a number of reasons.

First, in contrast to the power-of-appointment trust, under which all income must be payable to the surviving spouse annually or more frequently, the trustee of an estate trust can accumulate income within the trust instead of paying it out. If the trust is in a lower income tax bracket than that of the surviving spouse, the power to accumulate can result in income tax savings.

Second, because the spouse does not have to receive *all the income annually,* a trustee can either invest in *nonproductive* (non-income-producing) property or retain nonproductive assets, such as non-dividend-paying stock in a family-owned corporation.

These advantages must be weighed, however, against the certainty that any income accumulations (together with the original corpus) will be includible in the surviving spouse's estate. This in turn may result in increased administrative costs, be subject to the claims of creditors, and attract state inheritance taxes. (For example, compare this with the power-of-appointment trust, which, under the laws of a state such as Pennsylvania, is not part of the probate estate and the corpus of which is not taxed for state inheritance tax purposes at the death of the donee of the power.)

The third exception to the terminable-interest rule parallels the second: an interest in life insurance proceeds (or an endowment or annuity contract) will be treated as passing solely to the surviving spouse, if both of the following conditions exist:

- Under the settlement option, the surviving spouse is entitled to all the interest for life (or the right to installment payments of the proceeds for life).
- The surviving spouse has the right to appoint to himself or herself or his or her estate any proceeds or installment payments remaining.

This exception makes it possible to qualify life insurance proceeds under a settlement option if the surviving spouse is given the equivalent of a general power of appointment, even if there is a gift-over. For example, a settlement option could qualify for the marital deduction if it provided that (1) the surviving spouse is to receive *interest only* for life; (2) there is an unlimited right of withdrawal or the right to a one-sum settlement; and (3) if no withdrawal is made, any proceeds remaining are to be paid to the children born of the marriage of the insured and said spouse.

A fourth exception allows a qualifying terminable interest property to qualify for the marital deduction. A person can provide that his or her spouse will receive only the income from property and, at the death of the surviving spouse, it must pass to the person or persons specified in the will of the original transferor-spouse. This otherwise nondeductible terminable interest will qualify for the marital deduction—hence the name *qualifying terminable interest property (QTIP)* if certain requirements are met. This provision permits a spouse to provide for his or her surviving spouse through a transfer sheltered by the marital deduction and still retain control over the ultimate disposition of the assets. The QTIP is a way for a spouse to protect the interests of his or her other heirs (perhaps children from a prior marriage) while also providing for the surviving spouse.

There are four conditions that must be met before QTIP treatment will be allowed. (Keep in mind that other property besides that placed in trusts can satisfy these requirements and achieve the same favorable results.)

- The decedent-spouse (or donor, in the case of a lifetime gift) must make a transfer of property. The transfer can be in trust or through insurance proceeds or in other ways, such as the death proceeds of a nonqualified deferred-compensation plan.
- The surviving spouse (donee, in the case of a lifetime transfer) must be given the right to all the income. The income must be payable at least annually, and the surviving spouse must be entitled to that income for life.
- No one can be given the right to direct that the property will go to anyone (other than the spouse) as long as that spouse is alive. (It is permissible to give someone other than the surviving spouse the power to appoint QTIP property, if that power can only be exercised after the surviving spouse dies.)
- The first decedent-spouse's executor must make an irrevocable election on the decedent's federal estate tax return. The election provides that, to the extent the QTIP property has not been consumed or given away during the lifetime of the surviving spouse, its date-of-death value (at the surviving spouse's death) will be included in the surviving spouse's estate. In the case of a lifetime gift of QTIP property, the donor-spouse must file a similar election on the gift tax return so that the QTIP property will be in the estate of the donee-spouse, unless disposed of during the donee-spouse's lifetime.

In other words, under an elective provision even *terminable interests* passing to a spouse can now qualify for a marital deduction. Property passing to a surviving spouse for life with the remainder going to some other person(s) would be eligible for the marital deduction on the condition that the property would be subject to tax at the surviving spouse's death.

QTIP—The Problem of Unproductive Property

At first glance, it appears that the QTIP concept satisfies all needs for all people. Obviously this is not the case. If all or most of a client's estate consists of unproductive real estate (and/or stock in a closely held corporation that has not paid, and probably never will pay, any significant dividends), will the surviving spouse receive the statutorily required "all income at least annually"? Most authorities think that the answer is no.

The surviving spouse must be given an interest that realistically is expected to produce income (or will be usable by the spouse in a manner consistent with its value). Most closely held stock will never pay dividends or realistically be expected to produce an income consistent with its value. Therefore, without planning, the marital deduction could be lost. What can be done to save the marital deduction? If there is no state law giving the surviving spouse the power to require that trust assets be sold and that trust property be made productive in a reasonable period of time, the attorney drafting the marital formula must clearly insert a provision in the will or trust giving the survivor that power. If the surviving spouse can demand that the trustee sell the stock (or other unproductive assets) and use the proceeds to purchase income-producing property, the marital deduction can be saved (even if the power is never actually exercised).

Unfortunately, even if the surviving spouse is given the power to demand that the trustee sell the stock, there are practical problems.

For example, suppose that a client's objective was to pass the stock to his daughter at his wife's death. If the wife can force a sale, what assurance does the daughter have that she will be the purchaser? Who would purchase the stock if it was a minority interest? If it was a majority interest, what happens to the daughter's job if the stock is sold to a third party? Even if the wife is not given the power to require the trustee to sell the stock, can she obtain the corpus of the trust by electing against her husband's will? If the wife doesn't force a sale of trust assets, where will she obtain income sufficient to maintain her current standard of living?

Solutions include the creation of a life-insurance-funded irrevocable trust by the husband. At his death, the trust would provide income to the wife for life and then the corpus would pass to their daughter. This would relieve pressure on the wife to force the trustee to sell the stock in the QTIP trust. In fact, the irrevocable trust might provide income but make the surviving spouse's right to that income conditional on making no demand for a sale of QTIP assets. If she demands that the trustee sell the QTIP assets, she will lose her right to income from the irrevocable trust.

An alternative solution is a funded buy-sell agreement between the father and the daughter. If the daughter has the insurance proceeds at her father's death, she can purchase the stock from his estate. That way cash rather than stock goes into the QTIP trust. Another possibility is a recapitalization coupled with a Sec. 303 stock redemption and/or a cross-purchase agreement with the daughter.

OVERQUALIFICATION AND UNDERQUALIFICATION

Overqualification occurs when there is an underutilization of the estate owner's unified credit. The result is that more property than necessary (to reduce the estate owner's federal estate tax to zero) goes to the surviving spouse. Thus, at the surviving spouse's death, more property than necessary is exposed to tax. This is where property funding of a credit-equivalent bypass trust (CEBT) is useful. It assures an efficient use of both spouses' unified credit and prevents unnecessary *stacking* of assets in the surviving spouse's estate.

Underqualification means that less property passed to the surviving spouse in a qualifying manner than should have passed tax free. For instance, assume a wife had a $1 million adjusted gross estate in 1987 but left only $100,000 to her spouse in a qualifying manner. There would be a $300,000 underqualification ($600,000 would go to the CEBT and no tax would be payable; that leaves $400,000 that could qualify for the unlimited marital deduction). In other words, the marital deduction was underutilized by $300,000. (However, keep in mind that for tax and other reasons planners sometimes deliberately pass less than the maximum allowable marital deduction and thus deliberately underqualify.)

Formulas for Minimizing Tax

Obviously a clause is needed in the will that can provide, by formula, an amount or share of the estate that will effectively utilize the estate owner's unified credit and coordinate it with the unlimited marital deduction. These are appropriately known as *formula bequests*.

Because of the increasing unified credit, it is often desirable to provide that use of the marital deduction be limited to the amount required to reduce the estate owner's federal estate tax to the lowest possible figure after considering the unified credit allowable in the year of his or her death. For example, if the decedent's gross estate is $1 million and he leaves the full $1 million to his wife, there will be no federal estate tax at his death—but there will be a federal estate tax at the death of his wife that is equal to her tentative tax base less the then available unified credit.

If, instead of the unlimited marital share, the decedent had given to his spouse an amount exactly sufficient (and no larger) to reduce the federal estate tax due at his death to the lowest possible figure and had given the balance to his children (directly or through a CEBT), then (assuming the decedent dies in 1987) his children would receive $600,000 and his wife would receive $400,000. Upon his wife's subsequent death, there would probably be no federal estate tax due. In essence, what has been done is to "fund the residue" (the children's portion of the estate) to the extent of the exemption equivalent before funding the marital gift.

There are two types of *formula bequests*—the *pecuniary (dollar) amount* and the *fractional share*.

The pecuniary-amount bequest provides that the survivor will receive a fixed-dollar amount and takes into consideration not only property passing under the will but all property qualifying for the marital deduction. The pecuniary-amount bequest might read somewhat as follows:

> If my wife, Allene, survives me, I give, devise, and bequeath
> to her a sum of money that shall be exactly sufficient to reduce
> the federal estate tax (after applicable credits) due as a result of
> my death to the lowest possible number less the value of all
> interests in property, if any, that pass or have passed to her
> under other items of my will or outside my will, but only to the

15.18

extent that such interests are included in determining my gross estate and allowed as a marital deduction.

The fractional-share bequest is an attempt to accomplish the same goal by giving the surviving spouse a fractional share in the residue of the estate—that is, a fractional share of each asset, after specific bequests have been made.

How much should the surviving spouse be given under the marital bequest? Should the surviving spouse be given even less than the amount necessary to reduce taxes in the decedent's estate to zero? Should the surviving spouse only be given one-half of the estate? Will the time-use (or psychological) value of tax money saved on the death of the first spouse offset the cost, the (potential) increase in total taxes payable? Perhaps. Much depends on the use to which tax savings are put at the first death. If the money is used to insure or enhance the life-style of the surviving spouse, then it will result in a long-run benefit.

But if the excess of the amount necessary to *equalize the two estates* is invested by the surviving spouse and is eventually taxed at a higher rate when he or she dies, the net result will be fewer assets passing to the next generation. (There will always be—mathematically, at least—a tax saving by equalizing the estates, if it is assumed that the second spouse is merely accumulating and not spending the equalization amount.)

The example below (taken from Arthur Weiss and Linda Etkin, "New Law Overhauls Estate and Gift Taxes," *Journal of Taxation,* 55 [Nov. 1981]: 274) is based on the assumption that the husband dies first, and the wife lives 10 more years and is able to enjoy a 10 percent growth rate on her assets.

Unlimited Marital Deduction

Husband's estate

Gross estate	$3,000,000
Marital trust	2,400,000
(grows to $6,224,982)	
Gross residuary trust	600,000
Estate tax	0
Net residuary trust	$ 600,000
(grows to $1,556,246)	

Wife's estate

Gross estate	$6,224,982
Estate tax	2,695,491
Net estate	3,529,491
Residuary trust	1,556,246
To children	$5,085,737

15.19

<u>Equalization of Estates</u>
   <u>Husband's estate</u>

Gross estate	$3,000,000
Marital trust	1,500,000
(grows to $3,890,614)	
Gross residuary trust	1,500,000
Estate tax	363,000
Net residuary trust	$1,137,000
(grows to $2,949,085)	

   <u>Wife's estate</u>

Gross estate	$3,890,614
Estate tax	1,528,307
Net estate	2,362,307
Residuary trust	2,949,085
To children	$5,311,392
Excess through	
equalization	$ 225,655

The actual answer will vary according to the circumstances, needs, and desires of the parties involved. The time value of money, as well as the survivor's ability to consume or give away property, must be considered.

FORMS OF MARITAL BEQUESTS—ADVANTAGES AND DISADVANTAGES

There are many means of obtaining the marital deduction. One method discussed above is the outright transfer of property to the surviving spouse by will or through life insurance death proceeds. There are advantages to an outright bequest:

- The spouse has the right to use and manage marital assets as he or she desires.
- No trustee's fees or court accountings are required.
- Giving the spouse his or her marital share discourages him or her from electing against the testator's will.
- Assets the surviving spouse receives are available to his or her executor to meet estate liquidity needs.
- The surviving spouse can be given—and can safely retain—non-income-producing assets, such as the non-dividend-paying stock in a family-owned corporation.

But an outright bequest has a number of disadvantages:

- No protection is provided for a spendthrift spouse.
- There is no management where investment expertise is provided.
- The surviving spouse's creditor can attach the bequest both during his or her lifetime and at death.
- The surviving spouse can easily dispose of the bequest however he or she wishes during lifetime—even to the exclusion of his or her children, and in favor of a second spouse and children.

- Assets the surviving spouse has not given away or consumed will be included in his or her probate estate.

A second method of providing a marital bequest is by leaving property in a power-of-appointment trust. Typically the power-of-appointment trust gives the spouse a lifetime interest in the trust property, coupled with the right to specify the identity of the remainderperson during his or her lifetime or in his or her will. It usually also provides that if the surviving spouse fails to name the beneficiaries of trust assets, the trust corpus will go to a *taker in default*, a beneficiary named by the grantor of the trust. The trustee (and sometimes the surviving spouse) is often given additional powers over trust assets. These might include the right to use trust principal for emergencies or to make gifts to children and grandchildren.

The advantages of a power-of-appointment trust include these:

- As in the case of an outright gift, the surviving spouse will be discouraged from electing against the decedent's will.
- Protection is afforded to some degree against the surviving spouse's possible spendthrift habits.
- Protection is provided against the surviving spouse's creditors and the creditors of his or her estate.
- Principal distributions can be varied, depending on the surviving spouse's needs.
- The surviving spouse's right to dispose of the property during his or her lifetime can be limited.
- Probate of the trust corpus can be avoided when the surviving spouse dies.
- Management and financial guidance are provided for the surviving spouse.

But there are disadvantages of a power-of-appointment trust:

- Certain trustee's fees and accounting costs are involved.
- Assets in a power-of-appointment trust may not be available to the surviving spouse's executor for the payments of costs and taxes (unless he or she appoints the assets to his or her estate).
- Non-income-producing property, such as life insurance, cannot safely be obtained or retained in the trust.

The third form of marital bequest under a will is known as an *estate trust*. The type of trust described above is not required to give the surviving spouse all the income during his or her lifetime, but pays all the accumulated income and the corpus to the surviving spouse's estate when he or she dies. (During lifetime the surviving spouse can, of course, be given income or principal at the discretion of the trustee, but he or she personally has no lifetime right to demand either income or principal.)

Advantages of the estate trust include the following:

- Non-income-producing property can be purchased and safely retained by the trustee.
- Income tax savings can be realized by the accumulation of the income in the trust in years when the trust's income tax bracket is lower than the surviving spouse's bracket.
- Protection is provided against the surviving spouse's spendthrift habits, if any.
- Protection is afforded against the surviving spouse's creditors during his or her lifetime.
- The surviving spouse is unable to make lifetime assignments of trust property.
- Assets will be made available to the surviving spouse's executor on his or her death.

Disadvantages of the estate trust consist mainly of its inflexibility from the surviving spouse's viewpoint:

- The surviving spouse has no freedom to use and manage trust assets.
- The surviving spouse is restricted in disposing of any property in the trust during his or her lifetime.
- Assets in the trust will generate trustee's fees and accounting costs.

The fourth form of marital bequest is through the QTIP trust. The QTIP trust gives the spouse a lifetime interest in the property but no general power either during lifetime or at death. At his or her death, assets in the trust pass to the beneficiary or beneficiaries named by the testator.

The advantages of a QTIP trust include the following:

- The grantor can be more certain that the trust assets will eventually be received by the parties he or she has designated.
- Protection is afforded against the surviving spouse's spendthrift habits, if any.
- Protection is provided against the surviving spouse's creditors and the creditors of his or her estate.
- The surviving spouse is given no power to dispose of the property.
- Probate of the trust corpus is avoided at the surviving spouse's death.

Note that in many states a surviving spouse may be able to *take against* his or her spouse's will and thereby defeat some of the objectives and advantages described above.

Disadvantages of the QTIP trust include the following:

- There may be a false sense of security that the estate owner's objectives will be accomplished.
- Non-income-producing property can be safely used to fund the trust, only if the surviving spouse is given the power to demand that trust assets be made productive (income producing).
- The surviving spouse is restricted in the use of trust assets.

THE EXTENT TO WHICH THE MARITAL DEDUCTION SHOULD BE USED

There are a number of factors that should be considered in deciding how much of a decedent's gross estate should be transferred to his surviving spouse:

Factor	Consideration
Tax savings desired at first death	Maximum utilization of marital deduction is indicated
Tax savings—both estates	To extent not consumed or given away through present-interest gifts, marital-deduction assets may compound estate tax problems at second death
Lack of confidence in spouse's judgment	Marital assets will be subject to spouse's dispository desires, either during lifetime or at death
Fear of spouse's remarriage and aversion to new spouse's obtaining marital property	Right of new spouse to elect against spouse's will indicates use of less than maximum marital transfer
Size of surviving spouse's estate	Until size of surviving spouse's estate equals the exemption equivalent of the federal credit, assets should be transferred to her. But if his or her estate is as large as or larger than his or her spouse's or a sizable inheritance from a third party is likely, the use of sizable marital transfers is contraindicated.
Time value of money	Tax money saved by maximum use of marital deduction can be invested and may offset any additional tax on second death. Investment opportunities available to the surviving spouse must be taken into account.
Availability of spouse to of give away and consume marital assets	Spouse's age, health, number children and grandchildren, financial needs (including educational and health needs of children), living standard, and even inflation must be considered— generally, the younger the spouse, the greater his or her financial needs

Factor	Consideration
Income tax bracket of surviving spouse	If surviving spouse is already in high income tax bracket, additional income from marital assets may be counter-productive
Liquidity needs of decedent's estate	If decedent's estate is relatively nonliquid, maximum use of marital deduction is indicated
State death tax laws	Some states do not tax property subject to a power of appointment in donee's estate, unless power is exercised by donee. This makes it possible, in some cases, for property in a marital (spouse's) trust to escape state death taxation at his or her death.

ESTATE PLANNING FOR THE NONCITIZEN-SPOUSE

Ted Kurlowicz and Stephan R. Leimberg

The previous chapter discussed the unlimited marital deduction for federal estate tax purposes. The marital deduction provides an opportunity for a typical married couple to avoid federal estate taxes at the first death of the spouses. However, the marital deduction is not available for property passing to a surviving spouse who is *not* a U.S. citizen even if such spouse resides in the United States (referred to as a resident-alien). This change, brought about by TAMRA '88, reflects the concern in Congress that a resident-alien-spouse could receive assets in the marital transfer from the citizen-spouse and return to his or her home country with the family wealth. If a marital deduction were allowed under such circumstances, the property transferred to the resident-alien-spouse could completely escape federal estate and gift taxes. The United States does not have jurisdiction to tax a nonresident-alien for property located outside the country.

The denial of the marital deduction for transfers to a resident-alien follows the overall scheme intended for the federal estate and gift tax system. That is, the wealth accumulated by a married couple will, at the very least, be subject to transfer tax at the second death of the spouses. Simply, Congress is preserving its ability to tax the transfer of marital property at some point. The marital deduction is permitted, however, if the resident-alien-spouse is the first to die and transfers property in a qualifying manner to a surviving citizen-spouse. In this instance, the surviving spouse will be a citizen, and the United States will be able to impose tax whenever the surviving spouse makes a transfer of his or her property.

If a marriage includes a spouse who is either (1) a citizen of or (2) a resident of a foreign country, the transfers to *or* from such spouse may also be subject to foreign transfer taxes. In addition, property with a foreign situs might be subject to foreign transfer taxes even if transferred by a U.S. citizen. The United States has entered into foreign estate and gift tax treaties with many countries in an attempt to avoid the double taxation of certain transfers. The actual taxation of such individuals and their foreign property will depend on the specific treaty involved. The United States does allow a credit for foreign death taxes paid against the federal estate tax, as discussed in reading 18.

TRANSFERS TO A SURVIVING RESIDENT-ALIEN-SPOUSE

The general rule is that transfers to a resident-alien-spouse will not qualify for the unlimited federal estate or gift tax marital deduction. This creates a special concern for marriages that include a resident-alien-spouse. The transfer taxes facing such marriages will often depend on which spouse survives. If the survivor is the resident-alien, a substantial first-death estate tax may be payable. Fortunately, there are some exceptions to this harsh rule.

The Surviving Spouse Obtains Citizenship

Transfers to a surviving resident-alien-spouse will become eligible for the marital deduction if (1) the surviving spouse becomes a U.S. citizen before the decedent-spouse's estate tax return is filed and (2) the surviving spouse remains a U.S. resident after the death of the citizen-spouse.[1]

There are also estate tax benefits to the surviving spouse for obtaining citizenship *even* if his or her citizenship status is attained after the citizen-spouse's estate tax return is filed. As discussed below, the qualified domestic trust (QDOT) can be used to transfer assets to a surviving resident-alien-spouse while preserving the marital deduction for such transfer. The surviving spouse can avoid some or all of the disadvantages associated with receiving property in a QDOT by obtaining citizenship. To avoid the application of the QDOT rules, the surviving spouse who receives QDOT property must obtain citizenship prior to his or her death.

Qualified Domestic Trust (QDOT)

To alleviate some of the harsh estate tax implications associated with the denial of the marital deduction for transfers to a resident-alien-spouse, Congress created an exception for transfers to a qualified domestic trust. A QDOT is a unique transfer vehicle for marital-deduction transfers to surviving resident-alien-spouses. Unfortunately the QDOT rules also include a new type of transfer tax. Although the QDOT appears to provide all the usual tax benefits of the marital deduction, the discussion below demonstrates that the QDOT has several disadvantages not applicable to transfers between citizen-spouses. A QDOT is a marital-deduction trust that meets the following requirements:[2]

- At least one trustee must be an individual who is a U.S. citizen or domestic corporation.
- The trust terms must provide that no distribution can be made from the QDOT without the approval of the U.S. trustee.
- The executor of the decedent-citizen-spouse's estate must make an election to qualify such marital-deduction trust for QDOT treatment.
- The QDOT must be created in the form of the qualifying types of marital-deduction trusts discussed in the previous reading.

Qualifying Transfers to a QDOT

A QDOT is generally eligible to receive any transfer normally qualifying for a marital deduction. The QDOT can be eligible to receive property in the following forms:

- an estate trust
- a general power-of-appointment trust

- a QTIP trust
- proceeds of life insurance or retirement plans
- joint property passing by right of survivorship
- transfers of probate property through the decedent's will

The various terms of the estate, QTIP, and power-of-appointment trust were discussed in the previous chapter and are not further discussed here. It is clear that the QDOT must take the form of one of these trusts. In addition, any property passing to the surviving resident-alien-spouse will be eligible for QDOT treatment if such property is irrevocably assigned to the QDOT. Property can be transferred to the QDOT either (1) through a direct transfer by the decedent, (2) by the decedent's executor, or (3) by the surviving resident-alien-spouse. However, any irrevocable assignment of property to the QDOT *must* occur before the decedent-citizen-spouse's estate tax return is filed.

Thus the citizen-spouse's estate will be eligible for the marital deduction for property transferred through his or her will to a QDOT. This treatment is available regardless of whether the QDOT was a testamentary trust or an inter vivos pour-over trust.

The decedent's executor or the surviving resident-alien-spouse can also qualify property transferred *directly* to the survivor for the marital deduction simply by irrevocably assigning such property to a QDOT. For these purposes it is irrelevant whether the QDOT was created by the decedent, the decedent's executor, or the surviving resident-alien-spouse. Therefore QDOT treatment is available even if the decedent-spouse neglected to include a QDOT in his or her estate plan. The surviving resident-alien-spouse can preserve the marital deduction on property he or she receives by creating a QDOT and irrevocably assigning property received from the decedent-spouse to a QDOT in a timely fashion. Thus a surviving resident-alien-spouse can preserve the marital deduction by transferring property he or she received (1) through an outright bequest or intestacy, (2) as proceeds of life insurance on the life of the decedent, and (3) as survivor annuities[3] to the QDOT.

Taxation of QDOT Distributions

The transfer to a QDOT is unlike the typical marital-deduction transfer in many respects. Although the tax treatment applicable to the QDOT delays the estate taxation until the death of the resident-alien-spouse, this second-death taxation is based on a unique theory. The taxation of property distributed from a QDOT is based on the estate situation of the first spouse to die—that is, the citizen-spouse. The citizen-spouse is treated as the transferor, and the QDOT estate tax is calculated with the QDOT property included in the tax base of the citizen-spouse. Because of the marital deduction, however, the estate tax for property transferred to a QDOT is deferred until the QDOT corpus is distributed either (1) during the life of the surviving resident-alien-spouse or (2) at his or her death. The following events will trigger the QDOT tax:

- distributions of QDOT property to the surviving spouse except distributions of (1) income[4] or (2) on account of hardship[5]
- distributions of QDOT property at the surviving spouse's death
- failure of the trust to meet the QDOT requirements

The QDOT tax is imposed on any such taxable event and, similar to other transfer taxes, is determined cumulatively. That is, each additional QDOT taxable event will be added to previous taxable transfers to form the QDOT tax base, and each transfer may be subject to a higher marginal estate tax bracket. The notable distinguishing characteristic between the QDOT tax and the tax on a typical marital-deduction trust is that the QDOT tax is referenced to the decedent's transfer-tax base rather than the survivor's. The QDOT tax is calculated by adding the property to the citizen-spouse's estate and by computing the tax based on the rate applicable to such citizen-spouse's estate after the QDOT property is added.

This unusual tax treatment causes the estate tax imposed on a QDOT distribution to be different, perhaps substantially, from the second-death tax imposed on the normal marital-deduction trust. If the citizen-spouse has substantially more assets and is the first to die, the overall estate tax paid will be greater. This is because the transfer tax paid on the QDOT distribution will be based on the estate tax bracket of the wealthier spouse. Under these circumstances, the spouses will not receive the benefit of the surviving resident-alien-spouse's lower marginal transfer-tax rate. Conversely, this special QDOT tax treatment could be beneficial if the resident-alien-spouse is the wealthier spouse.

Availability of Credits. The credits available against federal estate tax are discussed later in reading 18. The unified credit was discussed in the previous assignment with respect to overqualification for the marital deduction. As that discussion indicated, an appropriately designed estate plan for a married couple could make optimal use of the marital deduction and the unified credits of both spouses. Under the optimal scenario, the married couple could leave assets of up to $1.2 million free of federal estate tax by fully utilizing each spouse's $600,000 unified credit equivalent. However, the QDOT transfer might eliminate the possibility of taking full advantage of the unified credit. Since the ultimate distribution of the QDOT corpus at the death of the surviving resident-alien-spouse is treated as if the decedent-citizen-spouse made the transfer, the unified credit of the surviving resident-alien-spouse is unavailable to shelter this transfer from QDOT tax. Thus the resident-alien-spouse will waste his or her unified credit unless he or she owns sufficient assets (approximately $600,000) outside the QDOT.

> *Example:* Suppose Tom, a U.S. citizen, is married to Sheila, a resident-alien. Tom has $1.5 million of individually owned assets, while Sheila has accumulated no personal wealth. Tom dies this year, and his will leaves $600,000 to a credit-equivalent-bypass trust to benefit his children from a prior marriage. The remaining amount, $900,000, ignoring taxes and other estate settlement expenses, is left outright to Sheila. If Tom dies this year, Sheila can qualify the transfer of the $900,000 for the

unlimited marital deduction by transferring such funds irrevocably to a QDOT before Tom's estate tax return is filed. The remaining $600,000 left in trust to his children will be sheltered from tax by Tom's unified credit. If Sheila dies next year, the $900,000 in the QDOT will be subject to tax as if it were included in Tom's estate. This $900,000 will incur an additional estate tax of $363,000 on this taxable QDOT event. This amount was subject to a marginal bracket of 43 percent. If the $900,000 were instead subject to Sheila's tax rates, only $114,000 of tax would be due. Sheila's estate would only be in a 39 percent marginal bracket and would, in this case, have the benefit of her unified credit leaving only $300,000 subject to estate tax. (As discussed below, the QDOT actually *is* in Sheila's estate. However, any tax due as a result of its inclusion in Sheila's estate will be avoided since her estate will receive a credit for the QDOT tax paid on the same distribution.)

Since the surviving spouse has the benefit of the QDOT for the remainder of his or her life, the transfer of the QDOT corpus at his or her death will, most likely, be subject to state death taxes. Since the federal tax—the QDOT tax—is treated as if the original decedent is making the transfer, the state death tax credit against the federal estate tax will be unavailable to shelter any QDOT tax. Thus the value of the property transferred at the death of the surviving spouse will be subject to multiple taxation where the QDOT tax is applicable.

A QDOT, similar to any typical marital-deduction trust, is included in the surviving spouse's gross estate at his or her death. Will the QDOT property be subject to both a QDOT tax and a federal estate tax imposed on the surviving spouse's estate? Fortunately there is a credit for a transfer tax paid on prior transfers of the same property. This credit will be further discussed in reading 18. The credit for tax paid on prior transfers is applied liberally to the QDOT taxable distribution. The net effect of this credit is that when the surviving spouse dies, no federal estate tax will be due to the extent that the same property transfer incurs a QDOT tax.[6]

MINIMIZING THE BURDEN OF THE QDOT TAX FOR SURVIVING RESIDENT-ALIEN-SPOUSES

The QDOT tax creates a problem for a married couple if one spouse is a resident-alien. This problem is particularly pertinent if the citizen-spouse is wealthier and is expected to be the first to die. Planning in these circumstances focuses on either (1) the avoidance of the transfer tax when distributions are made from a QDOT or (2) the use of a technique other than the QDOT to transfer wealth to the resident-alien-spouse. Among the techniques that could be used to minimize the burden of the QDOT are the following:

- The resident-alien-spouse could obtain citizenship prior to his or her death and avoid the QDOT treatment for subsequent distributions from the marital-deduction trust.

- Withdrawals could be made from the QDOT during the lifetime of the surviving spouse without tax to the extent that they qualify as hardship distributions.
- The remainder interest in the QDOT could be transferred to a charity. As discussed in the next reading, the charitable deduction will eliminate such transfers from the transfer-tax base.
- The surviving spouse could remarry. If the new spouse is a U.S. citizen, the surviving spouse could transfer QDOT property to the new spouse and qualify for the marital deduction. Of course, this technique is available only in limited circumstances and to the extent the surviving resident-alien-spouse has the ability under the terms of the trust to transfer the QDOT corpus.
- The citizen-spouse could minimize the need to fund the QDOT by making lifetime gifts to the resident-alien-spouse. As discussed earlier in reading 8, gifts to a resident-alien-spouse do not qualify for an unlimited gift tax marital deduction. However, the annual exclusion for transfers to a resident-alien-spouse is increased to $100,000 to the extent that such gifts would qualify for both the marital deduction and annual exclusion. Annual gifts from the citizen-spouse to the resident-alien-spouse over a number of years will increase the individually owned property of the resident-alien-spouse. This pattern of gifting will provide three benefits. First, the gross estate of the citizen-spouse will be reduced. Second, the wealth transferred to the resident-alien-spouse will reduce the need to fund a QDOT. Finally, the assets transferred to the resident-alien-spouse through lifetime gifts will be included in his or her gross estate and can be sheltered by his or her unified credit.
- Life insurance is particularly advantageous for estate planning in this situation. First, the resident-alien-spouse can purchase life insurance on the life of the citizen-spouse. Since the death proceeds will not be included in the citizen-spouse's gross estate, the proceeds will be received by the resident-alien-spouse free of QDOT tax. If such life insurance is owned by an irrevocable trust, the proceeds of such life insurance will escape estate taxation in both spouses' estates.
- Survivorship (second-to-die) life insurance policies are particularly useful in these circumstances. The QDOT tax is generally payable at the death of a surviving resident-alien-spouse and is generally more onerous than the typical second-death estate tax. For these reasons, survivorship life insurance is particularly suitable for a marriage in which one spouse is a resident-alien.

NOTES

1. Of course, the naturalization statutes provide some additional requirements to obtain citizenship. An applicant for citizenship must maintain a residence within the United States and have continuous residence and physical presence in the United States for 2 1/2 out of the 5 years prior to application.

2. The Treasury has been instructed to promulgate additional regulations regarding QDOTs to ensure that the tax imposed on the QDOT can be

collected. Presumably, Congress intends that such requirements will prevent the distribution of QDOT property outside the United States where any tax imposed on the QDOT might be uncollectible. At the time of this writing (June 1990), such regulations have not yet been drafted.

3. Congress has directed the Treasury to issue regulations to provide for QDOT treatment for a joint and survivor annuity. These roles will be necessary to permit such treatment since distributions from a qualified retirement plan or an IRA cannot technically be assigned to a QDOT. It is likely that the regulations will provide some method for the IRS to collect any tax due on such distributions.

4. Income distributions are defined to be the actual income of the trust for accounting purposes. As discussed later in reading 19, taxable income and accounting income are not necessarily the same. Congress has directed the Treasury to issue regulations limiting the flexibility of the trust terms with respect to the definition of *income* to prevent the abuse of the QDOT tax.

5. Hardship distributions of corpus will not attract the QDOT tax. However, what constitutes a hardship distribution has yet to be defined.

6. However, if the resident-alien-spouse is the wealthier spouse, the credit for the QDOT tax paid may be less than the resident-alien's estate tax liability with respect to the same transferred QDOT property. The credit for tax paid will not eliminate the surviving spouse's estate tax under these circumstances.

An estate tax charitable deduction is allowed for the full value of property transferred to a qualified charity, but only if the property is includible in the donor's gross estate. As with the income tax rules pertaining to gifts to qualified charities, there are specific rules governing charitable gifts of property included in an estate. Furthermore, it is possible for a charitable contribution made during the donor's lifetime to generate both an income tax deduction and an estate tax deduction if the value of the property is includible in the donor's gross estate. Inclusion of the value of a lifetime transfer in the gross estate may occur if the donor retained some interest in the property or powers over the property for life. Also a gift of a life insurance policy made within 3 years of the donor's death to a qualified charity that is includible in the donor's gross estate will qualify for the deduction.

The charitable deduction is presently and has been an unlimited deduction for property passing to a qualified charity as defined in the Code. Qualified charitable organizations include

- corporations operated exclusively for religious, charitable, scientific, literary, or educational purposes, including the encouragement of art and the prevention of cruelty to children or animals
- the United States, any state or political subdivision, or the District of Columbia, provided that contributions are made exclusively for public purposes
- a fraternal society, order, or association, if the contributions are used exclusively for the charitable purposes listed above
- the use of any veteran's organization incorporated by an act of Congress or its departments, local chapters, or posts

DENIAL OF DEDUCTION

A charitable deduction for any of the above bequests will be denied if any part of the net earnings of these organizations inures to the benefit of a private stockholder or individual. Also the deduction will be denied if a substantial part of the charitable organization's activities involves preparation of propaganda or other methods that attempt to influence legislation. Likewise, a deduction will be denied if the charity engages in any political campaign in behalf of a candidate for public office or other prohibited transactions. Also a deduction will be denied if, at the time of the donor-decedent's death, the gift is contingent upon the happening of an event or some act unless the probability that this contingency will not occur is so remote that it is negligible. In addition, if the charitable beneficiary or a trustee has the power to use the property or funds contributed to the charity in whole or in part for noncharitable purposes or uses, the charitable deduction will apply only to that part of the property or money not subject to this power.

DISCLAIMERS

If property is transferred from a decedent's estate to a charitable organization because there has been a qualified disclaimer by a prior beneficiary, a charitable deduction will be allowed for amounts that are actually transferred to the charity. For purposes of the charitable estate tax deduction, a complete termination of a power to consume, invade, or appropriate property for the benefit of an individual prior to the exercise of such power is considered to be a qualified disclaimer if the termination occurs before the due date for filing the estate tax return. The requirements for a qualified disclaimer for federal estate tax purposes, which basically constitute an absolute refusal to accept the bequest made prior to the time the estate tax return must be filed, were discussed in detail in an earlier reading.

PAYMENT OF DEATH TAXES

If, under the terms of the will or provisions of local law, payment of death taxes or other deductible expenses is to be made from the charitable bequest, the charitable deduction will be reduced by those amounts used to pay debts or taxes. In other words, the deduction is limited to the actual amount that passes free and clear to the charity for its charitable purposes. If the will provides that taxes and administration expenses are to be paid from the residue and the charitable bequest is also payable out of the residue, the bequest will be diminished by the amount of expenses and taxes paid. This creates a complex circular problem because a reduction of the charitable deduction will have the effect of increasing the taxable estate as well as the estate tax. There is an estate tax regulation that addresses this situation where death taxes are paid from a deductible interest. It is called an *interrelated computation* but is beyond the scope of this material.

TYPES OF CHARITABLE BEQUESTS

In addition to outright bequests of entire interests, charitable gifts can be in other forms including

- powers of appointment
- partial interests
- charitable remainder trusts
- guaranteed annuity interests
- split gifts

Powers of Appointment

A charitable deduction is allowed for property that was includible in the decedent's gross estate because the decedent possessed a general power of appointment over the property that passes to a charity by virtue of an exercise, release, or lapse of that power. It is considered to be a deductible bequest by the decedent to a charitable beneficiary.

Partial Interests

A charitable deduction will be allowed for the value of less than an entire interest passing to a charity provided that certain complex rules are met. The following make up the types of interests that may be bequeathed to a charity that will qualify for the charitable deduction:

- a testamentary gift of an undivided portion of the decedent's entire interest in property not in trust. An undivided portion means a fraction or percentage of each interest or right owned by the decedent in the property. Furthermore, the decedent's interest in a fraction of every part of the whole must persist over the entire term that his or her interest in the property exists.
- a remainder interest in a personal residence. A charitable deduction is allowed for the transfer by the decedent at death of a remainder interest in his or her personal residence. The residence need not be the decedent's principal residence. It includes any residence used by the decedent for any part of the year (even as a vacation home). The charitable remainder interest pertains to the residence itself as opposed to any proceeds received on the sale of the residence.
- a remainder interest in a farm transferred by the decedent at death, not in trust, to a qualified charity, or a transfer of a partial interest in property to a charitable organization exclusively for conservation purposes. Special rules must be adhered to upon the transfer of these partial interests either in real estate or for conservation purposes.
- remainder interests in trust to charitable remainder trusts and pooled income funds

Charitable Remainder Trusts

If the decedent transfers a remainder interest in property to a charity in trust, it must be made in the form of a charitable remainder unitrust, annuity trust, or pooled income fund. Otherwise, no estate tax charitable deduction will be allowed. These arrangements usually provide for an income interest to a noncharitable beneficiary with the remainder to the charitable organization. The trust instrument must provide that payments of the unitrust or annuity amounts begin as of the date of death if the charitable interest is to qualify for the estate tax charitable deduction. Gifts made in one of these forms are the only way to provide for income to individuals who are noncharitable beneficiaries while making a gift at the same time to a charitable organization that qualifies for an income, estate, or gift tax deduction.

Annuity Trusts

A charitable remainder annuity trust is one that provides a fixed annuity to the income beneficiary that is worth not less than 5 percent of the initial net fair market value of the property paid in trust. This amount must be paid at least annually to one or more noncharitable beneficiaries who are alive when the trust was created. Upon the death of the last income beneficiary or at the end of a term of years not greater than 20 years, the remainder interest must be held for or paid to a qualified charitable organization.

Unitrusts

A charitable remainder unitrust differs from the foregoing in that a fixed percentage (not less than 5 percent of the net fair market value of the trust assets as annually revalued) is paid at least annually to one or more noncharitable income beneficiaries. Again, as with the annuity trust, the remainder interest will be paid to or held for the benefit of a qualified charitable organization, either at the death of the last income beneficiary or after a term of years not greater than 20 years.

In essence, this form of trust differs from the annuity trust in that the annual income is more in the form of a variable annuity. Both types of trusts may be created during lifetime or under a person's will. Another distinction made between the two trusts is with regard to payment of income. In the annuity trust, if trust income is insufficient to meet the annual payment, the income beneficiary must be paid out of principal. In the case of the unitrust, however, the trust may provide that if income is insufficient, no payment will be made out of principal. Payments may be made from income only. In any year that a trust has more than enough income to meet its present payments, the deficit of earlier years may be paid at that time. Also there may be no further contributions to an annuity trust after the initial payment is made. However, additional contributions may be made to a unitrust.

Pooled Income Funds

A pooled income fund is much like a mutual fund maintained by a qualified charity. The fund contains commingled donations from many sources. In effect, a decedent's donation *purchases* units in the fund with the income attributable to these units being paid at least annually to the decedent's beneficiary. Of course, the remainder interest must be irrevocably earmarked to the charitable organization.

Guaranteed Annuity Interests or Lead Trusts

Another type of interest, a guaranteed annuity interest, may qualify for an estate tax charitable deduction whether or not it is made in trust. This type of gift works in reverse of the remainder trusts, hence commonly called *charitable lead trusts*. It involves a transfer by the decedent of an income interest in property to a charity with the remainder to a noncharitable entity. Unless this interest is in the form of a guaranteed annuity interest or unitrust interest, the charitable deduction will be disallowed. These guaranteed interests refer to the right to receive a determinable amount at least annually for a specific term or the life or lives of individuals living at the time of the decedent's death. The guaranteed annuity must be paid by an insurance company or a similar organization regularly engaged in the business of issuing annuity contracts. A guaranteed unitrust interest refers to the right to receive payment of a fixed percentage of the net fair market value of the property that funds the unitrust at least annually. The unitrust interest must be paid by an insurance company or any other similar organization as mentioned above.

Split Gifts

For transfers made after 1981, a donor-decedent may create a charitable remainder trust and obtain a deduction for both the charitable and noncharitable bequests. If a spouse is the only noncharitable income beneficiary for life, the estate will obtain a marital deduction for the income interest to the surviving spouse as well as a charitable deduction for the gift of the remainder interest to the charity. The result is that no transfer tax will be imposed on the creation of a charitable remainder annuity or unitrust for either the remainder or income portion, provided that the income interest to a spouse qualifies under the *new qualifying terminable-interest rules*. Thus a split gift to a spouse and charity in the form of a charitable remainder annuity or unitrust may pass entirely estate tax free by use of the combined marital and charitable deductions.

VALUATION

The gift of a partial interest (including a remainder interest to a charity) is valued at the fair market value of the interest on the appropriate valuation date. This may be the date of the gift or the date of death. The fair market value of an annuity, life estate, term of years, remainder, reversion, or unitrust interest is its present value. The present value of remainder interests in charitable remainder annuity trusts, unitrusts, or pooled income funds is determined under the income tax regulations. The present value of a guaranteed annuity interest is determined under estate tax regulations. The present value of a unitrust interest is found by subtracting the present value of all interests in the transferred property other than the unitrust interest from the fair market value of the transferred property.

As set forth in prior readings, the taxable estate is found by deducting from the gross estate all allowable estate debts, taxes, and administration expenses. Further reductions that may be applicable are the marital deduction and the charitable deduction. The result is the taxable estate.

In this reading the remaining steps necessary to compute the federal estate tax are discussed. These include

- who must file an estate tax return
- the determination of the tentative tax base
- the determination of the estate tax before credits
- the determination of the net federal estate tax payable

A convenient chart for computing the federal estate tax can be found on page 18.13.

In addition, the reading discusses the procedures for filing the estate tax return and paying the estate tax.

WHO MUST FILE AN ESTATE TAX RETURN

The personal representative of the estate of every U.S. citizen or resident must file Form 706—The United States Estate Tax Return—if the value of the gross estate plus adjusted taxable gifts on the date of death exceeds the statutory filing requirement. As will be seen later, this statutory filing requirement is the equivalent of the allowable unified estate and gift tax credit in the year of death. For 1987 and thereafter, the gross estate and adjusted taxable gifts must exceed $600,000 for filing to be necessary. In other words, the statutory filing limitations stated above are applied to the value of all property included in the gross estate, plus the total amount of taxable gifts made after 1976 that were not included in the decedent's estate. (Note that the value of adjusted taxable gifts is included for this purpose at the date-of-gift value, not the value at the date of death.) This is what is meant by the unified estate and gift tax system. The value of these lifetime gifts also plays a part in establishing the rate of estate tax to be applied.

DETERMINATION OF TENTATIVE TAX BASE

Once the taxable estate is determined, the amount of adjusted taxable gifts made after 1976 is added to the taxable estate. The result is the tentative tax base.

Adjusted taxable gifts are taxable gifts made after 1976 that are not includible in the decedent's gross estate. Consequently the following are excluded from treatment as adjusted taxable gifts:

- post-1976 gifts within the amount of the annual exclusion ($3,000 annual gift tax exclusion for gifts made after 1976 and prior to January 1, 1982; $10,000 annual gift tax exclusion for gifts made after December 31, 1981)
- gifts made to a spouse that qualified for the gift tax marital deduction
- gifts that qualified for the gift tax charitable deduction
- gifts that have already been included in the decedent's gross estate for whatever reason. In this latter category is the value of certain transfers that were included in the decedent's gross estate because the decedent retained certain interests, rights, or powers in the property for life, or because such interests were retained initially and were given away less than 3 years before death.

Estate Tax Treatment of Split Gifts

Inclusion or Exclusion of the Gift Value

If the split gift does not exceed the annual exclusion amount ($20,000 per donee), nothing is included in the gross estate or adjusted taxable gifts of the donor-decedent.

If the split gift does exceed the annual exclusion (but is not includible in the gross estate because of retained interests or powers), the excess over the annual exclusion amount becomes an adjusted taxable gift in the estate tax computation of the donor-decedent.

If a donor-decedent made a split gift within 3 years of death and retained certain interests or powers (for example, retained income for life) or transferred certain types of property (such as insurance policies on his or her life), the entire value of the gifted property is brought back into the estate of the donor-decedent.

If subsequent to the death of the donor-spouse the consenting spouse died (within 3 years of the gift), the consenting spouse's portion of the gift is not includible in his or her estate since the entire value of the gift had already been included in the donor-spouse's estate.

Includibility of Gift Tax Paid within 3 Years of Death

With respect to the gift taxes paid on the split gift, only the gift tax paid by the donor-spouse is includible in the estate. Indeed, the gift tax paid by the consenting spouse is includible in his or her estate at his or her subsequent death. (On the other hand, if the donor-spouse pays the entire gift tax, then the total amount of the gift tax is included in the donor-spouse's estate and no gift tax is included in the consenting spouse's estate.)

When the entire gift is includible in the donor-spouse's estate, any tax actually paid by the consenting spouse is in fact allowed as a credit in computing the donor-spouse's estate tax; therefore any credit allowed in the donor-spouse's estate is not allowed as a credit for gift tax paid by the consenting spouse.

The foregoing concept involves computations beyond the scope of this reading and is for informational purposes only.

DETERMINATION OF ESTATE TAX BEFORE CREDITS

Under the Tax Reform Act of 1976 a unified estate and gift tax system was created. This means that the same rate schedule will be applied to transfers during both the decedent's lifetime and at his or her death. The system uses a cumulative approach to all transfers made during lifetime culminating in the final gratuitous transfer of property at death. Cumulating taxable lifetime gifts with dispositions at death has the net effect of increasing the tax rates applied to the taxable estate by adding adjusted taxable gifts to the value of transfers taking effect at death. Since the estate and gift tax rate schedule is a progressive one, any individual who made lifetime taxable gifts after 1976 will be subject to a higher combined estate tax rate than would occur if the computation did not include lifetime gifts. That is the rationale for adding adjusted taxable gifts to the taxable estate to arrive at the tentative tax base—the amount to which tax rates are applied. In other words, this unified rate schedule (on page 18.14) is applied to cumulated transfers and the result is the tentative tax.

Once the tentative tax is determined, gift taxes generated by taxable gifts made after 1976 in excess of the unified credit amount are subtracted from this figure. The determination of the amount of reduction allowable because of taxes attributable to post-1976 taxable gifts is made as follows:

- Total all post-1976 taxable gifts.
- Compute the gift tax payable by applying the unified rate schedule in effect at the decedent's death (on page 18.14) to the total taxable gifts. In other words, all the post-1976 taxable gifts are treated as if they were made at one time—the date of the decedent's death.
- Reduce the gift tax payable by the allowable unified credit for the year of the decedent's death (for example, $121,800 for 1985; $192,800 for 1987 and thereafter).
- If the gift tax payable exceeds the allowable unified credit, subtract the excess from the tentative tax.

The result is the estate tax payable before credits.

DETERMINATION OF NET FEDERAL ESTATE TAX PAYABLE

Once the estate tax is computed, there are five possible credits that may be applied against the tax to arrive at the net federal estate tax payable. As with income tax credits, these credits are allowed as a dollar-for-dollar reduction of the estate tax. They are

- the unified credit
- the state death tax credit
- the credit for foreign death taxes
- the credit for gift tax paid on pre-1977 gifts
- the credit for taxes paid on prior transfers

No refund is allowed if the sum of the credits exceeds the estate tax otherwise payable.

Unified Credit

The unified estate and gift tax credit came into existence for estates of decedents dying after December 31, 1976. The term *unified credit* was adopted because it is a credit that may be used as an offset against gift as well as estate taxes. Actually the credit must first be used to offset gift taxes on lifetime transfers. Any remaining unified credit will be applied as a credit against the federal estate tax. The unified credit was gradually increased each year until it reached its current level of $192,800 in 1987. A unified credit of $192,800 is equivalent to $600,000 of taxable transfer. Thus, the unified credit is commonly, albeit mistakenly, referred to as a $600,000 credit; stated correctly, the $600,000 amount is a credit equivalent.

The unified credit also has the effect of eliminating the lower brackets allocated to taxable transfers below the credit-equivalent amount of $600,000. As the rate schedule on page 18.14 indicates, the first dollar of estate tax imposed above the credit equivalent is paid at a marginal rate of 37 percent. An interesting fact from a planning point of view is that any transfer that actually creates an estate or gift tax payable is subject to a higher marginal rate than that imposed on individual income by the federal income tax system.

Credit for State Death Taxes

Subject to statutory limits, there is a credit against the federal estate tax for any estate, inheritance, legacy, or succession taxes actually paid to a state if the state death tax is attributable to property included in the gross estate. The Internal Revenue Code prescribes a graduated rate table for determining the maximum state death tax credit allowable (IRC Sec. 2011). That table is contained at the end of this reading. The credit for state death taxes is further limited to the federal estate tax liability after reduction by the unified credit. The credit is computed by applying the statutory rate table to the adjusted taxable estate, which is the taxable estate reduced by $60,000 ($60,000 refers to the amount of the specific estate tax exemption allowed prior to 1977).

To summarize, the allowable credit for state death taxes is limited to the *lesser* of the following amounts:

- state death taxes actually paid

- the federal estate tax liability
- the statutory limits for the maximum amount of the credit

Credit for Foreign Death Taxes

There is a credit allowed against the federal estate tax for taxes actually paid by the decedent's estate to any foreign country for any estate, inheritance, legacy, or succession taxes. The purpose of the credit for foreign death taxes is to prevent double taxation. It is allowable only to the estate of a decedent who was either (1) a citizen of the United States or (2) a resident who was not a citizen at the time of death. Nonresident aliens are denied the foreign death tax credit. The credit exists for taxes actually paid by the decedent's estate to any foreign country, U.S. possession, or political subdivision of a foreign state.

Credit will be given for death taxes paid on property located within the foreign country to which the tax is paid that is also included in the decedent's gross estate for federal estate tax purposes. In other words, the property taxed by a foreign jurisdiction must also be taxed by the United States under our estate tax system. Thus the United States will recognize that the same property was taxed doubly and will allow a credit for taxes paid to the foreign jurisdiction. This credit is limited to the proportionate share of federal estate tax attributable to the property located in and taxed by the foreign country.

The maximum credit allowed is the lesser of (1) the amount of foreign death tax imposed on the property situated in the foreign country that was also included in the decedent's gross estate for federal estate tax purposes, or (2) the amount of federal estate tax attributable to that same property located and taxed in the foreign country that also is included in the decedent's gross estate for federal estate tax purposes. In comparing the two taxes to determine which is the lesser, the exchange rate for converting foreign currency into U.S. dollars in effect when each foreign tax payment is made is used. No credit will be given for interest owed or penalties connected with the payment of foreign death taxes.

If the federal estate tax was attributable to a remainder or reversionary interest in the foreign property and an election was made to postpone payment of that part of the tax, the credit will apply to the portion of foreign death taxes that are paid and claimed as a credit before the time for payment expires. The credit must be claimed within the later of (1) 4 years from the time the estate tax return is filed; (2) before any extension for paying the tax has expired; or (3) within 60 days after the Tax Court has reached a decision on a petition for redetermination of a deficiency.

Credit for Gift Tax Paid on Pre-1977 Gifts

Gift tax payable on post-1976 gifts becomes part of the computation for determining estate tax liability under the unified gift and estate tax system as explained earlier. Therefore no separate credit is allowed for taxes attributable to these gifts. However, a credit still exists for federal gift tax paid by a decedent on taxable gifts made before 1977 if the property is included in the gross estate. This concept can be illustrated by the following:

> *Example:* A grantor, Michael, established a trust in 1975 for the benefit of his son. The grantor reserved the right to all income from the trust during his life. The gift of the remainder interest was a taxable gift on which gift tax was paid. The grantor died in 1985 and the trust property was includible in his gross estate because of the retained life interest. A credit will be allowable (within certain technical limitations) for the gift tax attributable to the gift.

Additional complications arise if there are several pre-1977 gifts to which this could be applicable. A discussion of the rules regarding these complications as well as the technical limitations of this credit are beyond the scope of this reading.

Credit for Tax on Prior Transfers

Circumstances may arise in which a decedent has inherited property from someone who died less than 10 years before the decedent's death or within 2 years following the decedent's death and the property transferred to the decedent was already taxable in the estate of the transferor-decedent. To avoid double taxation on double transfers of property occurring within a reasonably short time period (that is, 10 years before or 2 years after), a credit is allowed against the federal estate tax paid by the present decedent as a result of this inherited property being included in the decedent's gross estate.

Amount of Credit

If the decedent's death occurs within 2 years before or after the transferor's death, the credit is limited to the lesser of (1) the amount of the federal estate tax attributable to the transferred property in the transferor's estate; or (2) the amount of the federal estate tax attributable to the transferred property in the present decedent's estate. If the transferor died within 2 years before or 2 years after the death of the present decedent, the allowable credit for the tax on the prior transfer is determined by (1) or (2) above. In other words, the full credit will be allowed if both deaths occur within 2 years of each other. However, if the transferor died more than 2 years before the present decedent, the credit will be reduced by 20 percent for each 2-year period in excess of 2 years.

> *Example:* If the transferor died 3 years before the present decedent, 80 percent of the credit will be allowable. The allowable percentages are provided in the following table:

TABLE 18-1

Percent Allowable	Period of Time between Transferor's Death and Death of Present Decedent
100 percent	up to 2 years after
100 percent	up to 2 years before
80 percent	2 to 4 years before
60 percent	4 to 6 years before
40 percent	6 to 8 years before
20 percent	8 to 10 years before
0 percent	more than 10 years before

A formula for determining the credit is contained in the Treasury regulations. The Code further defines how the property transferred to the present decedent from the transferor's estate shall be valued.

Allowance of Credit

Property included in the transferor's gross estate that is eligible for the credit includes any beneficial interest in property received by the present decedent from the transferor. The credit may also be allowed with respect to property received by the present decedent as the result of the exercise or nonexercise of a general power of appointment by the transferor-decedent. Of course, if the present decedent was the surviving spouse of the transferor, the credit will be disallowed to the extent that property included in the transferor's gross estate qualified for the marital deduction. The credit pertains to many types of property interests that the present decedent received from the transferor, including annuities, life estates, terms for years, remainders, and other interests. The necessary ingredient is that the present decedent inherited these interests from the transferor and became the beneficial owner of the interest. Determining the credit may be further complicated if property for which the credit on prior transfer was sought is also subject to a generation-skipping tax. The interaction of the credit and the generation-skipping tax are complex and beyond the scope of this reading.

PAYMENT OF ESTATE TAX BY THE PERSONAL REPRESENTATIVE

One of the primary duties of the personal representative is filing the federal estate tax return when due and seeing that estate taxes are timely paid. He or she must also timely file any estate income tax returns when they are due. If the estate is sizable enough to warrant filing a federal estate tax return, the return is due and the tax is payable no later than 9 months after the decedent's death unless an extension is granted (IRC Sec. 6075(a)).

The personal representative is required to gather and retain records as well as supplemental data supporting the amounts stated or claimed on the federal estate tax return. If the estate assets are insufficient to pay all the decedent's debts, the decedent's federal tax liabilities must be paid first. This includes the decedent's income tax liabilities up to the time of death, the income tax liability of the estate, and the estate tax liability. An executor (or administrator) will be held personally liable for the tax if he or she was aware of a potential tax liability or failed in the responsibility to determine if any such tax obligations existed prior to distribution of the estate's assets and the executor's discharge from responsibility (IRC Sec. 2202). In other words, an executor will be liable if he or she was either aware or should have been aware of the existence of tax obligations. In addition, if the estate is insolvent, the individual beneficiaries will be responsible for paying any federal estate tax accruing from the inclusion of their inheritances in the decedent's gross estate.

Extension for Filing

Generally a personal representative may obtain an extension for filing a return if it is either impossible or impractical to complete the return within the 9-month period after the decedent dies. This extension is limited to 6 months, unless the personal representative is abroad (IRC Sec. 6081(a)). However, an extension to file must be received and granted by the Internal Revenue Service before the time for filing the return expires. An extension of the time for filing an estate tax return does not prevent interest from accruing on any unpaid taxes beginning on the date the return was originally due (IRC Sec. 6601(b)(1)). Also an extension of time to file does not automatically extend the time for payment. Penalties of 5 percent per month up to 25 percent will be added to the final tax liability unless reasonable cause is shown (Treas. Reg. Sec. 20.6081-1(a)). Thus if it is impossible or impractical to file a return by the due date, consideration should be given either to paying the estimated amount of estate tax by the due date for filing or to obtaining an extension for payment of the tax.

Extension for Tax Payment

There are mitigating circumstances that will be acceptable for the IRS to grant an extension of time to pay the estate tax. An extension of time for up to 12 months to pay the estate tax will be granted if the Internal Revenue Service determines there is reasonable cause (IRC Sec. 6161(a)). While no definition of reasonable cause is given in the Code or regulations, the following situations are provided in the regulations as a basis for granting an extension of time to pay the tax:

- Although an estate includes sufficient liquid assets, assets are located in several jurisdictions and cannot be marshaled readily by the executor, even though he or she makes a diligent effort to do so by the time for filing the return.
- A great part of the estate consists of assets that will provide future payments, such as annuities, copyright royalties, contingent fees, or accounts receivable. Since these assets constitute the major part of the estate, the estate does not contain sufficient cash to pay the estate tax within the due period. Borrowing against these assets would inflict considerable losses upon the estate.

- The estate includes a major asset that cannot be collected without litigation. It is unknown whether this asset will ever be collectible, and the size of the gross estate is not determinable at the time for filing the return.
- Unless the estate borrows at a higher than normal rate of interest, it does not have sufficient funds to pay the entire estate tax when due as well as to provide reasonable subsistence for the decedent's spouse and dependent children during the remaining period of estate administration. Also funds are insufficient to satisfy claims currently due against the estate despite reasonable efforts by the personal representative to convert assets in his or her possession into cash (other than an interest in a closely held business to which Sec. 6166 applies).

While the initial extension for *reasonable cause* pertains to a 12-month period from the time the estate tax return is due, a finding of reasonable cause may allow a deferral of payment of estate taxes for reasonable periods up to 10 years for decedents dying after December 31, 1976 (IRC Sec. 6161(a)(2)).

Extension of Time to Pay Tax on Closely Held Business Interest

There is a special provision that allows the personal representative to elect a deferral for payment of estate tax attributable to the inclusion of a closely held business or farm in the decedent's gross estate if certain conditions are met (IRC Sec. 6166). The law provides that an executor may elect to defer payment of estate tax attributable to inclusion in the estate of a farm or other closely held business if that business consists of more than 35 percent of the adjusted gross estate. If the estate qualifies, such an election may be made at the sole discretion of the estate's personal representative. Payments of tax attributable to the business interest may be deferred for 5 years from the due date. Interest only on the unpaid balance is due annually for the initial 5 years. In the fifth year and thereafter, the tax plus installments of interest on the unpaid balance is payable in equal installments over a maximum of 10 more years. Note that the total payment period extends over 14 years rather than the 15 years it appears to be initially because the first installment of tax becomes due simultaneously with the last payment of interest. To determine whether more than 35 percent of the adjusted gross estate is made up of a closely held business or farm, the adjusted gross estate is defined as the gross estate reduced by deductible debts, expenses, claims, and losses, but before reduction by the marital or charitable deductions (IRC Sec. 6166(b)(6)).

For purposes of the 35 percent rule, an interest in a closely held business is defined as (1) an interest in a proprietorship, (2) an interest in a partnership carrying on a trade or business with no more than 15 partners or where 20 percent or more of its assets helped determine the decedent's gross estate, or (3) stock in a corporation with no more than 15 shareholders or where 20 percent of its voting stock is included in the decedent's gross estate (IRC Sec. 6166(b)(6)(1)). Property owned by a corporation, partnership, estate, or trust is regarded as owned proportionately by its shareholders, partners, or beneficiaries. In addition, for purposes of this election, interests in two or more closely held businesses are treated as a single closely held business if 20 percent or more of the total value of each business is included in the decedent's gross estate (IRC Sec. 6166(c)). Also all stock and partnership interests belonging to a decedent and any family members will be aggregated in order to meet the requirements of stock ownership. The family members whose interests are considered as held by the decedent are the decedent's brothers, sisters, spouse, grandparents, children, and grandchildren. For purposes of this election, stock in a closely held business must be stock that is not readily tradable. At the time of the decedent's death, this refers to stock that is neither listed on a stock exchange nor for which a market exists in over-the-counter trading.

In some cases an executor may be uncertain if the estate will need to defer payment of tax or will qualify for deferred payment of tax. In that event, he or she may file a protective election with the estate tax return. Filing such an election preserves the executor's right to elect estate tax deferral. Since the election is contingent on the value of the closely held business meeting the percentage requirements, the executor will have a period of 60 days to make a final election after it is determined that the estate qualifies for the extension.

Special 4 Percent Interest

The present law contains a special 4 percent rate of interest attributable to the deferred estate tax on the first $1 million of closely held business or farm property included in the gross estate. It should be noted, however, that the tax for which the 4 percent rate is available is reduced by the unified credit. The remaining amount accrues interest at the applicable federal rate on underpayments.

It is also interesting to note that interest begins to accrue on the date the tax was required to be paid without regard to any allowable extensions. However, the adjusted gross estate is determined on the date the estate tax return is filed, including any extensions of time for filing (IRC Sec. 6166(b)(6)). This differential allows the estate to deduct the interest payments that accrue up to the date the return is actually filed. Thus an estate that barely misses qualifying under the 35 percent rule may qualify for tax deferral by delaying filing and accruing interest. The interest deduction accrued from 9 months after the date of death to the date of filing will increase the amount of deductible expenses from the gross estate in arriving at the adjusted gross estate. This will decrease the value of the adjusted gross estate and increase the percentage of the closely held business or farm relative to the adjusted gross estate. Thus an estate that came close to qualifying but failed to do so under the 35 percent eligibility rule may now qualify for installment payment of tax.

Acceleration

Under certain circumstances the estate will forfeit its right to installment payment of tax. If any of the following actions occur, all remaining unpaid estate tax will become due and payable immediately upon notice and demand by the Internal Revenue Service. The events that will cause acceleration are

- late payment or failure to pay any individual installment
- withdrawal of 50 percent or more of the assets (including cash and property) from the business
- distribution, sale, exchange, or disposition of 50 percent or more of the value of the business interest to anyone other than a beneficiary who is entitled to receive the interest under the decedent's will or under state intestacy laws

These withdrawals are cumulative. If the decedent's interest in a closely held business is transferred because of either the death of the original heir or the death of any subsequent transferee receiving the interest as a result of the prior transferor's death, acceleration of taxes will not be triggered if each subsequent transferee is a family member of the transferor.

Furthermore, acceleration will not be triggered by late installment payments of tax by the executor in the first 6 months. An executor will now be given a grace period of 6 months after each installment is due within which to pay the tax without causing acceleration of the unpaid tax. However, late payment will cause the estate to lose the benefit of the 4 percent interest rate with respect to that payment. In addition to the higher interest rate, the estate will be required to pay a penalty of 5 percent for each month or part of a month that the payment is overdue.

Since an executor may be held personally liable if other distributions are made from the estate prior to payment of the estate tax, installment payment of the estate tax could leave executors vulnerable over a long period of time. To alleviate this problem, there is a special lien procedure available that will relieve the executor from personal liability for the entire installment period. It may be elected if the executor, as well as all parties having any interest in the property to which the lien will attach, files a written agreement consenting to creation of the lien in favor of the federal government instead of a bond. This agreement must name a responsible individual to deal with the Internal Revenue Service on behalf of the beneficiaries and all other parties who consented to the lien. A bond may not be required by the IRS except to the extent that no adequate security exists for the unpaid principal plus interest.

SEC. 303 REDEMPTIONS

Sec. 303 of the Code allows a redemption of stock for the purpose of paying funeral and administrative expenses and death taxes without the redemption being treated as a dividend. If the redemption qualifies, it will be treated as an exchange, and the gain will be treated as capital gain if the stock was held as a capital asset in the hands of the decedent at the time of the exchange. In order to qualify for capital-gains treatment under this section, the decedent's stock must represent more than 35 percent of his or her adjusted gross estate. Ownership of 20 percent or more of the stock of each of two or more corporations may be aggregated to satisfy this 35 percent test.

If any redemption is made more than 4 years after the decedent's death, capital-gains treatment will be available only for the distribution that represents the lesser of (1) the amount of the qualifying death taxes and funeral and administration expenses unpaid immediately before the distribution, or (2) the aggregate of these amounts paid within one year after the distribution.

This favorable tax treatment applies to the distribution by a corporation only to the extent that the interest of a shareholder is reduced directly or through a binding obligation to contribute to the payment of the estate's expenses or taxes. In other words, the party whose shares are redeemed must be the one who actually bears the burden of the estate and other death taxes or funeral and administration expenses in an amount equal to the redeemed value of the stock. That rule can be illustrated by the following example. Assume a block of otherwise qualifying stock is left to a surviving spouse in a manner that qualifies for the marital deduction and that the decedent's will provides that the marital bequest will bear no portion of taxes or administrative costs (a common provision). In that case the stock left to the surviving spouse could not be redeemed under Sec. 303 even though in all other respects it qualified, because there is no liability on the marital bequest to pay death taxes or administrative costs.

It should be noted that if a redemption qualified for capital-gains treatment under Sec. 303 or under other Code sections, an estate will recognize no taxable gain because the stock will receive a new stepped-up basis. However, should a redemption not qualify for capital-gains treatment, it will be treated as a dividend distribution, and the estate will recognize ordinary income on the full value of the stock on the applicable valuation date.

CHART FOR COMPUTING FEDERAL ESTATE TAX

	STEP 1	(1)	Gross estate	_____
minus		(2)	Funeral and administration expenses (estimated as _____% of _____)	_____
		(3)	Debts and taxes	_____
		(4)	Losses	_____
			Total deductions	_____
equals				
	STEP 2	(5)	Adjusted gross estate	_____
minus		(6)	Marital deduction	_____
		(7)	Charitable deduction	_____
			Total deductions	_____
equals				
	STEP 3	(8)	Taxable estate	_____
plus		(9)	Adjusted taxable gifts (post-1976 lifetime taxable transfers not included in gross estate)	_____
equals		(10)	Tentative tax base (total of taxable estate and adjusted taxable gifts)	_____
compute		(11)	Tentative tax	_____
minus		(12)	Gift taxes payable on post-1976 gifts	_____
equals				
	STEP 4	(13)	Estate tax payable before credits	_____
minus		(14)	Tax credits	
			(a) Unified credit	_____
			(b) State death tax credit	_____
			(c) Credit for foreign death taxes	_____
			(d) Credit for gift tax for pre-1977 gifts	_____
			(e) Credit for tax on prior transfers	_____
			Total credits	_____
equals				
	STEP 5	(15)	Net federal estate tax payable	_____

UNIFIED RATE* SCHEDULE FOR COMPUTING ESTATE AND GIFT TAX APPLICABLE UNTIL 1993

If the amount with respect to which the tentative tax is to be computed is . . .	The tentative tax is . . .
Not over $10,000	18 percent of such amount
Over $10,000 but not over $20,000	$1,800, plus 20 percent of the excess of such amount over $10,000
Over $20,000 but not over $40,000	$3,800, plus 22 percent of the excess of such amount over $20,000
Over $40,000 but not over $60,000	$8,200, plus 24 percent of the excess of such amount over $40,000
Over $60,000 but not over $80,000	$13,000, plus 26 percent of the excess of such amount over $60,000
Over $80,000 but not over $100,000	$18,200, plus 28 percent of the excess of such amount over $80,000
Over $100,000 but not over $150,000	$23,800, plus 30 percent of the excess of such amount over $100,000
Over $150,000 but not over $250,000	$38,800, plus 32 percent of the excess of such amount over $150,000
Over $250,000 but not over $500,000	$70,800, plus 34 percent of the excess of such amount over $250,000
Over $500,000 but not over $750,000	$155,800, plus 37 percent of the excess of such amount over $500,000
Over $750,000 but not over $1,000,000	$248,300, plus 39 percent of the excess of such amount over $750,000
Over $1,000,000 but not over $1,250,000	$345,800, plus 41 percent of the excess of such amount over $1,000,000
Over $1,250,000 but not over $1,500,000	$448,300, plus 43 percent of the excess of such amount over $1,250,000
Over $1,500,000 but not over $2,000,000	$555,800, plus 45 percent of the excess of such amount over $1,500,000
Over $2,000,000 but not over $2,500,000	$780,800, plus 49 percent of the excess of such amount over $2,000,000
Over $2,500,000 but not over $3,000,000	$1,025,800, plus 53 percent of the excess over $2,500,000
Over $3,000,000	$1,290,800, plus 55 percent of the excess over $3,000,000

*The tentative tax is increased by 5 percent of the amount (with respect to which the tentative tax is computed) in the range of $10 million to $21,040,000. This 5 percent surcharge eliminates the benefit of the graduated rates and unified credit.

CREDIT FOR STATE DEATH TAXES

If the **adjusted taxable estate*** is . . .	The maximum tax credit shall be . . .
Not over $90,000	.8 of 1 percent of the amount by which the taxable estate exceeds $40,000
Over $90,000 but not over $140,000	$400, plus 1.6 percent of the excess over $90,000
Over $140,000 but not over $240,000	$1,200, plus 2.4 percent of the excess over $140,000
Over $240,000 but not over $440,000	$3,600, plus 3.2 percent of the excess over $240,000
Over $440,000 but not over $640,000	$10,000, plus 4 percent of the excess over $440,000
Over $640,000 but not over $840,000	$18,000, plus 4.8 percent of the excess over $640,000
Over $840,000 but not over $1,040,000	$27,600, plus 5.6 percent of the excess over $840,000
Over $1,040,000 but not over $1,540,000	$38,800, plus 6.4 percent of the excess over $1,040,000
Over $1,540,000 but not over $2,040,000	$70,800, plus 7.2 percent of the excess over $1,540,000
Over $2,040,000 but not over $2,540,000	$106,800, plus 8 percent of the excess over $2,040,000
Over $2,540,000 but not over $3,040,000	$146,800, plus 8.8 percent of the excess over $2,540,000
Over $3,040,000 but not over $3,540,000	$190,800, plus 9.6 percent of the excess over $3,040,000
Over $3,540,000 but not over $4,040,000	$238,800, plus 10.4 percent of the excess over $3,540,000
Over $4,040,000 but not over $5,040,000	$290,800, plus 11.2 percent of the excess over $4,040,000
Over $5,040,000 but not over $6,040,000	$402,800, plus 12 percent of the excess over $5,040,000
Over $6,040,000 but not over $7,040,000	$522,800, plus 12.8 percent of the excess over $6,040,000
Over $7,040,000 but not over $8,040,000	$650,800, plus 13.6 percent of the excess over $7,040,000
Over $8,040,000 but not over $9,040,000	$786,800, plus 14.4 percent of the excess over $8,040,000
Over $9,040,000 but not over $10,040,000	$930,800, plus 15.2 percent of the excess over $9,040,000
Over $10,040,000	$1,082,800 plus 16 percent of the excess over $10,040,000

***For purposes of this section, the term *adjusted taxable estate* means the taxable estate reduced by $60,000.**

Trusts and estates are separate tax-paying entities. As such, both trusts and estates may provide opportunities for tax saving through income allocation among taxpayers so that the most favorable tax planning will be achieved. While income tax saving is not the primary purpose of either trusts or estates, the potential tax saving should not be overlooked by the financial services professional. Knowledge of this area will enable the financial services professional to make recommendations regarding the creation of trusts, which may be structured so that the trustee is given discretionary powers to either accumulate or distribute income earned by the trust. A critical question is, To which tax-paying entity should the income be taxed and in what proportion? Should it be taxed to the taxpayers to whom income may be allocated or to the trust or estate, the beneficiaries, or the grantor? Because of poor planning, the grantor will sometimes be the inadvertent taxpayer. In addition, the new rules pertaining to the unearned income of children under 14 years of age (kiddie tax) may have an impact on planning. In order both to maximize tax saving and to avoid taxing the wrong taxpayer, rules pertaining to income taxation of estates and trusts should be understood.

ESTATES AND TRUSTS

The creation, elements, and purposes of trusts were described in detail in assignment 4. At this time, it is appropriate to briefly describe the decedent's estate.

A decedent's estate exists for a limited time—the estate appears when the decedent dies and then it ceases to exist when all its functions are ended. It exists for a finite time because its purposes are limited. One primary purpose is to effectuate the orderly, legal transfer of property. Until this task is accomplished, the personal representative must manage and safeguard the property within his or her control. The personal representative has a duty to keep the property both invested and income producing. Income earned from estate assets is taxable to the estate. As a separate taxpayer, the estate must file timely income tax returns. One of the first tasks of the personal representative is to obtain a special tax identification number for the estate.

TAX STATUS OF ESTATES AND TRUSTS

The estate maintains its separate tax status until it is closed, which may take several months or years. An estate's duration will vary with the complexity of estate assets. The estate may contain a business interest or assets in a foreign country as well as other complicated ownership interests or rights that require it to be held open for an extended time period. Technically estates should not be closed before the federal estate tax return is filed and cleared, if one is required. The typical length of time that an estate remains open is one to 3 years. The state has an interest in the settlement and distribution of a decedent's estate to its beneficiaries. Furthermore the personal representative may become liable to beneficiaries and creditors of the estate for negligence or fraud and the management of estate assets, and therefore the personal representative also has an interest in settling the estate. An estate should not be kept open without reason. The tax benefits derived from the use of an additional taxpayer are not sufficient reasons by themselves to keep the estate open unduly, and an estate that unreasonably prolongs administration will lose its status as an estate for tax purposes. However, there are income tax benefits to be derived from properly using the estate as a separate tax-paying entity. These benefits should not be overlooked by the personal representative.

Similarities

There are many similarities between estates and trusts. The personal representative has duties and responsibilities similar to the trustee of a trust. Both administer property in a fiduciary capacity. Property is transferred from the decedent to the estate in a manner similar to the transfer of property by a grantor to a trust. Both decedents and grantors are responsible for the creation of the estate or trust. Beneficiaries of an estate have a relationship to the estate similar to that of the beneficiaries of a trust.

Differences

There are, however, important differences. An estate comes into existence involuntarily by operation of law upon the decedent's death. A living trust is created intentionally and voluntarily by a specific action of the grantor. Estates exist for a limited time period. Trusts generally exist for many years and possibly span more than one generation. The primary function of many trusts is to provide sound, professional asset management. Use of a trust can give the grantor a sense of security, peace of mind, and possibly some control over the management of one's property. The trustee's primary duty is to be a good manager. Whether an individual or institution, the trustee will be in charge of the management of the trust property for the duration of the trust. This period may extend over a long time. On the other hand, an estate serves as a temporary receptacle for assets pending distribution to the new owners. The personal representative functions primarily as a liquidator who must marshal the decedent's assets, advertise the estate for the benefit of creditors, and pay its debts, expenses, and taxes. The personal representative must settle any claims against the estate and has a duty to keep the property income producing until its distribution. Another significant difference between the two entities is their relationship to the court. An estate is created by operation of law and is supervised by the court until it is terminated. A trust, on the other hand, is generally a private arrangement. Unless a court accounting is requested by the beneficiaries, the trust will neither have direct contact with the court nor be guided by the court in its actions or investments in most cases.

Trusts and estates are subject to the same rate of income taxation. However, they are subject to a slightly different computational system of taxation than are individuals, corporations, or partnerships, because they exist for the benefit of others. Not operating as mere conduits, they are taxable on income withheld but receive deductions for income distributed. If Congress had chosen to tax estates and trusts in a manner similar to corporations, double taxation would have resulted. If taxed like a corporation, the trust or estate would be taxed on income earned during its taxable year. Beneficiaries would then be treated as shareholders who would be taxed on the distribution when received, just as dividends are taxable to shareholders in the year received. The result would be double taxation. This tax burden undoubtedly would have detracted from the desirability of maintaining trusts.

Alternatively, if a trust or estate was taxed as a partnership, all income would be passed through to the individual beneficiaries in a similar manner to partners. Using this method would be detrimental in cases where the grantor did not intend beneficiaries to be entitled to the income automatically. First of all, there would be a potential conflict with the law of trusts. Trustees normally derive their powers from the trust instrument. Taxation as a partnership would defeat the right of the grantor to give the trustee discretion to accumulate or distribute income. Also a personal representative of an estate does not have a duty to distribute income before the estate makes final distribution to the beneficiaries. Under the theory of partnership taxation, a beneficiary would pay tax on amounts not yet received.

Having considered these various possibilities, Congress, in its wisdom, wisely adopted a hybrid method for income taxation of estates and trusts, which is known as the *sharing concept*. The general rule is that the trust or estate will pay income tax on amounts of income retained, while the beneficiaries will pay tax on trust or estate income distributed, or deemed distributed, to them. The result is that trust or estate income is generally taxed only once. To the extent it remains in the estate or trust, income will be taxed to that entity. To the extent distributed, income will be taxed to the beneficiaries (with certain limitations, discussed later). With estates, the personal representative has discretion regarding retention or distribution of income. As for trusts, the trust instrument will provide the standards and directions for taxation of trust income. Much depends on the type of trust and the trustee's exercise of any discretionary powers regarding distribution or accumulation of trust income.

The income tax rates for trusts and estates are shown in the following table:

TABLE 18-1

Taxable Income (TI)	Tax Payable
$ 0 to $ 5,000	15% of TI
$ 5,000 to $13,000	$ 750 plus 28% of (TI above $5,000)
$13,000 to $26,000	$2,990 plus 33% of (TI above $13,000)
over $26,000	28% of all TI

Income Taxation of Estates

Decedent's Final Return

An executor or administrator has the duty to file two different types of income tax returns for a decedent—a decedent's last life return and an estate's income tax return.

A deceased taxpayer's tax year ends with the date of death. For example, if Greg dies on March 30, an income tax return must be filed for the short year of January 1 to March 30. The return must be filed on the regular due date, April 15, of the following year. The amount of income and deductible expenses that must be reported depends on the deceased taxpayer's regular method of accounting.

For cash-basis taxpayers, only income actually or constructively received must be reported. Deductions can be taken only for expenses actually paid during the decedent's lifetime. If the decedent was on the accrual method, the return will show all income and deductions accrued through the date of death.

Even though the decedent did not live the entire year, he or she is still entitled to use the full standard deduction and personal exemption. If the taxpayer has a surviving spouse, the spouse can still file a joint return with the decedent for the year of the decedent's death.

Income in Respect of a Decedent

Since this is the final income tax return for the individual, if he or she was a cash-basis taxpayer, income that was earned but had not been received by the date of death would not be included in the decedent's final return, because the individual did not actually or constructively receive the item by the date of death. For example, an insurance agent's renewal commissions paid after death cannot be included in a last life return, assuming the deceased agent was a cash-basis taxpayer.

Income that the decedent would have included in gross income had he or she lived does not escape taxation. Instead, it will be taxed to the recipient of that income. In other words, the estate or the beneficiary who receives it will be taxed on it in the same manner that it would have been taxed to the decedent. If it would have been ordinary income to the decedent during lifetime, it will be ordinary income to the estate or beneficiary.

You will recall from assignment 8 that income in respect of a decedent is also subject to estate taxes. The estate or beneficiary that includes in income an item of income in respect of a decedent is entitled to a deduction on the same income tax return for the amount of additional federal estate tax attributable to inclusion of that item in the decedent's gross estate.

Additional Considerations

As a taxable entity, an estate must pay tax on its income. If the income of the estate consists of dividends from stock and interest from bonds, these items will constitute the gross income of the estate. Likewise, if there is rental income, royalty income, income from the sale or exchange of property, or income from a business carried on by the executor or administrator, then the income of the estate will include those items as well.

Because an estate is considered a separate tax entity, it has not only income but also deductions. Since an estate calculates income tax like other taxpayers, total miscellaneous itemized deductions must exceed 2 percent of adjusted gross income to be deductible by the estate. However, expenses that are incurred solely by reason of estate or trust administration are deductible in full. An estate may deduct reasonable amounts paid for administration costs, including executor's fees, and legal fees in connection with the administration of the estate. (As mentioned in an earlier reading, some of these expenses may be taken on either the income tax return of the estate or as deductions from the gross estate to obtain the adjusted gross estate for federal estate tax purposes.)

An estate is also entitled to a deduction for amounts of income distributed. It is not entitled to the standard deduction. An estate may take a $600 personal exemption. As previously mentioned, to the extent that the estate retains income, it will be taxed; to the extent that the beneficiaries receive income, they are taxed. Furthermore estates that are open for tax years ending 2 or more years after the decedent's death are subject to the estimated tax rules. In contrast to beneficiaries of trusts, beneficiaries of estates are not subject to taxation under the *throwback rules* that will be discussed later.

The only beneficiaries who will not pay income tax on distributions of income from estates are those who receive specific bequests under the will in three installments or less. For example, assume that the will of the decedent, Leslie Little, states: "I give $5,000 to my favorite nephew, Al, and all the rest, residue, and remainder to my cousin, Jeffrey Little." During the first year of the estate, assets held by the executor generate $16,000 of income. The executor distributes $5,000 to Al and $11,000 to Jeffrey. Since Al's $5,000 was a specific bequest, he is not taxed. This amount is considered a distribution of estate corpus for tax purposes. In this case Jeffrey would be taxed on the $11,000 he received, and the estate would be taxed on the remaining $5,000 of income. On the other hand, if Leslie's will stated that the $5,000 bequest to Al was to be paid in five equal annual installments, and in the first year he received $1,000, he would be taxed on the $1,000 only if the payment is made out of income. Beneficiaries will be taxed on any specific bequests that are required to be paid out of income.

Aside from the foregoing rule regarding specific bequests, there is an *income-first rule* requiring that all distributions are deemed to be paid out of income first, even if the executor, administrator, or trustee in fact distributes corpus in the form of cash or property. For example, assume in the previous example that the distribution to Jeffrey consisted solely of stock. Jeffrey would still be deemed to have received income.

Income Taxation of Trusts

Trusts that are deemed irrevocable (nongrantor trusts—see below) are considered separate taxpayers. They may be testamentary (made irrevocable on the death of the testator) or inter vivos (living) trusts. Income from property in revocable trusts (grantor trusts) will be taxed to the grantor rather than to the trust, because the power to revoke the instrument gives the grantor control over the trust assets. Trustees of irrevocable trusts may be given discretionary powers to distribute or accumulate income. To the extent a trustee exercises the right to distribute that income and sprinkle it among more than one taxpayer within the family group, the income may be shifted to a lower tax bracket and can be sheltered by multiple personal exemptions.

Trust Income—General Taxation

The essential concept of trust taxation is that trust income is taxed once, either (1) to the beneficiary(ies) or (2) to the trustee. If a trustee is required to distribute the entire income of the trust annually, that income will be taxed to the recipient(s). However, some trusts authorize the accumulation of all or part of the income at the trustee's discretion. The tax law does not tax prospective beneficiaries on amounts they may never receive.

A system has been devised that taxes the trustee on income accumulated by the trust and the beneficiary on income receivable. To thwart tax avoidance, the beneficiary is taxed on the amount *distributable* to him or her rather than on the amount actually paid to him or her. This prevents the trustee from arbitrarily deferring payments in an attempt to keep trust income in lower brackets. Although the details of trust taxation are quite complex, in essence the taxation of trust income can be capsulized: Income that is accumulated by the trust is taxable to the trust; income that is payable to the beneficiary is taxable to the beneficiary; and income either accumulated or distributed by a grantor trust is taxable to the grantor.

Simple Trusts

The income tax law classifies trusts into two types—simple and complex. Whether a trust is simple or complex may change from year to year.

A simple trust is one in which the trust agreement requires that all trust income be distributed currently to the beneficiaries. In any year a simple trust may not make distributions from amounts other than current income. Principal may not be distributed and no charitable gifts can be made by this type of trust; otherwise, it will be deemed to be a complex trust for that taxable year. The trustee may be given a power to distribute corpus, but as long as no distribution is actually made during the tax year, the trust is considered simple for that year.

A simple trust is treated as a separate tax entity subject to a $300 personal exemption. As such, it has—subject to certain exceptions—the same deductions as an individual. It also has a special deduction for income that is distributable to its beneficiaries. The net result is that a simple trust does not pay tax on income it pays out. The beneficiary of a simple trust in turn will report the income received—or receivable. In other words, a simple trust acts like a funnel—a conduit for passing the trust income from the grantor to the beneficiaries.

Most trusts operate as simple trusts. For example, a trust that provides income "to my wife for life with remainder to my children" or "income to be distributed to and among my spouse and children in such amounts and such proportions as my trustee may determine" is a simple trust until and unless a distribution of corpus is made.

Complex Trusts

The second type of trust is known as a complex trust. A complex trust is any trust that is not a simple trust; that is, a complex trust is one in which the trustee either must—or may—accumulate income. The trustee of a complex trust—unlike the trustee of a simple trust—can also distribute corpus (principal). The trustee can also make gifts to charities. A complex trust—like a simple trust—is a separate tax-paying entity. It is allowed a special deduction for actual distributions of income but pays tax on any income it does not distribute. Generally the same rules that govern complex trusts apply also to the income taxation of a decedent's estate.

It is impossible to understand the taxation of trusts, unless the term *income* is defined. Actually, there is income in the trust sense and income in the tax sense. Most states have a Principal and Income Act that allocates receipts and payments between estate or trust income and principal. For example, if the trustee is required to pay out "all the income," then under the trust law definition the trustee would not be required to pay out capital gains or other items classified as corpus (as opposed to income). Capital gains are excluded from the trust law definition of income, and are treated as additions to corpus rather than income. But generally the grantor or decedent may override these rules. For example, gains from property could be designated by the grantor as trust income.

But note that a capital gain is every bit as much income in the tax sense as dividend income, rental income, or interest on a loan. Therefore it is possible that even though a trustee of a simple trust is required to distribute all the income (and thus that amount is taxable to the beneficiaries rather than the trust), the difference between the total income in the tax sense and the total income in the trust sense will be taxable to the trust.

> *Example:* Suppose a trust received $3,000 in capital gains from the sale of trust assets and $5,000 from dividends on stock it held. A trust that was required to pay out "all the income" to the beneficiaries would only make a distribution of $5,000 (the amount of dividends). The beneficiaries, rather than the trust, would be taxed on that $5,000. However, the remaining income in the tax sense, $3,000, would not be distributable by the trust and therefore would be taxed to the trust. For this reason, a simple trust may be taxed even though it is required to distribute all of its income in the trust law sense.

A complex trust that is required to distribute all its income currently has an exemption of $300. For a complex (sometimes called an *accumulation*) trust that is not required to distribute income, the regular exemption is $100. No type of trust (or estate for that matter) may deduct the standard deduction allowed to individual taxpayers.

Distributable Net Income

The mechanical approach to the sharing concept (the trust pays income tax on the amount it retains while the beneficiaries pay tax on the income of the trust distributable to them) occurs through the utilization of a concept known as distributable net income (DNI). In general, distributable net income means taxable income before the deduction for distributions and before the $300 personal exemption for simple trusts ($100 for complex trusts), but after the exclusion of capital gains and losses. The concept of DNI is used to achieve three main results. First, it provides a limit on the deduction that a trust or estate may receive for amounts distributed to beneficiaries. A second function is to limit the amount of distribution that may be taxable to the beneficiaries. The third purpose of DNI is to establish the character of the amounts taxable to the beneficiaries. As a general rule, income retains the same character in the hands of the beneficiaries as it had in the hands of the trust. Thus tax-exempt income to the trust will retain its tax-exempt status when distributed to the beneficiary.

The first purpose of DNI ensures that the trust or estate receives a deduction for amounts it distributes and provides a limit for that deduction. For example, assume that a trust earns $10,000 in taxable income and distributes $6,000 of that income to its sole beneficiary. The DNI is $10,000. Accordingly the estate or trust deducts $6,000. The trust will be taxed on the amount it retains, $4,000.

The second purpose of DNI is to limit the portion of distributions that are taxable to beneficiaries. If the trust in the above example distributed $12,000 to the beneficiary, the trust would be allowed to deduct $10,000, the DNI. The trust therefore would have no tax liability. The beneficiary would be taxed on $10,000 of the $12,000 received. The first $10,000 would be considered to have come from income, while the remaining $2,000 would be considered an income-tax-free distribution of trust corpus. The DNI rule does not allow a trustee to determine whether income or corpus has been distributed. Instead, arbitrarily and automatically, all amounts distributed are first deemed to be income—to the extent of DNI.

According to this arbitrary DNI rule, a beneficiary can be taxed even if the distribution received is actually from corpus. For example, assume a trust has interest income of $10,000 that the trustee decides to accumulate. If the trustee then decides in the same tax year to distribute $10,000 of corpus to one of its beneficiaries, the beneficiary will be deemed to have received $10,000 of income, even though the trustee is actually making a distribution from corpus.

The third function of DNI is to ensure that the character of the amounts in the hands of a beneficiary is the same as that in the hands of a trust or estate. Therefore, if dividends are received by a trust and distributed to a beneficiary, the dividends retain their character as dividends.

Likewise, if the trust receives tax-free income (such as from a municipal bond), the income remains tax free in the hands of the beneficiary. This result is achieved mechanically by limiting the trust's deduction to DNI determined without regard to tax-free income.

> *Example:* Assume a trust has $4,000 of tax-exempt interest and $6,000 of dividend income. Its distributable net income is $10,000, but the DNI for deduction purposes is $6,000. The $10,000 distributed would be the same in the hands of the beneficiary as it would be in the hands of the trustee—$4,000 of the interest would be tax exempt and $6,000 of the dividend income would be taxable, because the DNI received by the beneficiary will be $6,000.

Effect of Multiple Beneficiaries. When there is more than one beneficiary, each is taxed on his or her share of DNI. When special items are distributed (such as tax-exempt interest, dividends, and so forth), a beneficiary is considered to have received a proportionate share unless the trust agreement earmarks a particular type of income for a specified beneficiary. This makes it possible to pay out tax-exempt income to high-income-tax-bracket beneficiaries and to pay other income to lower-bracket beneficiaries as well as to pay other income to lower-bracket family members. (The distribution provisions cannot be arbitrary and must have some significance apart from their tax sense.) For example, it would be permissible to require that 40 percent of the trust corpus be invested in tax-exempt securities and that the grantor's spouse receive all such income.

Grantor-Trust Taxation

Trusts are typically created when a grantor with substantial assets creates a trust and contributes the trust property for the benefit of less wealthy family members. Quite often, one purpose for this transfer is to shift income, and the taxation thereof, from a higher-bracket grantor to lower-bracket beneficiaries, resulting in the availability of a greater amount of funds to the beneficiaries than if the grantor had received the income and paid the aftertax proceeds to the beneficiaries directly.

Trusts would be very popular indeed if the grantor could shift the taxation on trust income to lower-bracket beneficiaries while maintaining substantial control over the trust property and income. Congress recognized this as a possibility for abuse and devised the grantor-trust rules, which provide that the income from a trust will be taxed to the grantor if the grantor retains certain proscribed powers and controls over the trust. The grantor-trust rules will also apply if the spouse of the grantor, living with the grantor at the time of creation of the interest, is given any of the proscribed powers that invoke the grantor-trust rules. In the case of a grantor trust, the trust is disregarded for income tax purposes and all income, deductions, and credits attributable to any portion of a trust declared a grantor trust will be taken into account directly on the grantor's individual income tax return. The financial services professional should be aware of these rules to alert a client-grantor whose trust could be inadvertently designed as a grantor trust.

Trust Income Available for the Benefit of the Grantor. Grantor-trust taxation will be applied to all or part of the income of a trust if provided for the grantor or the grantor's spouse without the consent of an adverse party. Furthermore, the income will be taxed to the grantor for any portion of the trust if the income may be provided for the grantor or the grantor's spouse at the discretion of the grantor or nonadverse party. In the same manner, a trust will be considered a grantor trust if it accumulates taxable or tax-exempt income for future distribution to the grantor or the grantor's spouse. The grantor will also be taxed on any portion of a trust in which the income may be applied to pay premiums for life insurance on the life of the grantor or the grantor's spouse.

The income from a trust that is applied to satisfy the legal support obligations of the grantor is paid to the benefit of the grantor and will also cause grantor-trust tax treatment. However, the grantor will not be taxed on this income if it is merely payable for a support obligation of the grantor at the discretion of the trustee unless the income is actually so applied.

Revocable Trusts. The revocable trust described in an earlier reading is an example of a trust in which the grantor has strings attached to the trust property and income. In this case, the grantor has not completed a transfer for tax purposes if the power is retained, at any time, to return the trust property to the grantor's possession. For this reason the revocable trust is taxable as a grantor trust, and its creation will not alter the federal income tax picture of the grantor or the beneficiaries. The grantor will also be treated as the owner of the trust if the power to revoke the trust is similarly held by either the grantor's spouse or a nonadverse party. For the purposes of the grantor-trust rules, a nonadverse party means any individual who does not possess a substantial beneficial interest in the trust that would be adversely affected by the exercise or nonexercise of any power held by the individual with respect to the trust. For example, an adverse party would be a trust beneficiary who loses the benefit of the trust if the grantor revokes.

Reversionary Interest. Grantor-trust tax treatment will occur for any portion of the trust in which the grantor retains a reversionary interest in either the trust corpus or the trust income if, at the creation of the portion of the trust in which the grantor holds the reversionary interest, the value of this reversionary interest exceeds 5 percent of the value of this portion of the trust. The IRS valuation rules are to be used to determine the value of any reversionary interest. Generally, the trust income interest would have to be gifted for a period of over 30 years (this assumes current AFMR of 10.6) before the grantor-trust rules can be avoided. Thus, a temporary gift of an income interest followed by a reversionary interest in the grantor will rarely cause a shifting of income for tax purposes.

As an exception to the reversionary-interest rule, the grantor will not be treated as the owner of the income portion of trust if the reversionary interest will take effect at the death of the beneficiary who (1) is a lineal descendant of the grantor and (2) has not attained age 21. These reversionary-interest provisions apply to transfers and trusts made after March 1, 1986.

Controls Retained by the Grantor. The grantor-trust rules contain a series of proscribed controls and powers that the grantor might desire to retain over a trust. These are included in the grantor-trust category to prevent the grantor from shifting taxation of the trust income while retaining enough control over the trust to possess substantial beneficial enjoyment of the trust income and property.

Power to Control Beneficial Enjoyment. Grantor-trust tax treatment will occur if the grantor retains (1) the beneficial enjoyment of the trust corpus and/or (2) the power to dispose of trust income without the approval or consent of an adverse party. The general rule provides that the grantor will be taxed on the income when the grantor or nonadverse party holds the right to add or delete beneficiaries, to alter the shares of the beneficiaries in the income or principal, or to determine the timings of distributions. Fortunately this general rule is subject to several exceptions, which allow the grantor some flexibility in the design of the trust. Powers that may be held by the trustee, regardless of who possesses them, that do not cause grantor-trust taxation include the following:

- the power to apply income toward the support of the grantor's dependents except to the extent that the income is actually applied to satisfy the grantor's legal support obligation
- the power to appoint the income or principal of the trust by will, other than income accumulated in the trust at the discretion of the grantor or nonadverse party
- the power to allocate income among charitable beneficiaries
- the power of the trustee to sprinkle or accumulate income, including

- the power to invade corpus for the benefit of a beneficiary or beneficiaries provided that the trustee's power is limited by some definite standard (for example, the power to distribute corpus for the education, support, maintenance, or health of a beneficiary)
- the power to withhold income temporarily from a current-income beneficiary
- the power to withhold income during the legal incompetency or minority of a current-income beneficiary (this provision allows accumulation for the minor-beneficiary of a Sec. 2503(c) trust)

- the power, exercisable only by an independent trustee (an individual not subordinate to the grantor), to sprinkle income and principal among a class of beneficiaries
- the power to apportion income by a trustee (not the grantor or the grantor's spouse) among a class of beneficiaries guided by some reasonably definite standard in the trust instrument

Administrative Powers. Certain powers of administration over a trust held by the grantor or a nonadverse party will create grantor-trust taxation. Basically the powers included in the grantor-trust rules are ones that allow the trust to be operated substantially to the benefit of the grantor. These powers include powers to dispose of trust property or income for less than adequate consideration or the power to obtain a loan from the trust without adequate interest or security.

Taxation of Unearned Income of Children under 14—The "Kiddie-Tax" Problem

A popular income-tax-planning technique—shifting income from a high-bracket individual to his or her lower-bracket children—was curtailed severely by the Tax Reform Act of 1986. The new rules provide that a portion of the unearned income of a child under 14 years of age is taxed at the top rate of the parents. This provision applies to all net unearned income of the child under age 14, including income from a trust, and it applies regardless of when and from whom the child received the income-producing property. Therefore, as seen below, there is limited income tax saving if a parent transfers property to a trust that pays out income to a child-beneficiary under age 14. In fact, trusts in existence before these new rules were established are also subject to this new penalty.

Calculating the Kiddie Tax. The procedure for calculating the kiddie tax is quite complex and will not be described fully here. However, the law provides that the child will pay the parent's tax rate on net unearned income. The net unearned income of the child is the child's unearned income less the sum of the $500 standard deduction plus an additional amount, which is the greater of (1) $500 or (2) allowable deductions directly related to the production of the child's unearned income. The intent of this procedure is to apply no tax to the first $500 of unearned income due to the standard deduction. The next $500 of unearned income will be taxed at the child's bracket, and income in excess of $1,000 will be taxed to the child as if included in the parent's income for the year—at the parent's highest marginal bracket.

Example 1: Sara Jones, aged 13, receives $800 of unearned trust income and no earned income in 1988. Sara's $500 standard deduction is allocated against this, leaving a net unearned income of $300, which will be taxed at Sara's tax rate.

Example 2: Suppose instead that Sara had $1,400 of unearned trust income and no earned income in 1988. After applying Sara's $500 standard deduction, a net unearned income of $900 remains. The first $500 is to be taxed at Sara's rates, while the remaining $400 will be taxed at the parent's top federal income tax rate for the year.

Planning the Trust to Deal with the Kiddie-Tax Rules. It is obvious that the kiddie tax provides little or no income tax benefit to shifting income to children under 14 years of age. However, there are still some estate planning benefits to transferring income to children along with many personal nontax benefits for the creation of trusts for minor children. To minimize the impact of the kiddie tax when planning a transfer in trust for minor children, the client might consider the following:

- The trust can be designed to accumulate income until the child reaches age 14 or later. You will recall from the grantor-trust rules that while the child is a minor, a Sec. 2503(c) trust can be used to allow the trust to accumulate income that will be taxable to the trust. Income paid out to the child from the Sec. 2503(c) trust after the child attains age 14 will be taxed at the child's, not the parents', marginal tax rate. In general, the trust document may provide discretion for the trustee to temporarily withhold income from a trust beneficiary without the application of the grantor-trust rules.
- The trust property can be invested in assets in which income will be deferred—presumably until the child-beneficiary reaches age 14. Examples of investments that are suitable for this purpose include the following:

  - Series EE U.S. government bonds defer income until the bond is redeemed. For this purpose, the child must not already own Series EE bonds on which each year's income is being declared.
  - Growth stocks could be purchased with trust assets that pay little or no current dividends. The stock can be held until the child reaches age 14, at which time any gain would be taxed at the child's bracket.
  - Deep-discount tax-free municipal bonds can be purchased that mature after the child reaches age 14. The current interest will be tax free and any later gain will be taxed at the child's tax rate when the bond is redeemed.
  - Life insurance or annuity policies can be purchased on the life of the child-beneficiary without incurring either a grantor-trust or kiddie-tax problem. Any gain on a policy held until after the child reaches age 14 will be taxed at the child's rate. These policies are highly liquid since they may be surrendered at any time for the cash surrender value and, unlike stocks or bonds, are not subject to

19.13

market risk. However, it is important to remember that tax on the policy earnings is deferred only if the policy meets the statutory guidelines for the definition of life insurance.

Income-Tax-Saving Possibilities through Multiple Trusts

One technique for saving income taxes through trusts is to use separate or multiple trusts. Rather than create a single trust in which each beneficiary is given a fractional interest, a grantor may create one trust for each beneficiary. In other words, instead of providing that the residue of a testator's estate is to be held in trust and that each of the testator's four children is to receive one-fourth of the income each year with a one-fourth share of principal on termination, the testator could provide for separate trusts for each beneficiary. If the same assets were divided into four equal shares and held in separate and distinct trusts with one for each child, each trust would have its own exemption, and each would be subject to the lowest tax rates. The income tax difference can be significant.

It is possible to create several trusts for the same or different beneficiaries. If the tax law recognizes the existence of multiple trusts, then the income will be taxed separately to each trust, which means that each trust receives a separate exemption, and each trust is treated as a separate tax entity for all income tax purposes. Conversely, if multiple trusts are considered by the IRS to be one trust, only one exemption will be allowed. All the trusts will be treated as one entity for income tax purposes.

The grantor's intention is examined by studying the various trust instruments to determine whether or not more than one trust was established. The IRS will not question the separate tax status of multiple trusts if (1) the trusts have substantially different grantors and/or substantially different beneficiaries; (2) the trusts have substantially independent purposes or objectives, such as different dispositive goals for each beneficiary; and (3) the principal purpose for creating multiple trusts was not avoidance, deferral, or mitigation of the progressive income tax rates. The trusts should also be separately maintained (that is, separate books and records should be kept for each trust, each trust should have its own bank account, and separate returns should be filed).

Accumulation of Income in Trusts

One frequently used technique of estate planning is to give a trustee the discretionary power either to pay income to beneficiaries or to accumulate it. If a beneficiary has other sufficient income, a trustee may decide to retain income from the trust and pay it out in some year when the beneficiary is in a lower tax bracket or in more need of the money. If the beneficiary has more than sufficient income, it is improper tax planning for the terms of the trust to require a distribution of income since the income, if distributable, is taxable to the beneficiary whether or not it is actually received.

Throwback Rules. The technique of accumulating income within a trust is particularly effective when income beneficiaries earn high salaries or receive substantial amounts of passive income (for example, dividend, rent, interest). For example, in 1988 assume a trust has $4,000 (15 percent marginal tax bracket) of taxable income. If it distributes the entire amount to a single beneficiary in the 33 percent marginal tax bracket who earns $45,000 of taxable income, the liability resulting from the receipt of trust income would be $1,320. Conversely, if the income was retained, the tax paid by the trust would be $600, resulting in $720 of savings. But this *savings* is temporary. When the accumulated income is eventually distributed to the beneficiary, it will be taxed under the so-called throwback rules.

The essential purpose of the throwback rules is to tax a trust distribution of previously accumulated income in substantially the same manner as the distribution would have been taxed had it been paid to the beneficiary in each of the years when the income was actually earned by the trust. In essence, this tax system *throws back* the income to the year it was earned starting with the first year of an accumulation and bringing amounts forward. Accumulations prior to a beneficiary turning 21 years of age or during legal incompetency are excluded from the amount subject to the throwback rules.

In essence (but not in actuality), the beneficiary recompute each of the past years' income as if he or she had actually received the income (which in fact was accumulated by the trust). Once the total additional tax payable by the beneficiary (if any) is computed, the beneficiary may then take credit for taxes actually paid by the trust during the accumulation period.

Purchase of Life Insurance by a Trustee

A trust instrument may authorize a trustee of a testamentary trust to purchase life insurance on the lives of the beneficiaries. State law must be examined to see if there is a prohibition against the use of income for this purpose. From a tax viewpoint, income used to purchase life insurance on the lives of beneficiaries is considered as accumulated income; therefore income used to purchase life insurance by the trustee of the testamentary trust will be taxed to the trust. However, trust income used for premium payments for insurance on the life of the grantor of the trust (and/or on the life of the grantor's spouse) will be taxed to the grantor.

Authorizing a trustee to purchase life insurance on the lives of the beneficiaries can yield substantial benefits. For example, if one of the beneficiaries—a single daughter—has taxable income of $43,500 in 1988 (apart from the trust income), and if the trustee distributed $4,000 to her (which is all the trust income), the additional income tax would amount to $1,120 (assuming a 28 percent bracket for the daughter). This leaves $2,880 that can be used as premiums to purchase life insurance on the daughter's life. But if a trust itself purchased the insurance with income, the income tax would be $585 because of the trust's lower income tax bracket of 15 percent ($4,000 − $100 accumulation trust personal exemption, or $3,900 taxable). This would leave $3,415 of trust income to purchase life insurance or $535 more for premium payments by having the trust pay the premiums.

One of the principles of proper tax planning is that income should be divided among family members whenever possible in order to lower the rate at which the income will be taxed as well as to take advantage of the multiple individual personal exemptions. For example, assume a grantor's daughter, Jane, is a lawyer earning about $32,000. If the grantor left income-producing property in trust with the provision that the income was payable to Jane, $10,000 of additional income would net the daughter approximately $7,200. But if the same $10,000 was spread among the daughter and her three children for tax purposes, the total intrafamily *net dollars* might be more than if all the income were paid to Jane. However, you should recall that the kiddie tax is applicable to the unearned income of children under 14. The trust income distributed to children under age 14 will essentially be taxed as if included in Jane's income for the year resulting in no tax savings if the income is shifted to Jane's children under age 14. Any income shifted to Jane's children age 14 and over may result in tax savings if the children are in the lowest (15 percent) bracket.

Assuming Jane's children are all 14 and over, one way to accomplish the objective of shifting income to lower brackets is to require the trustee to pay the income to Jane and her children in four equal shares. Yet the same tax savings may be accomplished with more flexibility if the trustee was authorized, rather than mandated, to pay income to Jane or any one or more of her children at the trustee's discretion. The trustee could then allocate income among the family members in any manner that seemed desirable from tax year to tax year. In exercising that discretion, the trustee would consider the individual needs of the various beneficiaries, the ultimate use to which the income would be put, and the collective as well as individual tax burdens.

There are also nontax advantages to clauses that *sprinkle* income according to needs. An example would be a testator who would like to provide for the family of a deceased child but does not want to pay income for the lifetime of a deceased child's spouse. The testator may fear that if the surviving spouse remarries, income will go to the new spouse or the new spouse's children rather than to the testator's grandchildren. The sprinkle clause in a trust enables a trustee to pay income to the spouse only as long as the children are young or have varying needs and as long as the spouse does not remarry.

Another possible flaw, besides the kiddie-tax problem, in the use of a sprinkle clause to provide financial protection to the family of a deceased child of the grantor: if trust income is used to support a dependent, that income will be taxed to the person who is obligated to provide the support. In a trust with a sprinkle clause, to the extent that the trustee applies income for the support of a minor, the IRS may attempt to tax this income to the parent. "Obligation to support" means the duty imposed by law to support another person.

However, trust income generally is not considered to be used for the support of a dependent. There are a number of reasons that income will not be considered to be used for the discharge of the parent's obligation. First, if the beneficiary is over the age of majority, the obligation to support that child may be limited. Some states are beginning to recognize that support obligations include college costs. However, a family court decree may create an obligation to support postmajority child costs. Second, a trustee would generally accumulate income when a minor is involved. Third, if the finances of a parent are limited, income used by the trustee for support may be over and above the parent's obligation.

Conservative planning suggests that a trust provision be included stating that income may be used only if the parent's funds are inadequate for the desired purpose. Alternatively, such funds can be used to provide nonsupport items such as toys, music lessons, travel, entertainment, cars, or other items that will not fall into the category of "legal obligation to support."

CONCLUSION

Trusts and estates, creatively structured, can provide significant tax advantages for the beneficiaries. Full utilization of tax planning opportunities for estates, trusts, and beneficiaries is generally overlooked by all but the most sophisticated tax planners. While the income taxation of estates and trusts is complicated to learn, it may be worth the effort when considering the potential results achievable in tax savings.

AN EXAMINATION OF THE GENERATION-SKIPPING TRANSFER TAX

Ted Kurlowicz

INTRODUCTION TO THE GENERATION-SKIPPING TRANSFER TAX (GSTT)

A generation-skipping transfer tax (GSTT) was first enacted in 1976. However, when Congress decided to make sweeping revisions to the federal tax code in 1986, it seemed appropriate to make decisions about the GSTT. Indeed, the rules pertaining to this transfer tax enacted more than a decade earlier were extremely complex and contained obvious loopholes. In fact, the IRS never developed a form to report transfers subject to the tax. Congress was faced with the choice of either eliminating the GSTT theory completely or, alternatively, totally revamping the statute. The latter choice was followed.

First, the new law totally repealed the prior system of taxing generation-skipping transfers and replaced it with a completely different framework for the imposition of the tax. Rather than the rate of tax being equal to the estate tax bracket of the transferor (as under the old approach), the new approach imposes a flat rate on taxable transfers that is equal to the highest current unified federal estate and gift tax rate—55 percent currently and 50 percent after 1992.

TAXABLE TRANSFERS

The GSTT applies when a taxable transfer is made to a transferee more than one generation level below the transferor. For example, a generation-skipping transfer would occur if a grandparent transfers property to a grandchild. However, the GSTT applies only if the transfer avoids estate or gift tax one generation level above the transferee. That is, the GSTT applies only if a generation is "skipped" by the estate and gift tax system. For example, a gift from a grandparent to a grandchild that causes estate and gift tax on such transfer at the parent's level will not invoke the generation-skipping tax. It is important to remember, however, that estate or gift tax in addition to GSTT may be applicable on such generation-skipping transfers, since a *grandparent* will probably be subject to the federal estate and gift tax system as well as the GSTT system when making gifts to a grandchild. Thus the same transfer could incur transfer taxes in excess of 100 percent of the amount of the transfer.

The GSTT is imposed on gifts, bequests, or other distributions to skip beneficiaries. A skip beneficiary is either (1) a person who is at least two generations below the level of the transferor or (2) a trust in which the beneficiaries are skip persons and from which no nonskip person will benefit.

The taxes are imposed on three possible taxable events: direct skips, taxable terminations, and taxable distributions.

Direct Skips

As defined in the estate and gift tax system, a direct skip is a taxable transfer to a skip person. A direct skip can either be an outright transfer or a transfer in trust for the benefit of an individual. A transfer in trust will be treated as a direct skip if

- the trust benefits only one individual,
- no portion of the income or corpus may be distributed to anyone else during the beneficiary's lifetime, and
- the corpus will be included in the beneficiary's estate if he or she dies before the termination of the trust.

Thus a transfer to a life insurance trust will qualify as a direct skip if the trust meets the requirements above and provides current withdrawal powers, such as the Crummey withdrawal powers discussed in reading 8. A direct skip will not be treated as a taxable generation-skipping transfer if, at the time of the transfer, the parent of the skip person is already deceased. In this instance the GSTT is eliminated because the grandchild is the natural recipient of the grandparent's wealth if the grandchild's parent is deceased.

> *Example:* In 1990 James Dallop left a fully occupied apartment that he had owned for 14 years to his grandson, Scott, under the terms of his will. This transfer will *not* be considered a direct skip triggering the GSTT if Scott's parent who is the son or daughter of James predeceases James. If Scott's parent who is the son or daughter of James is alive at the time of James's death, the generation-skipping tax will apply to this direct-skip bequest. In either event, the regular federal estate tax will apply to this transfer.

Taxable Distributions

In addition to direct-skip situations, the new GSTT may apply to what is known as a taxable distribution.

A taxable distribution is any distribution of either income or principal from a trust to a person two or more generations junior to the trust settlor's generation. The recipients of a taxable distribution are called skip beneficiaries. To be taxable as a generation-skipping transfer, the distribution must otherwise escape federal estate and gift taxation at the first generation level below the original transferor.

The taxable amount in this scenario will be the net value of the property received by the skip beneficiary reduced by any amount he or she may have paid in order to receive the property. In addition, the taxable amount will include any GSTT paid by the *trustee* on such taxable distribution. The reason for this "gross-up" rule is that the GSTT liability falls on the skip beneficiary, not the trustee.

> *Example:* Ethel Bally created an irrevocable trust in early 1987 for the benefit of her son, Carlos, and her grandson, Julio. In December of this year the trustee made a distribution of $10,000 of trust income to Carlos and $8,800 of trust income to Julio. The distribution to Julio will be characterized as a taxable distribution that will trigger GSTT. Note that the original transfer to the trust in 1987 could have been subject to taxation through the gift tax rules at that time.

Taxable Termination

A taxable termination is defined as a situation in which there is a termination of a property interest held in trust by death, lapse of time, release of a power, or otherwise, that results in skip beneficiaries holding the property interests in the trust.

Four miscellaneous points must be noted.

- A taxable termination cannot take place if a skip beneficiary could not receive a distribution after the termination.
- A taxable termination cannot occur as long as at least one nonskip beneficiary has an interest in the property.
- There will be no taxable termination if an estate or gift tax is imposed on the trust property one generation level below the transferor at the time of the termination.
- A partial termination subject to GSTT is possible if a specified, separate portion of the trust is available only to skip persons after the termination.

The taxable amount in the case of a taxable termination is the value of all property involved reduced by any amounts paid by the recipient for the property and any expenses, debts, and income or property taxes triggered by the property in question.

> *Example:* In Rosemary Campo's will, she directed that the income from her marketable securities was to pass to her daughter, Kim, for life with the remainder interest to pass at Kim's death to Rosemary's granddaughter, Heather. When Kim died, her life interest in the trust property was terminated and Heather received the underlying property. Heather is the skip beneficiary. A taxable termination has occurred at Kim's death.

EXEMPTIONS AND EXCLUSIONS

Although the scope of the new GSTT is broad and could have a dramatic effect on a client's tax planning, it must be emphasized that there are several exemptions to, and exclusions from, this tax.

The most basic exemption is that every taxpayer is permitted to make aggregate transfers of up to $1 million during either lifetime or at death that will not attract the GSTT. Furthermore, since the transferor's spouse also has a $1 million exemption against generation-skipping transfers, a total family exemption of $2 million is available.

It should also be mentioned that certain transfers are excluded from the definition of the term *generation-skipping transfer*. These include transfers from a trust if the transfer is subject to federal estate or gift tax with regard to an individual in the first generation below the transferor; transfers that would qualify as gift tax free as direct payments made for a donee's educational or medical expenses; certain transfers qualifying for the annual $10,000 gift tax exclusion; and certain transfers that have previously been subject to the generation-skipping transfer tax.

Allocating the $1 Million Exemption

One important planning aspect of the GSTT is the allocation of the $1 million exemption. The exemption can be allocated at the option of the transferor, and, at the very least, the transferor should give some thought to selecting the appropriate transfer to which the exemption should be allocated. The mechanics of the GSTT, which are discussed below, demonstrate that the allocation of the exemption can cause transfers to be exempt, nonexempt, or partially exempt from tax. The best strategy is to leave transfers nonexempt if such transfers are expected to benefit only nonskip persons. To the extent possible, transfers that are likely to benefit skip persons should be made exempt.

> *Example:* P creates a life insurance trust that includes sprinkle provisions to provide benefits to his children and grandchildren. In his will, P leaves his probate estate in a marital trust for the life of his spouse, M, with a remainder to the Red Cross. P should allocate the exemption to each premium payment gifted to the life insurance trust. Unless the total premiums paid exceed the $1 million exemption, the entire trust will be exempt and thus all distributions to P's grandchildren will avoid GSTT. On the other hand, allocating the exemption to the marital trust would be inappropriate since it is highly unlikely that this trust will benefit a skip person.

Annual Exclusion Transfer

The $10,000 annual per-donee exclusion from gift tax was discussed in reading 8. Similarly an exclusion from the GSTT is available for direct skips. A direct skip is either (1) an outright gift providing the donee with immediate possession or (2) certain gifts in trust providing a present interest to a skip person. For GSTT purposes, the annual exclusion is more restrictive than the gift tax annual exclusion for gifts in trust. The gift in trust qualifies for the exclusion if it provides a present interest such as a current income interest or Crummey withdrawal power. In addition, the trust must limit distributions of income and corpus to a single beneficiary and must provide that the corpus will be included in the estate of the beneficiary if he or she dies prior to the termination of the trust. Thus, since only one beneficiary is permitted, the GSTT annual exclusion cannot be used on the typical inter vivos trust with sprinkle provisions. It is possible, however, to create separate trusts for each grandchild, such as a Sec. 2503(c) trust, that will qualify for both the gift tax and GSTT annual exclusions.

Exclusion for Transfers for Educational or Medical Expenses

Tuition or medical expense payments on behalf of a donee are also excluded from both gift tax and GSTT. Such gifts must be provided directly to the educational institution or medical provider for expenses incurred by the donee. The transfers excludible under this provision are not limited in amount, but the tuition payment exclusion is limited to transfers to educational institutions eligible for income tax deductible charitable contributions covering the direct tuition costs for the education or training of the donee.

Medical expenses eligible for the exclusion are those expenses normally deductible by the donee (subject to the 7.5 percent floor) under the income tax rules.

CALCULATION OF THE GSTT

The GSTT is calculated by a somewhat unusual process, which is discussed herein primarily to demonstrate the effect of the $1 million exemption. The GSTT is determined by multiplying the taxable amount by an applicable GSTT rate. The taxable amount is the value (less certain expenses) of any direct skip, taxable termination, or taxable distribution.

The applicable GSTT rate is the highest federal estate and gift tax rate (55 percent prior to 1993) multiplied by an inclusion ratio. The inclusion ratio is determined by the following formula:

$$\text{Inclusion ratio} = 1 - \frac{TE}{VT - (ET + CD)}$$

TE = transferor's exemption allocated to the transfer
VT = value of the transferred property
ET = amount of federal estate tax or state death tax recovered from the trust attributable to the transferred property
CD = charitable deduction attributable to the transferred property

Assuming no estate tax or charitable deduction, the inclusion ratio is one (and the applicable rate is 55 percent) if no exemption is allocated to the transfer. If the amount of the exemption is allocated equivalent to the value of the transferred property, the applicable rate is zero and the transfer is exempt from GSTT. It is possible, of course, to have an applicable rate ranging from zero percent to 55 percent if the transfer is only partially exempt. However, a partially exempt trust should generally be avoided unless the transferor has insufficient remaining exemption to fully shelter the trust from

GSTT. Partially exempt trusts will generally increase the complexity and fiduciary costs associated with the administration of the trust.

LIABILITY FOR THE TAX

The liability for tax payment depends upon the type of generation-skipping transfer. Therefore the transferor must consider the net amount to be received by the skip beneficiary in choosing the transfer mechanism.

For direct skips, the tax is imposed on the transferor or his or her estate. Therefore the direct-skip beneficiary receives the full amount of the transfer while the remainder of the transferor's estate is diminished by the transfer.

In the case of a taxable distribution, the liability for the tax falls on the transferee. That is, the tax that is imposed will reduce the amount of the transfer available to the beneficiary. Since the rate of tax is 55 percent before 1993 (and 50 percent in 1993 and thereafter), the amount of the taxable distribution available to the skip beneficiary is substantially reduced after the GSTT liability.

The tax is paid by the trustee in the event of a taxable termination. Thus, at the time of the termination, the skip person will receive the proceeds reduced by the tax.

The GSTT is imposed by statute on the property transferred unless the transferor specifically allocates the tax elsewhere by the terms of his or her will or trust document. As with the federal estate and gift taxes, a lien is applicable against the transferred property for collection of the tax.

PLANNING FOR THE GSTT

Since the GSTT is imposed at the highest marginal federal estate tax bracket, the tax will represent the highest percentage burden of any federal tax in the future. Since generation-skipping transfers are also potentially subject to estate or gift taxes, the combination of estate or gift tax and GSTT rates may exceed 100 percent of the amount of the transfer.

Obviously this new tax creates a substantial tax incentive to transfer property in a manner exempt from the tax. Gifts of appreciating property are good targets for lifetime gifts to take advantage of the $1 million exemption. The exemption will be applied to the value of the property at the time of the transfer, and any posttransfer appreciation will not be subject to the tax and need not be sheltered by part of the exemption. In addition, the exemption can be used to provide for skip persons through transfers in trust. The exemption must be allocated against current additions to the trust on a timely filed gift tax return. However, the appreciation on the corpus will avoid GSTT if all *additions* to the trust are sheltered by the exemption. Therefore because the GSTT exemption is leveraged, wealthy clients can transfer appreciating property that will eventually expand into substantial wealth at a huge total transfer-tax savings.

The irrevocable life insurance trust discussed earlier is an excellent device for using the $1 million exemption against the GSTT. Unless the trust has one beneficiary, the premium additions to a Crummey life insurance trust will not be eligible for a GSTT annual exclusion. However, the gift tax annual exclusion will be available, and the $1 million exemption will shelter the trust from GSTT unless aggregate premiums exceed $1 million. In this manner, substantial wealth may be transferred to the trust and avoid the gift tax or GSTT. The cash contributed to the trust can be used to purchase a life insurance policy on the life of the grantor. Therefore the appreciation in the life insurance policy and subsequent proceeds at the death of the grantor are beyond the reach of the estate tax or GSTT. The life insurance received by the beneficiaries will prevent the diminution of the grantor's estate caused by the total transfer taxes imposed on any wealth *retained* by the grantor until death. For example, suppose a $1 million policy is placed in the trust and will be paid up with 10 annual premium contributions of $15,000. The grandparent can then shelter such a transfer with $150,000 of his or her exemption, instead of using the full exemption on a different type of $1 million gift.

Each spouse should make full use of his or her $1 million exemption. The allocation of the exemption in the wills of both spouses should be carefully planned. The spouses should avoid wasting the exemption by allocating both exemptions to the same assets. A popular method is to provide the executors of the will with discretionary power in allocating the exemptions. After viewing the facts at the time of estate administration, the executor will then allocate the exemption where it is most appropriate. The exemption should be allocated to a transfer, perhaps a credit-equivalent bypass trust, that is most likely to benefit skip persons. In addition, the executor should avoid allocating the exemption to a transfer if the surviving spouse's exemption will be available.

If one spouse does not have sufficient assets to use his or her exemption, an interspousal transfer may be indicated. By using the unlimited marital estate or gift tax deduction, the wealthy spouse can transfer assets to the other spouse without incurring transfer tax. These assets may enable the less-wealthy spouse to use the $1 million GSTT exemption.

Finally, wealthy grandparents should consider other excludible transfers. For example, direct-skip gifts of $10,000 ($20,000 if split with a spouse) to a Sec. 2503(c) trust can be made without gift tax or GSTT liability. In addition, grandparents could pay a grandchild's tuition directly to an educational institution without incurring gift tax or GSTT. A systematic pattern of such gifts could both reduce the estate tax and GSTT base of the grandparent and provide helpful assistance to the children or grandchildren.

ADVANCED ESTATE PLANNING TECHNIQUES

Ted Kurlowicz

Recent tax reform has increased the significance of planning for federal transfer tax reduction. In many ways, the planning for estate and gift tax reduction can result in far greater gains to the taxpayer than planning for other taxes. This is particularly true for wealthy individuals with substantial estates. Reasons for the recent increase in the importance of estate planning include

- the federal transfer tax rates have increased in relation to the marginal income tax rates. (Marginal income tax rates peak at 33 percent with a flat 28 percent rate applicable to high income earners. The federal estate and gift tax rates have a 55 percent maximum, with a 5 percent additional surcharge for certain large estates.)
- the generation-skipping tax is applicable to many transfers to skip beneficiaries at a flat rate of 55 percent
- the combination of federal estate or gift taxes with generation-skipping taxes could result in a marginal rate in excess of 100 percent for certain transfers to skip beneficiaries
- that the new anti-estate freeze statute presents a new estate tax trap for the unwary, since it may cause additional unforeseen estate or gift taxes if property gifted during a donor's lifetime is returned to his or her gross estate

To prevent the Treasury from confiscating the wealth of those individuals who accumulate substantial assets, estate planning is particularly important. Although many popular estate planning techniques have been curtailed or eliminated by the anti-estate freeze statute, various methods of preserving the assets that wealthy individuals hope to pass on to their heirs still remain.

INSTALLMENT SALES

An installment sale can be a useful technique for financial and estate planning purposes. An installment sale is a taxable sale of a property where the income tax reporting of gain is accounted for under the installment accounting provisions of the Internal Revenue Code. An installment sale is any sale in which at least one principal payment is received in a year other than the year of the sale. The installment reporting provisions are the general rule when this definition for an installment sale is satisfied. However, the seller can elect to use normal accounting for an installment sale and recognize all gain in the year of sale.

Advantages of Installment Sales

From the seller's standpoint, an installment sale of property can provide both income and estate tax benefits. If installment reporting is available, the gain of the sale of property in exchange for an installment note will be delayed and recognized gradually over the installment period. Thus it is possible to sell highly appreciated property without immediate recognition of the full taxable gain. On the other hand, the ability to elect out of installment reporting will provide the taxpayer with the possibility of recognizing all gain immediately. For example, a taxpayer may elect to recognize all gain at the time of an installment sale in a year when the taxpayer either has little other income or shows a loss for income tax purposes. Under these circumstances reporting the gain immediately on an installment sale will prevent the taxpayer from wasting other deductions and tax benefits. The flexibility of an installment sale's reporting rules permits a taxpayer to defer gain recognition and, to some degree, plan the timing of gain recognition on the sale of property.

The installment sale also provides estate tax saving possibilities for the seller. The installment sale is a particularly useful device for family estate planning, which usually occurs when a senior family member wishes to pass property on to a successor in the family. For estate planning purposes an installment sale is one method of "freezing" the seller's estate and shifting the appreciation potential to a junior family member. If performed properly, the installment sale will shift the postsale appreciation to the junior family member without paying any transfer taxes will be payable on the property transferred to the junior family member if the installment note is equal to the fair market value of the property at the time of the sale. It is important to remember, however, that the rules of Sec. 2036(c) could apply to an installment sale of property to a family member. These rules will be further discussed below.

From the buyer's standpoint, the installment sale permits the buyer to defer some or all of the principal payments on the sale. This is particularly important for buyers without the funds for the entire purchase price. Quite often, the purchase and sale would be impossible without the payment deferral available in an installment sale.

Income Tax Treatment of an Installment Sale

The sale of appreciated property in exchange for an installment note will provide that some or all of the purchase price will be payable at some date in the future. From the seller's standpoint, the future payments can be broken down into three components for income tax purposes. One component of each annual payment on the installment note will be treated as a return of the seller's original basis of the property. This return of basis is not taxable since the seller is merely recovering his or her cost of the property. A second component of each payment received will be treated as taxable gain. Finally, the third and final component of each payment will be deemed interest. This interest will be taxable to the seller as ordinary income.

Under the installment sale rules, the taxable gain component is recognized proportionally over the period in which the installment payments are made. The formula for recognizing gain from any particular installment payment is as follows:*

$$\text{Capital gain} = \text{payment received during the year} \; \times \; \frac{\text{gross profit}}{\text{total contract price}}$$

Example: Tom Taxplanner would like to sell his vacation home to his daughter, Julia. The vacation home is valued at $200,000 and Tom's basis in the property is $50,000. Julia proposes an installment sale with a $50,000 down payment and the remaining principal payable in 10 annual installments of $15,000 beginning one year from settlement. Ten percent interest will be payable on any unpaid balance. Tom's gross profit is $150,000 and the contract price is $200,000. Thus Tom will recognize 75 percent ($150,000 divided by $200,000) of each payment as taxable gain. The amounts received by Tom are taxable as follows:

	Return of Cost	Taxable Gain	Interest
At settlement	$12,500	$37,500	—
Year 1	3,750	11,250	$15,000
Year 2	3,750	11,250	13,500
Year 3	3,750	11,250	12,000
Year 4	3,750	11,250	10,500
Year 5	3,750	11,250	9,000
Year 6	3,750	11,250	7,500
Year 7	3,750	11,250	6,000
Year 8	3,750	11,250	4,500
Year 9	3,750	11,250	3,000
Year 10	3,750	11,250	1,500

Interest on the Installment Sale

Under the current rules, there is no income tax rate differential for long-term capital gains. In addition, interest paid by a buyer on an installment sale is potentially deductible. Thus it might be to the benefit of the buyer to recharacterize some of the purchase payment as interest if the interest on the transaction will be deductible. Since there is no rate differential between long-term capital gains and receipt of interest, this recharacterization should not affect the seller. On the other hand, the buyer may wish to minimize the interest element of the installment sale if the interest will be nondeductible.

---

*This formula is simplified to some degree to demonstrate the gain recognition process without adding federal income tax complexity beyond the scope of this reading.

Under these circumstances it may be more advantageous for the buyer to characterize the payments as principal. The additional amount of principal will provide the buyer a higher basis, which may be available for depreciation deductions at a later date. Certainly the interest rate might be a consideration in the negotiation process for the installment sale.

Unfortunately the tax rules provide for target rates of interest on installment obligations under either the imputed interest rules (Code Sec. 483) or original-issue-discount (OID) rules (Code Sec. 1271–1274). These rules minimize the flexibility by specifying a rate of interest that is deemed to apply for installment obligations falling within these rules. These rules will not be further discussed; however, the estate planner should be aware that the appropriate tax advice should be sought for determining the rate of interest on an installment obligation.

Estate Tax Treatment of Installment Obligations

The estate tax treatment of the installment obligation depends on the following factors:

- Does the seller survive the term of the installment note?
- Does Sec. 2036(c) apply?
- If Sec. 2036(c) applies, does the installment note qualify for the safe harbor?

If the seller survives the retained-interest term and Sec. 2036(c) is not applicable, neither the installment note nor the property sold will be included in the seller's gross estate. Under these circumstances a successful freeze has been effected. The seller has removed the property from his or her estate and received a fixed number of installment payments in exchange for the property. To the extent these payments have been consumed or gifted away by the seller during his or her life, the value of the property will be removed from the seller's gross estate. In addition, any postsale appreciation on the property will avoid inclusion in the seller's transfer tax base. Suppose in our previous example that Tom lives 20 additional years after selling the vacation home to Julia. If Tom spends all the sale proceeds received from Julia, neither the property nor the installment payments will be included in his gross estate. Even if the vacation home property appreciates substantially, this additional amount benefits Julia without any transfer taxes imposed on Tom. Thus Tom was successful in transferring a substantial piece of property to Julia at a frozen contract price without any adverse estate and gift tax consequences.

If the seller dies during the installment term, the date-of-death value of the remaining installment payments will be included in the seller's gross estate. The date-of-death value of the remaining installment payments is determined by discounting the remaining installment payments to present value using 120 percent of the AFMR applicable at the date of death. These valuation methods were discussed in reading 11.

When Is Sec. 2036(c) Applicable? Sec. 2036(c) is applicable to installment sales of *enterprises* between family members (the affected related parties are discussed in reading 9). Sec. 2036(c) appears to be applicable to such installment sales since the nature of the sale is an estate freeze. That is, the appreciation on the enterprise is inherently shifted to the buyer. Presumably, the seller retains a fixed stream of income payments from the buyer. Thus the steps to invoke Sec. 2036(c) are satisfied because the seller transfers a disproportionate share of appreciation in an enterprise (in which the seller holds a substantial interest) while retaining an interest in the enterprise. The committee reports and the IRS guidance seems to make it clear that for Sec. 2036(c) purposes it makes little difference that the note requires the buyer (not the actual enterprise) to make the payments on the installment note.

Despite Sec. 2036(c) concerns, there are still potential estate tax planning uses for the family installment sale. First, virtually any type of installment sale freeze is possible for *non*enterprise property. Thus personal use property such as residences, heirlooms, and art collections can be sold to family members for an installment note without Sec. 2036(c) concerns. Second, Sec. 2036(c) provides for a safe harbor for installment obligations. Installment sales meeting this safe harbor are exempt from Sec. 2036(c).

Safe Harbor Installment Sales. Initially, there was much concern about the effect of the anti-estate freeze rules of Sec. 2036(c) on loans or installment sales of enterprise property between family members. You will recall that even full fair market value sales to family members might not avoid the grasp of the statute. Technical corrections gave us some relief in the form of a safe harbor for loans through provisions in Sec. 2036(c). Installment sales between family members will not be affected by the statute as long as the debt incurred by the purchaser meets the requirements of *qualified debt*.

Debt is considered *qualified* if

- the debt unconditionally requires fixed payments that do not extend beyond a period of 15 years (30 years if the debt is secured by real property) from the date of issue
- only interest and principal are payable and interest dates and rates are fixed (or set by a fixed relationship to a specified fair market interest rate)
- the debt is not subordinated to claims of general creditors (however, the debt may be subordinated to specified creditors)
- the debt does not provide for voting rights (or restrict the voting rights of current shareholders) except in the case of default
- the debt is not convertible (and provides no option to be converted) into any interest in the enterprise other than qualified debt

Congress also responded to the concern that the initial anti-estate freeze law would restrict the ability of a parent to loan money to a child's new business. For this reason a safe harbor for qualified start-up debt was included in the technical corrections.

Qualified start-up debt includes cases in which

- indebtedness unconditionally requires a payment of a sum certain in money
- the debt was received in exchange for cash to be used in an active trade or business
- at no time before or after the loan has the lender transferred any property other than cash to the enterprise. (Specifically included in these instructions is the prohibition of the transfer of goodwill or preferred customer lists to the borrower. This prevents a parent from, in effect, transferring benefits in a family business to an enterprise formed by an heir.)
- the lender has at no time held an interest other than the qualified start-up debt (this includes an interest as a director, officer, or employee)
- the borrower is an active participant in the management of the enterprise
- the terms of the debt do not provide voting or other convertibility rights as specified under the definition of *qualified debt*

The safe harbor provisions for various types of loans to enterprises or installment sales are helpful because they indicate what *can* be done. However, it is unclear whether everything that does not meet the safe harbor requirements is dangerous simply by negative implication. Generally, it is considered prudent to design an estate planning transaction to fit within these safe harbors.

Clearly, the material on installment sales contained in this reading is still valid for the income tax and estate planning treatment if the buyer and seller are unrelated. The material is similarly valid for installment sales between family members if the safe harbors are complied with. A parent could certainly sell enterprise property to a child in an installment sale that meets qualified debt requirements and therefore effectively freeze the size of his or her estate to the amount of the sale proceeds received from the transaction.

Because of negative implication in the safe harbors, a parent should not transfer enterprise property to a child in an installment sale transaction where the payments are unspecified or contingent on profits, despite the fact that this type of transaction is common in the installment sale area and despite the complicated regulations that are available to determine the federal income tax treatment of contingent principal payments. The retention of an installment note paying such contingent payments would probably be deemed a retained interest by the transferor-parent and therefore would cause the enterprise transferred in the transaction to be returned to the parent's gross estate at death.

Self-Canceling Installment Notes (SCINs)

A self-canceling installment note (SCIN) is an installment obligation that, by its terms, terminates the buyer's obligation at the seller's death. Thus the buyer has assumed the benefit of the mortality risk because the payments could terminate prior to the actual terms of the sale. This mortality component is bargained for, and the buyer should pay a higher price for the property since payments will be canceled if the buyer dies prematurely. The SCIN is a useful device to freeze a seller's estate tax value of the property that is sold for a SCIN. If the seller dies, the payments terminate and only the unconsumed amounts of the sale proceeds already received are included in the seller's gross estate.

SCINs will create problems with the anti-estate freeze statute if enterprise property held by a parent is sold to a child in exchange for a SCIN. SCINs are not unconditionally payable in fixed periods to a specified maturity date. The nature of the SCIN causes the number of actual installment payments to be indeterminate since the actual length is contingent on the duration of the seller's life. IRS Notice 89-99 specifically indicates that a SCIN will not qualify for an installment sale's safe harbor for qualified debt.

SCINs could, however, be a safe and useful estate freezing technique when the property transferred to a child is nonenterprise property. For example, property, such as a vacation home, can be transferred to an heir for a SCIN to reduce the senior family member's gross estate.

Private Annuities

The anti-estate freeze law also has some effect on transactions involving a sale of property for a private annuity. A private annuity is issued by the buyer in exchange for property to pay the seller a specified stream of income for the seller's life. The buyer cannot be in the business of selling commercial annuities. Since the annuity terminates at the seller's death, it will be excluded from the seller's gross estate if Sec. 2036(c) is not applicable.

Although private annuities have unspecified duration and thus do not fall within the safe harbor of qualified debt, they will be subject to the anti-estate freeze statute only if the other provisions of the statute are met. As with SCINs, a private annuity will be useful for estate planning purposes only if (1) the parties to the sale are unrelated or (2) the property sold is not treated as an enterprise for Sec. 2036(c) purposes.

GRANTOR-RETAINED INCOME TRUSTS (GRITs)

A GRIT is a type of trust taxable under the grantor-trust rules (discussed in reading 19). It is not an income-shifting device, and the grantor will continue to be taxed on the income in the trust. It is a value-shifting technique designed to transmit assets from a grantor (presumably an individual with substantial wealth) to one who is a natural object of his or her bounty without the full transfer-tax cost. The success of this technique depends on many factors (particularly the longevity of the grantor), and although it is not indicated in every case, this trust arrangement is expected to become more popular since GRITs that meet a safe harbor test are exempt from the anti-estate freeze rules of Sec. 2036(c).

Basic Design of the GRIT

The grantor of a GRIT establishes an irrevocable trust and retains the trust income for a fixed period of years. The remainder interest following the grantor's retained term consists of the trust property including, of course, any unrealized appreciation of the trust property during the grantor's term. The remainder interest is transferred irrevocably when the trust is *created* and will be distributed directly to, or held in trust for, the remainderperson at the end of the grantor's term.

As we will discuss below, this technique is indicated when a single individual or a married couple has a sizable estate and will not need the retained-income interest or the trust property beyond the specified term of years. The remainderperson, typically the grantor's child, will receive this interest with substantially reduced transfer-tax costs than would have been incurred had the grantor not made the transfer or retained the income interest until death. Some examples of trust property that can be transferred to a GRIT are income-producing real estate, closely held stock, and other assets with substantial appreciation value along with current income payments. Other possibilities include the grantor's residence or vacation home—assets that generally are passed to children.

> *Example 4:* Tom and Jane Fatcat, both aged 55, have substantial wealth. They own a large home in the Philadelphia area and a beautiful vacation home in Cape May, New Jersey. At age 65, Tom and Jane plan to fulfill a lifelong wish and retire to Florida. Since Tom and Jane will no longer need the vacation home, it is their objective to transfer ownership in the vacation home to their children at that time. Tom can transfer the vacation home to an irrevocable trust while retaining the income interest (in this case, the use of the vacation home) for a 10-year term, with the remainder interest to go to his children. If Tom lives for the entire term of the retained interest, the vacation home (including any appreciation subsequent to the transfer) will be transferred at a far lower transfer-tax cost.

Safe Harbor Requirements for GRITs

The application of the original anti-estate freeze statute to GRITs was unclear. Technical corrections resolved this dilemma by creating a safe harbor for certain GRITs if the grantor's retained interest meets certain tests. The retained income rights of the grantor is not to be treated as a 2036(c) retained interest if the following conditions exist:

- the grantor's retained income rights do not extend beyond 10 years
- the income rights must be retained by the grantor of the trust
- the grantor cannot be trustee of the trust
- the retained rights must be determined solely by reference to the actual income from the trust property (the grantor cannot retain a predetermined annuity payment)

- any reversionary interest retained by the grantor does not exceed 25 percent of the value of the retained-income interest

Since the anti-estate freeze law only applies to the transfer of appreciation and a substantial interest in an enterprise, the law should not apply to a GRIT funded by nonenterprise property. Thus a GRIT does not have to meet the safe harbor rules if the corpus consists of personal-use property. Since the grantor will have more flexibility in determining retained rights, the GRIT should be even more useful for nonenterprise property. Even if an enterprise is transferred to a GRIT, the safe harbor provides a useful estate freezing possibility. If the senior family member does not plan on remaining interested in the business for a period longer than 10 years, the business can be transferred through a GRIT mechanism for relatively low transfer-tax costs in comparison to outright lifetime or testamentary gifts of the business.

Federal Tax Considerations of GRITs

Assuming the safe harbor test is satisfied, the tax implications of a GRIT will depend upon whether the grantor dies or survives the term of the retained interest. As demonstrated in the following discussion, the risk of establishing this arrangement is low: if the grantor survives the period, the objectives of the arrangement are satisfied and a great deal of transfer tax is saved; if the grantor dies during the term of the retained interest, the transfer-tax picture is substantially the same as if the GRIT had never been established.

Gift Tax Consequences if the Grantor Survives the Retained-Interest Term

The GRIT is irrevocable, and a completed gift of the remainder is made for tax purposes when the grantor establishes the trust. The value of the property for gift tax purposes is reduced by the present value of (1) the retained-income interest and (2) any reversionary interest held by the grantor. The taxable gift at the time of the establishment of the GRIT is merely the present value of the remainder interest. This taxable gift constitutes a future-interest gift that does not qualify for the $10,000 annual exclusion. However, in many cases the grantor will have unified credit available that will shelter the entire transfer from any gift tax due.

The purpose of the GRIT is to reduce the overall transfer-tax costs of passing the grantor's assets to his or her beneficiaries. Therefore the key to this technique is establishing the highest value possible for the retained-income interest of the grantor. This will result in a low present value for the remainder interest, and therefore the total amount subject to gift tax can be minimized.

TAMRA created new rules for determining the present value of annuities, life estates, terms for years, and remainder interests. Essentially, these interest must be valued according to regulations prescribed by the IRS. These regulations can be found in either the estate or gift tax valuation regulations. The interest rate used in the valuation is based on the monthly rates published by the Treasury in the Internal Revenue Bulletin (I.R.B.). The rate will be 120 percent of the AFMR compounded annually.

The mortality component for this valuation table is based on the most recent mortality information available. This mortality component is applicable only if the grantor retains a reversion in the GRIT that is contingent on the grantor's death prior to the termination of the GRIT.

If no reversion is retained, the value of a remainder interest can be determined by multiplying a "remainder factor" by the value of the property placed in the GRIT. The remainder factor is determined by the following formula

$$\text{Remainder factor} = \frac{1}{(1 + i)^T}$$

i = 120 percent of the AFMR
T = the duration of the GRIT in years

If a reversion is retained, the computation is even more complex and software will generally be necessary to determine these valuation factors.

> *Example 5:* Assume the vacation home owned by Tom and Jane in the previous example is worth $350,000 at the time of the transfer to the GRIT. For gift tax purposes, the taxable amount of the transfer is equal to the present value of remainder interest left to Tom's children. This is a gift of the future interest, and thus the full amount of the remainder interest is subject to gift tax without the benefit of the annual exclusion. The remainder interest is currently worth
>
> $$\$350,000 \times \frac{1}{(1 + .106)^{10}}, \text{ or } \$127,796.$$
>
> This calculation is based on the current (May 1990) rate of 10.6 percent. If Tom has the full remaining unified credit, this transfer of a future interest worth $127,796 will result in no transfer tax at this time. If Tom survives the term period, the vacation home will pass to his children with no further transfer-tax costs. If there is no appreciation on the vacation home in that 10-year period, this technique will have saved Tom $122,212 in total transfer-tax costs assuming a 55 percent estate tax bracket. If the full value of the home was instead included in Tom's gross estate, the tax payable would be $192,500 ($350,000 taxed at 55 percent), whereas the tax payable for the gift of the remainder interest is only 55 percent of $127,796 (or $70,288). Furthermore, if the vacation home appreciates in value after the transfer to the GRIT, the transfer-tax savings will be even larger.

Estate Tax Consequences if the Grantor Survives the Retained-Interest Term

If the irrevocable trust is properly designed, none of the property will be in the grantor's estate if the grantor survives the term period. Of course, any income received by the trust during the term that is not consumed by the grantor before death will come back into the estate.

If the GRIT property consists of a substantial interest in an enterprise, the GRIT must follow the safe harbor requirements. Otherwise, the deemed gift rules of Sec. 2036(c) will cause the full gift taxation of the appreciation of the trust corpus at the time the grantor's retained term ends. In addition, if the original transfer to the trust is not considered a completed gift, the trust property could be returned to the grantor's estate. You will recall from the assignments covering estate inclusion that retained powers, such as the right to appoint trust principal to the grantor's creditors or to amend or alter the trust substantially, will cause the assets to be included in the grantor's gross estate. Financial services professionals should be aware that this technique will serve its objective only if the trust is truly irrevocable.

Unfortunately, successful use of this technique is not without its tax disadvantages. If the grantor survives the term of the retained interest, no trust property will be included in the gross estate, and therefore the basis step-up for the GRIT property at the grantor's death will not be available. This may result in a larger income tax if the remainderperson plans on disposing of the trust property at a future date.

The Grantor Dies during the Retained-Interest Term

The transfer-tax savings available through the use of a GRIT will only be realized if the grantor survives the term of the retained-income interest. You will recall from the estate-inclusion assignments that a transfer with a retained interest that does not end before the transferor's death is included in the gross estate under Sec. 2036(*a*). Therefore the full value of the trust property, not just the value of the remaining term, will return to the grantor's estate if the grantor fails to survive the term. However, the unified credit used on the original transfer, plus any gift tax actually paid, will be allowed as a credit against the estate tax due. Furthermore, the benefit of the income tax basis step-up will be available due to the inclusion of the assets in the gross estate.

The unexpired term of the grantor's income interest presents a problem if the grantor does not survive the term. Without dispositive planning for these payments, they will presumably be paid to the grantor's estate. This will prevent the beneficiaries from receiving the full trust property until the end of the term and may create a liquidity problem if the trust property cannot be reached during this time. In order to solve this problem, the following provisions might be considered for inclusion in the original trust terms:

- Accelerating the remainder interest to the remainderpersons if the grantor dies earlier than the expiration of the term will solve the delay problems in getting the property into the hands of the beneficiary. Unfortunately, this method will increase the value of the remainder interest and the associated transfer costs at the time of the establishment of the trust.
- A general testamentary power of appointment over (or reversionary interest in) the property exercisable only if the grantor dies during the

term will solve the problem of getting the funds at death into the hands of the beneficiary and will also increase the value of the grantor's interest (thus reducing the transfer-tax costs for establishing the trust). The transfer of the property to a marital deduction trust through the exercise of this power will, at least, preserve the marital deduction if the property if returned to the gross estate. IRS Notice 89-99 limits the use of the contingent reversion or general power to circumstances where the value of this contingent right is less than 25 percent of the value of the retained-income interest.

Since the planning value of the GRIT is eliminated if the grantor does not survive the retained-interest term, it is advisable to select a term that the grantor is likely to survive. For this reason, this technique is not a good planning device for a grantor in poor health or at an advanced age. If the term of the GRIT must be kept short due to the health or age of the grantor, the value of the remainder-interest increases, thus reducing the potential transfer-tax savings of the technique. However, the downside risk of attempting a GRIT is small since it leaves the grantor's estate with no greater tax liability than it would have had if nothing had been done.

Income Tax Consequences of a GRIT

The grantor-trust rules provide that the grantor will be taxed on the income from the trust during the retained-interest period. Therefore there is no income-shifting benefit from this technique until the property vests in the remainderperson.

PLANNING FOR ESTATE LIQUIDITY WITH AN IRREVOCABLE LIFE INSURANCE TRUST

The irrevocable life insurance trust can be of particular benefit for estate planning purposes. The irrevocable life insurance trust can provide the following benefits:

- Gift taxes can be avoided for premiums contributed to the trust.
- Estate taxes can be avoided when the proceeds are received.
- Generation-skipping transfer taxes can be avoided if the insured's exemption is allocated to the trust.
- The insured's transferable wealth can be enhanced through leveraging.
- The expenses and publicity of probate are avoided for transfers to the trust.
- Estate liquidity can be enhanced by the trust.
- The grantor-insured can control the disposition of the proceeds before the fact through the trust provisions.
- Income taxes are avoided on the corpus buildup and receipt of proceeds.

The estate tax treatment of life insurance was discussed in reading 10. Essentially there are two rules that create problems for the purposes of the irrevocable life insurance trust. If these two problems are avoided, the life insurance trust will be able to provide for heirs or to provide for the liquidity of the insured's estate without increasing the estate tax liability.

First, life insurance proceeds will be included in the insured's gross estate if they are payable to the executor. Therefore the grantor will generally avoid directly naming his or her estate as beneficiary of the trust. The hidden trap is indirectly causing the trust to be deemed payable to the executor, which could occur if the trustee is directed to pay the expenses of the estate or merely given the discretion to pay the expenses of the estate. Because these trust provisions will cause some, or all, of the proceeds to be included in the insured's gross estate, they should be avoided.

Trust provisions that can be used in the insurance trust to provide liquidity to the estate are discretionary powers to the trustee to loan trust funds to the insured's estate or to purchase assets from the estate. The loan or sale should follow normally acceptable commercial standards and should be within the explicit powers of the fiduciaries involved. The purchase of assets should be for fair market value, and the loan should be secured and bear adequate interest. These provisions will allow the cash proceeds held by the trustee to be transferred to the estate to increase estate liquidity without causing additional unnecessary estate taxes.

The second possibility for estate inclusion is the retention of any incidents of ownership by the insured within 3 years of death. Although this test sounds simple enough, it can be an additional trap for the unwary. First, the insured should possess no rights to the trust that would provide him or her with incidents of ownership in the corpus. Thus the trust must be a truly irrevocable, "no-strings-attached" gift. Therefore the insured should not be able to change beneficiary designations on the policy or within the trust once the trust is executed and should not be able to receive policy loan proceeds or use the trust as collateral for a loan. The IRS even takes the position that the insured cannot be trustee or merely retain the right to replace a corporate fiduciary with another.

Assuming a trust is drafted to avoid attributed incidents of ownership to the insured, there are further concerns. First, the insured should avoid obtaining incidents of ownership in the policy prior to the gift to the trust. This may be unavoidable if an existing policy is used to fund the trust. In this case, the insured must live 3 years after the transfer of the policy to the trust or Sec. 2035 will bring the proceeds back to the estate. This transfer is often recommended regardless of the Sec. 2035 risk. Quite often, an older insured may use an existing policy to fund an irrevocable trust as his or her estate tax concerns grow. The insured should do this when he or she is prepared to irrevocably name the beneficiaries of the trust and when it would be economically impractical to purchase a new policy within the trust.

If a new policy is used to fund the trust, it would be a serious estate tax mistake for the insured to acquire incidents of ownership. In this case, the 3-year rule will be a trap even if the intent is for the policy to be held in all events by an irrevocable trust. This is a real concern since the IRS seems to get particular pleasure in litigating this issue. As a result, the insured should participate in the process only as trust grantor and insured. The insured should not sign as applicant or owner on the policy application. The trustee will be the applicant and owner of the policy, and the trust should exist at the time of application. If the trust is not in place and the application and underwriting process must be started, the spouse or child of the insured could be the applicant and owner. Then a transfer to an irrevocable trust can be made when the trust is drafted. If these steps are followed, current case law indicates that the insured does not hold incidents in the policy even if the insured actually makes all premium payments to the trust.

The irrevocable life insurance trust can be designed to bypass both spouses' estates. The dispositive provisions should not provide the surviving spouse with any powers that will create inclusion in his or her estate. For example, the surviving spouse should not have a general power over the corpus or have unlimited invasion powers. However, the surviving spouse could be given a life estate with limited invasion powers (that is, the 5-and-5 powers discussed in reading 10). In addition, a discretionary invasion power in favor of the surviving spouse can be given to the trustee if the invasion is subject to ascertainable standards. In addition, a properly designed trust can be the owner of a second-to-die policy that covers the spouses and the second-death benefits will avoid inclusion in either spouse's estate.

As this discussion demonstrates, the irrevocable life insurance trust might be the most advantageous estate preservation technique available under current tax law. However, the potential hazards discussed above indicate that the trust should be drafted and administered only with the advice of an attorney experienced in estate planning matters.

ademption

when a will designates specific property (real or personal) to a beneficiary but at the date of death the property is not part of the estate. The beneficiary receives nothing unless the will substitutes another asset for that beneficiary.

adjusted gross estate

an amount calculated for the purpose of determining the availability of certain tax benefits (such as installment payment of estate taxes) and arrived at by reducing the gross estate by allowable debts, funeral as well as medical costs, and administrative expenses

adjusted taxable estate

the phrase now used in computing the state death tax credit. It means the taxable estate reduced by $60,000.

adjusted taxable gifts

all taxable gifts (total gifts less the charitable deduction, the marital deduction, and the annual gift tax exclusion) the decedent made after December 31, 1976—except for those gifts that were required for any reason to be included in the decedent's gross estate, such as gifts with retained interests or gifts of life insurance made within 3 years of death

administration

the management of a decedent's estate, including the marshaling of assets; the payment of expenses, debts, and charges; the payment or delivery of legacies; and the rendition of an account

administrator—executor

An administrator is appointed by the court to settle an estate. An executor is named by the estate owner in the will as the one to settle that estate. The administrator is always appointed by the court, and the executor is always named by the deceased in the will.

An administrator will be appointed (1) when the deceased left no will, (2) when the deceased left a will but failed to name an executor, (3) when the executor in the will failed to qualify or refused to serve and no successor was named, and (4) when the executor, after having qualified, failed to settle the estate (for example, if the executor died before settlement).

advancement

money or property given by a parent to a child, other descendant, or heir
(depending upon the statute's wording), or expended by the former for the
latter's benefit, in anticipation of the share that the child (for example) will
inherit in the parent's estate and intended to be deducted from the child's
eventual portion

adverse party

a beneficiary with an interest inconsistent with another beneficiary's interest
in the same trust property

afterborn child

a child born after the execution of a parent's will or trust

alternate value

for federal estate tax purposes, the value of the gross estate 6 months after
the date of death, unless property is distributed, sold, exchanged, or
otherwise disposed of within 6 months. In that case, the value of such
property is determined as of the date of such disposition.

annual exclusion

a gift tax exclusion of $10,000 that a donor is allowed each year for each
donee provided the gift is one of a present interest (donee must be given
an immediate right to possession or enjoyment of the property interest)

attestation clause

the paragraph appended to the will indicating that certain persons by their
signatures thereto have heard the testator declare the instrument to be his
or her will and have witnessed the signing of the will

beneficiary

(1) one who inherits a share or part of a decedent's estate or (2) one who
takes the beneficial interest under a trust. (For income beneficiary, see *life
tenant.*)

beneficiary—generation-skipping trust

any person with a present or future interest or power in the trust

bequest

strictly a gift by will of personal property as distinguished from a gift of
real estate, though often used to cover a gift by will of either personal
property or land, or both. "To bequeath" generally means to dispose of
property of any kind by will. (See also *devise* and *legacy.*)

Bequests are classified, generally speaking, as specific or general. A
specific bequest is a gift of a particular specified class or kind of property
(for example, a gift of the testator's diamond ring to a named individual or
a gift of designated stock in a corporation). A general bequest is one that
may be satisfied from the general assets of the estate (for example, a
bequest of a sum of money without reference to any particular fund from
which it is to be paid). Since a specific bequest designates a particular

item of the estate that is to be given, if that item is not owned by the decedent at the time of death, the gift fails.

charitable deduction

a deduction to a charitable organization (equal to the value of the gift) allowed against a reportable gift or as a deduction from the adjusted gross estate

codicil

a supplement or addition to an existing will, to effect some revision, change, or modification of that will. A codicil must meet the same requirements regarding execution and validity as a will.

collateral relations

a phrase used primarily in the law of intestacy to designate uncles and aunts, cousins, and so forth (for example, those relatives not in a direct ascending or descending line, like grandparents or grandchildren, the latter of which are designated as lineal relations)

community property

property acquired during marriage in which both husband and wife have an undivided one-half interest. Not more than one-half can be disposed of by either party individually by will. There are presently nine community-property states: Arizona, California, Idaho, Louisiana, New Mexico, Nevada, Texas, Washington, and Wisconsin.

contingent interest

a future interest in real or personal property that is dependent upon the fulfillment of a stated condition and may never come into existence

contingent remainder

a future interest in property dependent upon the fulfillment of a stated condition before the termination of a prior estate. For example, Hannah leaves property and securities to Tina in trust to pay income to Wanda during her lifetime. After Wanda's death Tina is to transfer the property to Socrates, if living when Wanda dies; otherwise the property will go to Cleopatra. Socrates has a contingent remainder interest (contingent upon outliving Wanda); Cleopatra has a contingent remainder interest (contingent upon Socrates not outliving Wanda).

corpus

a term used to describe the principal or trust res as distinguished from the trust income

credit estate tax

a tax imposed by a state to take full advantage of the amount allowed as a credit against the federal estate tax, also called a *gap* or *sponge* tax

deemed transferor

in generation-skipping transfers, the deemed transferor is the parent of the transferee who is more closely related to the grantor than the other parent of the transferee; or if neither parent is related, the parent having the closer *affinity* to the grantor. A parent related to the grantor by blood or adoption is deemed closer than one related by marriage.

descent and distribution

Descent refers to the passing of real estate to the heirs of one who dies without a will. Distribution refers to the passing of personal property to the heirs of one who dies without a will. Technically, the laws of descent relate to real property; those of distribution relate to personal property. Modern-day usage has substituted *intestacy* to designate the legal effect of dying without a will.

devise

a gift of real property under a will, as distinguished from a gift of personal property. (See also *bequest* and *legacy*.)

disclaimer

a complete and unqualified refusal to accept property or an interest to which one is entitled. It must be made timely and without consideration or without directions as to what happens to such disclaimed property. The terms *disclaimer* and *renunciation* are synonymous.

distributable net income

for fiduciary income tax purposes, the taxable income of the estate or trust for any taxable year, computed with certain modifications. (See Code Sec. 643(a).)

domicile

an individual's permanent home—the place to which, whenever the individual is absent, he or she has the intention of returning

donee

the recipient of a gift. The term also refers to the recipient of a power of appointment.

donor

the person who makes a gift. The term also refers to the person who grants a power of appointment to another.

estate tax

a tax imposed upon the right of a person to transfer property at death. This type of tax is imposed not only by the federal government but also by a number of states.

executor

See *administrator*.

fair market value

the value at which estate assets are included in the gross estate for federal estate tax purposes. The price at which property would change hands between a willing buyer and a willing seller, neither being under a compulsion to buy or to sell and both having knowledge of the relevant facts.

family allowance

the allowance of money from the estate to the family for support during administration

federal estate tax

an excise tax levied on the right to transfer property at death, imposed upon and measured by the value of the taxable estate left by the decedent

fee simple

an estate in which the owner is entitled to absolute ownership of property, with unconditional power to dispose of it during lifetime as well as the power to bequeath it to anyone at death

fiduciary

one occupying a legally defined position of trust (for example, an executor, an administrator, or a trustee)

fiduciary income tax return

the income tax return (Form 1041) filed by the fiduciary of an estate or trust

formula clause

a clause aimed at achieving the appropriate marital deduction and shifting all property in excess of that amount so that it will not be taxed again in the surviving spouse's estate

funded insurance trust

an insurance trust funded with cash, securities, or other assets whose income is used to pay premiums on the policies held in the trust

future interest

the postponed right of use or enjoyment of the property

general power of appointment

a power over the disposition of property exercisable in favor of any person the donee of the power may select, including the donee, the donee's estate, the donee's creditors, or the creditors of the donee's estate. For example, Alan creates a trust in which Bob has the power to designate the disposition of the property to any person he wishes, including himself, his estate, and his creditors.

generation-skipping transfer

a taxable distribution or a taxable termination from a generation-skipping trust or its equivalent

generation-skipping trust
> broadly defined in IRC Sec. 2611(b) as any trust that has younger-generation beneficiaries in more than one generation. Only a trust that has beneficiaries in at least two generations, both of which are below the grantor's generation, is a generation-skipping trust.

gift (for gift tax purposes)
> property or property rights or interests gratuitously passed or transferred for less than an adequate and full consideration in money or money's worth (except for bona fide sales) to another, in trust or otherwise, directly or indirectly

gift splitting
> a provision allowing a married couple to treat a gift made by one of them to a third party as having been made one-half by each, provided the non-donor-spouse consents to the gift

gift tax
> a tax imposed on transfers of property by gift during the donor's lifetime

gift tax marital deduction
> a deduction allowed for a gift made by one spouse to another, provided it qualifies. Outright gifts qualify; life estates qualify if the donee has the right to the income from the property for life and a general power of appointment over the principal.

grantor
> a person who creates a trust; also called *settlor, creator,* or *trustor*

grantor—generation-skipping trust
> any person who contributes or adds property to a generation-skipping trust

gross estate
> an amount determined by totaling the value of all assets that the decedent had an interest in, which are required to be included in the estate by the Internal Revenue Code

gross up
> The decedent's gross estate is increased by the amount of any gift tax the decedent or the estate paid on a gift made by the decedent or the decedent's spouse after December 31, 1976, within the last 3 years of the decedent's life.

guardian
> a person named to represent the interests of minor children

heir
> technically a person designated by law to succeed to the estate of an intestate (also designated as *next of kin*)

holding period

the period, with respect to substituted-basis property, during which the donor held the property (including *tacked-on* holding periods, where the basis of property has been carried over to the holding period of the donee)

holographic will

one entirely in the handwriting of the testator. In many states such a will is not recognized unless it is published, declared, and witnessed as required by statute for other written wills.

homestead exemption

a statute exempting the homestead and, often, specified chattels from the debts of a deceased head of a household, notwithstanding provisions of a will or the intestate laws

inheritance tax

a tax levied on the right of the heirs to receive property from a deceased person, measured by the share passing to each beneficiary, sometimes called a *succession tax*

insurance trust

a trust composed partly or wholly of life insurance policy contracts

intangible property

property that does not have physical substance (for example, a stock certificate or bond). The thing itself is only the evidence of value.

interest in property (for gift tax purposes)

present—an unrestricted right to the immediate use, possession, or enjoyment of property or income from the property

future—an interest other than a present interest

interpolated terminal reserve

the reserve on any life insurance policy between anniversary dates, regardless of whether further premium payments are due. It is determined by a pro rata adjustment upward (or downward in the case of certain term policies of long duration) between the previous terminal reserve and the next terminal reserve.

inter vivos trust

a trust created during the settlor's lifetime. It becomes operative during lifetime as opposed to a trust under will (testamentary trust), which does not become operative until the settlor dies.

intestacy laws

individual state laws providing for distribution of the property of a person who has died without leaving a valid will

intestate

the term for a person who dies without a will

irrevocable trust

for federal tax laws, a trust in which the grantor alone cannot retain any right to alter, amend, revoke, or terminate the trust. However, a trust that can be only revoked or terminated by the grantor with the consent of someone who has an adverse interest in the trust will be treated as irrevocable for income tax purposes.

joint tenancy with right of survivorship

the holding of property by two or more persons in such a manner that, upon the death of one, the survivor or survivors take the entire property by operation of law

joint will

The same instrument is made the will of two or more persons and is signed jointly by them. When it is joint and mutual, it contains reciprocal provisions. (See also *mutual wills.*)

lapse

the failure of a testamentary bequest due to the death of the devisee or legatee during the life of the testator

last will and testament

the usual term referring to a will. The phrase is an outgrowth of the old English law under which a *will* was a disposition of real estate and a *testament* was a disposition of personal property. The two terms originally meant different things. The difference is no longer recognized, however. Nothing is added by coupling *testament* with *will,* since the latter is sufficiently inclusive.

legacy

a gift of personal property by will. It would perhaps be proper to use the term *bequest* to include any disposition by will, the term *devise* to cover gifts of real estate, and the term *legacy* to cover gifts of personal property. However, both at law and in common practice, these terms are not used with any great respect for this distinction and often appear more or less interchangeably.

legatee

the person to whom a legacy is given

letters of administration

a written document granted by the judge of the court having jurisdiction over probate matters authorizing the person named therein to administer the personal estate of an intestate decedent

letters testamentary

a written document granted by the judge of an orphans', probate, or surrogate's court having jurisdiction to an executor named in a will, authorizing that person or entity to act as such

life estate
the title of the interest owned by a life tenant (income beneficiary)

life interest or life estate
an interest that a person has in property that endures only during lifetime, with no possession of ownership rights that may be transferred during life or at death

life tenant
the person who receives the income from a legal life estate or from a trust fund during the person's own life or that of another person (income beneficiary)

limited power of appointment
a power granted to a donee that is limited in scope (special power)

liquid assets
cash or assets that can be readily converted into cash without any serious loss of principal (for example, CDs or life insurance paid in lump sum)

lump-sum distribution
distribution or payment from a qualified employee benefit plan (which takes place within one taxable year to the recipient) of the entire account balance of an employee, which becomes payable to the recipient because of death or separation from the service or after age 59 1/2

marital-deduction trust
a trust consisting of all property that qualifies for the marital deduction

Mortmain Acts
state laws to discourage persons near death from naming charitable or religious organizations as beneficiaries under their wills. If a bequest to a charitable or religious organization is made within a certain period of time prior to the decedent's death or if the bequest is over a specified limit, other potential heirs may contest the will and the gift to the charity can be voided.

mutual wills
the separate wills of two or more persons, with reciprocal provisions in favor of the other person contained in each will

***needed* marital deduction**
also called a credit-maximizing formula or a marital deduction, but not the maximum allowable marital deduction, that is needed to reduce the taxable estate to an amount that is fully covered by the estate's exemption equivalent (that is, when the taxable estate produced a tentative estate tax that is fully covered by the estate's unified tax credit)

nonliquid assets
assets that may not be readily convertible into cash without a serious loss (for example, real estate or business interests)

G.9

nonprobate property
property that passes outside the administration of the estate. It passes other than by will or the intestacy laws (for example, jointly held property, life insurance proceeds payable to a named beneficiary, or property in an inter vivos trust)

nonreversionary trust
a trust in which there is no possibility of the grantor's regaining the property, having it return to the estate, or having a power of appointment over it

nuncupative will
an oral will that is declared or dictated by the testator during his or her last illness before a sufficient number of witnesses and afterward reduced to writing

posthumous child
a child born after the death of the father

pour over
a term referring to the transfer of property from an estate or trust to another estate or trust upon the happening of an event as provided in the instrument (for example, property disposed of by will *pours over* into an existing trust)

power
any power to establish or to alter beneficial enjoyment of corpus or income of the trust

power of appointment
a property right created (or reserved) by the donor of the power enabling the donee of the power to designate, within such limits as the donor has prescribed, who will be the transferees of the property

present interest
a present right to use or enjoy property

principal
the assets making up the estate or fund that has been set aside in trust, or from which income is expected to accrue (corpus). Trust principal is also known as the trust res.

probate
the process of proving the will's validity in court and executing its provisions under the guidance of the court. The process of probating the will involves recognition by the appropriate court of the executor named in the will (or appointment of an administrator if none has been named), and the determination of validity of the will if it is contested.

probate property
>   property that is passed under the terms of a will; if no will, it passes under
>   the intestacy laws (for example, individually held property or one-half of
>   community property)

qualified domestic trust (QDOT)
>   a trust that meets the requirements for a marital deduction for property
>   left to a surviving resident-alien-spouse. The trust must have at least one
>   U.S. trustee who approves distributions and is eligible for the marital
>   deduction if elected by the citizen-spouse's executor.

qualified terminable interest property (QTIP)
>   An otherwise terminable interest in property will qualify for the marital
>   deduction if the following requirements are met: the surviving spouse
>   alone must be given the right to all the income from the qualifying
>   property payable at least annually for life; no one else can be given the
>   right to direct that the property go to anyone other than the spouse during
>   the spouse's life; the decedent-spouse's executor must make an irrevocable
>   election on the decedent's federal estate tax return that all property
>   remaining at the surviving spouse's death will be included in the survivor's
>   gross estate valued on the date of the surviving spouse's death.

remainder interest
>   a future interest that comes into existence after termination of prior
>   interest. For example, Alexis (testator) created a testamentary trust under
>   a will in which the corpus is to be retained with income paid to Bill
>   (lifetime beneficiary) until Bill's death, at which time the corpus (remainder
>   interest) will be given to Carl (remainderperson).

remainderperson
>   the person who is entitled to receive the principal (corpus) of an estate
>   upon the termination of the intervening life estate or estates

reserve (life insurance policy reserve)
>   the difference between the present value of future benefits (death claim
>   and maturity value) and the present value of future net premiums for any
>   life insurance policy. The sum of the reserves for the individual policies in
>   force is the policy reserves figure that appears as a liability on the balance
>   sheet of a life insurance company. The term *reserve* is not synonymous
>   with *cash surrender value,* although the cash surrender value ultimately
>   equals the amount of the reserve after a policy (other than a term policy)
>   has been in force for a number of years.

resident-alien
>   a person who is not a U.S. citizen but does reside in the United States.
>   Such individual may receive transfers from a spouse qualifying for a marital
>   deduction from estate or gift taxes only under specific circumstances.

residuary estate
> the remaining part of a testator's estate after payment of debts and bequests. Wills usually contain a clause disposing of the residue of the estate that the testator has not otherwise bequeathed or devised.

residue
> the property that remains after any specific bequests, devises, and legacies have been made, and debts and expenses have been paid

reversionary interest
> a right to future enjoyment by the transferor of property that is now in the possession or enjoyment of another party. For example, Anthony creates a trust under which a parent, Berlinda, is to enjoy income for life, with the corpus of the trust to be paid over to Anthony at Berlinda's death. Anthony's interest is a reversionary interest.

reversionary trust
> a trust limited to a specified term of years or for the life of the beneficiary. At the termination of the trust, the trust property is then returned to the grantor.

revocable trust
> a trust that can be revoked, amended, or terminated by the grantor and the property recovered by the grantor

shrinkage
> a reduction in the amount of property that passes at death caused by loss of capital and income resulting from the sale of assets to pay death costs

sole ownership
> the holding of property by one person in such a manner that upon death it passes either by the terms of the will or, if no will, according to the intestacy laws

sprinkle or spray trust
> a trust under which the trustee is given discretionary power to distribute any part or all of the income or corpus among beneficiaries in equal or unequal shares

stepped-up-basis property
> all property acquired from or passed from a decedent not specifically excluded. "Acquired from or passed from a decedent" is interpreted in Sec. 1014(b) to include (1) property acquired by bequest, devise, or inheritance or by the decedent's estate; (2) property held in a revocable trust; (3) property subject to a general power of appointment; and (4) the survivor's share of community property.
>
> Stepped-up-basis property therefore includes items not traditionally thought of as generating capital gains (such as household as well as personal effects and cash). Stepped-up-basis property does *not* include specified property that is generally governed by other existing Code provisions.

tangible property

property that has physical substance—that is, it may be touched, seen, or felt. The thing itself has value (such as a house, a car, or furniture).

taxable estate

an amount determined by subtracting the allowable deductions from the gross estate

tenancy by the entirety

the holding of property by a husband or wife in such a manner that, except with the consent of each, neither husband nor wife has a disposable interest in the property during the lifetime of the other. Upon the death of either, the property goes to the survivor.

tenancy in common

the holding of property by two or more persons in such a manner that each has an undivided interest, which can be sold or gifted at any time, and upon the death of one is passed to the person(s) designated in the deceased tenant's will (or by intestacy) and does not pass automatically to the surviving tenants in common

terminal reserve

the reserve on a life insurance policy at the end of any contract year and, for policies on which premiums are still due, the amount of the reserve prior to the payment of the next premium

testamentary

a document, gift, or power not to take effect irrevocably until the death of the maker

testamentary trust

a trust created by the terms of a will

testate

a term used when a person dies having left a will

testator

a person who leaves a will in force at death

trust

a fiduciary arrangement whereby the legal title of property is held and the property is managed by someone for the benefit of another

trustee

the holder of legal title to property for the use or benefit of another

unfunded insurance trust

an insurance trust that is not provided with cash and/or securities to pay the life insurance premium. Such premiums are paid by someone other than the trustee.

unified credit against estate tax

   a credit to which the estate of every decedent is entitled, which can be applied directly against the estate tax

vested interest

   an immediate fixed interest in real or personal property, although the right to possession and enjoyment may be postponed until some future date or until the happening of some event. For example, Helga leaves real property and securities to Tim in trust to pay income to Sue during her lifetime. After Sue's death, Tim is to transfer the property to Steve and his heirs. Sue has a present vested life interest in the right to *income*. Steve has a future vested interest in the right to *property*. This is a vested remainder interest.

vested remainder

   a fixed interest in property with the right of possession and enjoyment postponed until the termination of the prior estate